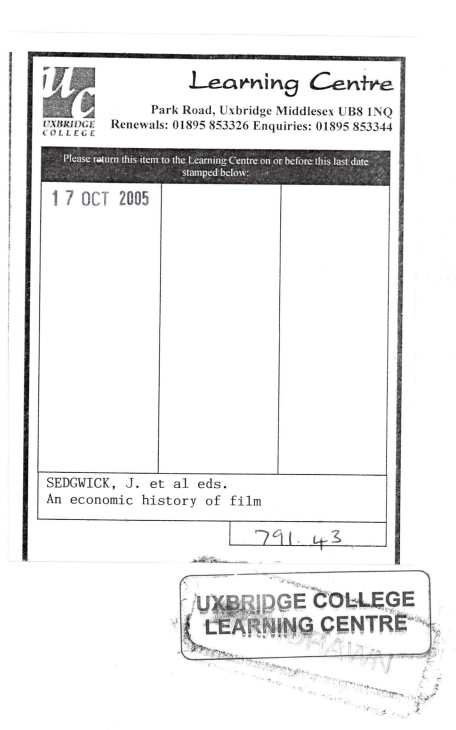

Learning Centre

Park Road, Uxbridge Middlesex UB8 1NQ
Renewals: 01895 853326 Enquiries: 01895 853344

An Economic History of Film

The economics of the movie industry has been curiously neglected by scholars, especially given the material circumstances in which film has been produced, distributed and exhibited in capitalist economies and its central importance in the lives of the huge numbers attracted to it as a commodity.

This book provides an economic framework for understanding developments in film history. Film is a peculiar commodity with a unique set of characteristics. The topic hence is interesting and covered with aplomb by the contributors to the volume. The book includes sections on:

- long-term trends in the film industry
- the transformation of film from a primitive commodity to a heavily branded product
- the operation of the studio system
- the end of the studio system in post-war America
- the role and payment of stars
- Hollywood's approach to risk during the 1990s.

Experts from the UK and North America have come together in these pages and the result is a readable, insightful and enlightening book that will gain many fans amongst those with an interest in the economics of film, economic historians, film historians and aficionados of the movie industry generally.

John Sedgwick is Principal Lecturer in Economics at London Metropolitan University, UK. **Michael Pokorny** is Principal Lecturer in Economics at the University of Westminster, UK.

Routledge explorations in economic history

An Economic History of Film

**Edited by John Sedgwick and
Michael Pokorny**

Routledge
Taylor & Francis Group

LONDON AND NEW YORK

First published 2005
by Routledge
2 Park Square, Milton Park, Abingdon, Oxon OX14 4RN

Simultaneously published in the USA and Canada
by Routledge
270 Madison Avenue, New York, NY 10016

Routledge is an imprint of the Taylor & Francis Group

© 2005 Selection and editorial matter, John Sedgwick and Michael
Pokorny; individual chapters, the contributors

Typeset in Times by Wearset Ltd, Boldon, Tyne and Wear
Printed and bound in Great Britain by MPG Digital Solutions, Bodmin

British Library Cataloguing in Publication Data
A catalogue record for this book is available from the British Library

Library of Congress Cataloging in Publication Data
A catalog record for this book has been requested

ISBN 0-415-32492-0

To Daphne, Carole, Martha and Rachel
and
To Annemarie, Helen, Robert, Elizabeth, Laura and Sarah

Contents

Figures

Tables

Acknowledgements

The initial stimulus for this book derived from the development of a final year undergraduate module in the Economics of the Film Industry, a module delivered to students with a relatively limited background in formal economics. It was largely in response to demands from successive cohorts of these students for a suitable reference text that we undertook the task of putting this book together. Particularly insistent in their demands were Christiane Barrow and Emma Sherlock, and their enthusiasm and the quality of their work provided a convincing justification for undertaking this task. We must also acknowledge the input of Bernard Hrusa Marlow, who uncomplainingly read the entire manuscript, making numerous suggestions for improvements. Indeed, we owe Bernard a general debt as he has monitored our work closely over the years, and has become uncomfortably (for us) familiar with our failings, but he has also been a rich source of suggestions for corrections, improvements and clarifications, all made with immense patience and modesty. Any remaining deficiencies are no doubt attributable to our inability to recognise the subtlety and relevance of his observations.

We also wish to acknowledge the following publishers for permission to reproduce material that constitutes most of the chapters in this book: Exeter University Press for sections of Chapter 1, Presses Inter-Universitaires Européennes/Peter Lang for Chapter 2, the Business History Conference and *Enterprise & Society* for Chapter 3, the Western Economic Association International and *Economic Inquiry* for Chapter 4, University of Chicago Press and the *Journal of Law and Economics* for Chapter 5, the Economic History Association and the *Journal of Economic History* for Chapter 7, Kluwer Academic Publishers and the *Journal of Cultural Economics* for Chapters 8 and 11, and University of Chicago Press and the *Journal of Legal Studies* for Chapter 9.

Introduction

This book is about the *business* of the film industry, and examines this business within a historical context. Given the extent to which Hollywood has dominated the industry, almost from its inception, Hollywood will necessarily be the focus of much of the analysis. The tools of analysis are those of economics, although every effort has been made to keep technical detail to a minimum so as to ensure that the subject matter of this book is accessible to a general readership. Indeed, this book has been written not for the economist/economic historian per se, but for the reader seeking a broader understanding of the film industry, irrespective of his or her own discipline background.

In the post-Second World War period, Hollywood attracted relatively little interest from the economist, for the simple reason that as an industry it is minuscule, and until relatively recently, it was an industry in decline. Even within the context of the growth in movie production over the past ten years,[1] consumers' expenditure on movie-going in the US accounts for just 1 per cent of total recreational expenditure, in contrast to the 'classical' period in the 1930s and 1940s when this was regularly in excess of 20 per cent.[2] In terms of employment, Hollywood is a relatively small employer of specialised and somewhat idiosyncratic labour, offering limited scope to the economist as a model for generalisation.

However, while movie-going remains a relatively minor recreational activity, movie 'consumption' has grown strongly throughout the 1990s, stimulated by evolving technology that allows for high-quality movie viewing in the home. In 2000, adult consumers spent an average of 69 hours per year watching movies, 57 hours of which were spent consuming movies via home video/DVD. The time spent watching movies in movie theatres has been virtually unchanged since 1970.[3] Not only do these technological advances ensure a much wider distribution and consumption of current movie production, they have also opened up a new market for the film studios' extensive back catalogues of films. Indeed, given their wide availability, these back catalogues now represent highly valuable assets, having become a stimulus for, and focus of, the frequent changes in studio ownership that have occurred within the industry in the recent past.

So certainly, as an economic phenomenon, the strong growth of Hollywood in the 1990s, together with the manner in which the industry has been transformed by technological change, has stimulated the interest of the economist.

Traditionally the film industry, and Hollywood in particular, has been analysed in cultural terms, the dominant analytical paradigm deriving from cultural theory. It is self-evident that Hollywood has had, and continues to have, an extensive cultural impact internationally, and constitutes a powerful medium for exporting American cultural values, with the myriad of implications this has, both economic and non-economic. This book does not have any pretensions with regard to supplanting or competing with this paradigm. Rather, the intention is to emphasise the economic/business dimensions of the industry, thereby broadening and deepening the context within which any cultural analysis takes place. The basic proposition of this book is that to fully understand the cultural impact that Hollywood has had, and continues to have, it is also necessary to understand the economics and economic history of the industry.

Notes on contributors and contributions

John Sedgwick and Michael Pokorny are Principal Lecturers in Economics at London Metropolitan University and the University of Westminster respectively. In Chapter 1 they outline the distinctive contribution that economic reasoning can make to film studies. They then go on to analyse the distinctive nature of film as a commodity before finally identifying some long-term industry characteristics and trends, and thereby provide a context for the chapters that follow.

Gerben Bakker is a Lecturer in the Department of Accounting, Finance and Management at the University of Essex. In Chapter 2, Bakker examines the problems European film companies faced in the United States between 1907 and 1920. Initially, in the 1890s and early 1900s, companies such as Edison, Biograph and Vitagraph set up foreign subsidiaries. However, up until the mid-1910s, when the US industry was caught up in patent battles and later a patent monopoly, European film companies took a leading share in world markets. From the mid-1910s, with the emergence of the feature film, American companies reversed this trend and started to push European producers out of the American market whilst setting up foreign distribution networks. Analysing the business strategies of the European film companies in America during the 1910s, this chapter explains how their ultimate decline led to Hollywood becoming the centre of international film production and distribution.

In Chapter 3 Bakker shows how motion pictures changed from technological novelties into heavily branded consumer products. The high sunk costs and short 'shelf-life' of movies led film producers to borrow branding techniques from other consumer goods industries. They tried to build audience loyalty around a number of characteristics, but eventually learned that stars and stories were the most effective factors in generating brand awareness and persuading consumers to see a new film. Data from the USA, Great Britain and France showing the disproportionate distribution of income and fame among stars, confirms their roles as persuaders.

F. Andrew Hanssen is Associate Professor of Economics at Montana State University. He shows in Chapter 4 that, during the silent era, film companies rented most of their films to exhibitors for flat per-day fees, but that the technological 'shock' of the coming of sound led to the widespread replacement of flat fees by revenue sharing. Hanssen examines the reason for this and finds that sound technology altered the structure of incentives, significantly reducing the scope for exhibitor shirking, reducing the cost of dividing attendance revenue *ex post* and raising the difficulty of negotiating lump-sum fees. Hanssen draws upon materials from Warner Bros. archives to substantiate his case.

He follows this in Chapter 5 by examining the way in which block booking developed, the nature of the optimisation problem, and the specifics of block-booking contracts. Rejecting the conventional explanation that the practice prevented exhibitors from 'oversearching' for film product, he argues that block booking was primarily intended to provide films cheaply in quantity, a claim made by movie producers of the time. He draws evidence from a series of commercial contracts between exhibitors and Warner Bros. during the 1930s and 1940s to support his interpretation of this business behaviour.

In Chapter 6, Michael Pokorny and John Sedgwick examine the risk environment faced by studios through an examination of Warner Bros.' ledger entries of rental income and production cost of each of their film releases during the Depression era, 1929-1941. The authors find that the studio adopted a portfolio approach to film production, balancing the greater risks associated with big-budget productions with the less volatile net earnings generated by their medium- and low-budget films. The budgetary categories within the portfolio are reflected in the studio's use of stars where it is not at all clear that the high-profile stars who appeared in big-budget films, with the exception of Errol Flynn, can be said to have attenuated the risks associated with such investments. However, there were clear and stable returns to 'workhorse' stars such as Bette Davis during her middle-budget period with the studio.

John Sedgwick in Chapter 7 argues that, whilst the average revenue of films fell in the USA during the post-Second World War period, the 'hit' end of the market sustained itself as consumers were drawn increasingly to particular attractions. The growing inequality in the distribution of revenues meant that the risks associated with high-budget productions could no longer be balanced against the steady earnings of medium-budget films. During the 1950s, the 'majors' all became distributor–financiers as they reduced their exposure to the risks associated with film production by replacing portfolios generated through internal command infrastructures with arm's-length contractual agreements with independent producers. In doing this they retained their dominant position in the industry.

Steven Albert currently works as a Lecturer of Economics and Research Methods in the School of Advanced Studies at the University of Phoenix Online. In Chapter 8 he sets out his case for stars as markers of quality characteristics. For Albert, audiences make choices between films using information from previous films, and this process generates a particular distribution of financially successful films among film types. Movie stars can be used to mark these successful film types. Thus, their star power originates not only from 'box office appeal' but also from 'marking power'. Evidence of 960 top-twenty films released in the United States and Canada between 1940 to 1955 and 1960 to 1995 is consistent with this model. Sedgwick, in the previous chapter, adopts Albert's approach to stars as markers and broadly confirms his results for the period 1946 to 1965.

Mark Weinstein is an Associate Professor in the Marshall School of Business, University of Southern California. In Chapter 9 he examines the development of profit, or revenue-sharing contracts in the motion-picture industry. Contrary to popular belief, such contracts have been in use since the start of the studio era. However, early contracts differed from those seen today. The evolution of the current contract is traced and evidence regarding the increased use of sharing contracts after 1948 is examined. Competing theories of the economic function served by these contracts are examined, with the conclusion that these contracts are not the result of a standard principal–agent problem where the contract is designed to induce optimal effort by the agent. Rather, they may arise because of contracting issues between studio managers and studio shareholders, or because these contracts can help resolve the information asymmetries between the talent and the studio.

This is followed in Chapter 10 with Michael Pokorny's examination of the recent performance of the film industry in the USA, with a particular emphasis on the risk environment of film production. He utilises a data set that contains details of the performance and characteristics of over 4,000 films released in the USA between 1988 and 1999. An analysis of the relative performance of a range of distributors/studios is presented, and places particular emphasis on the manner in which the distributors constructed their annual portfolios of films, and how risk can be interpreted within such a context. While recognising the volatility of film financial performance on a film-by-film basis, the chapter suggests that the analysis of financial performance only makes sense within the context of the aggregate performance of the film portfolio, and compares and contrasts such performance across the major Hollywood distributors.

Finally, Keith Acheson, Professor of Economics at Carleton University, Ottawa, and Christopher J. Maule, Professor Emeritus at the same

University, argue in Chapter 11 that the integrated international marketing of films and related merchandise, and close financial ties between distributors and producers, have evolved to cope with the risks of piracy, cost containment, opportunism and revenue uncertainty. In search of an explanation of why America remains the centre of this institutional and contractual web, the authors examine the impact of two world wars, the rapid commercialisation of new technologies in the United States by aggressive managers, an open financial system and the ethnic diversity, linguistic homogeneity and size of the domestic market.

Notes

1 Between 1990 and 1999 the number of films released by the major Hollywood producers increased by 30 per cent, and the real average (negative) cost of each film increased by 59 per cent, implying a more than doubling of output, in crude real value of output terms. Source: Vogel (2000), Tables 2.4 and 3.2, employing a price deflator (1996 prices) of 0.865 for 1990 and 1.046 for 1999.
2 Vogel (2001), Table S1.1.
3 Vogel (2001), Table 1.2.

Reference

Vogel, H. (2001) *Entertainment Industry Economics*, 5th edn, Cambridge: Cambridge University Press.

1 The characteristics of film as a commodity[1]

John Sedgwick and Michael Pokorny

This book has been designed to appeal to film studies scholars wanting to know more about the history of film as a commercial enterprise, and hence the context within which films were made by capitalist organisations seeking profits. It is thus concerned with the business of the making, distribution and reception of a product that has played a very important part in the cultural and aesthetic lives of consumers in vast numbers across the globe during the course of the twentieth century. The work is novel in that it specifically uses microeconomic tools of analysis to help explain film business practices. However, it does so from a pragmatic viewpoint: if the authors featured in this book find an aspect of economic theory useful in coordinating and interpreting evidence from the archive, they use it. In this they are explicit. Here is the evidence, they say, and this particular theory helps make it intelligible. In doing this, the authors may be open to criticism: the evidence they provide may seem to be shaky in that its selection and its manner of collection may be questionable – of course, we believe this not to be the case! Furthermore, their interpretation of the evidence may also be challenged along with their choice of theory to illuminate their findings. But in all cases the methodologies used and interpretations arrived at by the authors are made explicit and accessible – deploying only where necessary basic statistical and model-building techniques – and based upon what we believe to be solid empirical evidence either collected by the authors from the archive or already available in the public domain.[2] Almost certainly there are dimensions to our choice of theories that will appear to be narrow or limited to scholars from non-economic backgrounds. We ask for their patience with, and understanding of, our position as economists/economic historians who, in reading articles and books about the aesthetic, philosophical, sociological and ideological evaluations of films, often cannot avoid being aware that many viewpoints confidently, sometimes zealously, asserted depend in part on implicit empirical assumptions that could be checked, tested and possibly refuted.[3]

The book, then, is conceived not as a definitive work but rather as a contribution to understanding the inner workings of the film business and particularly Hollywood over the twentieth century. It is a corpus of work that needs to be added to. Hollywood is at the centre of the film industry and has been since the 1920s. The success and ubiquity of its film products across the globe from this time makes it impossible to define indigenous national film industries separately from Hollywood. We do not take a normative position with regard to Hollywood and its global dominance but, rather, try to explain how it got to this position and then maintained it. Our contributors show that, as businesses operating in a capitalist environment, the studios that made and make up Hollywood acted rationally in the pursuit of profit in response to the business environment that they found themselves in at each particular historical juncture. For example, it should come as no surprise that the 'major' distributors during the Classical period – defined by Bordwell *et al.* (1985) as dating from the mid-1920s to 1960 – pursued booking policies with independent exhibitors that privileged in-house product. This is what one would expect in bilateral trading relations where the power relationship between the parties was highly skewed in favour of the studio. However, it should also not come as any surprise that, during the same period, because the vertically-integrated parent companies were large-scale cinema owners, studio in-house cinemas would screen the products of rival studios in preference to their own in-house product where the former offered the prospect of higher box office revenues (Hanssen, this volume, Chapter 5; Huettig 1985).

Broad trends

Starting with the pre-rental, pre-feature days of the sale, at so many cents, pence or francs per foot or metre, of short films often occupying no more than three minutes of screen time, in which actors were anonymous, and popular genres included travelogues and interest films, our contributors chart the evolution of film as a commodity-type, and stars as its derivative commodity-type, to the point where today theatrical release on average generates less than one-fifth of a film's earnings. Film became, along with recorded sound, the earliest form of entertainment commodity to be organised through mass industrial methods and it dominated the paid-for entertainment markets of the USA and Britain in the period before the mass diffusion of television. Its importance to television programming and the further stimulation it has received through the widespread take-up of video technology has extended its reach during the past twenty years. Further, film is now a strategically important element in the product mix of the global communications and entertainment conglomerates, such as News International.

In order to provide some context for what follows in this book, it is useful at this stage to present some broad statistical indicators of the evolution of the film industry through the twentieth century. Statistics relating to the industry are most readily available for the US market, which is hardly surprising given the dominance of Hollywood. Thus while we will here describe the evolution of the demand for film in the US market only, this evolution will have had important repercussions for the industry world-wide.

Figure 1.1 shows the percentage of total US consumers' expenditure on recreation accounted for by movie-going, from 1929 to 1999 (Vogel 2001). There are two notable features of this figure. First, the overwhelming dominance of movie-going as a recreational activity during the 1930s and 1940s – up to 25 per cent of recreational expenditure went on movie-going – and second, the very rapid decline in the importance of movie-going in the post-Second World War period. There were a number of reasons for this rapid decline – not least being the rapid diffusion of television – and these reasons are explored more fully in Chapter 7. Indeed, so sudden and precipitous was this decline that, at the time, the very survival of the industry was in serious doubt. But survive it certainly did, via a range of strategic responses. Chief amongst these was an increased emphasis on the production of 'hit' films, films with increasing production budgets and films that could be clearly differentiated from the output of television. This increasing emphasis had, in fact, begun in the late 1930s, but the difference in the 1930s was that the risks associated with high-budget film production were attenuated by the relative success of lower-risk medium-budget films. These ideas are explored more fully in Chapter 6. In the post-war period, however, television was able to effectively and efficiently replicate the lower- to medium-budget output of Hollywood, drastically altering the risk environment of filmmaking. The success of high-budget filmmaking,

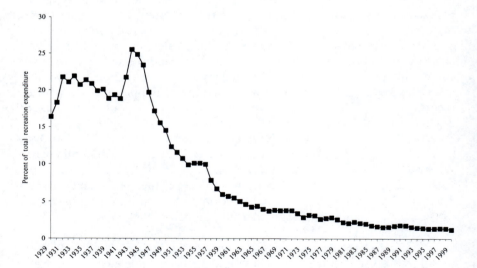

Figure 1.1 Expenditure on movie-going as a percentage of total recreation expenditure, 1929 to 1999.

with its high production values that television was unable to match, was now crucial to the success of Hollywood – high-budget films could no longer be treated as experimental and be cross-subsidised by medium-budget production as was the case in the 1930s. Nonetheless, recovery was slow and was not fully achieved until the late 1970s. This is reflected in Figure 1.2, which shows the number of US-produced films released onto the US market from 1929 to 1999, and where it can be seen that the volume of films released only began to increase from about 1980. However, Figure 1.2 overstates the decline in output of Hollywood in the post-war period and understates the increase for two reasons. First, there has been a secular increase in real average film production costs over the period, so that the value of output is markedly different from the volume of output. Detailed data on film production costs are notoriously difficult to obtain, but two comprehensive data sets are available for the 1930s and the 1990s (see Chapter 6 and Chapter 10, respectively, for further details). Thus there has been a more than five-fold increase in the real average production cost of films between the 1930s and 1990s, with the implication that the value of output (measured as the number of films released multiplied by average real production costs) has increased nearly three-fold. The second reason that Figure 1.2 understates the growth of Hollywood, particularly during the 1990s, is that modes of film consumption have changed radically, with movie-going accounting for as little as 20 per cent of film revenues, the remainder coming from consumption in the home, via video and television. In other words, while movie-going may have declined, relatively, as a recreation activity, movie consumption has not.

Figure 1.2 Total number of US-produced films released in the USA, 1929 to 1999.

Film as a commodity

Underlying the history of film is a set of characteristics that define and distinguish film as a commodity-type.[4] These characteristics conceptually delimit the manner in which film as a commodity-type has been developed by capitalists in search of profits and used by consumers in pursuit of utility. This ontological approach to film as a commodity serves as an example of a general methodological approach for investigating how different institutional practices have emerged historically among industrial configurations: it provides a framework for analysing how the 'system of provision' associated with film differs from that of other commodity-types such as painting, or theatrical performance, or tractors. It is an approach that contrasts with the 'horizontal' analyses in which economists typically search for and examine features common across industrial divides, such as rates-of-return on investment, industrial concentration and price elasticity of demand. It is thus helpful to understand film as a 'system of provision' – defined by Fine and Leopold (1993: 4) as a system that 'unites a particular pattern of production with a particular pattern of consumption ... [in] ways, in which each is moderated by the connections between them'.

Following Lysandrou (2000), we can say that commodities exist on two levels: as a fantastic array of things, both physical and intellectual; and as a set of prices. The latter implies that money is an integral aspect of commodity production allowing consumers the prospect of comparing commodities abstractly in relation to one another. Commodities, hence, can be conceived of as products that are assigned a price by the producing agent and placed in a social space (market) for potential buyers to locate and consider. The product is confirmed, or not, as a commodity when its price is realised through the act of transaction exchange. The theory of horizontal differentiation, built upon the seminal work of Hotelling (1929), shows that where differentiated products are offered at the same price consumers will rank them according to personal benchmark criteria, learned from previous consumption experience (Beath and Katsoulacos 1991: 5). On this basis, consumers are able to establish their most preferred product. Clearly, differences in price will affect that order as consumers trade-off price against utility. Where products are rejected by customers, or not even entered into commodity space, their existence will be confined to a separate domain; they do not exist as commodities, but as either quasi-commodities where their supply is guaranteed through the support of an outside agency such as Government, or as non-commodities which are distributed as gifts.[5]

As shown in Figure 1.3 there are two existential aspects to film as a commodity. The first, material, aspect is as strips of photographic representations on celluloid copied from and identical with an original master (template), which are the object of transactions between producers, distributors and exhibitors. These transactions are based on anticipa-

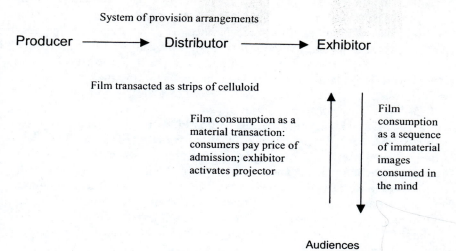

System of provision arrangements

Producer ——————▶ Distributor ——————▶ Exhibitor

Film transacted as strips of celluloid

Film consumption as a
material transaction:
consumers pay price of
admission; exhibitor
activates projector

Film
consumption
as a sequence
of immaterial
images
consumed in
the mind

Audiences

Figure 1.3 Production and consumption relations.

tions arising from the second, immaterial, aspect, which is the form in
which film is consumed in the mind of each member of the cinema audience, i.e. as a sequence of projected images.

Each token (separate film as a unique production) has its status as a
commodity confirmed, or otherwise, by audiences, through admissions to
the cinemas in which its sequence of projected images can be viewed. If it
is not shown (i.e. if the reels of celluloid do not undergo the appropriate
mechanical processes in a projector), it is not seen. *Qua* projected image, it
has no separate existence.

The basis of its reception will be those expectations of pleasure –
however defined – which audiences bring to the experience of film
viewing. The expectations that audiences have acquired from previous
film-going experiences are likely to be strongly formed within cultures in
which film-going has been a genuinely popular leisure activity, implying
that film-goers will hold firm preferences as to what they like. In Sedgwick
(2000), the framework developed by Gilad, Kaish and Loab (1987) is
adopted in which consumers search for consonance and reject dissonance
in making choices. However, a film-goer's expectations should not be
regarded as a state of mind bounded once and for all, but rather as a
modifiable set of ideas subject to change as distinctive aesthetic regimes
emerge and affect the way in which things are looked at and pleasures
derived.

In learning what they like, audiences are engaged in a discovery process
(De Vany and Walls 1996). The same is true, of course, for film entrepreneurs (Sedgwick and Pokorny 1998: 196–197). The exchange of a film

screening for the price of a cinema admission results optimally in pleasure and profit for consumers and suppliers respectively. Historically, this dynamic has brought about a convergence of structural, stylistic (aesthetic), ethical and narrative conventions that prevail for a certain length of time but then are replaced by others. For instance, Bordwell *et al.* (1985) have identified a set of filmmaking conventions that characterise what they have termed the 'Classical' period of Hollywood production, *c.*1925–1960. This mega-periodisation of film has been continued by Gomery (1998) who argues that, subsequently, there have been two 'New Hollywoods'. For Gomery, changes in aesthetic practices should be understood as the consequence of new business strategies which emerged in the face of: a) declining attendances from 1946 to the mid-1970s in the North American market; b) the change in the age composition of the audience; and c) the emergence and widespread diffusion of video, satellite, digital and multi-screen technologies. In an earlier work, Gomery (1992) explained Hollywood's studio system during the 'Classical' period in a similar business-strategy manner, a thesis that has been examined and elaborated in detail by Thomas Schatz (1998).

Film commodity characteristics

Carroll (1998: 196) has given the following functional definition of mass art work:

> *x* is a mass artwork if, and only if, 1. *x* is a multiple instance or type artwork, 2. produced and distributed by a mass technology, 3. which artwork is intentionally designed to gravitate in its structural choices (for example, its narrative forms, symbolism, intended affect, and even its content) towards those choices that promise accessibility with minimum effort, virtually on first contact, for the largest number of untutored (or relatively untutored) audiences.

Carroll's work is important because it provides a means of formally distinguishing between avant-garde, popular and mass art. For Carroll, accessibility is the key to reception. He writes that mass art 'is made with the intention that it be assimilated with minimum effort' (p. 35) but which nonetheless requires that audiences are actively engaged in interpreting 'narrative meaning' (p. 45). Drawing on the work of Walter Benjamin, Carroll goes on to argue that mass artworks are made possible by technologies of production and distribution 'capable of delivering multiple instances or tokens of mass artworks' (p. 188) 'to populations that are mass in that they cross national, class, religious, political, ethnic, racial and gender boundaries' (p. 185).

Film as a commodity corresponds exactly to these criteria, but to understand how it does so requires an exploration of those characteristics that distinguish the film commodity from other commodity types, including other mass art commodities.[6] They are:

1 the non-diminishable, indivisible, indefinitely enlargeable, infinitely reproducible, but excludable nature of the film image.
2 the slow physical deterioration of the means of producing the film image.
3 the rapidity with which pleasure derived from consumption declines relative to the anticipation of new pleasures – rapidly diminishing marginal utility.
4 uniqueness.
5 short product life cycles, particularly in the era before the mass diffusion of television.
6 the dedicated expenditure of time and attention on the part of consumers which could be put to alternative uses.

Characteristics '1' and '2' are technologically based and distinguish film from other art-type commodities such as books and records, not simply as physical entities, but also in terms of how they have facilitated the evolution of film as a 'system of provision'.[7] The set of characteristic '1' highlights the public-good aspect of film as well as its productivity potential.[8] Unlike the technologies of phonograph and radio, those of film projection made the household an unsuitable place for mass film consumption.[9] Given that the film image is indivisible – it is *non-rival* in that one person's consumption of it does not impair that of another – the early entrepreneurs needed ways of excluding consumers so as to be able to assign prices. The first commercial presentation of 'motion pictures' in New York in 1894 fulfilled this requirement by means of peep-show machines installed in 'Kinetoscope Parlors'. They soon showed the disadvantages, notably from the point of view of expansion to meet public demand, of the individualised-viewing regime for assigning prices, and within a year (Paris, 1895) the first public presentation of a film on a screen had taken place. Initially music-hall/theatre venues, converted shops/nickelodeons, or fairground tents were the sites of this technical and socio-psychological organisational innovation in public exhibition that enabled prices 'of admission' to be charged. However, by 1910 in the three largest markets, those of the USA, Britain and France, exhibition was increasingly dominated by purpose-built cinemas, the size (seating capacity) of which was not determined technologically but rather by an entrepreneur's assessment of the potential demand for film in a particular socio-economic location. In other words, cinemas could be, within limits, as large or small (and as luxurious or basic) as thought appropriate for business purposes.[10]

That any single film could be screened universally was a great incentive to the second generation of American film entrepreneurs which, from the mid-1910s onwards, was the first to produce from Hollywood. Kristin

Thompson (1985) has shown how internationally widespread the distribution links of these new production companies had become by the beginning of the 1920s, based initially on networks of overseas agents but, from the First World War onwards, increasingly through their own in-house distribution arms. The rationale behind extending the distribution reach was simply that, given a set of film production costs that were sunk (i.e. could not be retrieved for alternative uses once paid because, outside of distribution/exhibition, the reels of film would only be worth the scrap value of the celluloid and the photosensitive silver compounds) films should be distributed as widely as possible, up to the point where the additional revenues obtained from distributing into one more movie theatre just covered the additional costs associated with the making of new prints, the transportation of new and/or existing used prints, and publicity and distribution overheads. Whilst helping to quicken the pace at which costs could be amortised, the extension of the market also encouraged producers to increase the budgets of their major productions in the expectation that their specific qualities (including their stars) would be attractive to new audiences.

The relatively slow physical deterioration of film negatives to a state in which they were unusable by the distributor for striking new projection prints meant that the stock of a film commodity as a sequence of images did not decline mechanically in step with consumption (characteristic '2'). As mentioned earlier, during its proto-industrial period – up to *c.*1908 – film was sold by the foot/metre, leading to the stockpiling of films because local audience interest in a film subject declined at a rate faster than deterioration of the film stock on which it was held. In turn the oversupply of films in the market meant that producers had difficulty in selling new films to exhibitors. This problem was resolved at first through the emergence of a second-hand market and then with the introduction of a system of rentals as producers attempted to restrict the supply of films in circulation. This development was also informed by emerging audience taste for more highly differentiated films with stronger narrative story structures, in conjunction with the frissons from recognising and being attracted to some of the artists that appeared in them.

Characteristics '3', '4', '5' and '6'. As argued earlier, it is audiences who legitimise films by confirming them as commodities. From a different tack, Carroll argues that a film will only be an example of mass art when it is easily comprehensible as well as readily available. From this, it follows that where audiences find a film 'difficult' or 'challenging' it is less likely that it will attract a mass audience, although it might well still be confirmed as a commodity were it to be given a limited distribution, say, amongst art-house cinemas. Part of the explanation as to why films need to be easily accessible for them to be popular with audiences is that ambiguity and complexity detract, for many, from the pleasures derived from film-going, making the activity a less pleasant experience than anticipated.

One aspect of this is that, once seen, films are comparatively rarely revisited, at least at the cinema.[11] Accessibility implies that consumers are able to make sense of the film commodity, at their own personal level, to the extent that a second viewing would add little more to their appreciation of its qualities and might indeed reduce that remembered pleasure, in that repetition may lead to boredom. Furthermore, where consumers can choose between a variety of film programmes at similarly priced local cinemas, the opportunity cost of seeing film A for a second time is clearly demarcated in terms of not seeing films B to Z, amongst other uses of their time.

Linked to this is the fact that each film is unique, consisting of a set of structural characteristics that differentiate it from all other films in a way that is not true for most industrial products. But the requirement of accessibility on the part of audiences and their search for acceptably novel film-going pleasures have ensured that films are not randomly different from one another. Highly successful films send back signals of audience preferences, as revealed through the box-office, to the originating studio and also to its rivals. Box-office success has regularly engendered clusters of films with similar story and aesthetic characteristics, forming, over time, lineages that are subject to life-cycle tendencies (Sedgwick 2000: Chapter 8).

Empirical regularities

One of the most striking discoveries about the history of Hollywood film – from the time in which products were widely and systematically distributed across the US market, *c.*1915 – is the existence of a set of empirical regularities that have shaped the manner in which film as an industry has been organised. Arthur De Vany and David Walls (1996, 1997, 1999) in a series of articles, collected in De Vany (2004), have provided evidence of the highly unequal distribution of film revenues, as well as the stochastic (random) nature of box-office success of both films and the stars who appear in them. Furthermore, in articles with Eckert and Lee, De Vany has questioned the validity of anti-trust regulation when applied to the film industry (De Vany and Eckert 1991; De Vany and Lee 2004). From De Vany and Walls and our own studies at different historical junctures (Pokorny and Sedgwick 2001; Sedgwick 2000, 2002; Sedgwick and Pokorny 1998) it has been established that:

1   the distribution of box office revenue is highly skewed, meaning that only a very small number of films can expect to enjoy the considerable revenues available to the 'hits' of the year, and that a high degree of volatility exists between the revenues accruing to 'hit' films occupying the same berth in the charts during the course of that year and, by implication, between seasons.

2   the mode, median and mean revenue of films released during any one season fall in the lowest decile band of the distribution.
3   the life cycle of individual film subjects – when confined to theatrical release – is short: prior to the mass diffusion of television, this was, of course, the only medium through which films were consumed.
4   there is a positive relationship between the cost of production and the revenue generated by films in any one season, but this relationship is heteroscedastic – it becomes increasingly unstable the higher the production budget.
5   risk taking can be attenuated where studios place portfolios of films onto the market.

A number of these regularities can be illustrated through two extensive data sets. The first relates to all the films released by MGM, RKO and Warner Bros. in the USA from 1930 to 1942, a data set comprising of 1,796 films. The second relates to 2,116 films released onto the US market between 1988 and 1999. In both cases, data are available on the revenues generated by each of these films (distributor rentals in the case of the 1930 to 1942 data set and box office revenues in the case of the 1988 to 1999 data set). In addition, cost of production data is available for each film (actual costs for 1930 to 1942, and estimated costs for 1988 to 1999). Finally, data on the profitability of each film, deriving from theatrical release, is available, the actual profits generated by the films of MGM and RKO for 1930 to 1942, and estimated profits for Warner Bros., and estimated profits for the films released in the 1988 to 1999 period (see Chapter 6 and Chapter 10 for further details of these data sets).

Figure 1.4 presents a scattergraph of distributor rentals against production costs (in constant 1929 prices) for the 1930 to 1942 data set, and Figure 1.5 presents a scattergraph of box office revenues against production costs (in constant 1987 prices) for the 1988 to 1999 data set. Both graphs imply that the risk environment of filmmaking has been remarkably consistent over time – high-budget films tend to generate higher revenues, but this relationship is a far from stable one, and becomes increasingly less stable as production budgets increase. This can be seen more clearly in Figures 1.6 and 1.7, which show a scatter of film profits against production budgets. Broadly, these two figures reflect very similar profitability and risk environments – profit performance becomes increasingly variable as production budgets increase, with high-budget films being capable of generating substantial profits but, equally, these films can generate sizeable losses. The environment is one in which exceptional outcomes dominate, although these exceptional outcomes are relatively rare. In statistical terms, these 'outlier' observations severely inhibit the identification of stable, underlying models of film production – indeed, they virtually ensure that such models do not exist – and yet these outliers cannot be simply dropped from any detailed statistical analysis – these

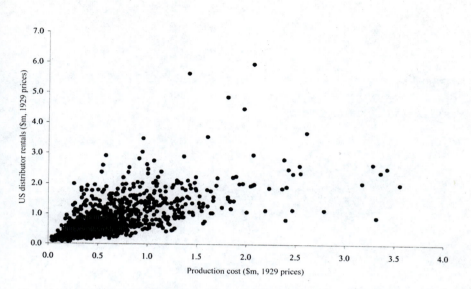

Figure 1.4 Scatter of distributor rentals against film costs, 1929 prices, 1930 to 1942.

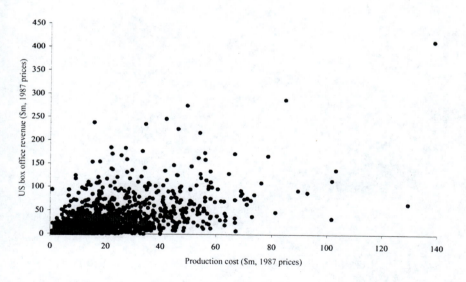

Figure 1.5 Scatter of box office revenues against film costs, 1987 prices, 1988 to 1999.

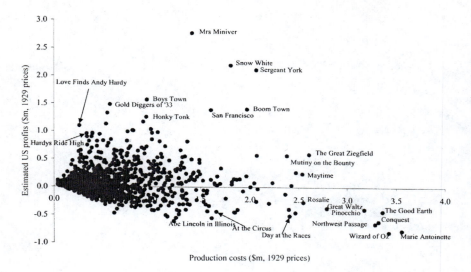

Figure 1.6 Scatter of US profits against film costs, 1929 prices, 1930 to 1942.

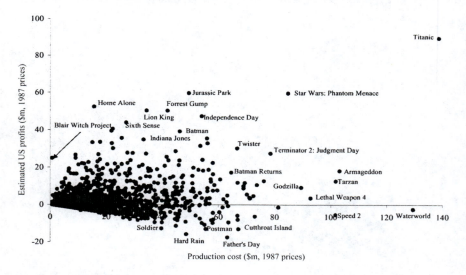

Figure 1.7 Scatter of US profits against film costs, 1987 prices, 1988 to 1999.

mega-hits (and mega-flops) are in many respects the essence of Holly-wood.[12]

While Figures 1.6 and 1.7, superficially, reflect a relatively unchanged filmmaking environment, there are some substantive differences between the two data periods. Very-high-budget film production in the 1930s was relatively unsuccessful, whereas in the 1990s these films were a major source of profits for the industry. Thus, if we consider films costing in excess of $1.4m (in 1929 prices) in the 1930s, and those costing in excess of $50m (in 1987 prices) in the 1990s, then such films accounted for about 4 per cent of all films produced in both periods. In the 1930s these films, in aggregate, generated a rate-of-return of just 5 per cent, compared to a rate-of-return of 13 per cent on all films produced in the period. In the 1990s these films generated an aggregate rate-of-return of 30 per cent, exceeding the 21 per cent generated by all films. In both cases these high-budget films absorbed about 16 per cent of production budgets. Although there was considerable variability in the performance of these high-budget films from year to year, there were a number of years during the 1990s when these films generated in excess of 50 per cent of total annual profits (in 1996, when these films absorbed just 18 per cent of total production budgets, and in 1997 when they absorbed 39 per cent of total budgets). There were, of course, other years in which these films were relatively unsuccessful – they generated losses in aggregate in 1993 – but apart from 1993, 1994 and 1995, the percentage contribution to aggregate profits of these very-high-budget films exceeded the proportion of production budgets that they absorbed. By contrast, high-budget production in the 1930s was largely unsuccessful. Very-high-budget films generated losses in four of the ten years in which high-budget production took place, and in only two of the six remaining years did the percentage contribution to aggregate annual profits of high-budget films exceed the proportion of production budgets that they absorbed (1936 and 1942). That is, financial success in the 1930s derived from medium- to lower-budget production, whereas in the 1990s it was higher-budget production that made the major contribution to financial success.

Conclusion

From these regularities it is difficult not to come to the conclusion that uncertainty is an integral element in making and watching films. Audiences do not know fully what pleasures they are going to get before they actually experience a film; producers do not know with any assuring degree of probability how their product is going to perform on the market. Clearly in these circumstances producers are very interested in learning how to attenuate this uncertainty. Historically, producers have devised strategies, according to their awareness and interpretation of the logic of the situations, that changes in technology, socio-political conditions and audience preferences presented to them. Some changes, such as the transition to 'talkies' following the commercial success of *The Jazz Singer* (1927), were starkly 'epochal' at the time; others, such as the post-1946 decline in admissions combined with the logistics of divorcement, found the moguls, company accountants and media analysts on differing learning curves for many years because, for those living through the times, the plethora of statistics from within and without the movie business made it difficult to achieve a consensus as to what the situation was.

This book is the first effort at producing an economic history of film across the twentieth century. From its pages it is apparent that the 'system of film provision' that prevailed largely unchanged from 1920 through to the emergence of television itself emerged from an earlier stage in which *ex ante* projection-based exhibition and rental-based distribution were not certainties but, rather, technical solutions to business problems. Audiences themselves came to learn to value both novelty and pleasure but in a form which was circumscribed by narrative, genre and star conventions. For instance, during the embryonic period of the film industry between 1896 and 1908, a film programme might include actualities, travelogues, event reconstructions, as well as dramatic and comic films. That hedonic film aesthetics prevailed over those that were more educational or interest-specific suggests that pleasure appears to be at the core of what audiences most enjoyed about the experience of film-going. It became intrinsic to the purpose for which films were made.

Notes

1 Aspects of this chapter are taken with permission from Sedgwick (2000).
2 See Jarvie (1995) for a discussion of film studies methodology.
3 See Salt (1992).
4 Care should be taken with the distinction made here between the characteristics of commodity-*types* and the characteristics of particular *commodities*. Film is a commodity-type, whereas a film such as *Gone With the Wind* (1939) was (and still is) a commodity.
5 In real-life complex markets, an item may succeed as a commodity at one stage, but fail at another. For example, a film producer may successfully sell a film to a distributor, so that relative to the producer the reels of celluloid have become a commodity. The distributor would only have bought the rights to the film on the basis of apparent potential. But war is declared and suddenly and unexpectedly the subject matter of the film is unacceptable. In the new context it has become unreleasable, so for the distributor its commodity-potential as a film is unrealised, indeed unrealisable, and the result is reels of celluloid which have little scrap value. (The events of September 11, 2001 left many projects mired in variations of this kind of jeopardy.)
6 In terms of numbers, film was the first truly 'mass' art. Annual figures for cinema admissions are of a different order of magnitude from those of museum admissions for non-mass arts such as painting. For example, in Britain during the mid-1930s there were close to a billion annual admissions to cinemas and approximately 2.25 billion in the USA.
7 With the exception of pay-per-view television, radio and TV art-type programmes, including films on TV, are more problematic in that whilst they might well be examples of mass art in Carroll's sense, they are not, strictly speaking, consumed as *commodities* by audiences even where they have been acquired by the programmers through market-based transactions. This is because they cannot be assigned prices for the reason that the technology that carries their transmission is inclusive. The commodity aspect to radio and television is the airtime purchased by advertisers, the price of which is related to the size and

type of audience listening to (or viewing) programmes around and within which adverts are placed. Accordingly, it can be argued that (in the absence of public service provision made fully available by the state – such as the BBC in the UK) films shown on 'free-to-air' commercial TV can be regarded as quasi *gifts* to its audiences.

8 The term 'productivity' here is based on the conception of film as an input from which audiences derive pleasurable outcomes (outputs). Hence, the productivity of a film is measured in terms of the size of its audience. One film will be more productive than another if its audience is greater.

9 It is interesting to speculate on whether cinemas would have had an existence had video and television technologies been extant at the end of the nineteenth century. In the same way that the phonograph and radio enabled a home-based pattern of consumption of recorded music and radio programmes, video technologies in conjunction with those of television have allowed film to be similarly consumed. The key difference between the consumption of recorded sound and films on videotape on the one hand, and radio and terrestrial TV programmes on the other, is that the latter two do not require specific software.

10 For the emergence of cinemas see Abeh (1994); Allen (1985); Balio (1985); Bowser (1990); Brown and Anthony (1999); Fuller (1996); Gomery (1992); Hendricks (1985); Hiley (2002); Low (1948); Low and Manvell (1948); Merritt (1985).

11 Before the 1940s, the re-issue of films for distribution was comparatively rare.

12 De Vany (2004: 1–6) argues similarly.

Bibliography

Primary sources

Eddie Mannix ledger, copied by Mark Glancy. The original ledger is held in the Howard Strickling Collection, The Margaret Herrick Library of the Academy of Motion Picture Arts and Sciences, Beverly Hills, California.

William Schaefer ledger, copied by Mark Glancy. The original ledger is held as part of the William Schaefer Collection at the University of Southern California Film and Television Archives in Los Angeles.

C.J. Trevlin ledger, made available by Richard Jewell. The original ledger is held at the University of Southern California Film and Television Archives in Los Angeles.

US Department of Commerce, Bureau of the Census (1975) *Historical Statistics of the US: Colonial Times to 1970*, Washington, DC.

References

Abel, R. (1994) *The Ciné Goes to Town: French Cinema, 1896–1914*, Berkeley, CA: University of California Press.

Allen, R. (1985) 'The movies in vaudeville: historical context of the movies as popular entertainment', in T. Balio (ed.) *The American Film Industry*, Madison, WI: University of Wisconsin Press.

Balio, T. (ed.) (1985) *The American Film Industry*, Madison, WI: University of Wisconsin Press.

Beath, J. and Katsoulacos, Y. (1991) *The Economic Theory of Product Differentiation*, Cambridge: Cambridge University Press.

Bordwell, D., Staiger, J. and Thompson, K. (1985) *The Classical Hollywood Cinema: Film Style and Mode of Production to 1960*, London: RKP.

Bowser, E. (1990) *The Transformation of Cinema 1907–1915*, New York, NY: Macmillan.

Brown, R. and Anthony, B. (1999) *A Victorian Film Enterprise: the History of the British Mutoscope and Biograph Company, 1897–1915*, Trowbridge: Flick Books.

Carroll, N. (1998) *A Philosophy of Mass Art*, Oxford: Oxford University Press.

De Vany, A. (2004) *Hollywood Economics: How Extreme Uncertainty Shapes the Film Industry*, London: Routledge.

De Vany, A. and Eckert, R. (1991) 'Motion picture antitrust: the Paramount Cases revisited', *Research in Law and Economics*, 14: 51–112.

De Vany, A. and Walls, W.D. (1996) 'Bose–Einstein dynamics and adaptive contracting in the motion picture industry', *Economic Journal*, 106: 1493–1514.

De Vany, A. and Walls, W.D. (1997) 'The market for motion pictures: rank, revenue, and survival', *Economic Inquiry*, 35: 783–797.

De Vany, A. and Walls, W.D. (1999) 'Uncertainty and the movie industry: does star power reduce the terror of the box office?', *Journal of Cultural Economics*, 23: 285–318.

De Vany, A. and Lee, C. (2004) 'Stochastic market structure: concentration measures and motion picture antitrust', in A. De Vany (ed.) *Hollywood Economics: How Extreme Uncertainty Shapes the Film Industry*, London: Routledge.

Fine, B. and Leopold, E. (1993) *The World of Consumption*, London: Routledge.

Fuller, K. (1996) *At the Picture Show: Small-Town Audiences and the Creation of Movie Fan Culture*, Washington, DC: Smithsonian Institution Press.

Gilad, B., Kaish, S. and Loab, P. (1987) 'Cognitive dissonance and utility maximization: a general framework', *Journal of Economic Behaviour and Organization*, 8: 61–73.

Gomery, D. (1992) *Shared Pleasures: a History of Movie Presentation in the United States*, London: BFI.

Gomery, D. (1998) 'Hollywood corporate business practice and periodizing contemporary film history', in S. Neale and M. Smith (eds) *Contemporary Hollywood Cinema*, London: Routledge.

Hendricks, G. (1985) 'The history of the kinetoscope', in T. Balio (ed.) *The American Film Industry*, Madison, WI: University of Wisconsin Press.

Hiley, N. (2002) '"Nothing more than a craze": cinema building in Britain from 1909 to 1914', in A. Higson (ed.) *Young and Innocent: the Cinema in Britain, 1896–1930*, Exeter: Exeter University Press.

Hotelling, H. (1929) 'Stability in competition', *Economic Journal*, 39: 41–47.

Huettig, M. (1985) 'Economic control of the motion picture industry', abridged from a publication of the same title published by University of Pennsylvania Press in 1944 and found in T. Balio (ed.) *The American Film Industry*, Madison, WI: University of Wisconsin.

Jarvie, I. (1995) 'Sir Karl Popper (1902–94): essentialism and historicism in film methodology', *Historical Journal of Film, Radio and Television*, 15: 301–305.

Low, R. (1948) *The History of British Film, 1906–1914*, London: Allen and Unwin.

Low, R. and Manvell, R. (1948) *The History of British Film, 1896–1906*, London: Allen and Unwin.

Lysandrou, P. (2000) 'The market and exploitation in Marx's economic theory: a reinterpretation', *Cambridge Journal of Economics*, 24: 325–347.

Merritt, R. (1985) 'The movies in vaudeville: historical context of the movies as popular entertainment', in T. Balio (ed.) *The American Film Industry*, Madison, WI: University of Wisconsin Press.

Pokorny, M. and Sedgwick, J. (2001) 'Stardom and the profitability of filmmaking: Warner Bros. in the 1930s', *Journal of Cultural Economics*, 25: 157–184.

Salt, B. (1992) *Film Style and Technology: History and Analysis*, 2nd edn, London: Starword.

Schatz, T. (1998) *The Genius of the System*, New York, NY: Pantheon.

Sedgwick, J. (2000) *Popular Filmgoing in 1930s Britain: a Choice of Pleasures*, Exeter: Exeter University Press.

Sedgwick, J. (2002) 'Product differentiation at the movies: Hollywood, 1946–65', *Journal of Economic History*, 62: 676–704.

Sedgwick, J. and Pokorny, M. (1998) 'The risk environment of film-making: Warners in the inter-war period', *Explorations in Economic History*, 35: 196–220.

Thompson, K. (1985) *Exporting Entertainment: America in the World Film Market 1907–1934*, London: BFI.

Vogel, H. (2001) *Entertainment Industry Economics*, 5th edn, Cambridge: Cambridge University Press.

2   America's master

The European film industry in the United States, 1907–1920[1]

Gerben Bakker

> What the mass media offer is not popular art, but entertainment which is
> intended to be consumed like food, forgotten, and replaced by a new dish.
>
> W.H. Auden[2]

Fear of economic dominance has played a fair part in the way Europeans
view America and Americans view Europe, and not only in present times.
At the end of the nineteenth century, with British investments accounting
for one-fifth of American GDP, polemical pamphlets stated that what
Britain had failed to accomplish with military means, it was now achieving
with economic ones. Just a few years later, similar fears emerged in
Europe, where American factories were making their appearance at a
rapid pace. Britain counted seventy-five American factories in 1900, and
up to the First World War, five more new ones were built every year. The
occasional fears of an America that would beat Britain in business were
exemplified by F.A. McKenzie, who published the pamphlet *The American Invaders* in 1902. In the same year, a campaign was started against the
invasion of American cigarettes (Emmott 1989: 5–8; 1992).

While during the rest of the century American economic fear remained
preoccupied with Communist Europe and Japan, European fears of
American economic dominance continued, as highlighted by Jean-Jacques
Servan-Schreiber in his influential *La Défi Américain* (1967: 40)

> While French, German, or Italian firms are still groping around in the
> new open spaces provided by the Treaty of Rome, afraid to emerge
> from the dilapidated shelter of their old habits, American industry has
> gauged the terrain and is now rolling from Naples to Amsterdam with
> the ease and the speed of Israeli tanks in the Sinai desert.[3]

Economic considerations have been but part of a broader view of America
that also encompassed fears of cultural intrusion. Already in 1900, British
members of parliament introduced a resolution denouncing the decline of
morals caused by American plays performed in London, and English

teachers were complaining about the invasion of Americanisms into the language around the same time (Zeldin 1990: 36; Kuisel 1993).

In the perceived struggle between Europe and America, the film industry is a battlefield of both an economic and cultural character: it was the main clashing point for most of the twentieth century. While many European intellectuals despised the 'cheap' American films, to their horror they witnessed how the European masses queued to see them, in numbers so large that the production of European films became hardly possible without state protection.

Between 1925 and 1928, eleven European governments introduced measures to protect their countries against the unlimited supply of American films.[4] The issue has not left the table since, and the debate heats up periodically. What has made the Hollywood dominance particularly hard to bear for some interest groups within European states is that American films not only deeply penetrated the European mind, but also ruled out an equivalent European alternative, because of the sheer economic power of Hollywood. The old continent, which stood at the roots of the modern film industry, had been overturned by its younger apprentice from the new world.

While the cultural and political aspects of the Hollywood dominance have been discussed considerably (De Grazia 1989; Elwood and Kroes 1994; Vasey 1997), the economic side has remained largely unexamined, and most attention has been paid to the period in which the Hollywood studios were the dominant film suppliers in the world. This chapter investigates the economic causes of Hollywood's dominance by examining the one period this century when American film companies did *not* control their home market and world markets, and instead European firms provided a large share of films shown. In this era, roughly the years from 1900 until the mid-1910s, European film companies not only held the largest market shares in their home markets, but they also were the major film suppliers in the United States. In some years, they supplied half of the films shown in America. Innovations like the newsreel and the feature film had their origins in Europe, but reached their zenith in the USA.

After the First World War, in the entire US market only a few European films were distributed. Never since have European companies managed to obtain a lasting presence in America, finding it difficult as a consequence to compete effectively with the Hollywood product in their home markets. During the remainder of the twentieth century, Europe's film industry never recovered. Since the mid-1920s, only protection, tax breaks and state subsidies have kept it afloat.[5]

It is this remarkable transition from economic dominance to insignificance that will be examined in this chapter. It will research how European film companies could be so successful initially, and what may have caused their collective downfall during such a brief period. By going back to this long-forgotten era, this chapter tries to answer an everyday question which many a European must have wondered about, namely 'Why do most movies come from Hollywood?' Furthermore, this contribution shows how expressions of popular culture are constrained and influenced by economic circumstances and historical accidents.

This chapter has been partially inspired by Kristin Thompson's pioneering *Exporting Entertainment*, which examines the inverse of this chapter, namely the rise to dominance of the Hollywood studios, although she also briefly addresses the decline of the European film industry (Thompson 1985; Uricchio 1996). To investigate the extent and timing of the shift, data series on market shares taken from trade publications have been used. The period examined starts in 1907, because it is only from that date that regular industry data are available, and because the earlier period is less relevant to the aims of this contribution. The period ends in 1920, when the European market share in the USA had become negligible and Pathé Frères, the largest European film company, sold its American subsidiary to Merrill Lynch.

Structure and development of the American market

An important characteristic of early American film production was the legal battle for the ownership of cinema technology. By 1907 two groups of producing companies emerged, both of which held competing patent claims: one around Edison, and one around the American Mutoscope & Biograph Company. In 1908 they pooled their patents and formed the Motion Picture Patents Company (MPPC), which aimed at controlling the whole film business. Film exchanges and exhibitors had to pay licence fees to the MPPC to use film stock and apparatus (Cassady 1959).

The MPPC had six American and two European members, the French Méliès and Pathé. Behind the trust stood Eastman-Kodak, which sold film-stock to MPPC companies on a three-year exclusive contract. In 1909, the patent trust extended its monopoly to distribution by buying the official (licence-fee paying) film exchanges, which were merged eventually into the General Film Company in 1910.

Nevertheless, the power of the trust quickly waned. Attracted by a rapidly growing market, many entrepreneurs made films without paying licence fees, packing bags around their cameras and claiming they used different technologies.[6] Moreover, in 1911, Eastman-Kodak's contract was modified to allow it to supply film-stock to non-MPPC companies. Another blow came when, in 1912, the US government sued the MPPC for violation of the Sherman (anti-trust) Act. In that same year, a court decision narrowed the MPPC's legal base, judging that its patents did not cover certain kinds of film technology.

Cinema consumption changed considerably in the early years. Around 1900, films in America were shown by travelling showmen, on fairs, and as parts of variety and vaudeville programmes. Between 1905 and 1907,

Nickelodeons emerged, small theatres with a few hundred seats, and from 1911 larger theatres emerged with 1,000 to 1,500 seats, generally in city centres and aimed at a middle-class audience. In 1909, *c.*6,500 cinemas existed, and in 1913 the number had doubled to 15,183, while the seating capacity of the average cinema had increased as well (Musser 1990; Balio 1985: 144; Cassady 1959).

During the same years, the length of an average film gradually increased from a couple of hundred feet – varying widely from one film to the next – at the turn of the century towards an industry standard of 1,000 feet (*c.*15 minutes) around 1911–1912, which in its turn was replaced by the feature film of three or more reels, again eventually reaching an industry standard of 90 to 120 minutes (six to eight reels). Watching a film changed from an activity lasting only a few minutes into an evening-filling event. The rapid growth of the film industry is further indicated by the increase in ticket prices, from 5 cents at the Nickelodeon to 25 cents for a feature, with peak prices as high as $1 for new special releases in city centres.

Figure 2.1 shows the total released length of films. This reflects the 'production capacity' of the film companies, and it can be argued that increases in this capacity reflect market growth.[7] The released length increased tenfold in the ten years between 1907 and 1916. Released length probably understates real market growth, as film budgets, rental prices and ticket prices increased, and more copies of individual films were rented and watched by more consumers.[8]

No systematic data on film budgets exist, but when available indications are used, it can be maintained that average film production costs increased significantly during the period 1907–1920. In 1908, the MPPC leased film to exchanges at 7–13 cents a foot (Cassady 1959), and if on average thirty copies would be sold, this means that the producer's revenue for a 500-feet film (the average length in 1908[9]) was on average about $1,650. This concurs roughly with estimates that put the average film budget at $1,000 for 1909 (Hampton 1931: 211). In 1914, films were estimated to cost on average between $10,000 and $30,000, and in 1921 the range was from $40,000 to $80,000 on average, and from $100,000–$200,000 for 'specials' (Balio 1985: 144; Hampton 1931: 205–211). Although the exact increase is unknown, a ten-fold increase – even if adjusted for longer film length – seems a conservative estimate.[10] As these costs were increasing, another shift occurred as well: films were no longer sold or leased by the foot for a fixed fee but rented for a percentage of box office revenue.

During this strong growth phase of the American market, European companies played an important role. In the early 1900s, European film companies generally exported films to the USA through American distributors, but they often saw their films illegally copied by American competitors (Musser 1990: 364–365). From roughly 1905 onwards, French companies became important. The Danish Nordisk film company started

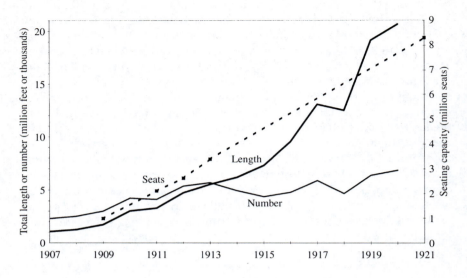

Figure 2.1 The size of the US film market, surrogate indicators, 1907–1920.

Sources

Number of films: 1907–1914: a representative group of samples is selected from samples of released films published in Thompson (1985: 213–214). These samples are based on weekly release schedules in the *Motion Picture World*. 1907–1911: for each year four seasonal samples are taken from Thompson's data (April, June, August, November or closest), the number of films in four samples is divided by four and multiplied by twelve to get a yearly estimate; 1912: yearly estimate based on two samples of releases during a month, and two samples of releases during a week; 1913–1914: yearly estimate based on one-week samples of mid-February, April, July, August, September, October.

1915–1920: yearly estimate based on number of films in one April sample (multiplied by twelve). It should be noted that the growth in yearly number of films might be over-estimated since, from 1919 onwards, film companies keep more and more older films (of the previous months) on their release schedule. This might be due to films being shown longer in individual cinemas, and getting longer 'runs'.

Released length: 1907–1914: average length of films in one April sample multiplied by total number of films. 1915–1920: total length of films in one April sample multiplied by twelve.

Total seating capacity: number of cinemas times average size.

Number of cinemas: 1909 and 1913: Balio (1985: 141). 1911 and 1912: Cassady (1959: note 92) 1921: Bordat and Etchevery (1995: appendix).

Average cinema size: 1922 taken from Bordat; 1913 is an educated guess based on the remark in Hampton (1931: 204), that the average size of a cinema increased 2.5 times between 1913 and 1922. This suggests a yearly growth in average cinema size of 9.5 per cent between 1913 and 1922. This rate has been used to estimate sizes for 1909, 1911 and 1912.

Note

The data in this figure are most indicative of annual changes. The absolute figures each year are educated estimates (see below) and might differ from the actual numbers. However, changes should reflect real changes in the market.

exporting films through an American company in spring 1907, and the next year had its own sales office (Mottram 1988).

Around 1907, the Pathé Frères company was the largest film producer and distributor in the world. Gaumont, its main French competitor was about a third its size. Other French companies, such as Éclair, Méliès and Lux, were much smaller. The French film companies thrived on exports. Pathé Frères, Gaumont, Méliès and Éclair all set up American studios, and some of them also had studios in Germany, Britain and Italy. Among the innovations French companies introduced in the American market were cartoons, the weekly newsreel and the cliffhanger-end-to-episodes characteristic of serials, which became popular during the 1910s.[11]

From 1911 onwards, several relatively small Italian companies introduced the long historical spectacle films in America, starting with *The Fall of Troy* (Itala) and *Dante's Inferno* (Milano). The films contained expensive historical sets and mass-scenes, and the films lasted three to four times as long as the standard American film, 45–60 minutes.[12] Production costs were high, but ticket prices were also higher, and the films became hugely popular (Cherchi Usai 1996). In New York and Boston, for example, *Dante's Inferno* played for two weeks, while the average American MPPC-film lasted only two days. Moreover, it was played in rented 1,000-seat legitimate theatres, at a ticket price of $1, while American films normally played in Nickelodeons with a few hundred seats for 5–10 cents (Gomery 1996: 46). The increase in budget, length and ticket price all became characteristics of the feature film as it emerged in the American market.

In the years from 1907 to 1910, the European share of the 'production capacity' used in the American market (as measured in released length) (Figure 2.2) seems to remain fairly stable, somewhere between 30 and 40 per cent, with a slight tendency to decline. Shortly before the war it had declined substantially to 20 per cent, and as the war started, the share dropped to only a few percentage points and remained hovering around 10 per cent for the rest of the 1910s. In absolute terms, European film exports to the USA had reached pre-war levels in 1920, but the American market had grown so much that the European share of the market had become marginal. This sharp decline was followed by a strong increase of the American market share in Europe (Figure 2.2). An intermediate position did not emerge, as would later occur in the music industry, with Europe still holding a significant market share in America.

Explanations for the decline of European films in the USA

The First World War as a direct cause

The First World War has often been mentioned as the cause for the dominance of the Hollywood studios. Kristin Thompson (1985: 41), for example, states that the home markets of the European film companies

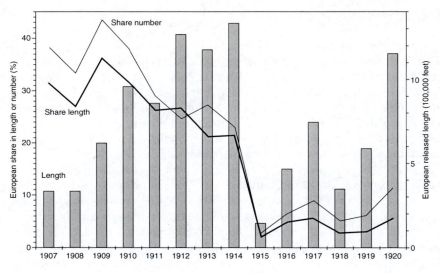

Figure 2.2 European share in American film releases, 1907–1920.

Notes and sources
European released length (bars): total yearly released length of European films calculated from April sample release schedules, *Motion Picture World* (see sources, Figure 2.1).

European share length (bold line): European released negative length divided by total released negative length (Figure 2.1).

European share number (thin line): European number of released negatives divided by total number of released negatives (Figure 2.1).

declined because of the war, while film production was seriously hampered. Furthermore, the war cut them off from the export markets outside North America and Europe that were essential to make profits, most notably the important Latin American and Australian markets. During this period, according to Thompson, the American film industry was able to develop unhampered and to take control of the export markets, blocking out European companies. European film companies were never able to recapture the markets and were doomed for the rest of the century.

As Thompson readily acknowledges, the decline of the European market share in the USA and in Europe itself had already begun a few years before the war (Thompson 1985: 215), indicating that other forces besides the war were at play. It can be argued, however, that without the war, the shift would not have been so extreme, and an intermediate position could have emerged.

It is not clear if and how much European film markets declined during the war. Available data suggest that the decline could not have been so dramatic. In France, for example, the market only shrunk in 1915, whilst in the other years it might have grown steadily, except for 1917, when it remained stable (Bakker 2001b).[13] The British market for films also seems to have remained largely stable during the war.

Film production was hampered by the war, as employees were called into service, and sometimes studios and facilities were sequestered by the government. The European film companies succeeded, though, in producing a steady supply of films, as is suggested by the stable market shares of French and British films in their respective countries during the war. They could even use their foreign-produced films as substitutes. Pathé's serial *Les mystères de New York* (1915–1916), produced by its American subsidiary, was extremely successful in France, as was Gaumont's French serial *Les Vampires* (1915–1916) (Uricchio 1996: 63).[14]

And even if, at times, film production slowed, this did not threaten the continuity of the firms. They often received government orders and government support, and the government would not allow them to go under. The equipment plants of both Gaumont and Pathé, for example, produced complicated devices such as bomb fuses. In Britain, the Urban Trading Company made highly successful war documentaries, in a joint-venture with the government. The newsreel departments of Pathé, Gaumont, Éclair and other European companies are likely to have benefited similarly from the war. Moreover, since the film market did not decrease dramatically, European film companies could always temporarily overcome a lack of films by buying rights to foreign films.

Had the war really ruined the film companies of the belligerent countries, then the film industry of neutral countries should have remained strong. An interesting case is Sweden. Figure 2.3 clearly shows that the American market share skyrocketed in the war years, while the Swedish share declined. In contrast, the market shares of domestic films in Britain and France remained remarkably stable, at the expense of foreign non-US films (Bakker 2001b).

The war did not fundamentally decrease the profitability of the European film companies, although it may have blocked the growth of turnover and profits. The profit figures of the three largest French film companies – Pathé, Gaumont and Éclair – declined only in the first year of the war, with only Pathé – then the largest European film company – suffering large losses in that year. During all the other war years, the three companies made substantial profits. Moreover, the profit figures of Pathé's European network of subsidiaries did not change in such a way as to threaten the continuity of the company (Bakker 2001b).

The Danish Nordisk company, which had Germany as its effective home market, expanded rapidly during the first years of the war, setting up a chain of first-class theatres in Germany and Switzerland. Only in 1917 did Nordisk face problems, as the German government blocked the importation of foreign films and forced Nordisk to sell its film business to the newly founded UFA firm for ten million marks, plus a 33.3 per cent stake in UFA.[15] However, after little more than a year, the German market was

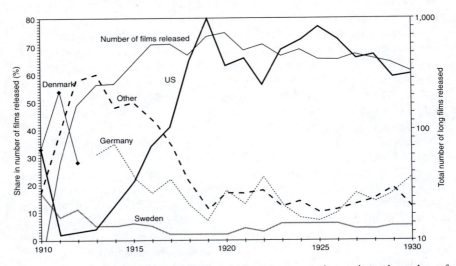

Figure 2.3 The structure of the US film market, concentration ratio and number of firms, 1907–1920.

Notes and sources
Four-firm concentration ratio: the combined share in released length of the four largest film-producing companies in an April sample of the *Motion Picture World* release schedule.

Number of firms: the number of film production companies in this sample.

open again. Nordisk at least did not go under and has continued to produce films to date.[16] The film industries of other neutral countries such as the Netherlands and Sweden grew somewhat during the war, probably because they could still supply the German market, while the allied countries could not (Uricchio 1996: 66).[17]

The second part of the 'war explanation' – the loss of foreign overseas markets – seems improbable as well. It is unlikely that the cutting off of the non-western export markets actually took place, since films are easily tradable. They are small in volume and weight compared to their value and the quantity necessary for export. Although the war made international trade in film more complicated,[18] these complications were not insurmountable. Also, in reality, the tariffs on raw film imports seem not to have increased during the First World War.

If the cut-off somehow did take place, though, then this could not have had a devastating effect on the European film industry. Overseas markets, with the exception of North America, were not essential to European film companies, who constituted only a small part of the world film market.

Export figures of French motion picture films from 1913–1918 show that the non-western market accounted for only 10 to 15 per cent of exports, and did not decrease. The same also holds true for Britain (Stephenson

1922). First of all, these figures show that exports continued during the war, and second, they probably overestimate the importance of non-western markets, those small markets to which copies (positives) were shipped. Negatives were usually sent to the more important markets, to be copied within the country.

From the late 1920s onwards, scales are available for the relative importance of national film markets in the world, which were based on the average rental price commanded by Hollywood films in each country. A 1926 scale shows that non-European and non-US markets constituted only 10–11 per cent of the world market.[19] According to a 1934 scale, which is more detailed, the total market outside Europe and the USA was 7.9 per cent of the world market, with Asia accounting for 3.13 per cent, Latin America for 2.67 per cent, and the British colonies of Australia, New Zealand and South Africa for 2.12 per cent.[20] Since non-western markets can be assumed to lag behind in the development of cinemas, it seems highly improbable that their importance in world markets was higher before the mid-1920s than after.[21]

For Pathé, the largest film company in the world at the time, the non-western markets accounted for only a small part of profits during the 1910s, and these markets continued to deliver profits to Pathé during the war years. The Australian subsidiary made only losses in the years 1911 to 1915, with these decreasing considerably during this period. The Asian subsidiary, based in Singapore, on the other hand, made its highest profits ever during the war years. No accounts were kept for the Latin-American subsidiaries, which probably meant that the size of these markets did not warrant a local subsidiary. Profits from this area must therefore have been incorporated into headquarters profits.[22] Since these profits only show a loss during 1914, and from 1916 onwards are on or above pre-war levels, the loss of Latin-American markets cannot have had a devastating effect on Pathé's profits (Bakker 2001b).[23] During the war, Charles Pathé made many trips to the USA to manage the subsidiary, and not a single one to Latin America or Australia.

The loss of Europe's overseas film markets was thus more a consequence of the rise of the American film industry than a cause.

The evolution of audience taste: feelings against foreign film

The downfall of European film in America might also find an explanation in a shift in audience tastes. It could be that consumers increasingly disliked foreign films. A detailed case study by Richard Abel on the attitudes of the American film business and audience towards the films of Pathé Frères indicates that, in the late 1900s, a feeling against foreign films emerged (Abel 1999). In 1910 the American trade press ran a 'smear campaign' against Pathé films. Abel writes: 'It was simply "common knowledge" that Pathé subjects often were inappropriate for the "happy, beautiful, virile age" in which (some) Americans supposedly imagined they were living' (Abel 1999: 136). The French competitor of Pathé, Gaumont, faced the same problems. In 1913 and 1914, the American manager of Gaumont wrote to headquarters that there was some resistance to foreign films. He complained that Paris was not able to supply him with feature films and that he had great difficulties acquiring them on the American market (Bakker 2001b: 210–212).

No matter what the changes in audience taste may have been, they are not important for the aims of this chapter; film companies can easily adapt to new tastes, given the short product life cycle and the mobility of film production and creative inputs. The question, then, is whether a difference in the capability to adapt to audience tastes existed between the European and the American film industry.

French film companies usually responded to taste changes by producing films in national markets. Pathé began producing in America in 1910, and its first American release was *The Girl From Arizona*, a western. Éclair also set up an American subsidiary, and even became specialised in the very American western genre. Méliès had already produced films in the USA since the early 1900s, under the name Star Films. Gaumont had produced films in New Jersey briefly in 1908, and started hesitantly to produce American films again in 1914. Its American manager writes:

> The one unfortunate phase of this development is the necessity of producing films in this country – a development to which I very much object and which I had hoped to avoid. However, the feeling is so strong against the use of foreign film that there was no alternative. We now have Mr. Gaumont's permission to go ahead on the understanding that the investment for 1914 shall not exceed $10,000, and that all expenses are written off year by year.[24]

These developments were mirrored by the American film distributor George Kleine, who built a huge studio complex outside Turin, in 1913. Driven by the success of the long Italian spectacle films he distributed in the USA, he wanted to produce these films with American actors instead, had the war not intervened (Cherchi Usai 1996).

Film companies also responded to audience tastes by adapting the films. The huge Danish Nordisk company, for example, found itself located at the crossroads of two worlds. For the German market and other western European markets, it produced films exclusively with happy endings. For the Eastern European markets, different, dramatic (quite unhappy) endings were shot (Brownlow and Gill 1998).

Since, in the end, the European efforts to adapt were unsuccessful, the question remains as to whether it was somehow easier for the American companies to adapt to changing audience tastes. Although the many immigrants in the United States could have played a role, the question can hardly be answered without avoiding tautological reasoning: the success of the American industry proves that it could adapt better. In the late 1920s, the Hollywood studios began to systematically screen scripts on parts that might insult any country, religion or interest group.[25] This constituted more of a rational business decision – that European companies could have made as well – than having anything to do with an American comparative advantage in adapting. The capability of US producers to adapt to audience tastes did not cause/precede Hollywood's dominance, but cemented it once Hollywood was dominant and hence was not a major factor in the decline of the European film industry.

The First World War as a European disadvantage in an escalation game

If changes in the American market structure are examined, a more speculative explanation for the downfall of the European film industry can be constructed, one still involving the First World War. A useful indicator of market structure is concentration, which measures the extent to which the market is dominated by the largest firms. Between 1907 and 1909, the four largest companies ('C_4-ratio') accounted for around 50 per cent of films released (Figure 2.4). From 1910 onwards, this ratio became significantly lower, between 20 and 30 per cent, but from 1918 onwards it suddenly increased dramatically, at the same time that the film market was growing at a rapid pace.[26]

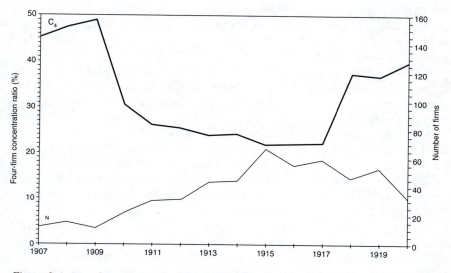

Figure 2.4 American share and other shares in Swedish releases of long films, 1910–1930 (source: adapted from Bjork 1995: 245–264).

Note
Long films are films of 750 metres or more.

Traditional industrial organisation theory supposes that, as market size increases, industrial concentration will fall, as more new entrepreneurs find it attractive to enter the market: the market has 'room' for more businesses.[27] This reasoning can explain why concentration (as measured by the C_4-ratio) fell so sharply in the USA around 1910. It is corroborated by the increase in the number of companies (Figure 2.3). At the same time, entry into the film business was made easier, given the waning power of the MPPC.

However, stable market shares experienced during the 1910s, up to 1918, and then increasing shares thereafter, in what was a rapidly expanding market, is at odds with this theory. A new approach to industrial organisation pioneered by John Sutton distinguishes between industries characterised by endogenous and exogenous sunk costs, and suggests that, in the case of the former, fixed investment on the part of firms can lead to increasing market share returns (Sutton 1991, 1998).[28] In the case of film, whilst a given increase in film budgets in a stable market might not have been sufficient to recoup the extra costs, an expanding market gave the 'escalators' a better chance to recoup their investment and leave their competitors in a more marginal position. This theoretical approach helps to explain the sharp increase in film budgets during this period.

These escalation strategies were not without risk, as many companies that tried them went bankrupt, and only a few successful companies ended up with larger market shares. The escalation game made it more difficult for new companies to attain significant market shares, since they needed increasingly large sums to spend on film budgets. The first companies to begin escalation had a substantial advantage, since they could outbid their more cautious competitors on creative inputs such as copyrights, star actors, directors and technicians.

In the American market, this process first brought about longer and more expensive films, until the industry reached the one reel (1,000 feet) standard around 1911–1912. In a second stage this mechanism led to further escalation, triggering the emergence of the long, big-budget feature film (approximately three-to-seven reels) as the new industry standard in the years 1915–1917, with heavily promoted stars, based on well-known stories, and having intensively advertised releases. After the birth of the feature film, the escalation continued, resulting in ever larger budgets and stars' salaries and ever more aggressive sales promotion (Bakker 2001a).

For European companies, an escalation strategy was less feasible than for their American counterparts. During the war, European companies faced an uncertain market environment, and while they were able to keep their existing business running, they could not or would not take the substantial risks involved in an escalation strategy. Once the war was over, European companies were in a position to adopt such a strategy, but it was too late.

Pathé could have adopted this strategy, since during the war it was large and profitable in the American market. Actually, it did invest considerably in filmmaking in the USA, and was the only European company that came close to joining the escalation process. However, Charles Pathé did not personally foresee that the feature film would emerge as the dominant and most profitable film format, and chose to concentrate his production on short films, serials and newsreels (Thompson 1985: 59).

For the two other large French companies, Gaumont and Éclair, an escalation strategy would have been more difficult. Although both companies had facilities in the USA, they were much smaller than Pathé, making an escalation strategy more risky.

The one large Danish company, Nordisk, was financially strong enough to have adopted an escalation strategy and, in fact, seems to have done so: the company was one of the first to release feature-length films. Until 1917, the German market must have been very profitable.[29] Nordisk, however, held only a small market share on the American market. Although the company had a US agent, relations between the two were not good, with them complaining continuously that the American market was not profitable (Mottram 1988). The release data show that Nordisk films counted only for a small part of all US releases. While the sudden loss of control over the German 'home' market did not threaten Nordisk's existence it did make a continuation of the escalation strategy difficult.[30]

The disintegration of the European film market

An implication of the foregoing theory is that, for products with high sunk costs, market size is all-important, since total average costs (nearly equal to sunk costs) will be dependent on the number of products sold. That is, variable and marginal costs are small in relation to fixed and sunk costs, and hence average costs fall rapidly with sales. The European film industry could be strong initially simply because sunk costs were relatively low, but as the standard level of sunk costs in the film industry grew, market size became ever more important, and the European companies found themselves increasingly at a disadvantage in their smaller home markets, relative to those firms operating in the American market.

The importance of market size was often stressed by contemporary business people. Charles Pathé, for example, wrote:

Having the advantage of their huge interior market, which, concerning box office revenue, represents forty to fifty times the French one, thus three quarters of the world market, the Americans can engage considerable sums in the production of their negatives, amortize them completely in their home market, and subsequently conquer the export markets all over the world, especially those of countries that cannot afford the luxury of having their own national film production.

The prime cinematographic importance of France in the world rested solely on its initial advantage and would have to disappear the day the building of the American film industry was finished. This day has come.[31]

As long as products are easily exportable, market size is closer to the size of the world market rather than to a particular domestic market. Unfortunately for the European companies, as sunk costs increased and market size became ever more important, the European market began to disintegrate and European film companies became increasingly locked into their small home markets. Both cultural and legal trade barriers increased. Before 1914, European countries were relatively open to each other's products, but during and after the war, consumers became more hostile to the products of enemy countries, especially with cultural products such as films.

This resentment was reflected in legislation, as German films were not allowed to be shown in France and Britain until the early 1920s, and Germany responded with a similar policy. Before 1914 legislation concerning film trade was minimal, since films were relatively new products. After 1914, however, taxes and duties increased and, in the 1920s, many European governments introduced special legislation controlling the number of foreign films that could be shown.

This disintegration of the European film market gave the largest market in the world, the American market, an additional advantage. Perhaps unintentionally, the European governments effectively starved each other's film industries. Although protection in the form of quotas was partially aimed at reducing the extreme market share of American films, it hurt the European film industry the most, since the size of the 'European home market' for intra-European trade was decreased still further.

As a consequence, in most European countries the market share of domestic companies remained stable at first, while shares of other European companies were pushed down by a sharply increasing American market share. In a second stage, American companies also pushed down the market share of domestic companies sharply, helped by the fact that the latter faced declining export markets. Access to the US market remained unchanged, and therefore cannot have been a reason for Europe's decline in the USA.[32]

Causes for Europe's failure to catch up after the war

If European companies could not participate in the escalation game during the war, the question remains as to why they were not able to simply catch up after the war was over. At that time, American companies had already been escalating costs for at least three years, and European companies were simply too late to join. The gap between their 1919 film budgets and the budgets needed to participate in escalation was simply too wide – much larger than the initial differences the American 'escalators' faced.

Another factor was the access to creative inputs such as actors, directors, cameramen, make-up artists, lighting specialists and set designers. Since US companies had been the first to escalate, they could outbid their European counterparts for these scarce inputs. Creative talent that initially developed in European markets would at a certain point outgrow these markets and maximise the rent captured by their popularity or their talent, which often meant going to Hollywood.[33] Europe was therefore a kind of laboratory out of which Hollywood could pick the most promising inputs.

A further consequence of this gap was that US companies could offer films of a relatively good quality on advantageous conditions (i.e. 'cheaper', having a better price/quality ratio, than European competitors) to European distributors and exhibitors. For goods, this business strategy might be called 'dumping'.

One consequence of the First World War was the emergence of American distributors world-wide. This was important for two reasons: since films are (copy)rights, out-sourcing distribution does not constitute a cost, but a rent that is captured by another company. A proprietary distribution network maximises the rent captured. Further, it guarantees access to the scare resource screen time during the short periods of the year in which most turnover is made, and enabled an American company to block out competitors. In the American market, a company that did not have access to enough screens during the short but essential periods around Christmas, Easter, 4th July and Thanksgiving would find it difficult to survive. In order to export profitably, a film studio had to have its own distributing agency in important foreign markets.[34]

Table 2.1 shows the foreign expansion of the American film studios. European companies were at a disadvantage since they lacked foreign distribution networks. The exception was Pathé, which was one of the largest distributors in the United States and had several other foreign distribution subsidiaries. The fact that Pathé was the only company that managed to keep a considerable and profitable presence in the American market during the war confirms just how important distribution networks had become in exporting films.[35] However, while American companies were setting up their international networks, Pathé was beginning to sell its foreign subsidiaries.[36]

Another factor making a catch-up difficult was that in advertising-intensive industries, once established, market shares of certain brands are difficult to reverse; history matters quite a lot.[37] Companies that simply were first to build a brand often maintain their market share for decades. If nationality is a criterion used by consumers to differentiate between films, then the fact that American companies were first to introduce the big-budget feature films on a regular basis into the world's film markets and

Table 2.1 Chronology of set-up direct foreign distribution subsidiaries by French and US companies, 1902–1927

Name of film company	USA	Canada	Britain	Australia	New Zealand	France	Germany	Italy	Sweden
French companies									
Pathé	1908–1921		*1904*	*1909*	*1909*		1912–1914	*1909*	1910
Gaumont	1908–1920		1902				1912–1914		
Éclair	1912–1917								
American companies									
Thanhouser						1914			
Essanay			1915						
American			1916						
Paramount			1920	<u>1917</u>		1921	<u>1925</u>		1923
Universal			1922	1921	1921		1926		1924
Fox		1919	1916			1919	<u>1925</u>	1919	
MGM		1925	<u>1927</u>			<u>1925</u>	<u>1925</u>		1923
Vitagraph			1916			1913/<u>1919</u>			
Warner						1925	1927		1927
First National (FN)									1923
Merged Warner/FN									
United Artists			1921	1921		1921			1922
Producers Distr. Corp.			1925						

Sources: French companies: company reports. Sweden: Bjork 1995. American companies: taken from the chronology in Thompson 1985.

Notes
Underlined dates mean the foreign distribution subsidiary was purchased instead of set up. Dates in italic mean that this is the earliest date the subsidiary is mentioned in the sources, but that it may have existed already for some time before. MGM in Sweden 1923: Metro Pictures, one of the predecessors.

capture a large market share with them may explain why European industries never managed to push back the American market share and reverse the situation. Europeans had acquired the regular habit of seeing American films, and this was difficult to change.

A final explanation for Europe's failure to catch up might be collusion among American companies against foreign competitors. When the Hollywood studios reached their zenith in the late 1920s, such collusion might have been possible and certainly did occur in foreign export markets, which was not illegal under American law. But before the mid-1920s, the market was too fragmented and too dynamic to make such collusion effective.

One might be surprised that such a brief period of four years (1914–1918) made such a difference for Europe's film industry, a difference that was never challenged, when US dominance in many other industries has been. However, the essential difference is that films are (copy)rights, and therefore, contrary to manufacturing industries, protection can be easily evaded, no foreign production plants are needed, and 'dumping' is easy because reproduction is low. For example, in the car industry, on the contrary, production costs, transportation costs, tariffs and the need for foreign production plants were all obstacles to absolute US dominance. Further, in the car industry no similar jump in endogenous sunk costs took place, since most costs are exogenous and dictated by technology. Moreover, the 'creative inputs' in the car industry (i.e. engineers and R&D) are less scarce than in the film industry. Even so, since cars are goods and not rights, no vertical integration is needed to maximise profit, and since 'perfect' selling contracts can be written, foreign distribution networks constitute less of an advantage.

Conclusion

At the dawn of the twentieth century, film emerged as a new and rapidly growing industry, which was international by its very nature. No one could have dreamed that this small, shabby, sinister and disreputable business would have grown in twenty years into an important international industry. Films were increasingly produced for an international market, but paradoxically film production changed from being spread internationally into an activity which was concentrated in one nation. By far the largest number of commercial films were produced in a single location, but shown in nearly every territory on the globe.

This production centre adopted most of the innovations that were pioneered in Europe, adapted them into a product that was a blend of these innovations, and exported this back to Europe and the rest of the world. America was like an apprentice who outclassed a master, and in the end left the teacher far behind. Since then, Europe has only been able to confront the creations coming from the melting pot of this sorcerer's apprentice with an attitude of intellectual and artistic superiority.

The main reason for this occurrence was that Europe was unable to take part in a significant development phase of the film industry between 1915 and 1917, because of historical accident. For partially different reasons, when the European film industry was in a position to participate, after the war was over, it was too late to catch up. When, in 1915, the feature film emerged in the American market as the dominant film format and market size increased rapidly, several American film companies started an escalation of spending on film budgets and film marketing. In contrast, while the war did not seriously damage the existing interests and continuity of European companies, they lacked the strong market growth and predictability of the future market environment to make a corresponding escalation strategy feasible. While many European companies were able to maintain their existing business interests, turnover and profitability, they failed to keep up with the rapid market growth and development in the USA.

After the war, when the European companies were in a position to respond to the escalation strategy, their options were limited. First of all, it was difficult to encroach upon entrenched market shares, as history shows for most advertising-intensive and some R&D-intensive industries. Since nationality functioned as a kind of brand name, and American films held the largest market share, the film audience had developed an appetite for American films, while films of other nationalities were seen as different, of a more exotic flavour.

Furthermore, to catch up, market size worked to the disadvantage of European companies. As fixed costs increased, market size mattered more, while the European market was actually disintegrating. Europe thus faced the dilemma of crafting films for the taste of its home market, and thus still managing to gain a substantial revenue in the home market and little in the foreign markets, or of crafting films for the taste of an international audience and obtaining a small revenue in the home market, but more risky and larger revenues in international markets. The option that appeared most sensible, making films in the USA for American taste, was made difficult by the absence of proprietary US distribution networks for European companies. Apart from Pathé, all companies would have to start from scratch in a market where concentration increased rapidly, and the main competitors were putting their foreign distribution networks into place.

The American companies, on the contrary, had already been able to take advantage of their market size simply because they were first to escalate. They could dump their films in Europe, impeding the start of a European escalation strategy. This initial advantage also enabled the Americans to outbid their European competitors on the scarce inputs for film – creative and technical talent and literary copyrights.

The interventions of European governments from the mid-1920s led to further disintegration of the European market. While intervention temporarily strengthened the position of domestic industries, in the long run it seems to have given an advantage to the American industry. The effect of quota legislation and other trade barriers was that, in most European markets, American companies gained market share over other foreign enterprises, and in a second stage a reinforced American industry was able to push down the market shares of the isolated domestic industries.

The consequence of all these circumstances was that, in the first half of the 1920s, many European companies gave up film production entirely. Pathé sold its American business, left filmmaking and concentrated on distribution and exhibition in France. Gaumont did the same, while Éclair went bankrupt. Nordisk continued as an insignificant Danish film company, and eventually went into receivership. The eleven largest Italian film producers formed a trust, which failed terribly, and one by one they fell into financial disaster. The well-known British film producer Cecil Hepworth also went bankrupt. By late 1924, not a single film was being made in Britain. American films were shown everywhere. Europe was a cinematographic Hiroshima. Finally, the apprentice had killed the master.

Notes

1 This chapter originally appeared in Luisa Passerini (ed.) *Across the Atlantic*, Brussels, Presses Inter-Universitaires Européennes/Peter Lang (2000): 213–240. © 2000 Gerben Bakker. All rights reserved. Reprinted with permission from the author. The author wishes to thank Paul Johnson, Massimo Motta, Mary Nolan, Jaime Reis, Bo Stråth and John Sutton for helpful advice and constructive comments, and more specifically Stephan Schroeder for information on the Nordisk film company. All remaining errors are, of course, the responsibility of the author alone. The author also wishes to thank NWO, the Netherlands Foundation for Scientific Research, and the Rens-Holle Foundation of the Netherlands, for financially supporting research done for this chapter.
2 In 'The poet and the city', in W.H. Auden, *The Dyer's Hand and Other Essays* (New York, Random House, 1948, 1962), pp. 72–92; p. 83.
3 Taken from the American translation (New York, Athenaeum, 1968), p. 29. This was the best-selling French book in 1967 and outsold André Malraux' *Anti-Mémoires*.
4 Glancy (1999: 11)
5 For a detailed case study of a medium-sized production company that formed an exception, and kept producing (low-budget) films profitably in Europe throughout the inter-war years (by differentiating its films as far away as possible from the Hollywood fare), see Bakker 2004.
6 Despite Pinkerton's detectives, hired by the MPPC, chasing them, the number of these 'independents' rose rapidly from 1909 onwards. Their films were shot as far away from New York, then the centre of the (MPPC-) film industry, as possible, in places like Cuba, Southern California or Mexico.
7 Since film lengths varied widely, total released length is a better indicator than the total number of released films.
8 For a more detailed discussion on the use of released length as a proxy, and on the statistical significance of the figures in Table 2.1, see Bakker (2001b).
9 Table 2.1.

10 For a more extensive and systematic treatment of this subject, see Bakker (2001a).
11 The first serial was 'What Happened to Mary Jane' – Edison, July 1912, 12 episodes. French Gaumont's 'Fantômas' – April 1913 – was the first French serial and the first to use the 'cliffhanger' characteristic, a technique that came to characterise the serial. The first American serial with a cliffhanger was Selig's 'Kathlyn' – December 1913. Thanks to Bernard Hrusa Marlow for this information.
12 This was 3,000–4,000 feet, which equates to 45–60 minutes.
13 These figures do not include the occupied territories.
14 When war broke out, Pathé intended to get its films supplied from studios in various European countries and the USA, which were either its own studios or studios with which it had distribution contracts. See Thompson (1985: 50–51, 58).
15 Information given by Stephan Schroeder. When Nordisk was allowed to sell its shares in Ufa, in 1919, they were only worth one-fifth of their 1917 value. See also Hayler (1926: 6–13); Kreimeier (1992: 39–40).
16 However, Nordisk only produced a few films in the 1920s, and did not manage to regain its position in export markets. In 1928 the firm actually did go bankrupt, but it was refounded in 1929 and still exists today.
17 See also the section on Sweden (page 31), which suggests the Swedish industry was not very strong in its domestic market.
18 The raw material of film, cellulose nitrate, was highly inflammable and, according to Uricchio (1996: 65), constituted a risk for war-essential materials on a ship and could complicate insurance. Cellulose nitrate could also be used for explosives, and Germany was totally dependent on the import of nitrates. Uricchio suggests that this also made international film transports more difficult.
      Both suggestions need further research. Film was not the only inflammable product (compare oil, explosives, weapons), and the small quantities of film shipped, compared with the complicated process to win back the raw materials from it, make the second point also doubtful. Even if the second point mattered, it would matter less for the non-western export markets.
19 This figure is calculated as follows: the whole non-European/US markets are *c*.22 per cent of the foreign market for US films. Generally it is said that the US film market was about two-thirds the size of the world film market (due to its large population, high income per capita and high cinema attendance per capita). At a conservative estimate, this figure is 50 per cent. The non-European and US markets, then, are 10–11 per cent of the world film market, with Australia and New Zealand counting for 4 per cent, Brazil and Argentina for another 4 per cent. See Seabury (1926).
20 The same method as above is used, conservatively estimating the US market as 50 per cent of the world market.
21 Differences in 1926 and 1934 figures seem to be due to the lesser reliability of the 1926 data.
22 The total profits minus the profits of the subsidiaries.
23 Further, research on the histories of European film companies until this date has not revealed any evidence of the Latin American and Australian markets being particularly significant, while other markets, such as the USA, are discussed as being important. Of course, this does not prove that it could not have been the case, but it certainly makes it less probable.
24 Bakker (2001b: 211).
25 Vasey (1997)
26 Released length represents more production capacity than market size (or

market share), but it can be argued that, in the long-term, changes in a firm's production capacity will more or less reflect changes in its market share. Second, it should be noted that using released length to measure concentration might somewhat underestimate real concentration. The method assumed that all films released generated equal revenue. In reality, however, revenues differed widely between films, and probably the films made by the biggest companies had bigger budgets, were wider and more expensively promoted, and had higher revenues; this implies that the shares of the biggest companies are higher than Table 2.2 indicates.

27 If exogenous costs and barriers to entry remain constant. For a more formal treatment, see Bakker (2001b).

28 Exogenous sunk costs are costs the level of which is 'dictated' by technology, and is more or less the same for all companies in the industry. Endogenous sunk costs are sunk costs the level of which can be decided upon by each individual firm and which can vary a lot between firms in an industry. Examples of endogenous sunk costs are advertising and Research & Development.

29 See above (pages 31–32).

30 The possibility of escalation strategies for Italian and British companies have yet to be researched, but the first intuition of the author, based on secondary literature, is that their possibilities for escalation strategies were limited.

31 Pathé (1940: 92–93). The quote concerns films of 1,500–1,800 m.

32 Rates for 1,000 feet of positive film declined from $207 in 1899 to $160 in 1909 to $97 in 1913 to $57 in 1922. Rates for 1,000 feet negative film changed from $206 in 1899 to $290 in 1913 to $172 in 1922 (all rates in 1982 dollars). (See Thompson 1985: 20–22.) Further, tariffs per se can only have a limited impact on foreign revenues of film companies, as a film essentially is a copyright and the number of viewings that this right generates in a foreign country cannot be taxed by customs. Unlike Europe, the USA did not introduce special legislation to limit the showing of foreign films through the imposition of quotas.

33 Although this chapter assumes that creative talent is scarce, one could also argue that it is unlimited. For the point made here it does not matter. Even in the unlikely case that the supply of creative talent was unlimited, after Hollywood studios would have bought the top actors, cameramen, directors, set-designers, lighting-specialists and so on, it simply would take time for other creative talent to fill the slots and reach the same position. Once this had happened, Hollywood studios could simply buy again.

34 Sutton (1998: 197–230) makes this argument for distribution in the pharmaceutical industry.

35 The biggest problem for Pathé's competitor, Gaumont, for example, was to get access to distribution in the USA. It had not been a member of the MPPC, and at first often released its films through George Kleine, an MPPC member. When the power of the trust waned, it started to release films by itself, but in 1913 and 1914 it made strong efforts to become a member of the patent trust, in order to have a guaranteed and continuous distribution outlet. After that failed, Gaumont's films were sometimes distributed nationally by others, sometimes by itself and sometimes as 'states right releases' (weekly release schedules in *Moving Picture World*).

36 On the sale of its American subsidiary to Merrill Lynch, see Perkins (1999).

37 See chapter, 'How history matters', in Sutton (1998: 205–226).

References

Abel, R. (1999) *The Red Rooster Scare: Making Cinema American, 1900–1910*, Berkeley, CA: University of California Press.

Bakker, G. (2000) 'America's master: the decline and fall of the European film industry in the United States, 1907–1920', in Luisa Passerini (ed.) *Across the Atlantic*, Brussels, Presses Inter-Universitaires Européennes/Peter Lang.

Bakker, G. (2001a) 'Stars and stories: how films became branded products', in *Enterprise and Society*, 2: 461–502.

Bakker, G. (2001b) *Entertainment Industrialised: The Emergence of the International Film Industry, 1890–1940*, Florence: European University Institute, Ph.D.

Bakker, G. (2004) 'Selling French films on foreign markets. The international strategy of a medium-sized company', in *Enterprise and Society*, 5(1): 45–76.

Balio, T. (ed.) (1985) *The American Film Industry*, Madison, WI: University of Wisconsin Press.

Bjork, U.J. (1995) 'The backbone of our business: American film in Sweden, 1910–1950', *Historical Journal of Film, Radio and Television*, 15: 245–264.

Bordat, F. and Etchevery, M. (eds) (1995) *Cent Ans d'Aller au Cinéma: Le Spectacle Cinématographique aux Etats-unis, 1896–1995*, Rennes: Presses Universitaires de Rennes.

Brownlow, K. and Gill, D. (as director/producer) (1998) *The Other Hollywood*, London: Photoplay Productions, in association with BBC, ZDF/Arte and D.L. Taffner.

Cassady Jr., R. (1959) 'Monopoly in motion picture distribution, 1908–1915', *Southern Californian Law Review*, 32: 325–390.

Cherchi Usai, P. (1996) 'Italy. Spectacle and melodrama', in Geoffrey Nowell Smith (ed.) *The Oxford History Of World Cinema*, Oxford: Oxford University Press.

De Grazia, V. (1989) 'Mass culture and sovereignty: the American challenge to European cinemas, 1920–1960', *Journal of Modern History*, 61: 53–87.

Ellwood, D. and Kroes, R. (eds) (1994) *Hollywood in Europe: Experiences of a Cultural Hegemony*, Amsterdam: VU University Press

Emmott, B. (1989) *The Sun Also Sets: The Limits to Japan's Economic Power*, New York, NY: Times Books/Random House.

Emmott, B. (1992) *Japan's Global Reach: The Influences, Strategies and Weaknesses of Japan's Multinational Companies*, New York, NY: Times Books/Random House.

Glancy, H.M. (1999) *When Hollywood Loved Britain*, Manchester: Manchester University Press.

Gomery, D. (1996) 'The Hollywood studio system', in Geoffrey Nowell Smith (ed.) *The Oxford History Of World Cinema*, Oxford: Oxford University Press.

Hampton, B.B. (1931) *A History of the Movies*, New York, NY: Covici-Friede.

Hayler, F. (1926) *Die deutsche Filmindustrie und ihre Bedeutung für Deutschlands Handel*, Universität Würzburg.

Kreimeier, K. (1992) *Die Ufa-Story. Geschichte eines Filmkonzerns*, München: Carl Hanser Verlag.

Kuisel, Richard F. (1993) *Seducing the French: The Dilemma of Americanization*, Berkeley and Los Angeles, CA: University of California Press.

Mottram, R. (1988) 'The great Northern Film Company: Nordisk Film in the American motion picture market', *Film History*, 2: 77–89.

Musser, C. (1990) *The Emergence of Cinema: The American Screen To 1907*, New York, NY: Scribner.

Pathé, C. (1940, 1971) *De Pathé Frères à Pathé Cinéma*, Paris: Premier Plan.

Perkins, E.J. (1999) *Wall Street to Main Street: Charles E. Merrill and Middle-Class Investors*, Cambridge: Cambridge University Press.

Seabury, William Marston (1926) *The Public and the Motion Picture Industry*, New York, NY: Macmillan.

Servan-Schreiber, Jean Jacques (1967) *La Défi Américain*, Paris: De Noël.

Stephenson, C.B. (1922) 'Moving pictures. The development of the industry abroad', *Commerce Reports*, 2 January: 34–38.

Sutton, J. (1991) *Sunk Costs and Market Structure: Price Competition, Advertising and The Evolution of Concentration*, Cambridge, MA: MIT Press.

Sutton, John (1998) *Technology and Market Structure. Theory and History*, Cambridge, MA: MIT Press.

Thompson, K. (1985) *Exporting Entertainment: America in the World Film Market 1907–1934*, London: British Film Institute.

Uricchio, W. (1996) 'The First World War and the crisis in Europe', in Geoffrey Nowell Smith (ed.) *The Oxford History Of World Cinema*, Oxford: Oxford University Press.

Vasey, R. (1997) *The World According to Hollywood 1918–39*, Madison: University of Wisconsin Press.

Zeldin, Theodore (1990) 'The pathology of anti-Americanism', in Denis Lacorne, Jacques Rupnik and Marie-France Toinet (eds) *The Rise and Fall of Anti-Americanism: A Century of French Perception*, Basingstoke: Macmillan.

3 Stars and stories

How films became branded products[1]

Gerben Bakker

> Men are like stars. Some generate their own light, while others reflect the brilliance they receive.
>
> José Martì[2]

In less than half a century, moving pictures grew from an emerging, fragmented business into a concentrated, large-scale industry. In 1900, film viewing was an inexpensive, brief, and haphazard activity; viewers saw many short films in borrowed venues like fairground tents, music halls, and theaters. By the 1930s, cinema-going had become a regular pastime, with audiences viewing one or two 'feature films' per program in purpose-built cinemas. In 1900, showmen and producers sold each other a supply of copies varying in quality and quantity through local or regional networks. By 1919, specialized distribution organizations rented films to cinemas and carefully coordinated logistical and promotional operations through international networks. In 1900, film production was low-cost and eclectic, involving many movies of different types and lengths. Forty years later, production concentrated on relatively few long, high-cost 'feature films,' which were carefully budgeted and heavily promoted.

A striking feature of this transformation was the multiplication of production costs. In the United States in 1909, the cost of making a movie ranged between $550 and $1,100 (Allen 1980: 219; Hampton 1931: 211).[3] By 1914, the average cost of a Fox feature was already $23,000, and it rose to $186,000 in 1927, shortly before sound became widespread. In 1929, Fox's sound films cost $308,000 on average. Similarly, Warner Brothers' average production costs increased from $90,000 in 1922 to $168,000 in 1927, and to $539,000 in 1940. RKO's costs nearly doubled from $220,000 per talking picture in 1929 to $424,000 in 1939. Metro-Goldwyn-Mayer (MGM), which specialized in high-budget films, saw its production costs escalate from $310,000 per picture in 1924 to $967,000 in 1939 (Koszarski 1990: 85; Glancy 1992, 1995; Jewell 1994).[4]

In Britain between 1905 and 1907, an average film cost no more than £100 to make, the most expensive production £600–£700. During the

1920s, average production costs grew to about £10,000–£12,000; after the introduction of sound at the end of the decade, they rose to around £17,000, and in the late 1930s to about £35,000 (Low 1949: 118; 1971: 276; Dickinson and Street 1985: 131).[5] In France in 1905, the relatively expensive 'trick films' made by Méliès for bourgeois audiences cost around 34,000–57,000 francs, while the negatives Pathé turned out cheaply and in large quantities cost only 16,000–17,000 francs (Abel 1994: 23).[6] In the inter-war period, average production costs increased from 410,000 francs in 1923 to over 1.9 million francs on the eve of the Second World War (Crisp 1993: 16).

These huge increases were not the result of exogenous forces such as new, costly technologies or sharp increases in the cost of raw materials. Except for the adoption of sound in 1927, basic cinema technology – and hence the minimum necessary costs of shooting a film – remained remarkably stable. The main causes of the cost explosion were endogenous: film producers started paying large sums for 'creative inputs' (actors, directors, and literary works) and for expensive stages, sets, scenery, and special effects (Bakker 2000). Why were film companies willing to increase their outlays so extravagantly throughout the period?

On the supply side, cinema technology industrialized the entertainment industry in three ways. First, it integrated markets by making entertainment a tradable product. Performers from Rio de Janeiro to Stockholm and from Kyoto to London competed with each other for the audience's money. Second, film technology automated entertainment: infinite reproduction of one performance at minimal cost enabled simultaneous showing in many places, maximizing the potential audience to the size of the population. Third, film technology standardized the quality of entertainment: it provided the same content whenever and wherever a film title was showing.[7] On the demand side, consumer expenditure for entertainment grew considerably between 1900 and 1940, further increasing the size of the internationally integrating market.

It could be argued that these three forces, by folding the stars of each local market into an international hierarchy, gave high-quality entertainers more 'capacity' to compete, allowing them to command higher rewards proportionate to their quality than before.[8] Pay for creative inputs might also have risen because film producers started to use them as brands to persuade consumers to see their movies, in order to reduce the *ex ante* uncertainty about a film's popularity. Yet another explanation might be that, as film companies increased their output, creative talent simply became scarcer and so demanded higher payments. But the rise in pay was not the same for everyone; a few creative inputs received large increases while others gained only modest increments, suggesting that scarcity cannot be the sole explanation (see, for example, Koszarski 1990: 95–116, 259–314).[9] Finally, it is possible that the eight Hollywood studios tried to prevent the entry of new companies by making the costs of creative inputs very high and keeping them under contract for long periods. This strategy was limited, because contracts could last at most seven years – though for brand names, 'eternally' protected by trademark law, such a strategy is more viable (see, for example, Kaldor 1950). In addition, the costs of creative inputs started to surge long before the eight studios dominated the industry, so the collusion explanation can be discarded.[10]

This chapter argues that the rise in pay for creative inputs occurred because film producers increasingly used them as brands and that films consequently came to resemble heavily branded products. Because film companies could not own them, artists and writers were able to capture in part the value of the brands they constituted. Thus market integration, standardization, and automation enabled both the process of branding and the higher rewards of high-quality talent.[11]

Looking at the period from the emergence of the film industry to the eve of the Second World War, before suburbanization deprived cinema of its position as a major mass medium (Gomery 1985),[12] this chapter will examine how creative inputs came to be used as brands, which branding techniques film producers developed, and how consumers perceived those brands. Because the international film industry was concentrated in the United States during this period, developments there receive the greatest attention. Britain is studied because it was the second largest film market in the world, although its own film industry was relatively weak, and France is included because it was home to Europe's largest film producers and distributors, although its own film consumption was low. After a discussion of the historical development of branding, microeconomic studies of both the production and the consumption of films are used to take a closer look at some aspects of the branding process.

The development of branding in the film industry

> The movie actor, like the sacred king of primitive tribes, is a god in captivity.
>
> Alexander Chase

During the period 1880–1930, market integration led to many business innovations such as single-price selling, branded products marketed nationally, department stores, mail-order firms, advertising agencies, market research, and distribution and delivery systems such as refrigeration (Fullerton 1988; Pope 1983; Church 1999: 410). The film industry shared several of these innovations, especially single prices, national branding, advertising, and market research, but the most important was probably the development of a dedicated distribution delivery system, the movie theater. Richard Tedlow observes a shift from regional to national branding and marketing, and the integration of manufacturing with retailing between 1880 and 1920. This coincides with a shift from 'low volume, high margins, moderate profits' to 'high volume, low margins, high profits' (Tedlow 1990; Church 1999: 410–411). In the case of entertainment, the film industry forced this shift upon the industry at large, by integrating regional and national markets and initiating a 'high profits, low margins, high volume' production model.[13] The key characteristic driving these developments was uncertainty: film producers incurred nearly all costs in advance, and they could not know beforehand the number of tickets that would be sold. They could not recover costs if a film failed to win audiences because a film negative – unlike real estate, a factory, or machinery – has a physical value close to zero. Uncertainty was a limited problem in the early film industry, as sunk costs remained relatively low and losses easy to bear. However, as production costs increased during the 1910s, film producers faced greater risks and higher potential losses.

In parallel, film consumers also faced uncertainty. Because film is an 'experience' product, moviegoers could not know beforehand if it would be satisfactory. When ticket prices were low and showings consisted of a succession of short films, this was not problematic, as moviegoers were willing to accept the limited risk of an unhappy experience. As ticket prices rose during the 1910s, however, and as film programs began to focus on a single, longer feature, consumers' risk increased.[14]

In response to this uncertainty and to the emergence around 1907 of fixed cinemas, which needed a regular, dependable supply of films, film companies first tried to rationalize production, moving from 'real-life' to fiction-based films. Producers could carefully budget and time their release, and they had the longest shelf-life. Initially, production costs were often lower than for non-fiction genres like news, sports, travel, documentary, or educational films (Allen 1980: 212; Abel 1994: 23).[15] In roughly ten years, the 'feature film' developed into the dominant film format. Paradoxically, in light of their notoriously high budgets and unpredictability of success in the present day, feature films appear to have originated in an attempt to reduce both costs and risk.

Second, film producers responded to uncertainty by trying to brand films. They wished to motivate the consumer to see the film and to compensate for the fact that potential moviegoers could not know the full quality before consuming a film.[16] Branding was particularly important to film companies because they continuously launched new products with short life-spans and therefore needed to persuade large numbers of consumers to buy the product 'now.' The process of branding became self-reinforcing, as greater outlays on branding increased the size of the risk and more assurances were needed that enough consumers would see the film. Moreover, one would expect branding to be relatively effective in the film industry, because rising monetary and opportunity costs would increase consumers' search activity, and they would thus become more receptive not only to advertising but also to reviews and word-of-mouth.

Film companies trying to turn films into branded products confronted a product life cycle too short to create brand-awareness of each individual film. They responded to this dilemma in three ways:

1 they extended the brand beyond one product into a series of successive products, using the trademark, the serial, or the star;
2 they acquired an existing brand about which consumers already had reached a high level of awareness, such as famous plays, novels, or music;
3 they increased the rate-of-return on their investment in branding to compensate for the short life of their products (films) by using the film itself as a brand to turn intrinsically unbranded (manufactured) products into premium branded products – for example, by the use of stars as spokespersons for products or by the licensing of what we today call 'merchandise tie-ins.'

The United States

At first, the technological novelty of film was sufficient to attract an audience, reinforced between 1900 and 1910 as additional novelties such as colored film and film with sound came into vogue.[17] Around 1907 the first fixed cinemas, 'nickelodeons,' emerged, with at most a few hundred seats. Companies used branding both to attract consumers regularly to the cinema and to convince cinema-owners of a product's quality and audience appeal. The main instrument first used in this way was the production company's trademark, which figured prominently on films and in advertisements. In the early 1900s, the French company Pathé, the largest film supplier in the United States, owed its dominant market position in part to its ostentatious trademark, a red rooster, which it promoted directly to audiences by displaying it prominently on its films and intertitles. American companies used their trademarks mainly in advertisements aimed at distributors and exhibitors (Allen 1980; Abel 1999: 17–19).[18]

With the formation of the Motion Picture Patents Company (MPPC) in 1908, a patent pool of previously litigating companies, trademark branding became widespread (Abel 1999: 17–19; Bowser 1990). The trademark not only informed consumers about a film's minimum quality, but also persuaded them to see the film by increasing the perceived quality. Over time, however, trademarks lost their importance as a branding device for the movie studios. A study of American trademarks in 1942 shows that trademarks could no longer have been important in persuading consumers to see a particular film (Handel 1950: 76). Respondents succeeded in matching the trademark to the correct film studio in only 30 percent of cases. Only for MGM and Paramount, with scores over 50 percent, may trademarks have played a limited role. Another survey finds the same situation for Britain in the late 1920s: only fifty-eight respondents out of 2,000 were able to mention a favorite film company, and only American studios received more than a few responses.[19]

In the early years of filmmaking, trademarks could facilitate product differentiation by informing consumers about genres. Essanay, for example, was known for comedies and Selig for westerns (Abel 1999: 93).[20] The use of genre as a brand was difficult, however, because it was non-proprietary. Moreover, numerous surveys showed that consumers' genre preferences were distributed very evenly, conferring little brand advantage on a studio specializing in one genre or another.[21]

In 1912, serials – films in twelve or twenty-four weekly installments of one or two reels (15–30 minutes) each – became popular. They reduced consumers' risk by spreading search costs over all installments and often piggybacked on consumers' existing brand-awareness of the popular dime novels on which the serials were based. As the Mutual Film Corporation advertised to exhibitors: 'A serial guarantees a secure audience' (Dall'Asta 1999a: 281–282). Serials expanded a film's shelf-life to three or four months, long enough to make heavy advertising viable and turn the film itself into a brand (Dall'Asta 1999b: 289). Advertising for serials was undertaken on a grand scale. Pathé, for example, offered a $25,000 cash prize in a fan competition and had an exclusive contract with the Hearst newspapers to print the accompanying stories.[22] Pathé also pioneered the simultaneous release, premiering a film in 500 cinemas, supported by advertising in local Hearst papers (Grau 1914: 242). Shortly afterward, the Thanhouser company reportedly spent $250,000 on a national advertising campaign and contest for its *The Million Dollar Mystery* (Staiger 1990: 13).[23]

In late 1915, film companies started to offer serials with episodes in sequel to replace those with independent installments that had prevailed before. The tactic proved insufficient to make the serial into the dominant film format, however, and it was marginalized by the feature film, which was emerging between 1915 and 1917, though specialized companies continued to make low-cost serials for smaller cinemas until the advent of television.

From the early 1910s, stars were increasingly used to brand films. The emerging independent companies lured away many of the MPPC companies' creative and technical talent by offering huge salaries. Whereas the MPPC studios sometimes refrained from printing the players' names in advertisements – out of fear that they would demand higher fees – the 'independents' publicized their stars prominently. In 1908, movie actors earned only $5 a day. In 1911, Mary Pickford earned $175 a week, then considered the highest fee attainable, but five years later she secured fifty times that much, and one hundred times as much in 1918 (Kerr 1990: Grau 1914).

The connections that audiences drew between stars and individual films were much stronger than their loyalty to abstract trademarks, and stars also had a longer product life cycle than the films or serials themselves. These advantages made the huge outlays on advertising stars profitable. As Rachael Low put it: '[Film actors] found themselves after a while in the possession of a monopoly similar to that of a trademark, with all the good-will attached to such an identification. The audience's familiarity with the players' faces gave a film in which they appeared a relative popularity not necessarily dependent on its quality' (Low 1949: 124). Long-term contracts made it attractive for studios to invest in promotion of their stars, allowing them to capture part of the rent from the stars' popularity.[24]

Stars became tradable properties, almost licensable like patents. In the late 1920s and 1930s, the eight Hollywood studios often rented stars to each other at 'market prices,' usually substantially above contract prices. Bette Davis, for example, was paid $143,000 a year by Warner Brothers in the late 1930s – about $30,000 a film; but when Warner rented Davis out to Goldwyn for *The Little Foxes* in 1941, the company received $385,000 (Shipman 1979; Albert 1998). Trademarked fictional characters such as Felix the Cat or Mickey Mouse offered the advantage that they were exclusive and permanent company property (Gaines 1991).

With the emergence of stars, film companies also started to use the popularity of existing properties such as short stories, novels, and plays to brand their films. This practice saved both promotion costs and time. It had taken years for literary works to build their fame, but their accumulated 'brand-awareness' could be instantly used by the film studios. In 1914, the average price for the film rights to a play was about $3,500, less for novels. Soon film companies started crowding each other out in their hunt for literary property rights.[25] In 1920, prices for successful plays had reached over $40,000. The most popular plays received even more: D.W. Griffith paid $152,000 for *Way Down East*, and in 1921 *Turn to the Right* (452 Broadway performances) sold for $218,000. In the 1920s, the screen rights of from 10 to 15 percent of Broadway productions were sold. Several film companies invested in Broadway in order to obtain lower prices, using Broadway as a brand-breeder. The advent of 'talkies' pushed up demand for film rights, the average price for a play reaching $74,000 by the late 1930s (McLaughlin 1974: 51–52).[26]

Stories had become more important as average film length increased, from about 500 feet (seven-to-eight minutes) in 1908, to 1,200 feet in 1914, and to 2,200 feet in 1917, when the five-reel (seventy-five minute) 'feature' had become the prevalent format, surrounded by a multitude of small films. Ticket prices increased synchronously, and from 1912 onward, large high-class cinemas of 1,000–2,000 seats emerged, often replacing the smaller, more 'popular' nickelodeons (Allen 1980; Kerr 1990; Gomery 1992).

A high promotion-to-sales ratio is characteristic of heavily branded products, and, although exact figures are lacking, it is clear that publicity was fundamental to film companies' success (Staiger 1990). The calculations of Walter W. Irwin, distribution manager of Vitagraph-Lubin-Selig-Essanay, illustrate how film developed into an increasingly branded product: in 1915 Irwin calculated that a cinema showing average features that changed each day had daily sales of $300 and a margin of $125 (42 percent). Film rental was 8.3 percent of sales, advertising 16.7 percent. If the cinema then shifted toward a weekly, highly publicized quality film, and doubled expenditures on both film rental and advertising, sales would grow to $550, the margin to $300 (54 percent), while film rental and advertising would be 9.1 and 18.2 percent of sales, respectively.[27] These rough figures suggest that consumers were receptive to increases in both advertising and quality.

Producers and distributors advertised stars extensively on postcards as early as the 1910s (Parsons 1927).[28] They issued fan magazines, generated publicity in the press, and featured their stars in movie advertising. By 1913, the popular *New York Evening Journal* sold $3,000 in movie advertisements daily (Grau 1914: 237). Film companies often had a special department to answer fan mail and sometimes recorded the number of letters per star.

Film companies also initiated other national advertising campaigns in addition to those launched for serials. In late 1913, Universal hired the Chicago advertising agency Witt K. Cochran for a $250,000 national campaign. Two years later, when Paramount increased the rental rate for its pictures, it embarked on a similar nationwide campaign. Within four months, other major producer/distributors such as Mutual, Triangle, World Pictures, and Metro Pictures had followed (Staiger 1990).[29]

In the 1920s, as cinemas changed programs less frequently and films had a longer run, promotion increasingly focused on individual films (Koszarski 1990). In 1928, Pathé launched a $75,000 national campaign aimed at consumers for Cecil B. de Mille's version of the life of Christ, *The King of Kings*. Paradoxically, by promising national consumer advertising, Pathé increased exhibitors' willingness to pay and could thus obtain higher rental prices. To make the advertising effective, Pathé had to orchestrate a 'wide' release, in 500 theaters at once. Thereafter, the practice of highly advertised wide releases gradually became established in the American industry.[30]

For eight FBO Productions pictures in 1927–1928, advertising expenditures ranged from $225,000, or 9.1 percent of production costs, for the most expensive picture to $4,500, or 1.4 percent, for the cheapest. Samuel Goldwyn's advertising campaigns of the early 1920s reached at least twenty-seven million people by his own account.[31] To launch Anna Sten as a star in 1934, Goldwyn and United Artists together spent $18,000 during the first week alone after her film's release. In late 1935, Paramount announced that it would spend $500,000 in three months to promote eight new films. Meanwhile, Metro-Goldwyn-Mayer was spending $3 million a year on advertising. It used 168 newspapers with a circulation of twenty-three million, forty national magazines with thirty-four million in circulation, and poster campaigns reaching two hundred million people a month. By 1947, the industry's annual spending on newspaper advertising had reached $52 million, making it the third largest advertiser in newspapers.[32]

As advertising costs grew, film companies discovered that they could increase the return on their investments in branding by licensing brands to manufacturers of otherwise unbranded products. This practice also made it easier to amortize the huge promotional expenditures for a movie, and 'merchandised products' in turn further promoted the film. Merchandising had the same advantage for manufacturers as stories did for film companies: instead of spending money for years to build their own brand, they could buy an instant brand.[33]

The first instances of merchandise 'tie-ins' appeared in the 1910s, when department stores offered for sale costumes worn by stars in Pathé serials (Staiger 1990: 11). In the 1920s, a whole line of products centered around Felix the Cat, and in the early 1930s child star Shirley Temple received a first royalty check of $75,000 for sales of Shirley Temple dolls (Kanfer 1997; Gaines 1991: 164).[34] In 1913, *Ladies World* doubled its newsstand circulation when it ran the weekly story of the Edison serial 'What Happened to Mary' (Grau 1914: 238). Star testimonials afforded another opportunity for brand extension. For example, between 1916 and 1921, Mary Pickford was the face of Pompeian Skin Cream (Grieveson 1999: 360). In many cases, the actors had no input in the uses to which their 'brand power' was put: to her disgust, actress Kay Francis watched herself figure in shoe polish advertisements.[35] A study of Canadian magazine advertising shows that testimonials by stars increased from 1.5 percent of all advertising during the 1920s to over 5 percent in the 1930s, while testimonials by experts declined from 7.5 to 4.5 percent (Leiss *et al.* 1990: 270).[36] Stars thus had become pure brands, enabling a triumph of persuasion over information. By simply attaching a star's name and image to an unbranded product, makers could multiply its value.[37]

Britain

The early British film companies made extensive use of trademarks, sometimes combined with advertising about technological wonders. The Urban Trading Company used its specialization in colored film to attract customers, using a patented color process branded as 'Kinemacolor' (Low 1949; Sadoul 1972: 46–47). The average length of films released in Britain increased gradually from 1907 to 1917, but remained shorter than those in the United States; in spring 1914, the British average was about 1,000 feet, compared to 1,200 feet in the United States.

French, American, and Italian companies supplied the majority of films shown in Great Britain, and it is not surprising that the first stars in Britain were American. The still-anonymous Mary Pickford became hugely popular there in 1910, and, when thousands of fans pressed for her name, the distributor of Pickford's films quickly christened her 'Dorothy Nicholson.' In late 1911, the Hepworth company, in a radical shift of strategy, adopted the star system. Previously unadvertised players suddenly covered whole film posters. 'The same players that had been with the company for several years without comment, were forced before the public on every possible occasion, on hoardings, in newspapers, on the walls of the underground' (Low 1949: 108, 126). Nevertheless, Hepworth was the exception, and most companies did not develop their own stars. In 1913, the newly formed London Film Company hired American actors, writers, and producers to make British films (Low 1950: 75–78). In the 1920s, British & Colonial hoped to attract more US revenues by putting American stars under contract. A decade later, producer Alexander Korda did the same, though by then a few British stars were obtaining substantial sums, including Gracie Fields, who earned about £40,000 per picture (Richards 1994: 164).

The small scale of the industry in Britain together with the proximity of the film studios to London's West End theaters, led film producers to 'rent' established stars from the stage. In 1911, Sir Herbert Tree received £1,000 for one day of acting in *Henry VIII*, and the producer highly publicized the film. To increase demand, the producer announced that he would burn all twenty copies after six weeks (and subsequently had to suffer the rage of exhibitors when he had second thoughts). At the time, £3,000 to £5,000 was not an exceptional fee for a famous stage actor or other well-known person for a starring role in a film. In 1919, the boxer Georges Carpentier, for example, received an offer of £6,000 (Low 1971: 95–96, 275). Of all registered stage actors in Britain between 1918 and 1936, as many as 65 percent had worked for the movies (Sanderson 1984: 215).

Stories became important from the early 1910s onward. The London Film Company promised to use the proceeds of a £40,000 public offering to buy the rights to famous plays and novels. Even in the 1920s, film rights commanded substantial sums, and ten years later story prices had increased dramatically; Herbert Wilcox had to pay £20,000 for the rights to the hit musical *Chu Chin Chow*, although average prices were lower. In the late 1920s, the price for an average play or novel ranged between £1,000 and £3,000, with lesser-known works fetching £400 to £1,500. An average original screenplay sold for about £350 (Low 1949: 133, 277). In the early 1930s, 490,000 francs (£6,000) were paid for Henri Bataille's *The Private Life of Don Juan*, £4,000 for Rudyard Kipling's *The Elephant Boy*, and £8,000 for *The Scarlet Pimpernel*. Some say that Alexander Korda acquired the rights to *Lawrence of Arabia* for £30,000, on the condition that they would never be transferred to an American company.[38]

France

In France, the main film companies had roots in the fine machinery industry, and they used technological features to lure an audience. The Pathé company pioneered colored film, and by 1910 the three main French companies – Pathé, Gaumont, and Éclair – each had its own coloring process. Attempts were also made to pioneer sound pictures, and in 1908 Gaumont tried in vain to market its sound system in the United States (Guy 1976: 100–109).

Also in 1908, Eclair noticed the popularity of the *Nick Carter* dime novel series and acquired the film rights.[39] Soon its French competitors launched their own serials, and American companies adopted the format in 1912. Before 1914, the star system did not play a large role in France. Actors were predominantly anonymous; posters did not feature their names, and Gaumont even ordered its illustrators not to draw any recognizable facial features on players, so that the public would not identify them (Aimone 1997: 84). The 'stars' of French films were fictional characters – mainly comic ones; it was the fictional name that was advertised and publicized, while the player could even be changed if necessary. As in Britain, however, companies occasionally used established stage stars, and then they prominently advertised their names (Abel 1994: 41).

As more and more fan mail piled up, film companies realized that identifiable stars might have some advantages. Gaumont, for example, received 300–400 letters a day for its star Renée Navarre. In 1913, it featured the star Musidora, who received the huge sum of 100 francs a day (Aimone 1997: 87). With exceptions such as D.W. Griffith or Thomas H. Ince, companies did not advertise the names of directors (Bousquet 1981: 67–75). During the 1910s, American stars became popular in France. In late 1915, Pearl White, starring in the serial *Mystères de New York*, became so famous that her costume – a simple skirt, black vest, narrow-brimmed hat, and white gloves – became fashionable among Parisian women (Abel 1984: 10). In the 1920s, as in Britain, some companies imported American stars, and some actors who saw their fame decline in the United States migrated to France to boost their careers – or end them (Hammond and Ford 1983). French observers lamented that their industry did not develop stars and remained unwilling to invest in long-term contracts; in France, a star's contract covered at most three films (Aimone 1997: 86; Crisp 1993: 31). French companies preferred stories over stars, especially in the early days. In 1897 Lumière filmed *Vues représentant la Vie et la Passion de Jésus-Christ* (Sadoul 1972: 20). Trading on the incontestable brand recognition of the New Testament, the film became hugely popular, and the American rights fetched $10,000. The lack of copyright on the material was also a drawback, however, as numerous imitations were promptly filmed. In 1908, Film d'Art started making films based on well-known French plays and novels and using famous stage actors. The fees involved were so large that the company came close to bankruptcy, and Pathé practically took it over. From 1909, the Société Cinématographique des Auteurs and Gens de Lettres, also backed by Pathé, focused exclusively on famous plays and novels, for which it had contacts with 300 authors (Sadoul 1972: 70, 73; Abel 1994: 40). They confined stage actors to minor roles for publicity purposes to keep costs down. In 1909 Eclair founded a competing subsidiary, Association Cinématographique des Auteurs Dramatique, which concentrated on classic plays and novels, until 1911, when it shifted toward contemporary, 'popular' works, especially police dramas and thrillers (Le Roy and Billier 1995: 36–37).

French film companies invested less in publicity than their US counterparts – at least after the First World War. A study by Henri Bousquet shows that, in 1919 about 30 percent of French films were heavily advertised in the trade press. By 1920–1921, the proportion had halved, to just over 15 percent, and in 1922 dropped further to about 10 percent. Comparable figures for American films in France are lacking, but it is likely that they were advertised more heavily (Bousquet 1981: 69–74).

Production strategies and consumer preferences

> The hero was distinguished by his achievement, the celebrity by his image or trademark. The hero created himself; the celebrity is created by the media. The hero was a big man. The celebrity is a big name.... A sign of a celebrity is often that his name is worth more than his services.
>
> Daniel Boorstin[40]

Overview

Paying creative inputs not only for their quality but also for the market value of their popular appeal should produce widely divergent payments rather than convergence to an industry average.[41] In addition, branded creative inputs (such as stars) should receive disproportionately higher pay than unbranded creative inputs (such as other players).

Budget breakdowns are lacking for most films, but Table 3.1 presents data on some American films for which information is available. The data show that the share devoted to players varied substantially, roughly between 10 and 25 percent. The share for copyrights fluctuated even more, from close to 0 to about 18 percent. Together, creative inputs make up 20 to 60 percent of the budget, though for productions over $200,000 the lower bound to this share lies around 30 percent.

These examples give information only on the order of magnitude, and breakdowns must have varied widely from case to case. As each film is an individual project, it is difficult to view these specific amounts as representative. In 1915 and 1916, for example, the average budget of an Artcraft Pictures film starring Mary Pickford was $165,000–$170,000, of which an unprecedented 75 percent was Pickford's salary (Koszarski 1990: 266). The average studio production costs shown in Table 3.1 help to arrange the cases as low-, middle-, or high-budget and so give some scale against which to measure individual cases. The average industry production cost in 1927 was $134,343, confirming the low budgets of the two MGM films listed for that year. In 1929 and 1931, the average costs were $186,230 and $175,495, and we can see that even the cheapest RKO

Table 3.1 Share of creative inputs in US film production costs, 1917–1937 (in percentages)

Year	Company	Title	All actors (1)	Lead actors (2)	Extras (3)	Director (4)	Screenplay (5)	Copyright (6)	Total creative inputs (1+3+4 +5+6) (7)	Total cost (in 1927 $s) (8)	Average studio cost (in 1927 $s) (9)
1917		'Average picture'	47.2	16.9		16.9	5.6		60.5	54,000	
1917		'Average picture'	48.0	33.9		14.1	11.8		70.6	23,000	
1922	Universal	The Way Back	15.2		2.6	10.0	5.0		43.6	35,000	
1924		'Est. of av. negative cost'	25.0					5.0	45.0		
1926	MGM	Mandalay	17.3		4.0	17.3	0.7	17.3	56.7	82,000	254,000
1926	MGM	The Scarlet Letter	16.6		6.3	16.6	4.8	16.6	61.0	212,000	254,000
1927	MGM	Wyoming	12.6	7.5	13.1	6.1	0.5	0.5	32.7	58,000	277,000
1927	MGM	Spoilers	11.3	2.3	3.5	13.4	2.4	2.4	33.1	23,000	277,000
1930	RKO	Swing High	13.8		8.0	3.4	4.2	0.5	30.0	286,000	363,000
1930	RKO	Night Work	13.4		5.9	7.1	1.9		28.2	188,000	363,000
1930	RKO	Her Man	11.9		8.4	7.0	5.5	1.6	34.5	387,000	363,000
1930	RKO	Holiday	19.6		2.9	5.1	2.1	11.4	41.1	320,000	363,000
1930	RKO	Her Private Affairs	11.4		3.0	7.6	2.4	3.0	27.4	207,000	363,000

1930	RKO	Paris Bound	12.7		2.8	8.8	1.0	5.6	30.9	279,000	363,000
1930	RKO	This Thing Called Love	18.5		1.6	6.6	1.5	5.5	33.8	235,000	363,000
1932	RKO	Truth about Hollywood	38.7	30.2	2.3	6.3	3.7	1.0	52.0	521,000	203,000
1932	RKO	Lady with a Past	26.6	20.7	4.9	11.1	6.0	2.8	51.4	685,000	203,000
1934	MGM	Manhattan Melodrama	24.5		10.3	4.2	7.3	7.3	53.7	405,000	596,000
1934	MGM	Copperfield	6.9		3.0	16.7	5.1	5.1	36.8	882,000	596,000
1937		'Average picture'	25.0			10.0	7.0	5.0	47.0		
		Average all films (excluding estimates)	16.9	15.2	5.2	9.5	3.8	5.8	40.4	300,000	

Sources: Bächlin (1945); Kennedy (1927); Schatz (1988); Koszarski (1990); Jewell (1994); Glancy (1995).

Notes

'All actors' = all major roles (the main characters in the film); 'Lead' is included in 'All actors'; 'Extras' = extras and small roles; 'Total' = share of all these creative inputs in total production costs; 'Total cost' = total production costs in 1927 dollars (rounded to nearest $1,000); 'Average studio cost' = average production costs for the respective studios during the respective year, based on *all* films.

movies were at the industry average and their others substantially above it.[42] In 1933, the industry average was \$159,427, placing the two 1934 MGM budgets far above average.

For Britain, few budget breakdowns are available. American observers noted that, in 1929, the average British film budget included about 20 percent spent on actors, 10 percent on the director, and 6.7 percent on the screenplay and copyright.[43] Table 3.2 shows the breakdowns of four high-budget films by London Film Productions in 1934. Even compared to US standards, these films were very expensive. The share of creative inputs varied considerably, between 27 and 42 percent.

Fifteen breakdowns were found for France, nearly all of them from Albatros, a medium-sized producer (see Table 3.3). The films listed cover only about 2 percent of all films made in France between 1924 and 1936, though Albatros was probably quite characteristic of film companies in inter-war France: film production was highly fragmented, but its distribution was highly concentrated (Bakker 2004). The average budget in France in 1923 was 410,000 francs, and in 1938 about 1.9 million francs, putting the 1924 films and the two 1930s films at or above the average. The share of creative inputs fluctuated between 15 and 35 percent, significantly lower than in the American cases. Total costs were also substantially lower than in the US studies, which suggests that, both absolutely and relatively, French companies spent less on creative inputs.[44]

How important were creative inputs in persuading consumers to attend particular films? Leo Lowenthal pinpointed a remarkable shift in consumer interest toward creative inputs, which occurred exactly when the feature film, with its 'famous players in famous plays,' rose to dominance. Analyzing biographical articles in popular US magazines, he found that, between 1901 and 1914, 74 percent of subjects came from business, politics, and the professions, whereas after 1922, more than half came from entertainment, especially from light entertainment and sports (Lowenthal 1961).[45]

If film studios were successful in using creative inputs to establish brands, then these inputs should be the main incentive for people to see a particular film.[46] How then did consumers make their choice? Sources on consumer preferences divide into three categories. The oldest are the polls conducted by fan magazines, which started as early as 1909.[47] Their representativeness is often questionable, as readers had to send in post-cards, and the subjects covered were limited. From the early 1920s onward, sociologists, psychologists, and citizens' organizations undertook surveys on the social effects of cinema, especially on children.[48] The third and most useful source is market research, which was done only sparsely before 1940 (Bakker 2003).[49] For Britain, the tabulated responses to surveys conducted by the Bernstein cinema chain cover moviegoers in and around London from 1927 to 1946.[50] For the United States, the market research reports of Audience Research, Inc. (ARI) are the major

Table 3.2 Creative inputs in production costs of six British films, 1931–1936 (in percentages)

Year	Company	Title	Actors (1)	Extras (2)	Director (3)	Screenplay (4)	Copyright (5)	Total (1 + 2 + 3 + 4 + 5) (6)	Budget (in 1927 £s) (7)
1931	Gainsborough	Hindle Wakes	14.6		7.0	18.9		40.5	32,000
1932	Gainsborough	Murder at Covent Garden	6.4	4.3	2.6	4.3		17.4	14,000
1935	London Films	The Scarlet Pimpernel	12.9	3.8	8.9	3.1	5.4	34.1	179,000
1936	London Films	Things to Come	5.3	5.0	13.9	2.6	0.4	27.1	284,000
1936	London Films	Moscow Nights	22.8	1.0	10.5	0.1	7.4	41.8	54,000
1936	London Films	The Man who Could Work Miracles	11.6	2.2	13.1	4.8	0.0	31.7	120,000

Sources: Aileen and Michael Balcon Collection, British Film Institute, File A57; David Cunynghame Collection, British Film Institute, File 'Weekly Production Costs – All Current Pictures.'

Notes
For the first two films, no disaggregated figures were available; costs of copyrights are included in 'Screenplay.' Total costs are rounded to nearest £1,000.

Table 3.3 Share of creative inputs in French film budgets and production costs, 1923–1939 (in percentages)

Year	Company	B	Title	All actors (1)	Lead actors (2)	Extras (3)	Director (4)	Screenplay (5)	Copyright (6)	Total 1+3+4+5+6 (7)	Costs in 1927 Fr. frs
1923	Albatros	1	Paris qui Dort	17.1	5.7	11.4	4.6	2.1		35.3	116,000
1924	Albatros	1	Kean	22.5		5.8	9.2	1.8		39.2	6,311,000
1924	Albatros	1	La Dame Masquée	7.2	1.9	13.1	2.5	0.3		23.2	461,000
1924	Albatros	0	Le Lion des Mogols	10.8	5.8	9.2	3.4	0.2		23.5	1,077,000
1924	Albatros	0	L'Affiche	11.7	7.0	8.4	5.1	1.3		26.5	570,000
1924	Albatros-Cinegraphic	1	Feu Mathias Pascal	17.9	9.7	6.9	7.7	0.8	8.2	41.5	897,000
1924	Albatros	1	La Proie du Vent	17.7	6.5	9.5	7.2	2.2		36.6	1,004,000
1925	Albatros	1	Les Aventures de Robert Macaire	12.8	6.4	7.9	6.3	1.3		28.2	1,039,000
1927	Albatros	1	Le Chasseur de Chez Maxim's	16.3	7.1	8.4	2.2	4.8		31.8	1,135,000
1927	Albatros	1	Un Chapeau de Paille d'Italie	18.4	7.1	1.8	5.9	5.9		32.0	842,000
1927	Albatros-Julisar	0	La Comtesse Marie	6.6	2.7	4.3	4.7		4.3	19.8	1,051,000
1928	Albatros-Sequana	1	Les Deux Timides	11.8	4.4	4.4	13.1	2.2		31.5	913,000
1930	Albatros	1	Procureur Hallers	7.8	3.1	4.7	7.8	1.3	1.3	22.8	
1931	Albatros	0	Un Coup de Téléphone	11.7		5.7	2.2	6.2		25.9	1,010,000

Year	Company	B	Film								Total
1931	Albatros	0	Le Monsieur de Minuit	7.9		2.5	5.7	13.1		29.2	1,135,000
1932	Albatros	0	Il a été Perdu un Mariée	12.0		3.2	3.5	5.7		24.4	924,000
1934	Albatros	1	La Porteuse de Pain	20.3	8.0	3.8	5.2	1.6	10.5	41.5	1,640,000
1934			Average film	25.0			6.8	1.7	1.7	35.3	
1936			Major film of average quality	20.0				2.5	2.5	25.0	
1936	Albatros-SFPF	1	Les Hommes Nouveaux	18.6	11.0	5.7	7.0	6.6		38.0	2,678,000
1936	Albatros	1	La Grande Illusion	25.2	6.5		4.6	2.5		32.4	1,815,000
1936	Albatros	1	Les Bas Fonds	11.4		3.5	4.9	13.3		33.2	2,397,000
1939	Albatros	1	A Bon Chat Bon Rat	30.2	13.8	3.4	1.7	3.4		38.8	2,234,000
1924	Albatros	0	L'Heureuse Mort	11.5		9.8		1.5		22.8	506,000
1926	Albatros	0	Carmen	6.9				0.2		7.1	624,000
1927	Albatros	1	Souris d'Hotel	9.7	3.9	6.1				15.8	619,000
1928	Albatros	0	Les Nouveaux Messieurs	11.6		11.2		5.4		28.2	1,385,000
1929	Albatros-Wengeroff	1	Cagliostro	22.4				1.8		24.1	479,000
1931	Film Sonor-SDFS	1	A Nous la Liberté	4.0		7.0		7.0		18.0	2,759,000
			Average all films (excluding estimates)	14.4	6.7	6.7	5.4	3.7	7.6	31.6	1,370,000

Sources: Collection Albatros, Bibliothèque du Film, Paris; Collection René Clair, Bibliothèque d'Arsenal, Paris; Bakker 2004; Bächlin (1945).

Note

Total production costs rounded at nearest 1,000 francs. In 'B' column, rows with '1' list budgeted amounts, rows with '0' list actual production costs.

source. George Gallup started the company in Princeton in 1938 and conducted research throughout the 1940s.[51] Universal Pictures also undertook some primitive market research, beginning in 1922. The company
ran a weekly advertisement in *The Saturday Evening Post*, signed by Universal's president Carl Laemmle, asking readers to state their favorite
stars and to answer some questions. Once, Laemmle even placed a job
advertisement for a 'Master Psychologist' who could 'analyze plot-situ-
ations' and 'forecast public reaction.'[52] Reportedly, Universal received
about 100 letters a day and built a substantial mailing list, from which it
selected 300 people whom it consulted frequently. When asked what
influenced them most to see a motion picture, the respondents answered,
in order of importance: the star, the 'popularity of story, book or stage
play,' the director, and the author.[53]

A more professional survey in 1933 conducted in Montclair, New
Jersey, with 5,130 children, also found that, besides the picture itself, stars
and stories were the main reasons to visit the cinema. A 1929 survey of
10,052 children in Chicago asked how the respondent selected a movie.
Again, stars and stories – if 'title' is considered related to story – were
among the main methods of selecting a film (Montclair Survey 1933;
Mitchell 1929: 161).[54]

The 1927 Bernstein questionnaire (Table 3.4) shows similar results for
Britain. Courtesy and service were reasons to visit the cinema for only 9
percent of respondents – and probably not even the main one for that
group, since more than one reason could be marked. Apart from the
picture itself, first the star and then the orchestra and the story were the
most important reasons.[55] A study by Annette Kuhn (1999) carried out
between 1994 and 1996 confirms these findings. Kuhn asked elderly

Table 3.4 Reasons for cinema-goers in and around London to visit the movies, 1927 (in percentages)

Reason	Male	Female	Unknown	Total
The picture	18.5	18.2	18.1	18.3
The star	14.2	14.9	15.3	14.5
The orchestra	14.3	12.8	14.9	13.8
The story	12.6	12.5	13.8	12.7
The varieties	11.3	10.3	10.0	10.8
Courtesy and service of the staff	9.2	9.4	8.3	9.2
Prices of admission	7.7	8.1	6.2	7.7
The producer	6.9	7.9	7.9	7.4
Publicity	5.3	5.9	5.5	5.6
Totals	100.0	100.0	100.0	100.0
Totals (absolute number)	3,222	2,378	470	6,070

Source: Bernstein Questionnaire, 1927, question 2: 'What attracts you to the cinema?' Sidney
L. Bernstein Collection, British Film Institute, London.

Britons about their cinema-going habits in the 1930s. The appearance of their favorite stars was an important reason to see a film for 75.3 percent, while 53.2 percent said publicity influenced their choice. 'Good acting/liked stars' was the most important reason why films made an impression on respondents (40.6 percent), followed by the story (35.0 percent).[56]

Stars

In mid-1929, 277 players were under long-term contract in Hollywood: the total stock of major and minor stars.[57] The available budget breakdowns for US films (see Table 3.1) supply scant information on the pay of the leading player, the star, but it is clear that stars received disproportionately more than their fellow actors. Sometimes the star's salary was half of all the actors' pay in total. The French case studies reveal slightly more than the US case studies: in the nine cases, the star received about as much as the rest of the cast combined. This supports the notion that stars' pay was not only for their service as an actress/actor (for example, payment according to a union/professional scale), but also for the popular appeal of their name. Even if the star worked a few days more than other players, the degree of difference remains striking.

Harvey Lehman's research on the box office potential of stars in relation to their age from 1915 to 1939 confirms this point (Lehman 1941).[58] He found that women reached their highest box office potential between 25 and 29 years of age, and men between 30 and 34 (see Figure 3.1). If companies were basing payment of stars only on the quality of their acting, the distribution would have been more even, or would have peaked at a later age, because quality and skill generally increase with age. Directors

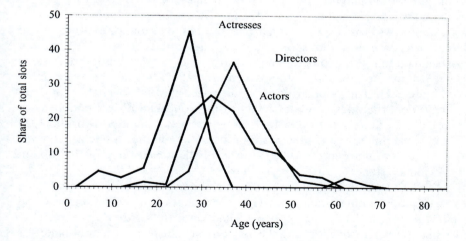

Figure 3.1 Age of the annual top-ten box office stars in earnings in the US, 1915–1939 (source: Lehman 1941).

reached their peak between 35 and 39 years. One might argue that talent is bound to be young in an emerging industry, but because the profession started before 1900, the oldest young entrant would have been 60 years old by 1939. If box office potential depended on quality, one would expect veterans to have won more top slots over time and that the peak would be less pronounced or would occur at a later age.

The existing data on the pay of actors/actresses and directors are also sparse, but available evidence from the late 1910s and 1920s confirms the high level of divergence (Koszarski 1990: 114–116, 212–213). As expected, the stars' salaries did not hover around an average, but diverged widely, even among the famous few. Between 1916 and 1923, stars' pay increased substantially across the board – for the top eighteen stars from \$73,968 to \$195,918 (in constant dollars). Income inequality among the stars remained remarkably constant, at a Gini-coefficient of 0.46 (see Table 3.5).[59] Interestingly, none of the stars in the 1916 list appeared in the 1923 list: stars were short-lived brands. Only four of the sixteen stars in 1916 were female, whereas in 1923 fifteen out of twenty-six were female, and women filled the top three slots. The top directors' pay for 1926 shows an income distribution similar to that of players (Gini = 0.47).[60]

The huge pay differences among stars suggest a similar degree of disproportion in their appreciation by consumers. The Bernstein polls of 1927, 1932, and 1934 indicate that the word 'star' lived up to its metaphor in this sense and that fame decreased disproportionately from larger to lesser players (see Table 3.5).[61] For example, in 1932 the most popular star, Norma Shearer, was named by 18.5 percent of respondents; the second, Constance Bennett, was named by 10.5 percent, and the sixth, Greta Garbo, by only 5 percent. The popularity distribution is quite similar for all three years and for both males and females, the Gini-coefficient hovering between 0.56 and 0.66. For the other years, the popularity distribution is about twice as disproportionate as the pay distribution. Although the data sets cover different stars, countries, and periods, nevertheless one can speculate that this gap between popularity and pay distribution represents the extent to which the studios captured the rents of the stars' fame (Figure 3.2). The popularity of 'small parts players' (available for 1934 only) confirms these findings in that this group had a distribution more equal than that of the stars. Interestingly, when compared with the 1928 Universal poll in the United States, four of the ten most popular US male stars do not figure in the 1927 Bernstein poll, nor do three of the top ten US female stars.[62]

A 1931 survey of Edinburgh schoolchildren shows a more equal fame distribution among stars, with Gini-coefficients of 0.49 for females and 0.34 for males. These results are probably a result of the survey method: while Bernstein encouraged the respondents to give as many names as possible, the Edinburgh children could give only one.[63] The Bernstein data better reflect the 'brand-awareness' of a star, as most consumers have

Table 3.5 Distribution of popularity and pay among top creative inputs and top films, 1916–1941

Year	Input or product	Measure	Gini	C4	C6	C8	HH	Ranks	N
1916	Actors/actresses	Pay	0.46	60	71	82	1,238	18	18
1923	Actors/actresses	Pay	0.46	43	58	66	674	32	32
1926	Directors	Pay/week	0.47	31	39	46	452	57	57
1927	Directors	Poll	0.55	60	72	79	1,066	24	c.2,000
1932	Directors	Poll	0.58	59	66	72	1,590	31	c.2,500
1934	Directors	Poll	0.60	40	53	62	637	42	2,460
1941	Directors	Poll	0.57	70	80	86	1,719	19	1,000
1927	Actresses	Poll	0.66	36	45	52	570	79	c.2,000
1932	Actresses	Poll	0.67	48	60	70	803	53	c.2,500
1934	Actresses	Poll	0.61	35	45	53	494	65	2,460
1934	Minor actresses	Poll	0.33	28	36	42	354	46	2,460
1931	Actresses	Poll	0.49	58	73	83	1,317	19	2,580
1940	Actresses	Poll	0.32	17	23	29	222	62	1,000
1927	Actors	Poll	0.61	29	40	48	401	73	c.2,000
1932	Actors	Poll	0.66	41	51	57	612	74	c.2,500
1934	Actors	Poll	0.56	28	37	45	372	73	2,460
1934	Minor actors	Poll	0.21	18	24	30	255	47	2,460
1931	Actors	Poll	0.34	46	60	71	820	19	2,580
1940	Actors	Poll	0.25	20	27	34	302	41	1,000
1932	Films in UK	Attendance	0.31	29	35	40	351	51	c.2,500
1932	Films in USA	Revenue	0.29	32	41	49	473	30	30
1941	Comics	Poll	0.61	34	42	48	441	82	1,000

Sources: Koszarski (1990); Jewell (1994); Glancy (1992, 1995); Mackie (1933); Audience Research, Inc.

Notes
'Gini' = Gini-coefficient (the area between the Lorenz-curve and the line of equality divided by the total area above the line of equality); 'C4, C6, C8' = combined share of 4, 6, 8 largest inputs; 'HH' = Herfindahl Hirschman index (sum of the squares of the market shares of each input); 'Ranks' = the number of creative inputs ranked in the rank order; 'N' = number of respondents.

several stars by whom they are attracted. The highest-ranked star in a Bernstein questionnaire is not necessarily the most appreciated, but rather the star who is a favorite of the most consumers.[64]

A 1940 Gallup poll showed a more evenly divided distribution, resulting from a different survey method: consumers had to go through a list of names and mark, without ranking, all the stars who would induce them to go to the theater. This method is bound to generate many hits for lesser stars, as refreshing the respondents' memories allowed them to mark as many names as they wanted. In the Bernstein case, the need for respondents' recall of stars was bound to give advantage to the biggest stars.[65]

Table 3.6 shows the popularity of stars over time. Over a period of a few years (1932–1934 and 1934–1937), 40 to 60 percent of the stars remained in top positions, but the correlation between the exact rank is limited, at most 0.53. This suggests that fame is an unstable and impermanent possession.[66]

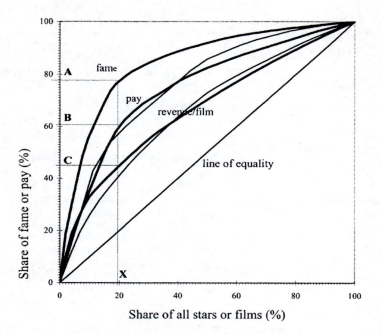

Figure 3.2 Distribution of fame and pay among creative inputs and films in Britain and the US, 1916–1932: Lorenz-curves.

Key
Fame: distribution of fame of the top film actresses among British moviegoers in 1932 polling data.
Pay, thin line: distribution of pay among the top film actors and actresses in the USA, 1916.
Pay, bold line: distribution of pay among the top film actors and actresses in the USA, 1923.
Revenue/film, thin line: distribution of tickets sold per film among British moviegoers in 1932, attendance data.
Revenue/film, bold line: distribution of box office revenue of top 30 films released by MGM, Warner Brothers and RKO in 1932 in the USA.

Reading examples
*   In 1932, about 20 percent of actresses (X) held about 78 percent of the fame of stars among British moviegoers (A).
*   In 1932, about 20 percent of American star actors and actresses (X) received 61 percent of stars' salaries (B).
*   In 1932, about 20 percent of the hit films (X) sold 45 percent of the hit film tickets (C).

Note
The diagonal is the hypothetical line if fame and pay would be distributed evenly among the stars or hit films.

The percentages of overlap for 1927–1932 are low because of the new demands posed by the advent of sound on directing, acting, and voice. Those for 1937–1946 are low because of the long period considered.

The question that remains, then, is whether the popularity of stars could predict the popularity of films. The data reveal that there is less equal dis-

Table 3.6 Popularity of creative inputs over time in Britain, 1927–1946

	Years	1	2	3
Actresses	1927–1932	30	−0.62	53
	1932–1934	51	0.35	53
	1934–1937	64	0.37	45
	1937–1946	23	−0.67	30
Actors	1927–1932	29	0.24	73
	1932–1934	51	0.53	73
	1934–1937	41	0.23	50
	1937–1946	18	−0.05	32
Directors	1927–1932	25	0.10	24
	1932–1934	52	0.33	31
	1934–1937	57	0.01	14
	1937–1946	33	−0.70	12

Source: Bernstein Cinemas, Sidney L. Bernstein Collection, British Film Institute, London.

Notes
1 = percentage of persons in first period that also appear in rank order next period; 2 = Spearman/Pearson coefficient of rank order correlation for persons that appear in both periods, where 1.0 is a perfect positive correlation, –1.0 a perfect negative correlation and 0 no correlation at all; 3 = number of rank positions over which the comparison has been made.

tribution of films than of stars.[67] While 10–20 percent of respondents liked the most famous star, only 3.8 percent saw the most popular film. This confirms the theory that companies needed stars as brands because it was difficult to brand the films themselves. The correlation between stars and film popularity, analyzed for the top fifteen stars, is rather low, for both males and females (see Table 3.7).[68]

Other studies confirm this low correlation, finding at most a 0.25 correlation between star popularity and box office revenue (see, for example, Kindem 1982: 79–93; Simonoff and Sparrow 2000). Because a film is the result of numerous interactions among many creative inputs, establishing a correlation is an especially difficult task. In this light, the huge sums spent on stars do not seem entirely justified. But the main value of the stars may have resided not in their power to guarantee a hit, but rather in their ability to guarantee publicity. Stars were giant promotion machines, which in a short time could create a high brand-awareness for a new film. As the surveys used here suggest, it is possible to gauge this brand-awareness and to express it in numbers.

Brand-awareness was a necessary, but not sufficient, condition for a film to reach high box office revenues. Even if a film failed, the star-as-brand had done his or her work by attracting people to the cinema in the first week. Whether a film would be a subsequent success or failure would likely depend more on its inherent quality – about which word-of-mouth and reviews transmitted information. As industry observer Howard Lewis noted in 1933: 'Granting that the star system is costly, its advocates believe that, in comparison with additional expenditures necessary to add color to a picture

Table 3.7 Top fifteen film stars and their films' relative popularity among moviegoers in and around London, 1932

Actors

Rank	Name	Film title	Film rank
1	Colman, Ronald	Devil to Pay	4
1		Raffles	12
2	Brook, Clive	East Lynne	22
3	Arliss, George		
4	Montgomery, Robert	Inspiration	34
4		Strangers May Kiss	7
5	Chevalier, Maurice		
6	Boles, John	Resurrection	30
6		One Heavenly Night	15
6		King of Jazz	17
7	Lynn, Ralph		
8	Walls, Tom	Plunder	9
9	Powell, William		
10	Beery, Wallace	Min and Bill	2
11	Bancroft, George		
12	Holt, Jack	Last Parade	38
13	Stone, Lewis	Inspiration	34
14	Cooper, Gary		
15	Farrell, Charles	Man Who Came Back	31

Coefficient of rank order correlation = 0.47

Actresses

Rank	Name	Film title	Film rank
1	Shearer, Norma	Strangers May Kiss	7
2	Bennett, Constance	Sin Takes a Holiday	27
2		Born to Love	20
3	Dressler, Mary	Reducing	10
3		Min and Bill	2
4	Chatterton, Ruth		
5	Gaynor, Janet		
6	Garbo, Greta	Man Who Came Back	31
6		Inspiration	34
7	MacDonald, Jeannette	Monte Carlo	13
8	Crawford, Joan	Dance Fools Dance	35
9	Harding, Ann	East Lynne	22
10	Dietrich, Marlene	Blue Angel	39
11	Carroll, Madeleine		
12	Francis, Kay	Raffles	12
13	Colbert, Claudette		
14	Davies, Marion		
15	Brent, Evelyn		

Coefficient of rank order correlation = 0.39

Source: Bernstein Cinemas, Sidney L. Bernstein Collection, British Film Institute, London.

without a star, such costs are relatively small. This is especially true, they aver, of expenditures for advertising and exploitation' (Lewis 1933: 119). Although stars did not guarantee a hit, they fully guaranteed publicity.

Stories

Just as with stars, film companies could use literary properties for two purposes: quality and fame. One can expect the price of a work to depend on four variables: inherently, on its quality and the ease of adaptation; relative to popular appeal, on its popularity (brand-awareness of the title) and its proven success.[69] Plays have all four characteristics, novels three (adaptation is less easy), short stories, articles, and other literary properties two (inherent quality and proven success), and screenplays only one (ease of adaptation). Therefore, one expects the prices of rights to plays to be higher than those of novels, and prices of novels to be higher than those of original screenplays.

The US film budgets in Table 3.1, fourteen of which use a literary work, show that the prices for rights varied tremendously (and the few French budgets suggest the same). Each year the Hollywood studios bought a wide variety of properties: besides plays and screenplays, they purchased short stories, comedies, radio programs, newspaper articles, and poems. The great majority were screenplays, and the literary works contained substantially more novels than plays.[70]

Nevertheless, the data for 1940 displayed in Table 3.8 show that the largest sums were spent on plays, followed by novels. The difference in prices is striking: plays commanded ten times more than original screenplays and twice as much as novels. This premium indicates the use of literary properties as brands. Even short stories commanded three times as much as original screenplays. Although the average prices for all literary works together fluctuated widely between 1937 and 1940 – from $14,391 to $11,921, to $9,686, to $18,229 – the sales of rights to Broadway plays shows a steady increase, from $500,000 in the 1924–1925 season to $1.1 million in 1931–1932, to a high of $3 million in 1944–1945 (Bächlin 1945: 175–176).[71]

The story departments of Hollywood studios bore some resemblance to the research and development centers of pharmaceutical companies. Paramount, for example, had story departments in both Hollywood and New York. The latter, close to the literary world, selected stories based on the studio's current story requirements, the states' censorship laws, and plots best suited to each Paramount player or director. Once a week, departments sent summaries of all reviewed material to the studio heads. If they were interested, an 'adaptor' quickly prepared a rough script. If that was approved, the studio head would assess the value of the story, set a price limit, and instruct the legal department to handle the purchase. The purchased story went into immediate production or to the studio's substantial catalog for future use.[72]

Table 3.8 Prices paid for literary properties by US film studios, by genre, 1940

Type of property	Number	Percentage share	Value ($)	Percentage share	Average price ($)
Stage plays	51	10	1,650,000	37	32,400
Novels	109	21	1,575,000	35	14,400
Original screen stories	323	63	1,000,000	22	3,100
Short stories	21	4	225,000	5	10,700
Miscellaneous	11	2	50,000	1	4,500
Total	515	100	4,500,000	100	8,700
Total (excluding 'Original screen stories')	192	37	3,500,000	78	18,200

Source: Bächlin 1945: 175–176.

Note
Average price rounded to the nearest $100.

Before 1940, Hollywood market research on stories was quite cursory. Universal asked in its 1928 survey whether respondents liked happy endings, and if Universal should retain unhappy endings when it turned books or plays into films. Most respondents favored happy endings, if not 'forced,' but wanted to keep original unhappy endings, although some would allow change if it 'did not detract from the story.'[73]

In the 1940s, film studios undertook more elaborate market research. For example, market researchers asked librarians in small towns about the most popular children's books. Apart from *Pinocchio*, *The Wizard of Oz*, and *Gulliver's Travels*, *Sue Barton Rural Nurse* turned out to be the favorite. It had never been filmed before, and the market researchers thus advised the acquisition of the rights to the Sue Barton novels.[74]

Film studios often bought stories because they thought them suitable for a particular star. A well-chosen combination of star and story brands could reinforce each other, just as 'miscasting' a star could damage film revenues. RKO, for example, questioned consumers on potential vehicles for Orson Welles. Did they prefer to see him in *Invasion from Mars*, *Heart of Darkness*, *Smiler with a Knife*, or *Cyrano de Bergerac*? Most chose *Invasion from Mars*, as they considered Welles a heroic personality. In the late 1930s and 1940s, the studios also habitually commissioned 'title tests' for new projects.[75] Studios realized that besides the fame of a work, the title itself was important, and it was the first or second thing consumers knew about a movie. It could be instrumental in informing and persuading the consumer.

For Britain, systematic data on prices paid for literary properties are minimal. During the 1930s, literary works rather than original screenplays were the basis for about half of all British films. Plays were the most popular genre, with more films based on plays than on novels and short stories combined. For France, data are also sparse. Between 1936 and

1939, over half of French films were adapted from a literary property, slightly more than in Britain, and French film producers used novels slightly more than plays. It is probable that both British and French film companies made more use of literary works than their American counterparts, perhaps because of their countries' grand literary traditions, and because of the small scale of the industry, which could probably sustain few specialized screenwriters or story departments.[76]

Few sources exist on consumers' preferences for stories, though Kuhn's findings for Britain support their importance. Most respondents (73.0 percent) favored 'Films of books and plays,' followed by 'Music and dance films' (43.1 percent), 'Epics, historical and adventure films' (35.6 percent), 'War films' (28.2 percent), 'Comedy' (18.4 percent), and 'Suspense and horror films' (18.4 percent) (Kuhn 1999: 538). The high prices paid for stories suggest that the distribution of fame among the most popular titles will be similarly disproportionate as that for stars. A 1941 ARI 'open question' poll about the respondents' most popular comic strip yielded a Gini-coefficient of 0.61, well within the range of that for players' fame.[77]

A 1940 ARI study in New York City suggests that, like stars, stories were poor predictors of a film's success, but were instead giant publicity machines, used to reach a high brand-awareness in a short time before and during a film's release. The researchers constructed a 'penetration index' and 'intensive penetration index' based on the percentage of people who 'had heard' or 'had heard a great deal' about a film. Ten pictures with a well-known title started their local promotion campaign with 19.5 points of penetration obtained at a cost of $27 per point, and an intensive penetration of 6.5 obtained at a cost of $119 per point. Sixty-five pictures with unknown titles started with 10 points and 3 points, respectively, obtained at $137 and $540 per point (Audience Research Institute 1940b). Clearly, it was much more difficult and expensive to create popular awareness of a new title than to work with one already known to moviegoers in another context.

Conclusion

This chapter has shown that the huge sums paid by the film industry for stars and stories were not as irrational and arbitrary as they sometimes may have seemed. They might have been just as rational and have had just as quantifiable a return as direct spending on marketing and promotion. Between 1900 and 1940, as the emerging film industry industrialized live entertainment and integrated its markets by standardizing the product and making the service tradable, sunk costs and uncertainty rose. To secure an audience, film producers borrowed branding techniques from other consumer goods industries, but films' short 'shelf-life' forced producers to extend the brand beyond one product by using trademarks or stars, to buy existing 'brands' such as famous plays or novels, and to deepen the product life cycle by licensing their brands. The growing and integrating market thus induced filmmakers to change film from a largely undifferentiated commodity into a heavily branded product.

The main value of stars and stories lay not in their ability to predict successes, but in their services as giant 'publicity machines' that optimized advertising effectiveness by rapidly amassing high levels of brand-awareness. The young age at which stars reached their peak, and the disproportionate income distribution even among the superstars, confirm that payment to stars was for their ability to generate publicity rather than only for the quality of their performances. Likewise, because 'stories' (pre-existing literary works) cost several times as much as original screenplays, their popular appeal was at least part of the reason for purchase. Stars and stories telegraphed a film's qualities to some extent, confirming that they contained at least two elements with which viewers were already familiar. Studies of consumer preferences corroborate the view that stars and stories provided the main incentives to see a film.

Gradually the film companies became adept at developing and leasing their 'instant brands' to other consumer goods' industries. In a self-reinforcing and symbiotic process, this merchandising, in its turn, widened and deepened the shelf-life of films. Thus, the process had gone full-circle: the motion picture, a branded *product*, had become a pure, short-lived *brand* without a product, which, when attached to a product of little value, could increase that product's perceived quality, multiplying the price and the quantity that could be sold. By making brands tradable, the feature film opened up a new chapter in the history of other consumer products and services.

Notes

1 This chapter originally appeared in *Enterprise & Society* 2 (September 2001): 461–502. © 2001 by the Business History Conference. All rights reserved. Reprinted with permission. The author thanks William J. Baumol, Douglas Gomery, Marcel Jansen, Stephan Louw, Massimo Motta, Jaime Reis, Robert Sklar, John Sutton, and the anonymous referees for comments and suggestions. Janet Moat and Saffron Parker of the British Film Institute, Emanuelle Toulet of the Bibliothèque d'Arsenal, and the staff of the Bibliothèque du Film provided invaluable help with sources.
2 José Martì, *Granos de or: Pensamientos seleccionades en las obras de José Martì* (Barcelona, 1941).
3 All US figures are in constant 1927 dollars.
4 Between *c.*1907 and 1917, costs increased in part because of the ten-fold increase in average film length.
5 All UK figures in 1927 pounds.
6 All French figures in 1927 francs.
7 Before sound film, standardization was limited by the local inputs of accompanying music and variety acts.
8 For upscale entertainment such as symphony orchestras or operas, an international market already existed and, in the late nineteenth century, emerging music hall and vaudeville circuits with circulating artists had already integrated the entertainment market nationally on a limited scale. Market integration caused costs to rise because, unlike trademarks or patents, creative inputs are

humans or controlled by humans (as in the case of literary works or music), and thus are able to capture at least in part the rents derived from their popularity.

9 A general increase in pay could have coincided with a more disproportionate income distribution.

10 From the late 1920s onward, they did collude in distribution, which eventually led to the Paramount Decree (1948) of the US Supreme Court that forced them to divest themselves of their cinemas (Gomery 1986: 24).

11 There is a largely theoretical debate within economics on the relationship between talent and pay. See, for example, Rosen (1981). For a more popular overview, see Cook and Frank (1995).

12 Until the 1950s, the music industry was not a mass industry like cinema. Radio reached its height in the late 1940s.

13 During the emergence of the feature film, high volumes coincided with increasing ticket prices because cinema substituted more expensive forms of entertainment.

14 Bächlin (1945: 96–98) addresses information asymmetries and the risks of film production, but not asymmetries among consumers. He mentions three other production risks: unpredictability of creative talents' efforts; risk that a film is not completed; impossibility of changing content after release. Bächlin notes that risk increases with production costs. He addresses 'consumption risk,' but by this he means simply the producer's risk that few people will watch a film. Sedgwick (2000: 23–38) gives a more formal economic analysis of film consumer risk than is presented here.

15 Allen locates the shift toward fiction films in the United States in 1907–1908, Abel around 1906 in France.

16 For a general overview on trademarks and branding, see Wilkins (1992); Casson (1994). A trademark often legally protects brands. Geographical origin (food) and product category (luxury products) may also constitute part of a brand image. Branded goods often have innovative packaging and design, a carefully designed distribution network, and a high promotion-to-sales ratio. Advertising seems to occur more for experience goods than for other goods. Davis *et al.* 1991 found an average advertising-to-sales ratio of 0.4 percent for search goods versus 4.0 percent for experience goods, examining 300 products in Britain in 1989. Branding can be exclusively informative or completely persuasive; in practice it is difficult to distinguish between the two, and in fact they are often mixed, but advertisements without any information on price, point-of-sale, or objective product characteristics are exclusively persuasive.

17 Edison's first slot machines appeared in 1894; in 1895 the Lumières added projection (Abel 1999: 40–47).

18 Abel argues that the combination of Pathé's trademark with its technologically superior stencil-colored films also helped to lure consumers to the Nickelodeons.

19 These were Famous Players (Paramount), MGM, and First Nation with thirteen, ten, and eight responses. For another question ('Name your favorite film producer') 158 respondents wrote the name of a studio instead of a producer: Fox, Famous Players, MGM, and First National received twenty-six, twenty-five, nineteen, and sixteen responses. The only well-known British companies were Gaumont-British (twenty-two) and Stoll (fourteen). Tabulated responses to the 'Bernstein Questionnaire,' questions 3 and 4, Sidney L. Bernstein Collection, British Film Institute, London (SLB), box BQ2 (1927).

20 Trademarks were also used to prevent illegal copying (Abel 1999: 14–19).

21 For example, *National High School Student's Poll* (1923); Kinema Theatre, *Market Research of Kinema Theatre, Fresno, California* (1924); Hepner (1929); all tabulated in Koszarski (1990: 29–31). See also Mitchell (1929: 167–168) and Handel (1950: 121).

22 This publicity also had an informative purpose: to provide information about the story beforehand. See 'Boosting Pathé Pictures: Pathé Frères makes alliance with the Hearst Dailies inaugurating big advertising campaign,' *Moving Picture World*, 19: 14 March 1914: 1392–1393; Singer (1996: 105–111).

23 This may be an inflated figure, as citing high numbers may have been part of the promotion strategy.

24 Most contracts gave the studio the rights over the image, voice, and likeness of the star. For example, actor Sidney Greenstreet was contractually bound to keep his weight above 250 pounds, and it was rumored that Buster Keaton's contract forbade him to laugh in public (Gaines 1991: 161, 148–159).

25 The *Film Daily Year Book* in the 1920s, for example, contained lists with best-selling books' sales figures.

26 All prices in 1927 dollars. Most rights were bought for a fixed fee, not a percentage. $10,000 might cover the play's production costs. In 1925, Fox Film Corporation invested $150,000 in plays, in return for half the stage profits and an option on screen rights, for which it paid $500 per week played, or equaled a rival bid, if made (McLaughlin 1974: 57, 66–67).

27 However, very few theaters were changing weekly at the time (Koszarski 1990: 34).

28 Parsons, advertising manager of Pathé Exchange, discerned three periods: 1907–1910: the formative period, when advertising is haphazard and unsystematic; 1910–1913: the transitional period when film companies create publicity departments; 1913–1923: when they massively escalate their advertising outlays.

29 Staiger argues that, as film producers and distributors increasingly asked for a percentage instead of a flat fee, consumer advertising became more profitable

30 'Pathé Exchange,' in H. Lewis (ed.) *Cases on the Motion Picture Industry*, New York, 1930, pp. 409–416.

31 'FBO Productions,' in ibid., 392–395; 'New Goldwyn plan for nationwide exploitation of motion pictures: 27,000,000 people reached by Goldwyn advertising' (Samuel Goldwyn 1921), as quoted in H. Leonard (ed.) *The Film Index: A Bibliography*, Vol. 2: *The Film as Industry*, White Plains, NY, 1985, p. 25.

32 'Paramount pictures to spend $500,000,' *Printer's Ink*, 173 (5 Dec. 1935, p. 83); the investment apparently paid off, as the film grossed $105,000 in that week. 'Goldwyn United Artists plunge heavily to pull over Anna Sten,' *Sales Management*, 34, 15 Feb. 1934, p. 136. Lawrence M. Hughes, 'Made-to-fit promotion plan wins prestige and sales for MGM,' ibid. 36, 1 June 1935, pp. 675, 702. (Rosten 1947: 116–124, 121).

33 This licensing enabled manufacturers of unbranded products to obtain higher margins. While the licensing fee as percentage of sales may have been considerably higher than the advertising-to-sales ratio of the market leader, the licensee did not have to incur the immense *absolute* advertising outlays of the market leader, which are necessary to create a minimum level of brand awareness and are fixed and sunk, independently of sales volume.

34 Temple's exceptional popularity enabled her mother to negotiate a special contract. Most actors got few of the studios' merchandising receipts.

35 Successful actors sometimes obtained special stipulations. Gene Kelly asked the studio not to retouch his scar on any photograph, and Ann Sheridan, after she had been heavily advertised as the 'Oomph girl,' obtained the right to veto all descriptive phrases about her made by Warner's publicity department (Gaines 1991: 148–159).

36 Testimonial advertising is persuasive, because the image of the star does not give information, especially in this period, as stars were not legally required to have used the product regularly. Only in 1980 did the Federal Trade Commis-

sion require that celebrity endorsers be 'bona fide users' (Gaines 1991: 159–160).

37 Putting Mickey Mouse on a T-shirt may enable the manufacturer to triple the price, while the shirt's inherent quality remains unchanged; only its *perceived* quality has increased.

38 London Film Productions Ltd. Weekly Cost Statement, 25 May 1935; Sir David Cunynghame Collection, British Film Institute, London; Letters Aldred Bloch, Paris, agent for the executors of Henri Bataille, to London Film Productions Ltd., 17 August 1933, 25 August 1933, London Film Productions Collection, British Film Institute, File F11; Audience Research Institute (ARI), 'Report XXVII: Lawrence of Arabia' (1940). McFarlane (1986) and Brown (1986) give an overview of British adaptations.

39 Nick Carter was originally published in the United States by Street and Smith, which licensed it to the German Dresdener Verlag, which in its turn marketed it in Paris through its French subsidiary (Le Roy and Billier 1995: 19).

40 Boorstin (1962: 61, 220).

41 In the short term, pay will also depend on luck, negotiation skills, and competitive bidding.

42 All in 1927 dollars.

43 'The European Motion Picture Industry in 1930,' *Trade Information Bulletin*, 752 (May 1931).

44 Market size does not matter for these differences, as films were internationally traded. French companies before the 1930s, for example, made the great majority of their revenues outside France.

45 Apparently, the shift coincides with the shift that Leiss *et al.* (1990) note for star advertising. Boorstin (*The Image*) draws especially on Lowenthal when concluding that a celebrity is 'a person who is known for his well-knownness' See also Caves (2000: 76).

46 It is true that some film scholars have argued that consumers went to the cinema primarily to be away from home, in a luxurious and sociable environment. See, for example, Koszarski (1990: 25–34). This argument concerns a different decision, however – choosing to go to the cinema as opposed to another activity is not the same as deciding which film to see. Moreover, the two choices are consecutive, not mutually exclusive. The minority of consumers who could attend only one cinema could still choose between going to a given film or waiting for the next movie.

47 *Moving Picture World*, 1909; see also, for example, 1930s British polls in *Picturegoer*.

48 For the US see, for example, Mitchell (1929) and a series of studies sponsored by the Payne Fund, one example of which is Blumer (1933). For Britain, see the 'Mass-Observation' studies of the late 1930s and early 1940s, some of which are published in Richards and Sheridan (1987). An early German example is Altenloh (1913), on cinema-going in Mannheim.

49 Corley (1987) gives an overview of market research in Britain before 1940. For other early case studies, see Collins (1994), Corley (1994), and Ward (1994).

50 Forms were distributed in about ten cinemas outside the West End. Returns ranged between 1,500 and 2,500. The main purpose was to garner publicity by extensively announcing the results in the press. Bernstein even offered a prize for the 'most complete' form returned. Obtaining market information seems to have been only a secondary purpose. On Bernstein and his cinemas, see Moorehead (1984). For detailed case-study analysis of the role of market research by Bernstein and Gallup in business strategies, see Bakker (2003).

51 For a detailed history, see Ohmer (1997). Another form of primitive market research were polls among exhibitors by the trade press, such as the yearly

polls of the *Motion Picture Herald* in the USA from 1915 onwards, and of *La Cinématographie Française* in France between 1936 and 1938 (Billard 1995: 211–219, 660–665).

52 *The Saturday Evening Post*, 21 July 1921.

53 'Universal Pictures Corporation,' in Lewis (ed.) (1930: 132–137); 'Report of answers to questions in advertisement,' printed in ibid., pp. 134–137.

54 The data do not show marked gender differences, but indicate that women are slightly more likely to go to see a star and that publicity influences men slightly more than women.

55 During the silent film era, the orchestra and variety acts were important elements of a film showing; after these disappeared, stars and stories must have become even more important.

56 Respondents could mark more than one: 31.7 percent saw whatever was on; 26.3 percent used recommendations of friends (Kuhn 1999: 536). Other categories were 'Music and/or dancing' (26.3 percent), 'Fantasy/escape/captivating' (18.1 percent), 'Realistic/true/identified with story/characters' (17.5 percent) (Kuhn 1999: 539). A current US study, allowing respondents only one answer, found a similar result, with 22 percent choosing a movie by the star, 18 percent by publicity, and 17 percent by the story (De Silva 1998).

57 *Motion Picture News*, 8 June 1929.

58 Pay of average actors cannot decrease greatly with age, as their income will not be far above union pay scales to begin with.

59 This does not mean that income inequality for *all* players remained constant. Making the comparison over equal ranks (18) yields similar results, inequality being slightly more in 1923 (Gini = 0.47).

60 For eight top directors, the Universal researchers could not state a fee; some of those, for example Maurice Tourneur, may have filled top slots.

61 Under the question, the numbers 1 to 3 were printed, but many respondents filled in more names, meaning that, for practical purposes, respondents could fill in as many names as they liked.

62 The actors are: Gary Cooper, Charles Rogers, Charles Farrell, Glenn Tryon; the actresses Dolores Del Rio, Joan Crawford, and Mary Philbin. The small (*c*.350) and self-selected sample may have made the Universal survey less representative.

63 Further, schoolchildren are less representative of the whole population.

64 In theory, many different popularity indexes are possible, depending on the number of names respondents can give. Not restricting the number can give good information.

65 ARI, 'Audit of Marquee Values' (Princeton, NJ, April 1940). ARI handed the respondents a card with players' names and asked: 'I'd like you to look at every name and to imagine that it is on the front of a theater. Which name would most make you want to buy a ticket?' This question is different, and complicated to understand.

66 ARI measured star popularity at short intervals, sometimes monthly or every three months, and observed considerable statistically significant fluctuations (ibid).

67 Respondents had to express their opinions based on fifty films shown at Bernstein cinemas. These responses were compared to film revenues. Since other cinemas were near, these data do not show all films at the respondents' disposal. For a detailed and comprehensive analysis of the number of film and star popularity in Britain during 1932–1937, using a statistical model based on exhibition records, see Sedgwick (2000: 55–101, 180–205). Since the data are based on exhibition and not on consumer polls or attendance figures, it is difficult to make a comparison with data presented here.

68 The coefficients of rank order correlation here yield limited information, because they compare two orders of different length. The correlation may be strengthened because all fifty films had been shown in the respondents' cinemas, and weakened because it does not include all films shown at these theaters. Several top-fifteen stars did not act in them. As reading all titles would take a while, many respondents left everything blank, and those who read the full list might be less representative.

69 The general price level depended on relative costs of original screenplays (a close substitute), studios' competitive pre-emptive buying, and market size.

70 Of the 5,688 literary properties bought by the Hollywood studios between 1935 and 1945, 64 percent were original screenplays, 17 percent novels, 7 percent plays, and 7 percent short stories (Motion Picture Association of America, Inc., *Annual Report* (1946), 26).

71 A study of the acquisition of literary properties at Warner Brothers confirms the above hierarchy of importance of works and roughly confirms the industry figures: between 1934 and 1941, the firm paid on average about $27,800 for a play, $15,400 for a novel, $9,200 for a short story, and $5,000 for an original screenplay (Gustafson 1983: 77). A Broadway boycott between 1937 and 1940 influenced fluctuations of all the Hollywood majors, except Columbia, against restrictions on their investments in Broadway (McLaughlin 1974: 282–284). All figures are in 1927 dollars.

72 'Paramount famous Lasky Corporation,' in Lewis (1933: 182–185). Gustafson (1983: 172–235) shows that the story department at Warner Brother's worked along the same lines in the 1930s and 1940s. Twentieth Century Fox even had an internal printed catalog of all the hundreds of stories to which it held rights, for circulation among its executives and creative personnel. Hollywood studios actively traded and exchanged their rights.

73 'Universal,' in Lewis (1933)

74 Not to be confused with *Sue Barton Student Nurse*, *Sue Barton Senior Nurse*, and *Sue Barton Visiting Nurse*. There were seven titles in the series, written by Helen Dore Boylston. See ARI, 'Report XXI: Sue Barton' (19 August 1940).

75 ARI, 'Report XII: Smiler with a Knife, Heart of Darkness or Invasion from Mars?' (15 May 1940); ARI, 'Report XIV: Cyrano de Bergerac' (18 May 1940); see, for example, ARI, 'Report XVII: Titles for man hunt story' (11 July 1940); Audience Research Institute (1942: 105–110).

76 These statements are based on time series for all British films produced during 1929–1939 as reported in Shafer (1983: 4–5) and Wood (1986: 122); and on time series for all French films produced during 1936–1939 as reported in Crisp (1993: 290). Because American data are on rights bought, and European data on rights used, they may not be fully comparable.

77 The disproportionate fame distribution may also explain first-mover advantages in advertising-intensive industries, where historically established market shares of branded products are hard to reverse. See the chapter 'How History Matters,' in Sutton (1991).

References

Abel, R. (1984) *French Cinema. The First Wave, 1915–1929*, Princeton: Princeton University Press.

Abel, R. (1994) *The Cine Goes to Town: French Cinema, 1896–1914*, Berkeley, CA: University of California Press.

Abel, R. (1999) *The Red Rooster Scare: Making Cinema American, 1900–1910*, Berkeley, CA: University of California Press.

Aimone, I. (1997) 'Un statut pour les acteurs: 1910–1920,' in P. Benghozi and C. Delage (eds) *Une Histoire Économique Du Cinéma Français: (1895–1995): Regards Franco Américains*, Paris: L'Harmattan.

Albert, S. (1998) 'Movie stars and the distribution of financially successful films in the motion picture industry,' *Journal of Cultural Economics*, 22: 249–270.

Allen, R.C. (1980) *Vaudeville and Film, 1895–1915*, New York, NY: Arno Press.

Altenloh, E. (1913) *Zur Sociologie des Kino: Die Kino-unternehmung und die Sozialen Schichten ihrer Besucher*, Heidelberg, 1913.

Audience Research Institute (1940a) Unpublished reports.

Audience Research Institute (1940b) 'New York City motion picture market study for RKO Radio Pictures Inc.' Princeton.

Audience Research Institute (1942) *Increasing Profits with Continuous Audience Research*, Princeton.

Bächlin, P. (1945) *Der Film als Ware*, Basel: Burg-Verlag.

Bakker, G. (2000) 'America's master. Decline and fall of the European film industry in the United States, 1907–1920,' in Luisa Passerini (ed.) *Across the Atlantic*, Brussels: Presses Inter-Universitaires Européennes/Peter Lang.

Bakker, G. (2001) 'Stars and stories: how films became branded products,' *Enterprise and Society*, 2: 461–502.

Bakker, G. (2003) 'Building knowledge about the consumer. The emergence of market research in the motion picture industry,' *Business History*, 45: 101–127; reprinted in A. Godley and R. Church (eds) *The Emergence of Modern Marketing*, London: Frank Cass.

Bakker, G. (2004) 'Selling French films on foreign markets. The international strategy of a medium-sized film company,' *Enterprise and Society*, 5: (forthcoming).

Barr, C. (ed.) (1986) *All Our Yesterdays: 90 Years of British Cinema*, London: British Film Institute.

Billard, P. (1995) *L'Age Classique du Cinéma Français. Du Cinéma Parlant à la Nouvelle Vague*, Paris: Flammarion.

Blumer, H. (1933) *Movies, Delinquency and Crime*, New York, NY: Macmillan.

Boorstin, D. (1962) *The Image, or What Happened to the American Dream*, New York, NY: Atheneum.

Bousquet, H. (1981) 'Economie et Publicité Cinématographique dans l'Immédiat Après Guerre,' *Cahiers de la Cinémathèque*, 33–34: 67–75.

Bowser, E. (1990) *The Transformation of Cinema, 1907–1915*, Berkeley, CA: University of California Press.

Brown, G. (1986) ' "Sisters Of The Stage." British film and British theatre,' in Charles Barr (ed.) *All Our Yesterdays. 90 Years of British Cinema*, London: British Film Institute.

Casson, M. (1994) 'Brands: economic ideology and consumer society,' in Geoffrey Jones and Nicholas Morgan (eds) *Adding Value. Brands and Marketing in Food and Drink*, London and New York, NY: Routledge.

Caves, R. (2000) *Creative Industries: Contracts between Art and Commerce*, Cambridge, MA: Harvard University Press.

Chase, A. (1966) *Perspectives*, New York.

Church, R. (1999) 'New perspectives on the history of products, firms, marketing, and consumers in Britain and the United States since the mid-nineteenth century,' *Economic History Review*, 52: 405–435.

Collins, E.J.T. (1994) 'Brands and breakfast cereals in Britain,' in Geoffrey Jones and Nicholas Morgan (eds) *Adding Value. Brands and Marketing in Food And Drink*, London and New York, NY: Routledge.

Cook, P. and Frank, R. (1995) *The Winner-Take-All Society*, New York, NY: Free Press.

Corley, T. (1987) 'Consumer marketing in Britain, 1914–1960,' *Business History*, 29: 65–83.

Corley, T.A.B. (1994) 'Best-practice marketing of food and health drinks in Britain, 1930–1970,' in Geoffrey Jones and Nicholas Morgan (eds) *Adding Value. Brands and Marketing in Food and Drink*, London and New York, NY: Routledge.

Crisp, C. (1993) *The Classic French Cinema, 1930–1960*, Bloomington, IN.: Indiana University Press.

Dall'Asta, M. (1999a) 'La Diffusione del Film a Episodi in Europa,' in G.P. Brunetta (ed.) *Storia del Cinema Mondiale*, Vol. 1: *L'Europa: Miti, luoghi, divi*, Turin: Einaudi: 277–324.

Dall'Asta, M. (1999b) 'Il Serial,' in G.P. Brunetta (ed.) *Storia del Cinema Mondiale*, Vol. 2: *Gli Stati Uniti: Tomo primo*, Turin, Einaudi: 289–338.

Davis, E.H., Kay, J.A. and Star, J. (1991) 'Is advertising rational?' *Business Strategy Review*, 2/3: 1–23.

De Silva, I. (1998) 'Consumer selection of motion pictures,' in B.R. Litman (ed.) *The Motion Picture Mega-Industry*, Boston: Allyn and Bacon, 144–171.

Dickinson, M. and Street, S. (1985) *Cinema and State: The Film Industry and the British Government, 1927–1984*, London: British Film Institute.

Eyles, A. (1998) *The Granada Theaters*, London: British Film Institute.

Fullerton, R.A. (1988) 'How modern is modern marketing? Marketing's evolution and the myth of the "Production Era,"' *Journal of Marketing*, 52: 108–125.

Gaines, J.M. (1991) *Contested Culture: the Image, the Voice and the Law*, London: British Film Institute.

Glancy, H.M. (1992) 'MGM film grosses, 1924–1948: the Eddie Mannix ledger,' *Historical Journal of Film, Radio and Television*, 12: 127–144.

Glancy, H.M. (1995) 'Warner Bros. film grosses, 1921–1951: the William Schaefer ledger,' *Historical Journal of Film, Radio and Television*, 15: 55–73.

Gomery, Douglas (1985) 'The coming of television and the "lost" motion picture audience,' *Journal of Film and Video*, 37(3): 5–11.

Gomery, Douglas (1986) *The Hollywood Studio System*, London.

Gomery, Douglas (1992) *Shared Pleasures: A History of Movie Presentation in the United States*, Madison, WI: University of Wisconsin Press.

Grau, R. (1914) *The Theatre of Science: a Volume of Progress and Achievement in the Motion Picture Industry*, New York, NY: Benjamin Bloom.

Grieveson, L. (1999) 'Nascita del divismo. Star e pubblico del cinema dei primordi,' in Gian Piero Brunetta (ed.) *Storia del cinema mondiale*, Vol. II: *Gli Stati Uniti*, Turin: Giulio Einaudi Editore.

Gustafson, R. (1983) 'The buying of ideas. Source acquisition at Warner Brothers, 1930–1949,' PhD diss., University of Wisconsin-Madison.

Guy, A. (1976) *Autobiographie d'une Pionnière du Cinema, 1873–1968*, Paris: Denoël/Gonhier.

Hammond, R.M. and Ford, C. (1983) 'French end games,' *Films in Review*, 34: 329–333, 383–384.

Hampton, B.B. (1931) *A History of the Movies*, New York, NY: Covici-Friede.

Handel, L. (1950) *Hollywood Looks at Its Audience*, Urbana, IL.

Hepner, H.W. (1929) 'Public likes, dislikes,' *Film Daily Year Book*.

Jewell, R.B. (1994) 'RKO film grosses, 1929–1951: the C.J. Tevlin ledger,' *Historical Journal of Film, Radio and Television*, 14: 37–49.

Jones, G. and Morgan, N. (eds) (1994) *Adding Value: Brands and Marketing in Food and Drink*, London: Routledge.

Kaldor, N. (1950) 'The economic aspects of advertising,' *Review of Economic Studies*, 18: 1–27.

Kanfer, S. (1997) *Serious Business: the Art and Commerce of Animation in America from Betty Boop to Toy Story*, New York, NY: Scribner.

Kennedy, J. (ed.) (1927) *The Story of the Films*, Chicago, IL: A.W. Shaw.

Kerr, C.E. (1990) 'Incorporating the star: the intersection of business and aesthetic strategies in early American film,' *Business History Review*, 64: 383–410.

Kindem, G. (1982) 'Hollywood's movie star system: a historical overview,' in Gorham Kindem (ed.) *The American Movie Industry: the Business of Motion Pictures*, Carbondale, IL: Southern Illinois University Press, 79–93.

Kinema Theatre (1924) *Market Research of Kinema Theatre*, Fresno, California.

Koszarski, R. (1990) *An Evening's Entertainment: the Age of the Silent Feature Picture, 1915–1928*, Berkeley, CA: University of California Press.

Kuhn, A. (1999) 'Cinema-going in Britain in the 1930s: report of a questionnaire survey,' *Historical Journal of Film, Radio and Television*, 19: 531–543.

Le Roy, E. and Billier, L. (eds) (1995) *Éclair: Un Siècle de Cinéma à Epinay-sur-Seine*, Paris: Calmann-Levy.

Lehman, H.C. (1941) 'Chronological ages of some recipients of large annual incomes,' *Social Forces*, 20: 196–206.

Leiss, W., Kline, S. and Jhally, S. (1990) *Social Communication in Advertising: Persons, Products and Images of Well-being*, 2nd edn, London: Routledge.

Leonard, H. (ed.) (1985) *The Film Index: A Bibliography*, Volume 2: *The Film as Industry*, White Plains, NY: Kraus International.

Lewis, H.T. (ed.) (1930) *Cases on the Motion Picture Industry*, New York, NY: McGraw-Hill.

Lewis, H.T. (1933) *The Motion Picture Industry*, New York, NY: D. van Nostrand.

Low, R. (1949) *The History of the British Film, 1906–1914*, London: George Allen & Unwin.

Low, R. (1950) *The History of the British Film, 1914–1918*, London: George Allen & Unwin.

Low, R. (1971) *The History of the British Film, 1918–1929*, London: George Allen & Unwin.

Lowenthal, L. (1961) *Literature, Popular Culture and Society*, Englewood Cliffs, NJ: Prentice Hall.

McFarlane, B. (1986) 'A literary cinema? British films and British novels,' in Charles Barr (ed.) *All Our Yesterdays. 90 Years of British Cinema*, London: British Film Institute.

Mackie, J. (1933) *The Edinburgh Cinema Inquiry Committee*, Edinburgh.

McLaughlin, Robert W. (1974) *Broadway & Hollywood: A History of Economic Interaction*, New York, NY: Arno Press.

Martì, J. (1941) *Granos de or: Pensamientos seleccionades en las obras de José Martì*, Barcelona.

Mitchell, A.M. (1929) *Children and Movies*, Chicago, IL: University of Chicago.

Moorehead, C. (1984) *Sidney Bernstein: A Biography*, London: Jonathan Cape.

Ohmer, S. (1997) 'Measuring desire: George Gallup and the origins of market research in Hollywood,' PhD diss., New York University.

Parsons, P.A. (1927) 'A history of motion pictures advertising,' *Moving Picture World*, 85 (26 March): 301, 304–305, 308–309.

Pope, D. (1983) *The Making of Modern Advertising*, New York.

Richards, J. (1994) 'Cinema going in worktown,' *Historical Journal of Film, Radio and Television*, 14: 147–166.

Richards, J. and Sheridan, D. (1987) *Mass-Observation at the Movies*, London: Routledge & Kegan Paul.

Rosen, Sherwin (1981) 'The economics of superstars,' *American Economic Review*, 71: 845–854.

Rosten, L.C. (1947) 'Movies and propaganda,' *The Motion Picture Industry: Annals of the American Academy of Political and Social Sciences*, 254 (November): 116–124.

Russell Sage Foundation/National Board of Review of Motion Pictures/Associated First National Exhibitors (1923) *National High School Students Poll, 1923*, New York.

Sadoul, G. (1972) *Histoire Générale du Cinéma*, Paris: Flammarion.

Sanderson, M. (1984) *From Irving to Oliver: a Social History of the Acting Profession in England, 1890–1980*, London: Athlone Press.

Schatz, T. (1988) *The Genius of the System: Hollywood Filmmaking in the Studio Era*, London and New York, NY: Simon & Schuster.

Sedgwick, J. (2000) *Popular Film in 1930s Britain: a Choice of Pleasures*, Exeter: Exeter University Press.

Shafer, S.C. (1983) 'Enter the dream hours: the British film industry and the working classes in Depression England, 1929–1939,' PhD diss., University of Illinois at Urbana-Champaign.

Shipman, D. (1979) *The Great Movie Stars: The Golden Years*, New York, NY: St. Martin's Press.

Simonoff, J.S. and Sparrow, H.R. (2000) 'Predicting movie grosses: winners and losers, blockbusters and sleepers,' *Chance* (August): 15–24.

Singer, B. (1996) 'Serials,' in Geoffrey Nowell-Smith (ed.) *The Oxford History of World Cinema*, New York, NY: Oxford University Press, 105–111.

Staiger, J. (1990) 'Announcing wares, winning patrons, voicing ideals: thinking about the history and theory of film advertising,' *Cinema Journal*, 29: 3–31.

Sutton, J. (1991) *Sunk Costs and Market Structure: Price Competition, Advertising and the Evolution of Concentration*, Cambridge, MA: MIT Press.

Tedlow, R.S. (1990) *New and Improved: the Story of Mass Marketing in America*, New York, NY: Routledge.

Ward, V. (1994) 'Marketing convenience goods between the wars,' in Geoffrey Jones and Nicholas Morgan (eds) *Adding Value. Brands and Marketing in Food and Drink*, London and New York, NY: Routledge.

Wilkins, M. (1992) 'The neglected intangible asset: the influence of the trade mark on the rise of the modern corporation,' *Business History*, 34: 66–95.

Wood, L. (1986) *British Film, 1927–1939*, London: British Film Industry.

4 Revenue sharing and the coming of sound[1]

F. Andrew Hanssen

At least since Adam Smith, economists have been intrigued by share contracts. There has been a proliferation of models, most of which tend to explain the share contract as resulting from some mix of optimal risk-bearing and optimal effort motivation.[2] A large number of researchers have attempted to test these models empirically. Sharecropping contracts, not surprisingly, are the most intensively examined (see the bibliography in Knoeber 2000), but similar studies have been conducted in many other areas. For example, Martin (1988) and Lafontaine (1992) examine franchise arrangements, Hallagan (1978) investigates contracts used to lease gold claims, Leffler and Rucker (1991) analyze a sample of private timber sale contracts, Goldberg and Erickson (1987) study long-term contracts for the sale of petroleum coke, Aggarwal and Samwick (1999) investigate incentive contracts between firms and their executives, and Chisholm (1997), Goldberg (1997), and Weinstein (1998) all examine profit-sharing contracts between film companies and "the talent."

This chapter differs in an important respect from most previous studies, which analyze a cross-section of contracts in an attempt to determine how (or whether) they vary according to the attributes of the contracting parties or the products being contracted for. Instead, it investigates an area where a sudden technology shock led to the rapid and widespread replacement of one form of contracting by another. The industry is the motion picture business, and the shock was the arrival of sound. During the silent era, the vast majority of first-run feature films were rented to cinemas for flat daily or weekly payments. Within two years of the release of the first sound picture, revenue-sharing contracts were the norm, and they remain the norm to this day.[3] My goal is to investigate the degree to which the standard economic concerns – moral hazard, risk sharing, and measurement problems – can explain this change. Because the contracting parties remained the same, the question becomes, what was altered in the nature of the product, or in its provision, so as to have correspondingly altered the incentives faced?

The chapter concludes the following. First, the coming of sound fundamentally changed the inputs; live music and other acts, supplied by the exhibitor and central to the show, were replaced by a soundtrack and short sound films, supplied by the film company. The benefit of deterring exhibitor shirking through the use of flat rental fees (which made the exhibitor full residual claimant) declined accordingly. The party whose effort makes the largest contribution to marginal product generally receives the largest proportion of the residual claims, and in the decades following the coming of sound, the proportion of residual claims collected by film companies rose steadily. In addition, average revenue per film increased with the coming of sound, while the cost of ensuring that exhibitors reported attendance revenue honestly – done by locating a film company's representative in the theater – remained the same. The *ex post* division of revenue (necessary for revenue sharing) thus became cheaper on a per-film basis. Finally, uncertainty about the value (in terms of expected attendance revenue) of the early sound films appears to have raised the cost of negotiating lump-sum rental fees, and thus promoted experiments with revenue sharing. However, while this may have contributed initially, it cannot explain the practice's persistence; uncertainty about film values declined as talking films became better known.

The nature of the problem

A film company contracts with an exhibitor so that they may jointly produce the final good: a movie presentation.[4] To that end, each supplies essential inputs. The film company provides the movie (itself assembled from a variety of inputs) and some sort of national advertising support. The exhibitor provides the theater (which consists of seating, projection equipment, a refreshment stand, and other support activities) and some form of local advertising. The output from this joint activity is attendance revenue: a certain number of consumers will pay the given price to see the film.

As researchers have pointed out, film attendance revenue is highly uncertain, even for a given quantity or quality of inputs (for example, De Vany and Walls 1996; Sedgwick and Pokorny 1998). Because the same price tends to be charged for all films (although it may vary across cinemas, times of day, and customer types), the uncertainty involves the number of people who will choose to attend at the given price.[5] A range of contract types is possible. The exhibitor could pay a flat fee for each day it shows the film, making it the full residual claimant. Or the film company could instead become the residual claimant by hiring the exhibitor for a flat payment. Or the two could enter into an arrangement to share attendance revenue in some proportion. In a world of perfect certainty, the parties would be indifferent between these alternatives; however, the real-world unpredictability of attendance revenue renders the choice of contract form meaningful. As noted in the introduction, there is substantial literature that seeks to explain the circumstances under which share contracts will be used. I will focus on four factors. The first two have been central to most studies of share contracting: moral hazard and risk aversion. The second two have received important, but more limited, attention: the cost of pre-sale measurement and the cost of dividing revenue *ex post*.

Moral hazard models typically assume that parties wish to enter into an agreement, but cannot observe the precise behavior of the other, nor infer it from the level of output, because output has a stochastic element that is costly to ascertain.[6] In the context of film exhibition, the film company enters into a contract with the exhibitor to reap gains from specialization – the exhibitor is better informed as to the appropriate level of local inputs. However, the assignment of residual claims creates incentive problems; for example, the exhibitor may choose to provide less than the efficient amount of local inputs if it keeps less than the full amount of the corresponding gain. Because of the inherent unpredictability of attendance revenue, determining whether or not the exhibitor has shirked in completing its duties is difficult. One way to ensure the efficient provision of the exhibitor's inputs without monitoring is for the film company simply to "sell" the movie to the exhibitor – i.e., to rent it for a flat fee. Of course, the film company also provides necessary inputs, and may also be inclined to shirk; for example, to provide lower-than-optimal quality films. The incentive for exhibitor shirking is greatest if the exhibitor sells its services for a flat fee, and weakest if it pays a flat rental for the film instead. Equivalently, the incentive for film company shirking is greatest if the film company receives a flat fee for its film, and is weakest if it pays the exhibitor a flat fee instead.

Risk may be another concern. A flat rental fee requires the exhibitor to bear all the risk of uncertain attendance revenue. If the exhibitor is risk averse, it will have to be compensated accordingly, most likely in the form of a lower per-film price. By replacing the flat fee with a share contract, the film company can bear some of that risk itself, and thus receive a higher per-film price.

Ensuring the honest *ex post* reporting of an *ex ante* uncertain output so as to permit sharing has been shown to be costly in many settings – for example, Allen and Lueck (1992), Lazear (1986), and Umbeck (1977). For example, a revenue-sharing contract between film company and film exhibitor requires that they divide attendance revenue after the showing of the film has been completed. However, only the exhibitor observes actual attendance in the course of performing its normal duties. And because this revenue is unpredictable, the film company cannot easily determine whether the exhibitor has reported honestly. Flat-fee rentals eliminate the need for the *ex post* division of output. They are thus most attractive, *ceteris paribus*, when that division is very expensive.

Finally, heterogeneous products (such as movies) inspire efforts by buyers to measure the quality of the goods before purchasing them. For many goods, such efforts are socially valuable, as they reward the most efficient producers and punish the least efficient. However, when the characteristics of the good are not affected by the amount of buyer measurement (for example, a movie does not garner larger attendance revenues just because exhibitors have expended efforts on predicting audience response) and buyers have equal valuations for the product, presale measurement is socially wasteful.[7] One way to reduce this wasteful measurement is to engage in a share contract. Buyers who provide payment in the form of a proportion of the output have less incentive to expend resources measuring product quality *ex ante* – they lose less if the product is of low quality and gain less if it is of high quality. The more difficult it is to determine the value of the goods prior to the sale, the more costly it is to negotiate flat payments, and the more attractive is a share contract.

In what follows, evidence is sought for the contribution of these factors to the switch from flat rental payments to revenue sharing that accompanied sound.

Background

The structure of film distribution

Both during the silent and sound eras, exhibitors were organized into runs: first-run, second-run, and so on. First-run theaters exhibited films first; they were located in prime downtown areas, were large and elaborate, and showed new releases for a week or more. Fourth- and fifth-run theaters were located in residential neighborhoods, showed films that had already been on the market for several months, and changed their films several times per week. The second- and third-run theaters fell between, being located in busier areas and exhibiting films for one to four days. Theaters within each run designation enjoyed a contractually set period of time that had to pass before a film could be sent to a lower-run theater (the "clearance"). For example, second-run theaters usually had to wait for three weeks beyond the end of the first-run showing to exhibit a film, and so on down the line. Finally, runs and clearances operated within a specified geographic "zone," over which the exhibitor was given exclusive privilege. Zoning eventually became quite complex, and even gave theaters in certain cities prior rights over those in other cities.[8]

A standard feature of exhibition contracts from the mid-1910s until 1948 (when the practice was banned) was block booking; films were not contracted for individually, but in blocks (see Chapter 5). An exhibitor would agree at the start of a season to show a certain number of a studio's films (the exact number was negotiable). These films were booked blind – exhibitors were unable to preview them before contracting (indeed, most had not yet been produced). In the course of the season, as the films were completed, they were made available to exhibitors, first-run first, and so on down the line. Contrary to popular belief, the blocks were not rigidly enforced; indeed, there was substantial *ex post* flexibility. The practice of revenue sharing enhanced a studio's willingness to permit such flexibility – it, as well as the exhibitor, gained when popular showings could be extended and unpopular ones cut short. However, evidence indicates that such flexibility was permitted even during the silent years, when flat rental payments were the norm. This is not surprising; an exhibitor's willingness to pay would have depended in part on the willingness of studios to interpret contractual obligations flexibly.

The "big five" film studios (MGM, Fox, RKO, Warner Brothers, and Paramount) were vertically integrated into exhibition; the "little three" (Columbia, Universal, and United Artists) were not. Four of the big five began purchasing movie theaters in the early 1920s, well before sound, which is typically dated from late-1927.[9] Nonetheless, these companies earned most of their revenue renting to cinemas other than their own. Except in the major cities (such as New York), the producer-owned chains did not overlap. And in any case, no single company made enough films to supply a given theater for an entire year.[10]

In sum, the structure of film distribution and exhibition largely predated the coming of sound and survived it with few major changes, at least until 1948 and the famous *Paramount* decision.[11]

The coming of sound

The potential for the simultaneous projection of pictures and sound existed nearly from the dawn of the movies – Thomas Edison is credited with inventing both the movie projector and the phonograph in the late nineteenth century, and he experimented with linking them.[12] However, it was not until the mid-1920s that technology had developed sufficiently to allow sound to be systematically synchronized with moving pictures. The lead in the introduction of sound technology was taken by Warner Brothers, who formed a joint venture – Vitaphone – with Western Electric in April 1926 to promote Western Electric's sound-on-a-disc system. Fox was the only studio to respond immediately; it contracted for the rival Movietone system, which placed the sound on film instead. The other movie companies adopted a "wait and see" attitude, agreeing in 1927 that none of them would convert to sound until they all did.[13] By moving first, Warner Brothers propelled itself into the top tier of movie companies.

The first public showing of a "sound" feature film occurred in 1926, when Warner Brothers fitted their version of *Don Juan*, originally intended as a silent feature, with synchronized music. The company then released several talking shorts (mostly comedy and musical acts) over the following months, while Fox produced a talking newsreel. But the dawn of the sound era is generally considered to coincide with Warner Brothers' release of *The Jazz Singer* in late 1927. *The Jazz Singer* actually contains only three short sound sequences, each a song by its star, Al Jolson, accompanied by a bit of dialogue (291 words in all). Like many of the very early sound features, it had been conceived as a silent film; a sound track was added later in the production process. It was extremely popular, earning $2 million through 1931 (Crafton 1997: 111), and made clear the appeal of sound motion pictures.

Despite the success of *The Jazz Singer*, many industry pundits initially regarded sound as a fad, and even supporters expected talking and silent films to coexist indefinitely.[14] It was soon clear that they were wrong. Warner Brothers released the 50 percent talking feature *The Lion and the Mouse* in May of 1928 (*The Jazz Singer* had been less than 10 percent talking), and the first fully talking picture, *The Lights of New York* (based on a Broadway play), the following July. The company reported a $2 million profit for the fiscal year ending August 1928 and announced that all its films planned for the 1928–1929 season would have sound (Crafton 1997: 113). United Artists made the same announcement in November of 1928 (*Variety*, 7 November 1928: 11), and Fox declared in March 1929 that it had made its last silent feature (Crafton 1997: 201). Other companies followed suit. Of the 200 films released in the last quarter of the 1928–1929 season, eighty-six were "100 percent talking," and fewer than twenty were purely silent.[15] *Film Daily Yearbook*, in its synopsis of 1928, wrote, "July was proving a heyday for the wired houses, and, conversely, the unwired ones were fighting with their backs to the wall." By 1929, most cinemas in the largest cities had been wired for sound, and by 1930, Hollywood had stopped producing silent films.

It is important to recognize that silent and sound films are different goods – a sound film (of the type we see today or even saw in the early 1930s) is not simply a silent film plus talking and music. Silent plots were by necessity much simpler than sound plots; the lack of dialogue meant that very complicated ideas and plot twists could not be communicated.[16] The cinematography was also different – wide-lensed views of the action alternated with tight closeups on the faces of the actors. The gestures and facial expressions that actors used were highly stylized – broad, sweeping movements and widening or narrowing of the eyes would indicate anger, anguish, happiness, and so forth, in ways that were recognized by contemporary audiences, but are far removed from how people actually behave (which is essentially what sound films show). As we will see, the transition to sound cost many actors their careers, because the skills necessary for stardom changed fundamentally.

Table 4.1 lists the number of films made, attendance, and box office receipts for the years for which data are available from the silent era to 1940. As column 2 shows, the coming of sound (in 1927–1928) was accompanied by a reduction in the number of films made. Column 3 lists

Table 4.1 Movie data

Year (1)	Number of feature films (2)	Weekly attendance (millions) (3)	Average attendance per film (4)	Annual box office receipts ($millions) (5)	Annual receipts ($millions) in 1967 prices (6)
1917	687				
1918	841				
1919	646				
1920	796				
1921	854				
1922	748	40	53,476		
1923	576	43	74,653	337	657
1924	579	46	79,447		
1925	579	48	82,902	367	670
1926	740	50	67,568		
1927	678	57	84,071	526	1,012
1928	641	65	101,404		
1929	562	95	169,039	720	1,403
1930	509	90	176,817	732	1,464
1931	501	75	149,701	719	1,577
1932	489	60	122,699	527	1,289
1933	507	60	118,343	482	1,242
1934	480	70	145,833	518	1,292
1935	525	75	142,857	566	1,377
1936	522	88	168,582	626	1,509
1937	538	85	157,993	676	1,572
1938	455	85	186,813	663	1,571
1939	583	85	145,798	659	1,584
1940	477	80	167,715	735	1,750

Sources: Steinberg (1980); *Historical Statistics of the U.S.* (1975).

average weekly attendance from 1926 to 1940, while column 4 lists attendance per film. As can be seen, total movie attendance increased sharply with the coming of sound (compare 1926 and 1927 to 1929 and 1930) despite the fact that the number of pictures on the market fell. And although both attendance and box office receipts then declined as the Great Depression took hold, sound films continued to attract substantially larger audiences than had silent films. Box office receipts are shown in columns 5 and 6. The average sound film earned revenues that were more than twice in real terms those of the average silent feature.

More detailed cost and revenue data may be found in two recently discovered files: the Eddie Mannix ledger of MGM films produced between 1924 and 1948, and the William Schaefer ledger of Warner Brothers films produced between 1921 and 1951.[17] Each lists by year the number of films produced, and the production cost, domestic rental revenue earned, and foreign rental revenue earned by film. Table 4.2 shows the number of films released and the mean and standard deviation for cost and domestic

Table 4.2 MGM and Warner Brothers cost and rentals ($000) in 1929 prices

Year (1)	No. of films (2)	Average production cost (3)	Standard deviation of col. 3 (4)	Average rentals (5)	Standard deviation of col. 5 (6)	Coefficient of variation of rentals (7)
MGM						
1924–1925	26	150.27	54.70	256.03	85.01	0.332
1925–1926	40	208.89	120.04	346.92	158.17	0.456
1926–1927	44	253.86	144.87	406.82	213.55	0.525
1927–1928	50	266.84	205.86	417.73	197.89	0.474
Silent	48	262.81	209.13	410.79	196.80	0.479
Sound	2	363.49	7.80	584.21	143.74	0.246
1928–1929	53	270.16	222.27	517.81	392.60	0.758
Silent	23	178.04	129.35	321.12	251.96	0.785
Sound	28	246.64	145.50	509.78	397.64	0.780
1929–1930	44	355.77	149.31	591.11	408.05	0.690
1930–1931	49	465.25	235.46	664.26	295.66	0.445
1931–1932	43	502.16	209.03	677.98	352.07	0.519
1932–1933	40	598.09	337.96	690.02	430.10	0.623
1933–1934	38	619.86	383.59	706.52	446.33	0.632
1934–1935	41	559.77	445.60	702.16	531.69	0.757
1935–1936	45	613.64	440.14	866.21	684.58	0.790
1936–1937	35	891.69	880.56	1,019.02	901.21	0.884
1937–1938	42	854.72	773.46	939.23	612.01	0.652
1938–1939	48	834.29	670.05	979.15	706.37	0.721
1939–1940	48	925.12	639.92	1,064.75	821.33	0.771
1940–1941	46	695.07	428.50	986.26	668.54	0.678
Warner Brothers						
1921–1922	3	86.98	35.86	361.22	171.61	0.475
1922–1923	12	152.21	65.74	348.19	107.64	0.309
1923–1924	17	139.93	108.73	281.57	78.14	0.278
1924–1925	18	100.59	38.13	202.14	38.28	0.189
1925–1926	40	114.16	75.39	176.34	115.77	0.657
1926–1927	29	161.80	123.88	274.66	243.55	0.887
1927–1928	38	101.48	72.26	299.07	355.29	1.188
Silent	25	89.89	49.76	172.02	66.36	0.386
Sound	13	123.76	98.72	543.40	519.40	0.956
1928–1929	36	180.20	171.03	700.88	660.12	0.942
Silent	1	140.33	n.a.	647.07	n.a.	n.a.
Sound	35	181.34	173.32	702.42	669.42	0.953
1929–1930	40	298.73	177.73	435.21	343.98	0.790
1930–1931	60	345.36	145.82	379.81	169.14	0.445
1931–1932	52	306.42	83.46	413.70	133.66	0.323
1932–1933	50	296.43	113.90	513.29	414.74	0.808
1933–1934	54	304.18	165.17	470.03	352.84	0.751
1934–1935	54	363.42	266.77	561.21	406.73	0.725
1935–1936	58	327.20	267.22	494.55	322.67	0.652
1936–1937	58	347.06	266.39	476.23	342.02	0.718
1937–1938	56	488.77	473.99	559.66	440.87	0.788
1938–1939	53	482.66	336.28	690.49	528.11	0.765
1939–1940	47	530.36	426.54	665.77	511.53	0.768
1940–1941	49	460.17	357.85	688.11	558.85	0.812

Sources: Eddie Mannix ledger and William Schaefer ledger – see Glancy (1992, 1995).

revenue per film (in constant 1929 dollars) from the early 1920s to 1940. Warners committed more quickly to the sound film than MGM: more than one-third of its films released in 1927–1928 had sound, as were all but one released during the 1928–1929 season.[18] MGM released only two sound films in 1927–1928, but more than half of its 1928–1929 releases had sound. And by the 1929–1930 season, neither company was making silent films any more. The average MGM sound film released during the transition years (1927–1928 and 1928–1929) cost 39 percent more than the average silent film of the same period to make and earned 40 percent more rental revenue, while for Warner Brothers during the same period, sound films cost one-third more to make and earned 50 percent more revenue. The average MGM film for all the silent years through 1926–1927 cost $204,000, while the average MGM sound film produced during the 1930s cost $630,000. The average Warner Brothers silent film cost $126,000, while their average sound film cost $366,000. Over the same period, MGM rental revenues tripled, while that of Warner Brothers doubled, so that revenues less production costs increased by the annual average of 53 percent for MGM, and by 21 percent for Warner Brothers.

The change in exhibition contracts

Motion picture exhibition dates back to the late 1800s. The first "movie theaters" appeared at the turn of the century; they were called nickel-odeons because they charged a nickel for admission. The motion pictures they showed were short and simple, consisting largely of scenes of passing trains, famous speeches, noteworthy landscapes (the subject and staging being chosen by the cameraman), or very basic narratives. Few of these films were more than ten minutes in length. They were sold outright to exhibitors, for a flat per-foot fee.[19] The principal problem facing the early exhibitors was obtaining an adequate supply of films; in order to operate successfully, a nickelodeon had to present three-to-five pictures per program, and to change programs frequently.[20] Nickelodeons there-fore began to trade films among themselves as local audiences tired of them. The practice was formalized, and a number of film "exchanges" were organized, the first in San Francisco in 1903.[21] The exchanges, typ-ically owned by the exhibitors they served, purchased movie shorts from producers and leased them to exhibitors for about one-fifth the purchase price.

The "feature film," which appeared c.1912, fundamentally changed the nature of movie distribution. The system of exchanges was set up to sell short films to nickelodeons, and nickelodeons were too small to show prof-itably the longer and more expensive features. Some of the first feature films were exhibited as "roadshows"; distributors rented out "legitimate" theaters for a percentage of the revenue. However, with the construction of large cinemas and the establishment of a national distribution system, flat rentals were adopted, although unlike the practice with short films, features were rented at prices that varied with expected revenue.[22] Paramount, the first national film distributor, was formed in 1914 through the merger of several regional film exchanges. W.W. Hodkinson, Paramount's founder, describes the company's early booking practices as requiring exhibitors "to pay ... $500.00 a week for one program each week ... I was getting $500.00 a week for a single feature in my first runs, as against the usual $50.00 for a day [for short films]."[23]

Flat fees remained the norm until 1927.[24] For example, a handwritten sheet of charges paid by the Wellesley Theater in Wellesley, Massachusetts for that year consists entirely of flat payments.[25] However, a fundamental change accompanied the release of *The Jazz Singer*. As Crafton writes:

> Instead of the traditional flat rental fee, Warner's took a percentage of the gate. The signing of the contract by the greater New York Fox circuit was regarded as a headline making precedent. The silent practice of renting for a flat fee was eventually replaced by this new percentage-of-the-gross pricing.
>
> (1997: 111)

A contemporary account adds, "In June 1929, prior to the opening of the motion picture selling season, it was apparent that percentage pricing would become the accepted method of sale that year.... In the past, practically all sales had been made on a flat rental basis." [26]

Individual exhibition contracts from the silent era are difficult to find. However, from the Adolph Zukor file at the Academy of Motion Pictures Arts and Sciences Library in Los Angeles, I obtained a copy of a 1917 contract between Paramount and the Woodley Theater at 831 South Broadway in Los Angeles. It specifies as follows:

> The total consideration of this contract is for seventeen (17) weeks of Paramount Pictures (Monday release) at eight hundred ($800) dollars per week, or a total of thirteen thousand, six hundred ($13,600) dollars.

The Woodley was a first-run theater; with the coming of sound, it would almost certainly have been paying a percentage of its revenue.

More is available for the early sound years. The most fruitful source for contract information is the Warner Brothers Archives at the University of Southern California, where a collection of boxes containing exhibition data was recently recovered from a New York building about to be demolished. The contents of these boxes has been only loosely catalogued, but they contain a wealth of data from the 1930s and 1940s on exhibition practices. Table 4.3 lists Warner Brothers films booked by nine West Coast

Table 4.3 Revenue sharing versus flat fees for top-billed features (1930–1931 season)

Season	Cinema	Location	Average weekly revenue ($)	No. of top-billed films where revenue shared	No. of top-billed films rented on a flat-fee basis
(1)	(2)	(3)	(4)	(5)	(6)
1930–1931	Aberdeen	Aberdeen, WA	1,667	19	3
1930–1931	California	Los Angeles, CA	997	2	31
1930–1931	Beverly Hills	Beverly Hills, CA	2,873	25	0
1930–1931	Capitol	Salem, OR	1,904	15	4
1930–1931	Elsinore	Salem, OR	1,752	21	0
1930–1931	Forum	Los Angeles, CA	1,238	2	23
1930–1931	Fresno	Fresno, CA	4,481	29	2
1930–1931	Tivoli	Los Angeles, CA	4,509	33	0
1930–1931	Uptown	Los Angeles, CA	2,961	35	0

Source: Warner Brothers Archives, University of Southern California.

theaters for the 1930–1931 season. As columns 5 and 6 show, revenue sharing was by then standard. Only two of the nine cinemas rented the majority of their top-billed features for flat fees, while 95 percent of the bookings of the other cinemas was on a revenue-sharing basis. The two exceptions were houses that earned substantially less revenue on average.[27]

Exhibition contracts from the very early sound years attempted to mimic their silent era equivalents. They included exhibitor guarantees – minimum payments due by the exhibitor whatever the total gross – set equal to the average rental of a silent film of that type, while all revenue above a specified amount (typically equal to the average silent take) would be shared.[28] But such guarantees quickly disappeared, to be replaced instead by exhibitor allowances for fixed expenses (see below). This was part of a steady movement away from making the exhibitor residual claimant, and toward making the film company residual claimant instead.

The Warner Brothers Archives contain a series of film commitment sheets, which specify the terms at which Warner Brothers-owned cinemas booked the films of rival studios. I collected data for Warner theaters in the Philadelphia area by season from 1931–1932 through 1942–1943 (no data were available for 1932–1933, 1933–1934, or 1939–1940). The number of theaters for which data were provided varied by year, ranging from as few as twelve in 1941–1942 to as many as fifty-seven in 1940–1941, with the average being thirty-six. The typical cinema in the data set booked approximately twenty movies per season from the specified company (either Fox or Paramount, depending on which was available).

Table 4.4 summarizes the data. Column 2 divides the films between those booked for flat fees and those booked on a share basis. Because all the Warner Brother theaters in the data set were first- or second-run, the only flat-fee bookings were for films that made up the bottom half of double features (second features were invariably rented for flat fees – see pages below). These comprised about one-quarter to one-third of all bookings, a proportion that stayed roughly constant over the period.[29] The amount of the typical flat rental payment, shown in column 3, changed little over the period, although it fluctuated somewhat by year. By contrast, the sharing percentages increased substantially, with the proportion of revenue going to the film company rising steadily. Column 4 lists the various rental percentages specified in each year's contract, column 5 lists the number of films booked at each percentage, and column 6 lists the average percentage rental paid. In 1931–1932, the average percentage paid to Paramount was 22.6, and the typical rental charges were 20 percent and 25 percent. By 1942–1943, the average percentage paid (now to Fox) had risen to 31.7, and the typical rental charges ranged from 25 to 40 percent.

Another useful source of information in the Warner Brothers Archives is the film billing sheet, which lists the rental prices charged to independent theaters for Warner Brothers' own films. Table 4.5 lists the average percentage paid to Warner Brothers by twelve independent theaters, also located in the Philadelphia area, by eight-year intervals from 1931–1932 to 1947–1948.[30] The fourth column shows the average weekly revenue for each theater, which increased steadily over the period (both attendance and ticket prices were rising). The average percentage of attendance revenue paid as rent by exhibitors rose from 18 percent to 38 percent between 1931–1932 and 1947–1948. The highest payments increased even more dramatically, from 25 percent in 1931–1932 to as much as 70 percent (60 percent in most cases) in 1947–1948. Film companies have always charged higher percentages for films expected to do better at the box office.[31] But while average revenue earned by the films in the sample rose by 33 percent between 1932 and 1948, the average sharing percentage more than doubled.

The percentage of attendance revenue collected by film companies has continued to rise since. Today, film companies receive 90 percent of revenue after an allowance for house expenses has been deducted. The contracts also specify alternative minimum sharing percentages of 50 to 70 percent, depending on the film and the cinema. If revenue less the house allowance multiplied by 90 percent is greater than revenue times the minimum, the film company collects the former; if not, it collects the latter.[32]

Table 4.4 Sample of Warner Brothers bookings from Paramount and Fox, 1931–1943

Year	No. of flat and share rentals	Average flat fee ($) 1929 prices	Percentage splits	No. of films rented at each percentage share	Average percentage rental	Studio supplying sample Warner Bros. cinemas
(1)	(2)	(3)	(4)	(5)	(6)	(7)
1931–1932	No. flat 125 No. share 423	51.5	20 25	199 244	22.6	Paramount
1934–1935	No. flat 284 No. share 893	55.2	20 25 30	449 327 117	23.1	Paramount
1935–1936	No. flat 245 No. share 507	38.3	20 25 30	233 178 96	23.6	Fox
1936–1937	No. flat 299 No. share 632	44.3	20 25 30 35	340 182 84 26	23.4	Paramount
1937–1938	No. flat 389 No. share 912	24.8	20 25 30 35	296 459 103 54	24.5	Fox

Year		No.	%	Rate	No. films	Avg.	Studio
1938–1939	No. flat	327	36.2	35	34	24.5	Fox
	No. share	565		20	193		
				25	271		
				30	67		
				35	34		
1940–1941	No. flat	624	64.7	35	123	25.6	Paramount
	No. share	1,088		20	360		
				25	356		
				30	249		
				35	123		
1941–1942	No. flat	85	51.7	40	2	27.6	Fox
	No. share	140		20	24		
				25	45		
				30	46		
				35	23		
				40	2		
1942–1943	No. flat	335	37.5	40	150	31.7	Fox
	No. share	984		25	246		
				30	312		
				35	276		
				40	150		

Source: Warner Brothers Archives, University of Southern California.

Table 4.5 Warner Brothers rentals to independent exhibitors

Year	Cinema	Location	Average weekly revenue ($)	Average weekly percentage going to Warners	High percentage for individual film	Low percentage for individual film
(1)	(2)	(3)	(4)	(5)	(6)	(7)
1931–1932	69th St.	Phil., PA	3,273	20.0	25	15
1931–1932	Ritz	York, PA	997	15.9	20	15
1931–1932	Savoy	Phil., PA	1,291	15.0	15	15
1931–1932	Seltzer	Palmyra, PA	882	19.3	25	15
1931–1932	Stanley	Chester, PA	4,691	16.8	25	12.5
1931–1932	Stanley	Camden, NJ	5,899	20.0	25	15
1931–1932	Wishart	Phil., PA	1,779	20.6	25	20
1931–1932	Wynne	Phil., PA	1,781	17.9	25	15
Average			2,574	18.2	23.1	15.3
1939–1940	69th St.	Phil., PA	4,499	26.0	35	15
1939–1940	Ritz	York, PA	1,674	22.2	35	15
1939–1940	Roosevelt	Newark, NJ	4,527	27.7	40	20
1939–1940	Savoy	Phil., PA	1,759	26.7	35	15
1939–1940	Strand	Bayonne, PA	907	18.5	25	15
1939–1940	Wishart	Phil., PA	2,885	23.8	32.5	15
1939–1940	Wynne	Phil., PA	2,973	29.2	40	25
Average			2,746	24.9	34.6	17.1
1947–1948	69th St.	Phil., PA	4,541	38.9	60	22.5
1947–1948	Ritz	York, PA	2,102	42.7	60	17.5
1947–1948	Ritz	Newark, NJ	4,398	38.6	60	25
1947–1948	Roosevelt	Newark, NJ	4,793	41.9	60	30
1947–1948	Savoy	Phil., PA	2,536	32.8	60	17.5
1947–1948	Strand	Bayonne, NJ	1,873	38.3	60	20
1947–1948	Tivoli	Newark, NJ	4,209	41.3	60	25
1947–1948	Wishart	Phil., PA	3,002	33.5	70	15
1947–1948	Wynne	Phil., PA	3,433	36.2	60	17.5
Average			3,432	38.2	61.1	21.1

Source: Warner Brothers Archives, University of Southern California.

The evidence

In this section, I will examine how film exhibition was changed by the coming of sound, the uncertainty that was created, and instances where share contracts were used during the silent era and flat rentals during the sound era.

How movie exhibitions were changed by sound

During the silent era, the "show" consisted of much more than the movie, also including a number of live performances of various types. For example, urban houses booked major vaudeville acts, and even the smallest and most rural theaters offered such things as "wooden shoe" dances, or "beautiful baby contests."[33] These acts were organized and/or booked by the exhibitor with little participation by the film company. In addition, the exhibitor had to ensure proper musical accompaniment to the film. A small, neighborhood theater would have had at least a piano player on its payroll, while large metropolitan houses employed entire orchestras.[34] House musicians were required to learn and play a new musical set whenever the program changed, which could be as often as three times per week. Organizing the musicians, and even choosing the music, was left entirely to the exhibitor.[35]

Live acts and music were not just a pleasant accompaniment to the film – accounts of the time indicate that they were considered at least as significant. Charlie Chaplin once said that as much as half the comic effect his films achieved was due to the background music.[36] Koszarski (1990: 53) describes a series of reports presented at the 1925 annual meeting of the Society of Motion Picture Engineers (that is, exhibitors): "What is most interesting about these reports is the emphasis placed on the composition of the show, and the theater's treatment of its films as just another troublesome item on the bill." Audiences evidently agreed; when a 1924 pollster asked film customers what aspects of a cinema appealed to them most, 28 percent cited the music, 19 percent the courtesy of the staff, 19 percent the comfort of the interior, 15 percent the attractiveness of the theater, and only 10 percent mentioned the films (Koszarski 1990: 30). Furthermore, 24 percent of exhibitors surveyed in 1922 said that the quality of the feature film "made absolutely no difference" to success at the box office; what mattered, they said, was the surrounding program (Koszarski 1990: 9). Advertisements of the time (see, for example, Koszarski 1990: 42, 49) tended to give as much print to the music and the live acts as they did to the title, actors, or plot of the feature film.

The coming of sound led to the dramatic reduction of live performances. In the first place, sound features had their own musical tracks, and so required no accompaniment. In the second place, it was cheaper and easier to present a short film of an orchestra or musical act than it was to show it in person.[37] Gomery (1992, 58) writes: "Filmed stage shows – short recordings of top vaudeville acts of the day – were substituted for the far more expensive live stage shows in all but the largest theaters." The 6 June 1928 edition of *Variety* proclaimed with a banner headline: "Stage Bands Passing." Two months later, the fabulous Roxy Cinema in New York City announced that it was phasing out live shows, and would instead emphasize sound films (*Variety*, 9 August 1928: 48). Two months after that, a headline announced of Grauman's famous Chinese Theatre in Hollywood, "Grauman's Abandons Pit Orchestra and Stage Shows – All Sound at Chinese" (*Variety*, 31 October 1928: 23). By the end of 1929, live acts were to be seen only at specialty houses.

Things changed for film companies as well, albeit not as dramatically as for exhibitors. For example, large soundproof studios had to be constructed and the roster of actors changed (see the next section). Furthermore, films of short comedy acts, vaudeville performances, newsreels, and so forth needed to be produced in large numbers, to replace the live acts formerly supplied by exhibitors. Double features also quickly became the norm, which meant that studios had to produce two types of feature films: high budget for the main act, and low budget for the second feature (see below). But the process of shooting, distributing, and marketing motion pictures was largely unaffected. Sound films were more costly to produce, on average, but also garnered higher revenues, on average (see Tables 4.1 and 4.2). However, the net effect of the disappearance of the live act was to substantially increase the relative importance of the movie company's inputs. Post-sound, patrons came to the theater for one major reason: to watch films.

The uncertainty of sound

Crafton (1997: 166) writes: "Sound epitomized what businessmen hate most: uncertainty." To begin with, no one was even sure what a sound film should look like. Should it simply synchronize music and add sound effects? Should it include dialogue? How much dialogue? Should certain types of films (dramas, for instance) include spoken dialogue, while others (comedies, for instance) remain silent? Many of the early "sound" productions in fact contained no dialogue at all (they still used title cards), but simply added synchronized music and sound effects.[38] Three ways of dealing with sound technology emerged initially: music and sound effects were added to existing silent features ("retro-fitting"), dual versions of new films were produced (both silent and sound), and films were made that were essentially silent in their nature and plotting, but had several "sound" scenes grafted on (*The Jazz Singer* is an example). By the 1929–1930 season, what had been a popular novelty was being criticized for being too loud and ostentatious, and the musical, initially considered the ideal platform for sound, was flopping (Crafton 1997: 268–269).[39]

The general sense of uncertainty was enhanced by the fundamental change sound brought about in the roster of movie stars. As De Vany and Walls (1999) point out, one of the few things that render film performance relatively more predictable is a predictably popular star. Yet with the coming of sound, the popularity of all existing stars was thrown into question. It is instructive to read movie advertisements from the late 1920s and early 1930s; although some of the names correspond, for the most part, one is dealing with two different sets of actors. A page-one article in 28 November 1928's issue of *Variety* makes this clear. "Film Stars Fading Away," reads the gigantic headline, while the sub-headline says, "Talking Films Make Big Change." Most of the big stars of the late silent era – John Gilbert, Vilma Banky, Corinne Griffith, Colleen Moore, Norma Talmadge – failed to make the transition to the talkies.[40] The skills required were fundamentally different – as noted, the silent actor communicated through facial expressions and gestures, while the sound actor used his/her voice.[41] Studios engaged in a panicked rush to sign stage stars; at least *they* knew how to talk. Some succeeded, but many more failed. When Lewis (1933: 121) writes that "motion pictures production underwent an almost complete revolution" with the coming of sound, he is referring to the fact that a whole new group of stars had to be developed. This made the revenue-generating potential of a given sound film that much more difficult to determine.

The last column of Table 4.2 show the coefficient of variation of film rentals (standard deviation divided by mean) for Warner Brothers and MGM. Some of the highest values occur for the transition years of 1927–1928 through 1929–1930.[42] A simple regression of rental revenue on production costs yields a silent era R-squared of 0.62 for MGM – 62 percent of cross-film variation in rental revenues can be explained by the production budget. That then fell to 0.21 during the transitional years of 1927–1928 and 1928–1929, to rise again during the sound years of the 1930s to 0.44. For Warner Brothers, the pre-sound R-squared was 0.62, the post-sound R-squared was 0.59, and the transitional R-squared was 0.39 (see Appendix 4 for results of the regressions).

Share contracts during the silent era and flat rentals during the sound era

Although the vast majority of silent feature films were rented to exhibitors for flat, daily fees, there were a small number of exceptions. As a study of the time noted, "Theaters exhibited special productions and roadshows on a percentage arrangement, but these were usually confined to higher-quality pictures which were expected to realize box office receipts that were substantially in excess of the average gross."[43] Such features were very different from (and very much more expensive to produce than) the films that exhibitors typically rented; in this sense they were analogous to the early sound films. For example, in 1927, the Pathé Company released the big-budget silent feature *The King of Kings*, directed by Cecil B. De Mille. Up to that time, Pathé had rented its films exclusively for flat fees, because its management had concluded that the necessity of checking receipts rendered revenue sharing too costly. However, *The King of Kings* was of potentially far greater drawing power than anything Pathé had previously produced. It therefore decided to rent the film to theaters on a share basis

> in order to secure rentals commensurate with the value of the picture.... The company believed that when an important attraction such as *The King of Kings* appeared in a program, it deserved a substantial proportion of gross admissions, a proportion greater than might be obtained by flat rental ("Pathé Exchange" 1928: 404–405).[44]

Pathé made one exception – it continued to charge a flat fee to movie houses located in "remote" towns, believing that the cost of checking receipts for those houses would be "prohibitive."

Turning to the sound era, there were several instances in which share contracts were *not* used. First, film companies continued to rent films to lower run theaters for flat fees. These lower-run houses changed bills as often as three times per week and were charged $7 to $15 per day per film (Balio 1993: 27). The reason for the flat charge was straightforward: the film company's cost of verifying that the attendance figures reported by the exhibitor were correct was simply too high given the tiny revenues that such houses generated – they both had fewer seats and charged lower admission prices (exhibition contracts specified minimum admission prices until forbidden from doing so in 1948).[45] This same rationale held for renting the expensive silent-era roadshows for flat fees to "small and remote" cinemas. Later-run cinemas generally pay flat exhibition rentals to this very day for exactly the same reason.

A second exception was the "B" movie. While "A" movies cost $300,000 or more to make and were sold on a percentage basis, B-films cost $50,000 to $200,000 and were sold for flat fees.[46] B-movies emerged primarily as a result of the double feature, which became the predominant mode of exhibition in the 1930s (Ricketson 1938: 78). B-films formed the bottom half of the double bill. Double features had initially presented a challenge to revenue sharing; given that the first feature was made by one studio and the second by another, how was one to identify the individual contribution of each so as to allow a share contract? The initial attempts to divide output between two separate films proved quite costly – representatives of each film company had to meet with the exhibitor to hash out appropriate percentages. It was quickly decided that a simpler and cheaper approach was to have on every bill one high-quality feature (the A-film) and one low-quality feature (the B-film), and to rent the high-quality feature on a percent-of-gross basis, and the low-quality feature for a flat fee.[47]

A third exception involved cinemas that continued to organize and present live entertainment into the sound era. They were a distinct minority, but included some important houses in large urban areas – Radio City Music Hall in New York presents live shows to this day. Although these theaters were of the type charged on a revenue-sharing basis elsewhere, when they presented live performances, they instead paid a flat fee for each film they rented.[48] Film companies were concerned that the theaters would otherwise lack the incentive to devote sufficient effort to the live shows, and that attendance revenue would suffer accordingly.

The implications

Shirking in the provision of inputs

Flat-fee rentals give exhibitors a greater incentive to provide the optimal level of their inputs than does revenue-sharing. As described above, those inputs were more extensive (and expensive) during the silent era.[49] Accounts of the time indicate that the silent film studios took very seriously the possibility of exhibitor shirking. A 1928 interview with a studio's sales manager concludes: "It was his belief that when an exhibitor did not have to guarantee a certain return to the distributor, the inclination was to ignore the [live inputs and] . . . let the picture do its own work" (Sidley Pictures Corporation 1930: 330). A contemporary scholar, Howard Lewis of Harvard Business School (1933: 190), recounts how silent-era experiments with revenue-sharing had highlighted what he called "the principle weakness in the system: inadequate exploitation [by the exhibitor]."

What about shirking by movie studios? There are two reasons to believe this to have been of lesser concern:

1   the cost of spotting shirking by film companies (in movie quality) was likely to have been lower than the cost of spotting exhibitor shirking (in the quality of live shows and music), and
2   a film company's incentive to shirk was likely to have been less, because the potential punishment was greater.

First, the poor performance of a film at a particular theater may be due to many things specific to the locale – the weather, local tastes, a local holiday – and accordingly, difficult to attribute to the exhibitor without actually attending the performance (and film companies sold to hundreds of first- and second-run theaters). By contrast, an exhibitor observed the contracted-for film in the course of normal duties. Second, studios made large and largely sunk investments in stars and inventories of movies (both finished and under production) that were justified by the anticipated stream of future revenues, which depended in turn on the company's reputation for providing films of a given quality.[50] By contrast, most of a cinema's value was in easily transferred physical assets and location.[51] Thus, shirking by the exhibitor, as potentially important (given the live show) in its effect on revenue as shirking by the film company, but more costly to observe and less costly to engage in, was the greater threat during the silent era, and flat rentals were used, accordingly.

With the coming of sound, the nature of the exhibitor's inputs changed, and so did concern about exhibitor shirking. In a simplified sense, one can think of sound as having reorganized the production process. A film presentation is created from a variety of inputs, including projection, seating, sight, and sound. During the silent era, only "sight" was supplied by the film company, and even that incompletely. Sound technology trans-ferred the responsibility for sound – sound effects and shows – to the film company, while the exhibitor's contribution to sight – the live act – was completely eliminated. A movement away from the flat fees that had made the exhibitor residual claimant became more attractive as a result. In fact, once sound films became the norm, film companies began to actively push for the removal of live entertainment from the cinema, presumably so that the revenue generated would depend more completely on their own efforts.[52] The importance of potential exhibitor shirking during the silent era is also indicated by the fact (as already noted) that exhibitors who con-tinued to present live shows into the sound era continued to be charged flat rental fees, although comparable cinemas without live shows rented films on a revenue-sharing basis. Film companies worried that revenue sharing would blunt the incentives of exhibitors to provide the optimal amounts of their important live inputs.

Finally, as Tables 4.4 and 4.5 demonstrate, the proportion of attendance revenue paid by exhibitors to film companies increased steadily in the decades following the conversion to sound. Today, film companies receive 90 percent of residual attendance revenue. Contracts have thus evolved from making the exhibitor full residual claimant to nearly making the film company the same.[53] This makes sense – the party whose effort has the greatest effect on marginal product generally receives the greatest propor-tion of the residual claims. Post-sound, the films were the reason that patrons visited a cinema. This was not true during the silent years, when the exhibitor's own live shows often surpassed the film in their attractive-ness to audiences.

Risk

Flat film rentals generate the optimal provision of exhibitor inputs, but at the cost of placing all the risk of uncertain audience response on the exhibitor's shoulders. The demise of the live act created the opportunity to shift more of that risk to the film company with less concern about exhibitor shirking. Sound also increased the uncertainty over film perform-ance, as described above, by changing the nature of the product and the roster of stars. Film revenues became more variable, as detailed above. All this would suggest the importance of efficient risk bearing to the choice of contract.

Nonetheless, other facts suggest that risk-bearing concerns were not central to the *change* in rental pricing. First, the uncertainty over audience reaction to early sound films, just like the uncertainty over audience response to the silent roadshows, did not appear to have generated concern about the riskiness of film revenue per se, but rather to have increased the difficulty in agreeing to an *ex ante* price, more on that below. Second, flat-fee rentals were still used (and are still used today) for lower-run theaters, which generally tend to be smaller, and are often located in smaller towns. These cinemas tended to be owned and operated by small businessmen, who most probably had a larger portion of their wealth in the operation than did the owners of the publicly held chains that rented films on a revenue-sharing basis. The small exhibitors were thus plausibly more risk averse, and certainly not less risk averse. But they paid flat fees anyway, while larger operations were charged a percent of the gross. While this does not mean risk-based concerns played no role in the overall choice of contract form, it does suggest that other factors dominated when it came to the switch from flat fees to revenue sharing.[54]

The cost of dividing output ex post

Lewis (1933: 192–194), in his early history of the motion pictures, examines of the use of share contracts and concludes:

> An important consideration was the dishonesty of some exhibitors and the distributor's inability to provide an adequate and economical box office checking system.... The seriousness of the problem of checking receipts at times threatened to disrupt the entire percentage system.

The basic problem was that exhibitors had a strong incentive to under-report attendance. To counteract that incentive, film companies randomly placed people in theaters to count the audience.[55] There were three ways of doing this: the checkers could take tickets at the door, they could count tickets after the box office had closed, or they could examine opening and closing ticket numbers. The first was disliked by exhibitors – the checker had to supplant the regular doorman, which, it was feared, would lead patrons to conclude something was wrong at the cinema; furthermore, important customers could be upset if free passes were questioned. The second method was quite laborious and required the checker to work late into the night (box offices normally did not close until 9p.m. or 10p.m). Film companies worried that checkers would simply submit false reports so as to quit early. The third method was the most widely employed, but could be stymied by the use of old tickets, or the redistribution of previously distributed ticket halves.[56]

Not only was putting a man in the theater costly, the checkers were often dishonest themselves. A film company contemplating revenue sharing noted that "it was common knowledge that checkers had resorted to various forms of theft, such as making agreements with exhibitors and reselling tickets" (Shaefer Pictures Corp. 1930: 339). Today, specialty firms exist, whose sole purpose is to check attendance figures on behalf of film companies.[57] There were also concerns among exhibitors, who worried that film companies would use the revenue figures to demand a higher price the next time around, or even to open a competitive movie house.[58] Given all these problems, Lewis (1933: 196) concludes that "it is doubtful that percentage pricing can be justified."

Yet sound pictures brought percentage pricing in their wake. However, what changed was not the monitoring problem, but the film's average gross, which increased substantially with the coming of sound (Tables 4.1 and 4.2). If one can assume that the cost of the monitoring remained roughly constant, monitoring costs per dollar of film revenue declined. Revenue sharing became relatively more attractive, accordingly.

The importance of the cost of the *ex post* division of output to the choice of contract form is illustrated by two of the uses of flat-fee rentals during the sound era, described above. First, smaller, lower-run cinemas were (and are) invariably charged flat fees, for the explicit reason that the cost of monitoring the exhibitor's reporting of attendance revenue was too high. For example, of the sample of nine West Coast theaters shown in Table 4.3, the two that rented primarily on a flat-fee basis had an average weekly revenue of $1,117 in 1930–1931, compared to $2,878 for the seven theaters that rented primarily on a revenue-sharing basis. Second, B-movies were rented for flat fees, because the cost of dividing revenue between two films shown simultaneously was simply judged to be too high.[59]

The cost of pre-sale measurement

Before contracting for a film, a film company and an exhibitor must negotiate the appropriate price. If there were no variation in film performance (that is, in attendance revenue), or very predictable variation, such negotiations would be simple. The fact that films are highly heterogeneous complicates the process by providing exhibitors with a strong incentive to seek to measure film quality before agreeing to a purchase. However, precise *ex ante* measurements are very costly, because a film's value (in terms of potential for generating revenue) can only be determined by observing actual audience response.[60] Given this costliness, one would expect that ways to avoid pre-sale measurement efforts would be found, and indeed, relatively little occurred in the film business. Exhibitors throughout the silent and sound eras dealt with the same companies year after year, and bought many of the same kinds of pictures. During the selling process, film companies would provide such information as the title, plot, actors, and/or director of the films under negotiation, insufficient for a precise prediction of audience response to that particular film, but enough to indicate the approximate value of the group of films that were being contracted for. As a result, contract negotiations could proceed with a minimum of film-by-film haggling.

What was required, however, was a clear and shared (between exhibitor and film company) agreement on the value of the "typical" film. As already noted, the principal reason why silent-era "roadshows" such as *The King of Kings* were booked on a revenue-sharing basis was that they were very different from the films typically rented, and thus much more costly to agree a flat price for. Indeed, there were occasional calls for a more general use of revenue sharing during the silent era on precisely the grounds that it would reduce haggling over rental prices.[61]

It is possible that the early sound films presented a similar problem. As noted, there was a fundamental lack of knowledge about what a sound film should be, and directorial, cinematographic, and acting techniques had to evolve to take advantage of the new technology's potential. Simultaneously, an entire roster of movie stars disappeared, and a new one emerged. During the transition period, the relationship between production costs and revenue was weaker, and the general variability of film revenue increased (see above). All of this would have raised the cost of determining the appropriate flat rental fee, and thus made revenue sharing relatively more attractive.[62]

If one were to judge entirely by contemporary accounts, one would conclude that the difficulty in negotiating flat rentals was an important spur to the use of revenue sharing.[63] However, as time passed, the sound film became less uncertain in its performance – a new roster of stars emerged, the technology was mastered, and appropriate film styles were developed. Revenue sharing persisted nonetheless. While it is thus possible that problems with pre-sale measurement helped promote the initial use of revenue sharing, they certainly cannot explain its persistence.

Conclusion

Silent films were rented by film companies to exhibitors for flat, per-day fees, ranging from as much as $1,000 per day for large, first-run cinemas in major metropolitan areas to as little as $7 per day for the smaller, lower-run houses. Revenue sharing was used only rarely, because film companies worried that it would reduce the difficult-to-monitor efforts made by exhibitors to support the film with live musical (and other) acts, and the cost of ensuring honest reporting of revenue (essential to a share contract) was seen as prohibitive given the amount each film generated.

The technology shock represented by sound altered the structure of the incentives in film exhibition, and thus changed the nature of exhibition contracts. Because sound eliminated the live act, it substantially reduced the contribution to attendance revenue of the exhibitor's inputs, and thus concern about exhibitor shirking. By contrast, the relative importance of the film company's inputs (specifically, the film) increased dramatically, and film companies claimed a greater proportion of the residual revenue as a result. Sound films also earned more on average than silent films, which decreased the cost of monitoring on a dollar-of-revenue basis. Finally, sound films were – initially at least – more difficult to evaluate, and thus more difficult to agree on a lump-sum rental for, than silent films had been.

Film companies were well aware of the effect of their choice of contract on the possibility of exhibitor shirking, and were concerned that a movement away from the flat fee would increase the exhibitor's incentive to shirk on the provision of inputs (that is why the initial share contracts included minimum guarantees). They were also aware that exhibitors could not be depended on to report revenue honestly, and that efforts to ensure honesty would be costly. The sound film, requiring less intensive exhibitor provision of inputs and generating more revenue on average thus impelled a switch to revenue sharing that has lasted to this day.

Appendix 4.1

Table A4.1 Revenue regression

Equation: Revenue = $\alpha + \beta$ (production cost)

Company	Period	α (standard error)	β (standard error)	R^2	# Observations
MGM	1924–1925 through 1926–1927	164.4 (439)	1.085 (0.081)	0.618	113
	1927–1928 through 1928–1929	299.7 (293)	0.669 (0.206)	0.206	104
	1929–1930 through 1940–1941	278.7 (387)	0.760 (0.038)	0.442	519
Warner Brothers	1921–1922 through 1926–1927	66.7 (102)	1.354 (0.097)	0.623	119
	1927–1928 through 1928–1929	133.8 (456)	2.605 (0.380)	0.395	74
	1929–1930 through 1940–1941	103.3 (217)	1.064 (0.034)	0.594	678

Notes

1 I would like to thank Darlene Chisholm, Rob Fleck, Dean Lueck, Ron Johnson, John Sedgwick, Mark Weinstein, and participants at seminars at Montana State University, The University of Southern California's Business School, and at the Western Economic Association Meetings in San Francisco for helpful comments. This research was completed while I was a National Fellow at the Hoover Institution; I would like to thank the Institution for its support.

2 See, for example, such review articles as Prendergast (1999) and Sappington (1999).

3 Revenue sharing was used in certain rare circumstances during the silent era, and flat fees continued to be used in some cases during the sound era.

4 In fact, a producer produces a film, and a distributor rents it to exhibitors. Today, these activities are often carried out by two independent firms, but during the period in question, the major studios both produced and distributed their films (and many exhibited them as well). I will therefore use the term "film company" throughout this chapter.

5 All uncertainty is thus on the demand side, in contrast to agricultural share contracts, which must account for major uncertainty in factors affecting supply (weather, for example).

6 One-sided moral hazard models (e.g. Holmstrom and Milgrom 1987) emphasize shirking by the agent and focus on the choice between optimal effort-motivation and optimal risk-bearing. Two-sided moral hazard models (e.g. Eswaran and Kotwal 1985; Allen and Lueck 1992) emphasize shirking by both parties, and typically assume that the contracting parties are risk neutral.

7 See Barzel (1982).

8 See Huettig (1944: 125–127) for more detail.

9 Paramount had more than 500 theaters by 1925, and more than 1,000 by 1929. Loew's/MGM had its nearly full complement of about 200 theaters by 1924. Fox initiated its big theater expansion program in the mid-1920s. Warner Brothers was an exception – it used proceeds from its early sound hits to go on a theater-buying spree. RKO was not formed until 1929, but its chain was made up primarily of theaters from the old Keith-Albee and Orpheum vaudeville circuits (RKO did add more theaters later, often taking over those that owed money to RCA for installed sound equipment). For more detail on the history and structure of vertical integration in the film industry, see Gomery (1992).

10 The biggest studios released fifty films per year at most, and even a theater changing films only once per week (two- and three-change policies were more common) would require fifty-two first features plus fifty-two second bills (double features were standard in the 1930s and 1940s).

11 Block booking, a fixed system of runs, clearances, and zoning, and studio ownership of cinemas were all banned by decree of the Supreme Court in *United States* v. *Paramount Pictures, Inc.*, 334 U.S. (1948). See De Vany and Eckert (1991) for a review of the case and Chisholm (1993) for a discussion of contemporaneous long-term contracts between studios and actors.

12 See Crafton (1997: 9). It would be more accurate to say that Edison's work was the culmination of a number of incremental developments dating back to the "magic lantern" of the mid-seventeenth century at least.

13 This is referred to as the "Big Five Agreement," because it was signed (in February 1927) by five of the most important film companies: Loew's (MGM), Universal, First National (later purchased by Warner Brothers), Paramount, and Producers Distributing Corporation. The firms agreed that for one year, none would adopt any sound technology unless (1) a standard had been identified as

best for the industry, (2) that technology was made available to all producers on equal terms, and (3) it was to be adopted by all simultaneously. See Gomery (1985) and Walker (1979) for more detail.

14 Jack Warner, the champion of the talking picture, said as late as 1928 that he expected most future films to be part sound and part silent (Crafton 1997: 174). Adolph Zukor, President of Paramount Pictures, was also quoted in late 1928 as saying: "By no means is the silent picture gone or even diminished in import-ance ... there always have been subjects which could not be augmented in value or strength by the addition of sound and dialogue" (*The Film Daily 1929 Yearbook*: 513). The author of a case study of a cinema considering the conver-sion to sound in 1928 writes, "It was difficult to judge the permanence of the appeal of sound pictures. Theatrical managers were convinced that the appeal at first was largely one of curiosity" (Clayton Theater 1930: 491).

15 Crafton (1997: 171). A silent-film version of the story of the sinking of the Titanic was abandoned in the summer of 1928 with the following explanation: "Until assured of a more popular market for an all-silent picture that will warrant the money it will cost..." (*Variety* 1 August 1928: 4). Several months later, a *Variety* article began with the following sentence, "With talkers now looked upon as the mainspring of the trade..." (7 November 1928: 5). That same issue announced that thirteen of the fourteen Broadway movie houses where high-profile films were given their debuts were showing sound movies that week.

16 The very pattern of cinema-going was different during the silent era – patrons would show up in the middle of the film and simply stay through the sub-sequent showing until they were back to the point where they had arrived. Walker (1979: 97) writes: "Silent movies had enabled the casual customer to drop in, and within a minute or two be locked into the story and characters. Mime-acting made the characters' predicaments easily intelligible; sub-titles gave people emotional cues to follow rather than narrative points to recall. But dialogue altered this: it demanded attention." Sound films initially discomfited both audiences and theater managers by requiring that all viewers arrive before the film began.

17 For a description and discussion of the data in the Mannix ledger, see Glancy (1992), and for the same for the Schaefer ledger, see Glancy (1995).

18 During the 1927–1928 and 1928–1929 seasons, roughly half of each company's "sound" films had musical scores and sound effects but no dialogue, or only selected talking sequences. However, by the 1929–1930 season, more than 95 percent of all the films that each released were fully talking.

19 See, for example, Balio (1985: 16) and Donahue (1987: 7).

20 See Merritt (1985).

21 By 1907, between 125 and 150 exchanges operated around the country. See Balio (1985: 17).

22 Harold Franklin, (1927: 27) President of West Coast Theaters, writes of the silent feature: "Rentals vary in accordance with the size of the city or commun-ity, as well as with the type and size of the theater, and also in accordance with the run – first, second, third, etc." By contrast, the General Film Company, which dominated the distribution of film shorts between 1910 and 1912, described its leasing practice as follows: "no account was taken of individual pictures or of individual actors or directors, and the flat rate per foot applied without regard to the number of separate pictures, the quality or character of the pictures, the size of the theater, or the town or city" (Lewis 1933: 17).

23 The quote is taken from a memo (dated 5 March 1958) which summarizes Hod-kinson's personal recollections and is addressed to George Seaton, then presid-ent of the Academy of Motion Pictures Arts and Sciences. The memo is on file at the Academy of Motion Pictures Arts and Sciences Library in Los Angeles.

24 Gomery (1980: 28) writes, "Prior to the coming of sound, most films were rented for a flat fee." Franklin, (1927: 27) writes of the silent feature: "In most instances, the rental is a flat sum, which is based on possible box office receipts. These are scheduled by experts who are familiar with the film rental possibilities." There were some exceptions; unusually big-budget features were released on a revenue-sharing basis. But such films were a distinct minority – less than 1 percent of the approximately 1,000 features produced per year, earning about 3–5 percent of film revenue.

25 This was also obtained from the Zukor file at the Academy of Motion Pictures Arts and Sciences Library in Los Angeles.

26 Shaefer Pictures Corp. (1930: 336). The 1928 Motion Picture Herald contains a debate on the merits of the newly implemented percentage pricing for "program pictures" (the typical films shown by most theaters on most days). On March 10, N.L. Royster, Secretary-Treasurer of the Theater Owners Association of North Carolina, complained that the new percentages being demanded are "exorbitant" as compared to the flat fees formerly paid (p. 29). On April 14, A.R. Bender, owner of Melba and Mecca Theater in Cleveland, Ohio, responds that, while this may or may not be so, "price haggling" has fallen substantially under percentage pricing, to the benefit of both parties (p. 25).

27 Smaller houses generally paid flat rentals throughout the sound era; see below.

28 See Lewis (1933: 191–192) and Willard Theater (1930: 592).

29 The balance of the second features (the number of first and second features must obviously match) would most probably have been booked from the "Poverty Row" studios that specialized in low-budget films and serials – Monogram, Republic, and so forth.

30 The averages are calculated using the eight weeks that begin with Christmas. Particular theaters were only sporadically covered by the available billing sheets.

31 For example, the 1939 MGM product offering consisted of four "super-specials" on which the rental rate was 40 percent of revenue; ten "lesser bombshells" with a 35 percent rental rate; another ten films at a 30 percent rate, and twenty B-pictures, mostly at flat rentals (these were used primarily as second features). See *Fortune*, August 1939, 20: 25–30.

32 See, for example, Friedberg (1993), Murphy (1983), and Litman (1998: 48). Today's percentages fall as time passes as well (i.e., the second week's percentage is less than the first's and so on), thus encouraging longer showings. The house allowance, or "nut," is typically calculated on a per-seat basis ($15 per seat, for example), with the rate depending upon the quality of the sound system, the configuration of the seats, and the overall condition of the theater. This practice has an effect somewhat similar to the "splits" employed in some exhibition contracts during the 1930s – the percentage of attendance revenue going to the film company increased after a specified total had been reached.

33 In *The 1925 Film Daily Yearbook*, for example, there is a "Manual of Exploitation," (pp. 677–678) intended to help exhibitors to design their own live shows.

34 The results of a 1922 survey indicated that 29 percent of respondents employed a full orchestra (the median size being five pieces), 50 percent had an organ and organist, and 21 percent had only a piano – see Koszarski (1990: 41). Large theaters invested substantially in their orchestras; for example, Publix Theaters, belonging to Paramount, boasted in 1928 that they were "the largest employer of stage talent of any circuit in the world." Their payroll included 1,000 chorus girls, 250 dancers, 34 blues singers, 51 opera singers, 25 comedy singers, 50 comedians, and 1,200 musicians (*Variety*, 25 April 1928: 1). Franklin (1927: 47)

notes that many first- and second-run American cinemas spent in excess of $200,000 per year on musicians' salaries alone.

35 It was rare that a picture would have its own specially written score; instead, stock pieces were chosen to conjure up particular moods. The film company would occasionally include a folder of such pieces with their shipment of the film, but more common was the "cue sheet," which provided a short description and the approximate length of the film's various scenes, so that the theater's music director (or piano player) could prepare the musical accompaniment on his or her own. Large orchestras maintained huge music libraries, and even the single pianist had access to such volumes as *Motion Picture Moods* (Koszarski 1990: 43).

36 From "Jacques Tati's silent comedies: surrounded by sound," by Bob Schwabach, *The New York Times*, 10 December 2000. To appreciate the importance of the musical track, one only has to compare the experience of watching a silent film without music, or with an inappropriate or poorly done track (both of which were standard for many decades after the coming of sound) with watching some of the more recent re-releases with specially written scores (Thames Television presented such a series several years ago.)

37 Indeed, it was reportedly the prospect of being able to replace live shows with short films of the best vaudeville acts that first sparked Harry Warner's interest in sound. When his brother Sam pointed out that he could have actors talk, too, Warner is said to have responded: "Who the hell wants to hear actors talk?" (see Walker 1979: 6). The early sound short mimicked stage shows completely, consisting of a single static shot of the act on a stage, with an orchestra observable in a pit in front of it.

38 This led to many disappointed and unhappy patrons and a push towards standardized labeling. One *Variety* article (6 June 1928: 48) suggested that a "sound" film could be defined as one with sound effects but no dialogue, while a "dialog" film be one that had spoken parts as well. The article concluded that the former were here to stay but, with respect to the latter, it was too early to tell: "They [dialogue pictures] are wholly experimental at present and probably for at least a year to come."

39 Recall the famous sequence from *Singin' in the Rain*, in which Gene Kelly and Jean Hagen, playing silent-film stars, struggle with the demands of their first sound feature. A real-life counterpoint occurred in the early talking film *Tenderloin* (1928), when popular silent actress Dolores Costello, playing a young woman menaced by gangsters, declaimed the immortal line: "Merthy, merthy, have you no thithter of your own?" The poor quality of the early recording technology did not help. A May 1929 issue of *The New York Times* printed a letter from an unhappy film-goer, who wrote: "One has to elongate one's ears and try to unravel from a concatenation of sounds what it's all about.... Do give us one delightful, quiet theater until it grows up" (quoted in Rogers and Allen 1947: 89).

40 See Griffith and Mayer (1957: 247–251) for a discussion of the effect of the coming of sound on the roster of stars; in particular, see the sub-section entitled "Kaput."

41 The following is from an August 1926 *Variety* article discussing the possibility of films with spoken dialogue: "Just how far that might start a panic among picture players who can't talk and have no dramatic experience or knowledge of elocution or diction is problematical. Its effect might reach far and also open up a more ready picture field for dramatic actors" (p. 25).

42 The coefficient of variation of film revenue is somewhat higher overall for the post-1929 sound years than for the pre-1927 silent years. Pre-sound (i.e. pre-1927–1928), the average Warner Brothers coefficient of variation was 0.466, and the average MGM coefficient was 0.438. Post-sound (i.e. post-1928–1929),

those coefficients averaged 0.704 and 0.661, respectively. This is due in part to the fact that film costs became somewhat more variable – companies began producing both high-budget "A" films and low-budget "B" films, the latter to show as the bottom of double features.

43 Wellington Theater (1928: 573). The "Standard Exhibition Contract" that formed the basis for all film company-exhibitor contracts limited the number of films designated as "roadshows" to two per season per film company; see *The 1929 Film Daily Yearbook* (pp. 801–815). The Warner Brothers Franchise Agreement defined roadshows as "any motion pictures released by a distributor which shall be exhibited in the main theatrical district of New York City and one other key point, on a prerelease basis; that is to say, on a basis whereby only two shows a day are given at advanced admission prices" (Goldstein, Incorporated 1929: 418).

44 A similar situation occurred with the release of the very popular 1928 silent feature *Lilac Time*, starring one of the silent screen's top actresses, Colleen Moore. A contemporary *Variety* article (15 August 1928: 43) notes, "On the strength of the Cathay Circle Showing, FN has booked *Lilac Time* in Long Beach at an 800 percent increase over the average rental for a Colleen Moore picture for that town. Heretofore, $600 has been an average rental figure [for her] ... *Lilac Time* was booked at a guarantee of $5000 with a 60–40 split over $16,000 and a minimum run of 3 weeks guaranteed."

45 The publication *Motion Picture Exhibition*, prepared for the 50th anniversary committee of the Motion Pictures and Distributors of America in October of 1939 (on file with the Academy of Motion Pictures Arts and Sciences Library in Los Angeles), shows the following distribution of theaters:

City/town population ('000)	No. of towns	No. of theaters	No. of seats ('000)	Average no. of seats
>500	13	2,251	2,427	1,078
200–500	28	1,104	1,010	915
100–200	52	783	755	964
50–100	94	801	761	950
20–50	276	1,202	1,054	877
10–20	494	1,341	923	688
5–10	845	1,626	1,006	619
2.5–5	1,351	1,954	962	492
1–2.5	2,874	3,221	1,113	346
<1.0	3,160	3,253	845	260

For a representative sample of films from the 1943–1944 season, the average studio earned nearly 50 percent of its revenue in first-run cities of 25,000 people or more (see Conant 1960: 69). Such theaters averaged nearly 1,000 seats, versus less than 500 for theaters in towns with fewer than 25,000 people. Nearly half of all theaters were located in towns of less than 5,000 people, but they contained only about one-quarter of all seats.

46 The B-film had several distinguishing characteristics. First, it starred actors who were either unknown, or who had only modest box office appeal (actors would occasionally make the leap from B movies to A movies – John Wayne and Mickey Rooney are two examples). Second, it was rapidly made, usually in less than three weeks, and sometimes in as little as one. Finally, it was shorter than the A-film, lasting only 50 to 70 minutes (John Wayne's B-Westerns were only 45 minutes long). For more detail, see Balio (1993, Chapter 8).

47 See Lewis (1933: 194). A *Variety* article of 1 April 1931 announced that the Paramount theater chain intended to rent all its second features for flat fees, because it considered the only other alternative to be "to show two pictures from one film company on the same bill," a practice too difficult to maintain. To reduce the exhibitor's incentive to rent lower than optimal quality B-films, the flat fee was typically deducted from gross revenue before the sharing percentage was applied. This created the contrary incentive, and some contracts therefore contained limits on the rental that could be deducted for a second feature. See Kenney and Klein (1983: 524).

48 See 1940 Congressional Hearings, cited in Kenney and Klein (1983: 526). Alternatively, these exhibitors sometimes leased films on a revenue-sharing basis, but were able to deduct the cost of the stage show from gross revenue up to some maximum before applying the sharing percentage.

49 In his text on (silent) cinema management, Harold Franklin (1927) estimates that the cost to exhibitors of live programs averaged 40 percent of gross receipts, versus film rental costs of less than 15 percent of gross receipts. By comparison, the average rental charge for sound films in the 1930s was roughly 20 to 30 percent of gross receipts (see Tables 4.4 and 4.5).

50 As Klein and Leffler (1981) point out, the prospect of repeat dealings can provide substantial incentive not to cheat. Movies were sold blind each spring, largely to the same group of exhibitors year after year. The exhibitors were willing to purchase blind because they expected the films to be of similar quality to films previously purchased from that studio.

51 This exaggerates somewhat. Run designations were very valuable – a first-run theater grossed significantly more than a second-run theater – and are fully under the control of the film company. Both Kenny and Klein (1983: footnote 70) and Hanssen (2000: 325) suggest that run designations could have been used to discipline erring exhibitors.

52 Crafton (1997: 252) writes: "Hollywood developed specific strategies to kill off live acts." Sound shorts were made that attacked live shows – one film company even released a short film entitled *Sentencing the Live Prologue to Death*. Crafton also quotes United Artists executive Joseph Schenck, who traveled around the country proclaiming: "Good pictures never needed acrobats or spangles."

53 Why was that final step toward making the film company full residual claimant not taken? Presumably because it continues to be efficient for a separate (and locally based) supplier to provide certain inputs – a clean theater, a courteous staff, an appropriate mix of complementary products (popcorn, etc.), and local advertising. Vertical integration may as yet be unfeasible for a variety of reasons, including anti-trust concerns (the *Paramount* decree required the major movie studios to divest themselves of their cinema chains).

54 It is alternatively possible that smaller cinemas, facing less local competition, had less variable revenues. Selling to them on a flat-fee basis might then have been an efficient form of risk pooling. However, there are two reasons to think this was not so. First, the proportion of revenue involved was relatively small; 20 percent or so at most. Second, the explanations given (in the past and today) for renting to smaller cinemas for flat fees invariably involve the cost of ensuring the honest reporting of revenue, not spreading risk.

55 In the early sound period, checkers were hired by the day at a cost of $5, plus $5 for expenses, plus transportation. Such checking was done sporadically and randomly; see Shaefer Pictures Corp. (1930) and Lewis (1933: 195) for what follows.

56 Harrold Weinberger worked as a checker, and then ran the West Coast check-

ing operations for MGM from the 1930s until the 1960s. He describes how checkers would engage in surreptitious observation of exhibitors believed to be cheating. For example, a checker would pose as a customer and buy one of the first tickets to the early show and one of the last tickets to the late show, and then compare the numbers on the two stubs to the reported attendance figures. Or if the theater was too small for him to get away with that, he would station himself at a point where he could not be seen (in a car parked across the street, for example) and simply count the people who entered. See the Harrold Weinberger transcript in the Academy Oral History Program at the Academy of Motion Pictures Arts and Sciences Library in Los Angeles.

57 For example, the *Motion Picture Almanac* (1985: 431) lists five firms under the category "Checking Theater Attendance."

58 See Sidley Pictures Corp. (1930: 334).

59 In a similar recent example, Mortimer (2001), finds that revenue sharing between video distributors and retailers was not widely adopted until low-cost computer networking systems to track video rentals were developed.

60 See De Vany and Walls (1996).

61 See, for example, a 24 December 1922 article in the *Morning Telegraph* of New York, in which movie producer C.C. Burr recommends the use of percentage pricing in order to reduce the amount of haggling that occurred in the contracting of films for exhibition.

62 In his examination of contingent compensation in the movie business, Goldberg (1997: 546, 549) suggests it is often intended to reduce haggling over such *ex ante* difficult-to-value items as script treatments and low-budget independent films. In a similar vein, Goldberg and Erickson (1987: 383) find that commission pricing (i.e., revenue sharing) contracts for petroleum coke were much less likely to specify the quality of the product than were fixed-price contracts, because the incentive to engage in costly pre-contract search was reduced. The authors write: "Contracting parties can avoid some of the ex ante costs of gathering information by using commission pricing. . . . Commission pricing reduces the value of special price information and, therefore, permits the parties to develop the information in a more timely, less costly manner."

63 For example, Lewis (1933: 190) writes:

> "Sound pictures were of unknown worth at the box office, though it was obvious from the time of their introduction that they possessed great novelty value. The producers and distributors, on the one hand, wished to prosper from the increased attendance; since they were unable to measure the potentialities of the sound film, however, they could not determine rental increases fairly and accurately. . . . Many exhibitors, on the other hand, wishing not to be burdened with higher flat rentals for pictures of unknown drawing power, acceded to the percentage rental system.

And an exhibitor of the time noted that "the fact that the new pictures were proving very popular and that he had no experience by which to judge their possibilities" convinced him to sign a share contract instead of pressing for the flat rentals that he had formerly preferred (Willard Theater 1928: 593).

References

Allen, D. and Lueck, D. (1992) "Contract choice in modern agriculture: cash rent versus cropshare," *Journal of Law and Economics*, 35: 397–426.

Aggarwal, R.K. and Samwick, A.A. (1999) "The other side of the trade-off: the impact of risk on executive compensation," *Journal of Political Economy*, 107: 65–105.

Balio, T. (1985) "Novelty spawns a small business, 1894–1908," in T. Balio (ed.) *The American Film Industry*, Madison, WI: University of Wisconsin Press, 3–83.

Balio, T. (1993) *Grand Design: Hollywood as a Modern Business Enterprise, 1930–1939*, New York, NY: Scribner and Sons.

Barzel, Y. (1982) "Measurement costs and the organization of markets," *Journal of Law and Economics*, 25: 27–48.

Chisholm, D.C. (1993) "Asset specificity and long-term contracts: the case of the motion picture industry," *Eastern Economic Journal*, 19: 143–155.

Chisholm, D.C. (1997) "Profit-sharing versus fixed-payment contracts: evidence from the motion pictures industry," *Journal of Law, Economics, and Organization*, 13: 169–201.

Clayton Theater (1930) "Selection of sound equipment to be installed, 1928," in *Harvard Business Reports, Vol. 8, Cases on the Motion Picture Industry*, New York, NY: McGraw Hill, 490–499.

Conant, M. (1960) *Antitrust in the Motion Picture Industry*, Berkeley, CA: University of California Press.

Crafton, D. (1997) *The Talkies: American Cinema's Transition to Sound, 1926–1931*, New York, NY: Scribner and Sons.

De Vany, A. and Eckert, R.D. (1991) "Motion picture antitrust: the Paramount cases revisited," *Research in Law and Economics*, 14: 51–112.

De Vany, A. and Walls, W.D. (1996) "Bose–Einstein dynamics and adaptive contracting in the motion picture industry," *The Economic Journal*, 106: 1493–1514.

De Vany, A. and Walls, W.D. (1996) "Uncertainty in the movies: does star power reduce the terror at the box office?" *Journal of Cultural Economics*, 23: 285–318.

Donahue, S.M. (1987) *American Film Distribution*, Ann Arbor, MI: UMI Research Press.

Eswaran, M. and Kotwal, A. (1985) "A theory of contractual structure in agriculture," *American Economic Review*, 75: 352–367.

Franklin, H.B. (1927) *Motion Picture Theater Management*, New York, NY: George H. Doran Co.

Friedberg, A.A. (1993) "The Theatrical Exhibitor," in J.D. Squires (ed.) *The Movie Business Book*, Englewood Cliffs, NJ: Prentice Hall.

Glancy, H.M. (1992) "MGM film grosses, 1924–1948: the Eddie Mannix ledger," *Historical Journal of Film, Radio and Television*, 12: 127–144.

Glancy, H.M. (1995) "Warner Bros. film grosses, 1921–51: the William Schaefer ledger," *Historical Journal of Film, Radio and Television*, 15: 55–73.

Goldberg, V.P. (1997) "The net profits puzzle," *Columbia Law Review*, 97: 524–550.

Goldberg, V.P. and Erickson, J.R. (1987) "Quantity and price adjustment in long-term contracts: a case study of petroleum coke," *Journal of Law and Economics*, 30: 369–398.

Goldstein, Incorporated (1930) "Maintenance of Broadway exploitation theater, 1929," in *Harvard Business Reports, Vol. 8, Cases on the Motion Picture Industry*, New York, NY: McGraw Hill, 417–425.

Gomery, D. (1980) "Hollywood converts to sound: chaos or order?" in E.W. Cameron (ed.) *Sound and the Cinema*, New York, NY: Redgrave Publishing.

Gomery, D. (1985) "The coming of the talkies: invention, innovation, and diffusion," in T. Balio (ed.) *The American Film Industry*, Madison, WI: University of Wisconsin Press.

Gomery, D. (1992) *Shared Pleasures: A History of Movie Presentation in the United States*, Madison, WI: University of Wisconsin Press.

Griffith, R. and Mayer, A. (1957) *The Movies*, New York, NY: Simon and Schuster.

Hallagan, W.S. (1978) "Share contracting for California gold," *Explorations in Economic History*, 15: 196–210.

Hanssen, F.A. (2000) "The block booking of films: reexamined," *Journal of Law and Economics*, 18: 297–328.

Holmstrom, B. and Milgrom, P. (1987) "Aggregation and linearity in the provision of intertemporal incentives," *Econometrica*, 55: 303–328.

Huettig, M.D. (1944) *Economic Control of Motion Picture Industry*, Philadelphia, PA: University of Pennsylvania Press.

Kenney, R. and Klein, B. (1983) "The economics of block booking," *Journal of Law and Economics*, 26: 497–540.

Klein, B. and Leffler, K. (1981) "The role of market forces in assuring contractual performance," *Journal of Political Economy*, 89: 615–641.

Knoeber, C.R. (2000) "Land and livestock contracting in agriculture: a principal–agent perspective," in B. Bouckaert and G. De Geest (eds) *Encyclopedia of Law and Economics, Vol. III*, New York, NY: Edward Elgar Publishing, 1133–1153.

Koszarski, R. (1990) *An Evening's Entertainment: the Age of the Silent Feature Picture, 1915–1928*, New York, NY: Scribner and Sons.

Lafontaine, F. (1992) "Agency theory and franchising: some empirical results," *RAND Journal of Economics*, 23: 263–283.

Lazear, E.P. (1986) "Salaries and piece rate," *Journal of Business*, 59: 405–431.

Leffler, K.B. and Rucker, R.R. (1991) "Transaction costs and the efficient organization of production: a study of timber harvesting contracts," *Journal of Political Economy*, 99: 1060–1087.

Lewis, H.T. (1933) *The Motion Picture Industry*, New York, NY: D. Van Nostrand, Inc.

Litman, B.R. (1998) *The Motion Picture Mega-Industry*, Boston, MA: Allyn and Bacon.

Martin, R.E. (1998) "Franchising and risk management," *American Economic Review*, 78: 954–968.

Merritt, R. (1985) "Nickelodeon theaters, 1905–1914: building an audience for the movies," in T. Balio (ed.) *The American Film Industry*, Madison, WI: University of Wisconsin Press.

Mortimer, J.H. (2001) "The effects of revenue sharing contracts on welfare in vertically-separated markets: evidence from the video rental industry," mimeo, Harvard University.

Murphy, A.D. (1983) "Distribution and exhibition: an overview," in J.D. Squires (ed.) *The Movie Business Book*, Englewood Cliffs, NJ: Prentice Hall, 243–262.

Pathé Exchange, Inc. (1930) "Basis changed from flat rental to percentage for superspecial picture, 1928," in *Harvard Business Reports, Vol. 8, Cases on the Motion Picture Industry*, New York, NY: McGraw Hill, 402–408.

Prendergast, C. (1999) "The provision of incentives in firms," *Journal of Economic Literature*, 37: 7–63.

Ricketson, F.H. (1938) *The Management of Motion Picture Theaters*, New York, NY: McGraw Hill.

Rogers, A. and Allen, F.L. (1947) *I Remember Distinctly*, New York, NY: Harper Brothers

Sappington, D.E.M. (1999) "Incentives in principal–agent relationships," *Journal of Economic Perspectives*, 5: 145–166.

Sedgwick, J. and Pokorny, M. (1998) "The risk environment of film-making: Warner Brothers in the inter-war years," *Explorations in Economic History*, 35: 196–220.

Shaefer Pictures Corp.(1930) "Method of checking receipts under percentage pricing contract, 1929," in *Harvard Business Reports, Vol. 8, Cases on the Motion Picture Industry*, New York, NY: McGraw Hill, 336–340.

Sidley Pictures Corporation (1930) "Sound pictures sold on a percentage basis, 1928," in *Harvard Business Reports, Vol. 8, Cases on the Motion Picture Industry*, New York, NY: McGraw Hill, 330–335.

Steinberg, C.S. (1980) *Film Facts*, New York, NY: Facts on File.

Umbeck, J. (1977) "A theory of contract choice and the California gold rush," *Journal of Law and Economics*, 20: 421–437.

Walker, A. (1979) *The Shattered Silents: How the Talkies Came to Stay*, New York, NY: William Morrow and Co.

Weinstein, M. (1998) "Profit-sharing contracts in Hollywood: evolution and analysis," *Journal of Legal Studies*, 27: 67–112.

Wellington Theater (1930) "Determination of flat rental prices to offer, 1928," in *Harvard Business Reports, Vol. 8, Cases on the Motion Picture Industry*, New York, NY: McGraw Hill, 572–589.

Willard Theater (1930) "Acceptance of percentage motion picture rental, 1928," in *Harvard Business Reports, Vol. 8, Cases on the Motion Picture Industry*, New York, NY: McGraw Hill, 590–595.

5 The block booking of films re-examined[1]

F. Andrew Hanssen

Introduction

Block booking is the selling of motion pictures as a group, or "block." On two occasions the US Supreme Court ruled it illegal: *United States* v. *Paramount Pictures, Inc.* and *United States* v. *Loew's, Inc.*[2] Scholars have debated why movie producers booked films in blocks. The producers claimed that it merely allowed them to economically provide in quantity a product needed in quantity.[3] The Supreme Court disagreed, and banned the practice on the grounds that it was used to force exhibitors to purchase films they did not want in return for receiving those they did. Stigler[4] pointed out the illogic nature of the Supreme Court's argument, and proposed that block booking was a form of price discrimination, akin to other tying arrangements. Kenney and Klein[5] rejected Stigler's explanation, and suggested instead that block booking was intended to resolve an over-searching problem, brought about by the fact that new information about film quality (in the form of early box office receipts) was revealed between the signing of the contract and the time when the exhibitor actually received and had to pay for the film. The Kenney and Klein explanation remains the most generally accepted among economists today.

A review of the actual details of movie contracts sheds new light on the debate. At the time of the *Paramount* decision, major films were rented to major theaters on a revenue-sharing basis. As a result, both producer and exhibitor gained when a film's run length could be adjusted in line with demand. In the movie business, the demand for a particular film is not revealed until it is actually exhibited.[6] Therefore, it would appear optimal to interpret *ex ante* (before demand is revealed) film exhibition obligations *flexibly ex post* (after demand had been revealed). But central to the Kenney and Klein hypothesis (as well as to the Supreme Court and Stigler explanations) is the assumption that block booking contracts had to be – and were – rigidly enforced *ex post*. Block booking could simply not do what each suggests unless post-contractual adjustments in exhibitor obligations were limited significantly.[7]

After investigating the history of the package selling of motion pictures and the way in which block contracts were applied, the conclusion is reached that movie producers were correct and block booking was simply intended to cheaply provide in quantity a product needed in quantity. Non-first-run exhibitors, operating a double feature twice-weekly-change policy, required a large number of films to fill their screens (200 or more per year), and wanted a sure and steady supply. At the same time, producers were able to reduce direct selling costs substantially by contracting for films in volume. Thus, films were sold as a package, with the size of the package depending on the exhibitor's needs. Selling in quantity is relatively common in retailer–wholesaler relationships;[8] what is somewhat unique to the film industry is revenue sharing, which generates different incentives *ex post* than are typically found.

The chapter begins with a review of the Kenney and Klein and quantity selling hypotheses, followed with an examination of the history of the bundling of motion pictures. It emerges that package selling originated in the early days of the silent cinema, when films were sufficiently homogeneous that they were sold by the foot. This, coupled with the fact that no new information was revealed between contracting and release, is consistent with the producer's explanation for block booking, but not with the Kenney and Klein hypothesis (nor with the Supreme Court's or Stigler's, for that matter). The chapter then examines the optimization problem facing movie producers and exhibitors once films became heterogeneous in quality (with the arrival of the feature film, *c.*1912), and find that *ex post* adjustments in exhibition obligations – specifically, the extension of popular showings and the abbreviation (or even cancellation) of unpopular ones – were common, although they are precisely what the Kenney and Klein hypothesis posits block booking was intended to prevent. Furthermore, exhibitors appear not to have taken full advantage of contractually permitted opportunities to redistribute revenue from producers to themselves *ex post*, although the Kenney and Klein hypothesis presumes that only (or at least primarily) the terms of the block contract deterred them from doing so. Finally, a review is conducted of the manner in which film distribution was affected by the ultimate banning of the block-booking practice, and the nature of movie distribution today. In each case, the evidence suggests that the primary objective of block booking was to cheaply provide in quantity a product needed in quantity.

This is not the first analysis to propose that block booking was simply an efficient means of selling in quantity.[9] However, it is the first to tie that hypothesis systematically to an investigation of the history of package selling in the movie business, and to the way in which block booking contracts worked. This chapter does not claim that there was no potential problem of the type discussed by Kenney and Klein in movie distribution. It does claim that block booking was not the means of resolving that problem. While the Kenney and Klein hypothesis may explain package-selling arrangements in other settings, it does not appear to be the reason that films were booked in blocks.

Explanations for block booking

Block booking to prevent oversearching

Kenney and Klein develop their hypothesis in a discussion of how the De Beers Company sells diamonds. De Beers offers diamonds as a package, and only as a package, priced at the average value of the diamonds therein.[10] Buyers are allowed to inspect the package before buying it, but those who reject a package are never invited back. Kenney and Klein suggest that the De Beers system serves to:

1 avoid oversearching by buyers (which would require De Beers to spend more money sorting diamonds), while
2 preventing De Beers from cheating on the quality classification (by allowing customers the right to inspect and reject any given package).

By transacting in this way, De Beers and its customers are able to reduce sorting costs substantially, and to share the savings that result.

Kenney and Klein then apply this model to the booking of films. Their essential point is that, while it is in the *ex ante* interest of both exhibitors and producers to minimize sorting, the incentives differ *ex post*. The blind selling of films saved on inventory costs,[11] but raised the possibility of opportunistic *ex post* search by exhibitors, given that box office receipts from earlier showings were available before films were actually received and paid for (exhibitors could potentially reject those films revealed by audience response to be over-priced).[12] Block booking, by requiring that all films contracted for *ex ante* be exhibited (or at least paid for) *ex post*, resolved that problem. Kenney and Klein (1983: 522–523) write:

> Block booking was used *solely* [emphasis added] as a way to prevent exhibitors from engaging in this post-contractual rejection of over-priced films.... Block booking, or the intentional over-pricing of ex post unexpectedly poor quality films, can be thought of in this context as a means of enforcing blindness, effectively preventing exhibitors from searching out and rejecting the poorest-quality films after first-run results become available.[13]

As evidence of the severity with which block contracts were enforced, Kenney and Klein cite the liquidated damages clause that took effect if an exhibitor rejected a film from the contracted block.[14] They also note that such things as run designation could be used to discipline exhibitors.[15]

Block booking as quantity selling

In their 1927 testimony before the Federal Trade Commission,[16] producers based their defense of block booking on the following:

1   it was wholesaling applied to motion pictures,
2   it reduced the cost of distributing motion pictures, and
3   it simplified the buying problem by allowing exhibitors to obtain a year's supply of pictures in one large purchase.[17]

In short, block booking provided exhibitors with an assured and steady supply while enabling producers to lower direct selling costs. Lewis writes of early package selling in the film industry: "What the distributors sold and what the exhibitors wanted was a *service*, that is, a constant supply of two or three reels of motion picture film furnished two or three or more times a week."[18] Film journalist A.D. Murphy writes: "[T]hen [*c.*1920] and now, a theater owner would go berserk not knowing what [new] film to put on the screen when a film showing had ended its run."[19] An exhibitor trade association noted in 1938: "The exhibitor is in the position of buying a sufficient quantity of quality product for his theater to insure a continuous supply of merchantable pictures. To quit block booking would be to greatly increase the price of pictures."[20] In 1923, Famous Players-Lasky, the production arm of Paramount, experimented with replacing block booking by the individual selling of films. It discovered that the new approach upped the number of sales calls from three-to-four to thirty-to-forty per exhibitor per year. To maintain individual selling, the company estimated that its sales force would have to be quadrupled, sales and overhead costs doubled, and price per picture raised by 40 percent. It instead abandoned the practice.[21]

Testable implications

Kenney and Klein recognize that block booking was desirable for the reasons put forward by movie producers, but focus on the rigid application of the block, which they suggest was necessary to resolve the oversearching problem. They thus posit that *ex ante* block booking contracts had to be enforced rigidly *ex post* (to a fair degree at least) to prevent that problem from arising. The oversearching problem occurred because films were of heterogeneous quality and new information about film quality was revealed between contracting and payment. Therefore, the investigation that follows will investigate:

1   the nature (homogeneous versus heterogeneous) of packaged motion pictures and the process of *ex post* information revelation,
2   the flexibility with which block contracts were applied, and

3   the degree to which contractual terms appear to have been a key factor in deterring *ex post* exhibitor opportunism.

If, over the history of motion picture package selling, it is found that

1   films were heterogeneous and new information about film quality was revealed after contracting but before payment,
2   block contracts were enforced with a fair degree of severity, and
3   exhibitors acted opportunistically to the degree permitted by the written terms of the contract,

the Kenney and Klein hypothesis is supported. If the reverse is found, the producer defense becomes the more plausible explanation.

A history of the block booking of films

The first full-time movie theaters emerged at the turn of the century, and were called "nickelodeons" for their practice of charging five cents admission.[22] Nickelodeons were typically small and uncomfortable, and were located in old dance halls or large shops (not until the late teens would theaters specially constructed for the showing of movies become common). The early movies that the nickelodeons showed were very different from what we see today, or even from what a viewer would see one decade later. First, films were quite brief, typically lasting only a few minutes,[23] and most were documentaries or scenes of landscapes and passing trains.[24] They were typically the product of a single cameraman, who would choose the subject, provide the necessary staging, and edit the result. Advance planning was minimal and no scripts were used, so film quality, as we would now judge it, was very low. This was less important than one might imagine; both quality and subject matter came a distant second to the novelty of seeing places and people in motion.[25] The relative unimportance of the individual film is revealed by the prevalent pricing practice: films were sold by the foot, and nickelodeons purchased the number of feet they required to make up a show.[26]

The principal problem facing nickelodeons was obtaining an adequate supply of films. In order to operate successfully, a nickelodeon had to present three-to-five pictures per program, and to change programs frequently.[27] Few could justify purchasing all the films they required, and instead began to trade films among themselves as local audiences tired of them. The practice was formalized, and a number of film "exchanges" were organized, the first in San Francisco in 1903.[28] The exchanges, typically owned by the exhibitors they served, purchased movies from producers and leased them to exhibitors for about one-fifth the purchase price.

It was at this time and in this context that the first block-selling arrangement emerged – the "program system."[29] Because new productions attracted larger audiences than previously displayed films, producers began to charge higher prices for prints of new releases, and to sell them on a subscription basis only. Each exchange signed a standing order with one or more movie producers for the weekly delivery of the producer's "program"; that is, for at least one print of every new picture the producer made.[30] The system was not controversial; many hours of film were required to meet the need for frequent program changes. Given the relatively undifferentiated nature of the product (several minutes of views of landscapes, passing trains, public speeches, and prize fights), it was simpler and cheaper for all concerned to commit to buy whatever was produced (indeed, they had to, in order to fill screen time) than to choose film prints one-by-one from a catalog.

Between 1905 and 1910, film-makers gradually switched from documentaries to narrative subjects. Narratives were easier to make; the storyline could be geared to the limitations of studio and surrounding locale. However, the quality of individual films remained low. The films often failed to tell clear and comprehensible stories, and instead focused on such things as magic tricks or chases, which could be sold in detachable units.[31] The preferred fare was slapstick comedy, usually violent.[32] The star system had not yet developed; actors were not even credited for their roles, and would not be for several more years.[33] Technology, rather than artistic or narrative skill, was considered central to success, and producers sought to differentiate their pictures by emphasizing the technical superiority of the production and exhibition equipment, rather than the narrative superiority of the films.[34] As late as 1911, writes Ralph Cassady (1959: 371): "there was relatively little preselection of subjects by exhibitors." The General Film Company, which dominated film distribution between 1910 and 1912, described its selling practice as follows:

> no account was taken of individual pictures or of individual actors or directors, and the flat rate per foot applied without regard to the number of separate pictures, the quality or character of the pictures, the size of the theater, or the town or city.[35]

In sum, when the first block-selling arrangements emerged, the movies they contained were highly homogeneous. While audiences may have responded more favorably to some than to others, films were short and quality was uniformly low.[36] As a result, all films were sold at the same price, by the foot, just like a grade of lumber or bushels of wheat. Furthermore, no new information was revealed between the signing of the contract and the receipt of (and payment for) the films. In short, there was no potential oversearching problem of the kind Kenney and Klein suggest motivated block booking.

As time passed, films changed. The biggest innovation was the appearance of the feature film, a multiple-reel effort that lasted one hour or more and was first seen among movies imported from Europe around 1911.[37] Between 1912 and 1914, nearly 300 feature films were distributed in the United States,[38] and by 1915, the feature film was the norm.[39] Feature films were rented, rather than sold outright, and required a concomitant change in distribution and exhibition practices. The nickelodeons, where single-reel films were shown, were generally too small to generate revenue sufficient to support the more expensive and much longer feature films, and were gradually supplanted by larger theaters. However, the exchange system of distribution was based on selling to nickelodeons. To serve these new, larger cinemas, the first national film distributor, Paramount Pictures, was formed in 1914 by the merging of eleven territorial exchanges.[40] It began by formally grading theaters from first- to fifth-run, based on size, location, and condition.[41] First-run theaters exhibited films first; they were located in prime downtown areas, were large and elaborate, and showed new releases for a week or more. Fourth- and fifth-run theaters were located in residential neighborhoods, showed films that had already been on the market for several months, and changed their films several times per week. The second- and third-run theaters fell between, being located in busier areas and exhibiting films for one-to-four days. Theaters within each run designation enjoyed a contractually set period of time that had to pass before a film could be sent to a lower-run theater (the "clearance"). For example, second-run theaters usually had to wait for three weeks beyond the end of the first-run showing to exhibit a film, and so on down the line. Finally, runs and clearances operated within a specified geographic "zone," over which the exhibitor was given exclusive privilege.[42] This categorization of cinemas into runs and stipulation of clearance periods and zones quickly became the industry standard.[43]

The avowed goal of Paramount's first president, William W. Hodkinson, was to establish a system that would guarantee exhibitors a steady flow of product.[44] Paramount initially distributed 104 films per year, enough to fill the playing time of houses that changed programs twice per week. Its variation on the old program system became known as "block booking."[45] Block booking and program selling differed in that the former involved a contract for a precisely-defined "season" (initially three months, eventually a full year), while the latter was a weekly arrangement of indefinite duration. However, in each case, the exhibitor contracted for a producer's entire output, or some part thereof. The evolution from service system to block booking occurred in several steps. Paramount initially provided exhibitors with a simple list from which they could choose as many films as they wanted, with all films rented at the same price (although that price varied with the size of the exhibitor's town).[46] Paramount (and its rivals) then began to set up film blocks around popular actors, and to charge higher prices for the blocks of the more popular stars.[47] Finally, star blocks were abandoned in the early 1920s in favor of the more flexible general blocks that would characterize block booking thereafter – an exhibitor could book as many films as it desired from the producer's entire offering, at prices that varied with the expected popularity of the film.[48] Although producers preferred to sell as large a block (to lease as many of its films) as possible to any given exhibitor, the number of films actually booked was negotiable.[49] However, the greater the number of films an exhibitor contracted for, the better the terms it received.[50]

Blocked films were sold "blind"; exhibitors were not provided with the opportunity to view the films before signing the contract (this was, of course, the practice with the program system as well). "Blind selling" is actually somewhat of a misnomer; exhibitors usually knew the titles, casts, and directors of the films they booked.[51] The rationale for selling blind was straightforward – it saved on inventory costs.[52] However, although the films were *contracted for* blind at the start of the season, they were not *paid for* until actually exhibited, usually some months later.[53] By this time, first-run receipts (at least) were observable, which created the problem described by Kenney and Klein.

The first block-booking contracts (in contrast to later practice) specified *exactly* which films were being leased, and an exhibitor was not required to show any film based on a different script or featuring a different star or director than specified at the time of the agreement (this would change). Furthermore, any film that was believed offensive to local audiences could be removed from the block at no penalty, given approval by an arbitration board.[54] Finally, these early contracts included the right to cancel up to 50 percent of the package at no penalty once the first-run results were available.[55]

Not all film producers sold their films in blocks. A prominent exception was United Artists (UA), formed in 1919, which did not actually produce films but rather distributed the films of various independent but affiliated producers.[56] Kenney and Klein[57] attribute UA's eschewing of block booking to its need for accurate measures of individual film values, so as to provide each producer with the return corresponding to his or her own films. Of course, UA could have sold the films of *each producer* in blocks (for example, a Charlie Chaplin block or a Mary Pickford block); indeed, the early "star" blocks described above were exactly that. However, the individual UA producers made only two or three films per year, and the savings in direct selling costs that would have resulted from block selling were correspondingly tiny. That a lack of savings in direct-selling costs (rather than a need to allocate revenue accurately) would explain UA's rejection of block booking is consistent with the observation that small film-production companies also tended to sell their films individually, despite the fact that they had no need to individually allocate revenue across separate individuals.

The introduction of sound in the late 1920s led to a switch from flat rentals to revenue sharing as the predominant form of exhibition payment,[58] but film prices continued to vary with the expected performance of the film.[59] Revenue sharing was used only for "A" (major) films; low-budget "B" films continued to be leased for flat fees. It was also applied only to first-run through third- or fourth-run theaters no matter what the film.[60]

In sum, by the time of the *Paramount* decision in 1948, the conditions outlined by Kenney and Klein were in place. Did block booking prevent oversearching, by forcing exhibitors to accept *ex post* all (or substantially all) films booked *ex ante*? To say more, I will turn to the nature of the optimization problem between producers and exhibitors, and to the details of block-booking contracts.

The optimization problem and block booking

The challenge facing film producers can be portrayed most straightforwardly by imagining that they are fully integrated into exhibition; many of them did indeed own theaters.[61] Imagine as well that there is only one producer/exhibitor, and it has only one film. It does not know how good or bad that film is – that is, how much revenue it will generate – until the film is actually shown to the general public. By that time, most of the costs associated with the film are sunk; advertising and exhibition costs being the exception. Therefore, the producer/exhibitor shows the film for as long as it can cover its direct exhibition costs.

If the producer/exhibitor has another film in its warehouse, the cost of showing "film 1" is not simply the monetary expenses associated with exhibition, but the lost opportunity to show "film 2" instead. Assume for simplicity that films are of two quality types: "low," which generates $1 per day, and "high," which generates $2 per day. All marginal costs associated with exhibition are 0. The producer/exhibitor then shows one film for a day, and if it generates $1, knows it is of low quality and immediately replaces it. If it generates $2, the exhibitor knows it is of high quality and lets it play.

Of course, a film does not generate a fixed level of revenue indefinitely – the audience for any single film declines over time, as more and more of those who want to see it actually have.[62] For that reason, large numbers of films are produced annually, and we see a regular turnover of features as time passes. Producer/exhibitors have cut-off points at which an old movie will be replaced by a new one. How quickly that cut-off point is reached depends on the film; today, highly popular films play for months, while unpopular ones may disappear in a week. With this additional twist, the optimization problem is the same as in the previous scenario, and the producer/exhibitor will adjust film playing time in line with demand.

If we drop the assumption that producers and exhibitors are one in the same, does the conclusion change? No. Given that films are priced on a revenue-sharing basis, producer and exhibitor still both desire to see popular films play for longer than unpopular ones.[63] They both therefore have the incentive to devise the most efficient (in terms of maximizing the joint profits, or revenues, given the mostly fixed-cost nature of the business) contract possible; they then can divide the rents that accrue.

The story changes somewhat when the possibility that there are several competing film producers is considered. As the audience for a particular film dwindles, the exhibitor still wishes to change it for another film. If that other film is the product of the same company as the original film, then the producer will share the desire; however, if the replacement instead comes from another studio, the producer prefers to see its original film keep playing instead, at least for the duration of the contracted period.

The movie distribution contract thus had to balance the need for flexibility with the risk that the exhibitor would use that flexibility to opportunistically replace the films of one producer with those of another producer, in the manner that Kenney and Klein suggest. How did the contracts do this? As mentioned in the previous chapter, the University of Southern California Film School maintains an archive of material from the Warner Brothers Company. Recently, several hundred boxes of exhibition contracts and various other bits of information relating to film exhibition were discovered in a New York building that was being demolished. Archivists, although still cataloging the find, allowed the author access. The material contained complete 1937–1938 schedules and box office receipts for all first-, second-, and third-run theaters owned by the Warner Brothers Company in the state of Wisconsin – twenty-eight theaters that played collectively more than 5,000 films over that period.[64] Those schedules provide information on the number of days that each film was booked, the number of days that each was actually shown, the revenue earned, and the applicable pricing arrangements.

Tables 5.1–5.3 summarize some of this information. Table 5.1 divides the films into two categories: those booked for a fixed number of days (1,

Table 5.1 Contracting – fixed versus variable number of days

Fixed number of days		Range of days	
Contract (number of days)	Number of films	Contract (number of days)	Number of films
1	18	1–2	71
2	111	1–3	4
3	122	2–3	2,313
4	234	2–4	880
5	23	3–4	1,337
6	3	3–5	98
7	96	4–5	1
Total fixed	607	*Total range*	4,703

Source: Warner Brothers Archive: University of Southern California.

Table 5.2 Number of days played versus contracted time

Contracted days	Actual days played			
	Less than contract	*Equal to contract*	*More than contract*	*Percentage within contract*
1	n.a.	17	1	94.4
1–2	n.a.	59	12	83.1
1–3	n.a.	1	3	25.0
2	30	79	2	71.2
2–3	380	1,823	110	78.8
2–4	74	711	95	80.8
3	25	88	9	72.1
3–4	403	810	124	60.6
4	19	100	115	42.7
3–5	17	79	2	80.6
5	7	15	1	65.2
6	1	2	0	66.7
7	10	83	3	86.5
Total	966	3,869	477	72.8

Source: Warner Brothers Archive: University of Southern California.

2, and so forth) and those booked instead for a range of days (1–2, 2–3, and so forth). The vast majority of films fall into the latter category. This makes sense: *ex ante*, one can predict only very imprecisely how a film will be perceived, but once the showing has begun, new information is learned that may make either extending or abbreviating the performance desirable. The most frequent contract in the sample was a two-to-three-day booking (typical for a second- or third-run theater), although two-to-four and three-to-four were also common. However, the flexibility did not end there: abbreviations and extensions *outside* the contracted range were also allowed. Table 5.2 relates the number of days a film was booked to the number of days it actually played. Only slightly more than 70 percent of films played for their contracted period. A total of 18 percent were taken off the screen more quickly than the contract called for, while 9 percent played for longer.[65]

Thus, films were booked for a range of days rather than a fixed period, and adjustments to that range were frequent. As a result, the runs of popular films could be extended and unpopular ones abbreviated, to the benefit of exhibitor and producer alike.[66] Of course, this meant that neither the exhibitor nor the producer knew *exactly* how many films would be required in the course of a year.[67] Producers therefore had to permit the *ex post* rejection of films from the contracted-for block; otherwise, exhibitors would hesitate to extend popular showings, out of concern that they would run out of time before they ran out of films. And, indeed, *ex post* rejections were allowed. Most prominently, block-booking contracts

Table 5.3 Causes of cancellation (FBO productions, 1927 and 1928)

Category	Cause of cancellation	Percent
1	Picture of same or previous year substituted for contract picture Allowance for gratis advertising Theater did not open Percentage return overestimated Exhibitor availed himself of cancellation privilege in contract Duplication in contracts corrected Error in contract corrected Exhibitor revoked contract before receiving approved copy Same picture previously sold, or now sold, to theater's opposition. Picture resold to same exhibitor on new contract Original pricing unreasonably high Pictures sold for uncontemplated run in exhibitor's area	33
2	Exhibitor has lowered price scale of theater Exhibitor claims picture not of suitable type Exhibitor used picture for shorter run than contracted for Exhibitor was ordered by Film Board to assume contracts left by predecessor Exhibitor refuses to give play dates until receiving price concessions Exhibitor demands cancellation of older product in return for buying new Exhibitor has no open dates Exhibitor is losing money at his theater Picture in question was flop at exhibitor's theater Exhibitor says he has changed type of picture presented by him	15
3	Cancellations arising from acts of FBO (no print available, etc.)	2
4	Theater closed	28
5	New owner refuses to accept responsibility for contracts of predecessor	17
6	Accounting adjustments/miscellaneous	5

Source: Harvard Business Reports (1930).

contained a "cancellation clause," which granted exhibitors the right to refuse a given number of films from the block *after* actual box office receipts were reported.[68] *Variety*, the industry newspaper, even ran weekly reviews of film receipts-by-city intended to help exhibitors decide which films to accept and which to cancel.[69] Film exhibitors could use the cancellation clause to adjust, at the margin, the number of films they actually accepted, and thus vary play dates in line with demand without worrying that they might not be able to show all the films they contracted for. The cancellation clause was a standard feature of block-booked contracts, and 10 percent was the standard minimum.[70] Paramount's early block-booking contracts had included the right to cancel up to 50 percent of the package at no penalty once first-run results were available.[71]

The cancellation clause was, in fact, only one of many sources of *ex post* adjustment of film exhibition obligations. FBO Productions (soon to become part of RKO) conducted a study in which it charted all non-penalized cancellations for two weeks in November 1927, two weeks in February 1928, and one week in March 1928, and categorized them by cause. Table 5.3 reproduces that information.[72] The first cause listed in category 1 makes perfect sense: the substitution of one of FBO's productions for another (presumably an unsuccessful picture for a successful one) – this benefited FBO and exhibitor alike. Cancellations were also permitted where pictures were deemed "unsuitable" to the exhibitor's audience,[73] where the exhibitor wished to trade old pictures for new (more on this below, directly), as well as for more mundane reasons, such as bookkeeping errors, violations of territorial promises, and theaters failing to open. The cancellation clause is listed, too (cause 5 in category 1), but so are shortened runs and lack of open dates, each considered sufficiently frequent occurrences to include them among the causes of cancellations. Interestingly, exhibitors were also permitted to cancel films when the price was simply revealed *ex post* to be too "high" (cause 11 in category 1). This is not as surprising as it might first appear; FBO dealt with the same exhibitors year after year, and repeat dealings provide a substantial incentive to take the interests of the other party to the transaction into account.[74] However, it does not suggest an overwhelming concern with limiting *ex post* search.[75]

Contractual flexibility is further demonstrated by the practice of "rolling over" unshown films into the following season, common in the industry at the time. Most of the rolled-over films were never actually shown, but were instead exchanged for agreements to show newer films. The FBO study[76] states:

> Sometimes these [rolled over films] were pictures which the exhibitors considered of unsatisfactory quality and, therefore, had neglected to select dates for, hoping that an opportunity to cancel them would present itself. Sometimes the exhibitor had contracted for too many pictures, and had not had time to exhibit all of them.

Table 5.4 illustrates this.[77] The top row lists the percentage of the 1927–1928 exhibitor film obligations by the year in which the film was released. As one would expect, the majority of booked films pertained to that same season; however, 14 percent were from the previous year, and 4 percent were from even earlier. As row 2 of Table 5.5 indicates, between July 2 and December 2 of 1927, 42 percent of the obligations from the

Table 5.4 Cancellation by year of release (FBO productions, 1927 and 1928)

	Pictures released 1927–1928	Pictures released 1926–1927	Pictures released 1925–1926	Pictures released 1924–1925
Percentage of outstanding obligations in 1927–1928	82	14	3	1
Percentage canceled during 1927–1928	2	42	63	73

Source: Harvard Business Reports (1930).

1926–1927 season, 63 percent of the obligations from the 1925–1926 season, and 73 percent of the obligations from the 1924–1925 season, were canceled, presumably in return for obligations to show newer films instead. The study notes that: "[E]very member of the sales organization knew that a large proportion of all cancellations consisted of adjustments made to exhibitors to further the sales of the new season's pictures."[78] Such cancellations were a loss for accounting purposes only; the study continues: "They [FBO's management] knew that the exhibitor had only so many days in the year to show pictures and that if all the time was taken up, the mere substitution of new pictures for old pictures was not a real loss of business."[79]

Exhibition contracts were thus extremely flexible, which suggests that block booking was not intended primarily to force exhibitors to respect their *ex ante* exhibition obligations – given the flexibility, it could not have served that purpose. But did exhibitors at least attempt to redistribute income from producers to themselves *ex post* to the extent that contracts allowed? If it is found that they did not, further doubt is shed on the hypothesis that block booking, itself, was necessary to keep oversearching in check.

First, a simple test can be conducted by examining the use of the cancellation clause. If the *ex post* rejection of low-quality films was limited only by the terms of the written contract, the cancellation clause should be evoked consistently up to its maximum (or close thereto). However, if the clause instead existed primarily to allow programs to be adjusted at the margin, it being difficult to predict precisely the number of films needed per year, fewer than the allowable number canceled should be expected. If exhibitors were persistently failing to take advantage of contractually permitted opportunities to rid themselves of the worst-performing films, doubt is shed on the premise that block booking existed solely to prevent such behavior.

In the Warner Brothers archive, a number of contracts can be found from the 1930s and 1940s between the Warner Brothers studio and several independent exhibitors in the Long Island area.[80] These contracts provide information on canceled films, which is summarized in Table 5.5. Eight

Table 5.5 The cancellation clause (Warner Brothers theaters, 1937–1938)

Name	Year	Films actually canceled	Films permitted to be canceled by contract	Difference
Edwards Theater	1933	8	10	2
Hampton Star	1933	3	10	7
Bellaire Theater	1935	6	10	4
East Islip Theater	1935	1	3	2
Bellmore Theater	1936	3	6	3
East Islip Theater	1936	3	6	3
Bellmore Theater	1937	2	6	4
West Hampton	1937	5	5	0
East Islip Theater	1938	1	6	5
Strand Theater	1938	4	6	2
Bellmore Theater	1939	3	5	2
Criterion Theater	1939	5	6	1
East Islip Theater	1939	5	5	0
Strand Theater	1939	5	5	0
Bellmore Theater	1940	4	6	2
Criterion Theater	1940	3	3	0

Source: Warner Brothers Archive: University of Southern California.

theaters altogether are represented, for a total of sixteen theater-years. The third column lists the number of films canceled during that year, the fourth the number of cancellations allowed by contract, and the fifth, the difference between the two. The cancellation clause was used to its fullest in only four out of the sixteen possible cases.[81] Of the ninety-eight possible cancellations, only sixty-one were invoked. Cinemas left three, four, five, and even seven cancellations unexercised, a substantial amount of foregone *ex post* search. Of course, a theater would be unwise to use up its cancellation options prematurely, but the numbers of cancellations left unexercised by the various exhibitors appear to be greater than a simple careful use of cancellation options would suggest. And although the contracts did not give *unlimited* cancellation rights, the actual limitations appear to have been far from binding.

A second test compares the number of days of film initially contracted for to the number of days of playing time actually available. The Kenney and Klein hypothesis suggests that, if given the opportunity to reject films from the block *ex post*, exhibitors will contract *ex ante* for more films than they can actually use.[82] At the extreme, one can imagine an exhibitor booking *all* available films, and simply keeping those revealed *ex post* to be the best. Of course, cancellation privileges were not unlimited; nonetheless, if it is indeed *solely* (or even primarily) the terms of the block contract that prevent this form of oversearching, theaters would have engaged in it to the degree that contracts allowed.

Looking for evidence among the Warner Brothers theaters, whose contracts are summarized in Tables 5.1 through 5.3, the number of days of film actually exhibited (which represents the amount of showing time available) are compared to the number of days of film booked at the start of the season. Because most contracts were for a range rather than a fixed number of days (see Table 5.1), the number of available days are compared to the minimum and maximum days contracted for, as indicated by the low end and the high end of the agreed range, from which it is possible to conclude that overbuying occurred if the minimum *ex ante* contractual obligation was greater than the number of available days. The results are shown in Table 5.6. The sample consists of the twenty of the twenty-eight theaters for whom the entire 1937–1938 season's bookings are available.[83] As the top row shows, although there were 12,299 available days among all these theaters during 1937–1938, only 10,812 days of films (minimum) were booked – certainly not evidence of overbuying. The totals for the individual theaters are listed on the following rows.[84] For only four of the twenty cinemas was there overbuying (in the sense of booking a minimum greater than the available number of days), and in two of those cases, the overbuying was by less than 3 percent. In three of the twenty cases there was actually "underbuying." It appears that cinemas were passing up contractually permitted opportunities to behave in the way that Kenney and Klein posit block booking was necessary to deter.

Table 5.6 Days bought versus days available (Warner Brothers theaters, 1937–1938)

Theater	Days booked (minimum)	Days booked (maximum)	Days available
Total	10,812	15,394	12,299
Egyptian	672	988	683
Garfield	616	947	679
Gateway	408	553	570
Kenosha	560	791	683
Lake	602	871	685
Majestic	467	677	551
Milwaukee	736	1,038	669
Mirth	559	821	639
National	687	971	633
Oshkosh	458	679	590
Princess	694	1,079	679
Rex	442	615	653
Rialto	394	558	613
Sheboygan	546	773	687
Uptown	612	939	680
Venetian	538	756	677
Vogue	526	763	595
Warner 1	659	659	656
Warner 2	636	916	677

Source: Warner Brothers Archive: University of Southern California.

Finally, as noted above, it is clear (given revenue sharing) that a producer benefits when showings of its films can be adjusted in line with demand, *except* if exhibitors use that contractual flexibility to replace the producer's own films with those of its rivals. In other words, *intra*-producer flexibility was desirable as far as producers were concerned, while *inter*-producer flexibility was not. The contracts did not specify between them. Which was occurring?

Table 5.7 compares days booked to days actually played by each of the major film studios for all twenty-eight Warner Brothers cinemas. For each of the eight producers, actual days played were in excess of the minimum number booked. For five of the eight, days played were between 15 and 20 percent above the minimum booked, while United Artists and Universal were between 24 and 28 percent above (each sold substantially fewer days of film).[85] The smallest gap between minimum days booked and days played is for Warner Brothers, but since Warner Brothers owned the cinemas, attempts at *ex post* opportunism do not appear a likely explanation.

In short, there is little in the way that contracts were applied to support the Kenney and Klein hypothesis. First, substantial *ex post* substitution away from poorly performing films was allowed (as revenue sharing would lead one to expect), while Kenney and Klein suggest that block booking existed to *prevent* exhibitors from doing this. Second, exhibitors evidently failed to take advantage of contractually permitted opportunities to oversearch, suggesting that the specific terms of the block contracts were not a binding constraint on such behavior.

The aftermath of the *Paramount* decision

What happened once block booking was banned – what took its place?[86] The question is not as straightforward as it sounds, because block booking

Table 5.7 Days bought versus days played by producer (Warner Brothers theaters, 1937–1938)

	Days booked (minimum)	*Days booked (maximum)*	*Days played*
Columbia	1,337	2,055	1,531
MGM	2,293	3,214	2,659
Paramount	2,104	3,059	2,382
RKO	1,635	2,280	1,872
Twentieth Century Fox	1,980	2,856	2,367
United Artists	622	834	769
Universal	877	1,445	1,119
Warner Brothers	2,253	3,036	2,346

Source: Warner Brothers Archive: University of Southern California.

was only one of several practices outlawed by the *Paramount* decision. Movie producers were also required to sell off affiliated theaters, forbidden from entering into franchise arrangements with other theaters, and prohibited from maintaining any fixed system of runs, clearances, and zoning. And there were changes in other things, as well, the most significant being the rise of television. What can be observed in the aftermath of the *Paramount* decision is that the number of films produced fell – in particular, studios stopped making the "B" movies that had supported double features. Movie attendance fell as well.[87]

Despite these changes, producers and exhibitors faced the same challenge as before: getting films to theaters in the right quantities. In the immediate aftermath of the *Paramount* decision, producers experimented with leasing films through competitive bids.[88] The attempts met with many complaints. One exhibitor commented: "[B]uying one picture at a time is a killer. If you are an individual operator, you have to be on the roam maybe five days a week and then try to run the theater at night." Another exhibitor said: "What is the difference if we buy them one at a time or buy them together; we still have to play them all."[89] Conant[90] writes that, after block booking was banned, "[m]any exhibitors ... found negotiating for each picture individually too time consuming and preferred to buy films in groups."

Competitive bidding was used primarily in competitive areas; in "non-competitive" areas (where a single theater served a well-defined audience) producers could still lease in blocks if the theater so requested, and it usually did. In fact, even in competitive areas, block booking was permissible if all theaters agreed.[91] As Simon Whitney[92] notes: "As late as 1958 about half the theaters [in competitive areas] leased some of their films in groups – for the labor of buying would otherwise have been impossibly heavy – although they signed an individual contract for each." Interestingly, the Allied Association of Motion Picture Exhibitors, a trade association that supported the Department of Justice's crusade to force the divorcement of production and exhibition, was so unhappy with the disappearance of package selling that it sponsored its own plan. Under that plan, 2,400 theaters would have contracted with an independent producer to make a feature film for them each month; a revival of block booking, for which the Justice Department granted an exemption.[93]

The movie distribution business is somewhat different today, in large part because of the rise of the multiplex (the many-screened cinema).[94] Rather than a detailed system of runs, movie studios now release their films widely all at once, on what is called the "national break."[95] A "general" (or broad) release entails opening a film on 2,000 or more screens at once, while a "limited release" involves 500–1,000 screens, with plans to open more later if popular response warrants.[96] Films continue to be leased on a percentage-of-gross revenue basis.[97] As before, revenue sharing means that both producer and exhibitor benefit when the most popular films get the most screen time.[98] The multiplex now allows cinemas to juggle films, so that seats and screen-time more closely conform to demand. A particularly popular picture may open on two or more screens at once, and then be shifted to smaller screening rooms as the audience dwindles over time.

What is the contracting process? Producers provide exhibitors with annual release sheets, which list movie titles, plot descriptions, casts, and projected release dates for the coming year.[99] Delays occasionally occur, but a film is typically locked into a particular release period (summer, Thanksgiving/Christmas, and so forth) about four months in advance. Exhibitors then rough out a tentative schedule. Because how long a picture shows depends, as always, on how well it is received, the schedule remains very imprecise until quite close to the opening date. Many states require producers to screen their films before offering them for contract; this is typically done two-to-four weeks before the anticipated release. Once the film has been screened, the exhibitor receives a call from the producer's salespeople naming that date and specifying the relevant terms: the percentage-of-gross to be charged and the number of weeks to be committed to.[100] Each week, exhibitors examine the previous week's gross and decide which films to keep and which to replace with the newly available films. They then inform the studios' salespeople. The films are ordered on Monday or Tuesday, and the print arrives the following Thursday, in time for Friday's opening (most films open on Friday). No written agreement accompanies the print;[101] the long-term nature of the relationship again means that each understands its obligations and has little incentive to breach them.[102]

Thus, although the oversearching problem has largely disappeared (because films are released everywhere at once), the prevailing practice bears a remarkable resemblance to the old block-booking system. Just as in the days of block booking, theaters work with the same producers year after year, contracting for roughly the same number of films. Serious contract negotiations occur once per year at most. Films are accepted as they are released, and play a variable amount of time, depending on demand. A film may occasionally be refused altogether if its anticipated performance is sufficiently poor – parallel to block booking's cancellations. But, by and large, most of what is produced gets played without movie-by-movie haggling. The major challenge remains getting films to exhibitors in large and regularly changing numbers at low cost.

Conclusion

Most analyses of contractual practice focus on a single dimension of a contracting problem. It might be more reasonable to suppose that contractual clauses serve multiple purposes. The question would then be not what single contracting problem explains a particular practice, but rather which of many problems was the practice's primary concern.

This chapter has investigated the block booking of films. Several explanations for block booking have been put forward, ranging from the Supreme Court's determination that it allowed movie companies to force exhibitors to buy films they didn't want, to Kenney and Klein's contention that it resolved a measurement problem that would have led exhibitors to opportunistically reject films *ex post* from a package priced at *ex ante* average value. The Kenney and Klein explanation is the one most accepted among economists today. However, the problem that Kenney and Klein describe did not exist when block booking first developed; the block-booking contract as applied was much more flexible than a primary concern with that problem would suggest, and exhibitors did not appear to take advantage of contractually permitted opportunities to act in ways that block booking was posited necessary to deter. Instead, the way the practice emerged and the manner in which it was used support the hypothesis that block booking was simply an efficient quantity-selling arrangement, as movie producers maintained in their defense.

All this is not to assert that potential exhibitor oversearching was not a problem that needed to be dealt with, but simply that block booking was not the means of doing so. What might have combated that problem? In the first place, there *was* substantial *ex post* substitution of poorly performing films for better performing films, but with the blessing of producers – because of revenue sharing, producer and exhibitor both gained when film runs could be adjusted in line with demand. However, the flexibility in exhibition contracts went further than that; for example, producers released exhibitors from obligations to show pictures when the price was proved *ex post* to be "unreasonably high," or if exhibitors simply had "no open dates." Such things are exactly what Kenney and Klein hypothesize that block booking was intended to prevent, but, in fact, producers had little to gain by taking advantage of exhibitors. And the reverse was true as well; there were a small enough number of producers given the number of films required that few exhibitors could face the loss of a studio's entire output with equanimity, and things such as run designation were central to a theater's profitability and fully under producer control.[103] In short, there were many potential weapons to be used against exhibitors who abused the flexibility of block-booking contracts.

Kenney and Klein recognize that repeat dealings are important, although they do not apply that observation to the oversearching problem.[104] It is clear that whatever the mechanism used to deter *ex post* opportunism – building reputations for honesty, penalizing errant exhibitors, or applying blocks rigidly – there is a cost involved. The cost of rigidly applying block booking would have been a serious decline in the ability of producers and exhibitors to adjust run lengths *ex post* in line with demand. The fact that such adjustments were common and blocks, as a result, very flexibly applied suggests that other mechanisms were used instead. In short, it appears highly unlikely that the problem outlined by

Kenney and Klein was a significant factor in the decision to sell films in blocks.

Notes

1 This chapter was published originally in the *Journal of Law and Economics*, Vol. XLIII (October 2000: 395–426). For their very helpful comments on this chapter, I would like to thank Rob Fleck, Ron Johnson, Andy Kleit, Francine LaFontaine, Dean Lueck, Scott Masten, Kathy Terrell, Doug Young, and seminar participants at the American Economic Association meetings in New York and at the Western Economics Association meetings in San Diego, as well as at Montana State University. I would also like to thank Lester Telser, who first brought block booking to my attention in his class on the theory of the core. Finally, I would like to thank two anonymous referees.

2 *United States* v. *Paramount Pictures, Inc.*, 334 U.S. (1948) and *United States* v. *Loew's, Inc.*, 371 U.S. (1962). The *Paramount* case dealt with contracts between filmmakers and film exhibitors, while *Loew's* involved the sale of old films to television stations.

3 See the arguments made by the various defendant producers in the *Paramount* case, such as Loew's (76), Paramount (107), RKO (134), Columbia (155), Universal (174), Warner Brothers (213) and Twentieth Century Fox (234), as well as the discussion to follow.

4 Stigler (1968: 5).

5 Kenney and Klein (1983).

6 De Vany and Eckert (1991). See also De Vany and Walls (1996) and De Vany and Walls (1997) for a more detailed examination of the optimization problem faced by film producers and exhibitors.

7 Kenney and Klein (1983: 524–527). Although Kenney and Klein discuss the role of revenue sharing, they do not explore its implications for block booking, focusing instead on its effect on each party's incentive to provide such complementary inputs as clean theaters (exhibitors) and high-quality films (producers). Contingent pricing, they conclude, economized on brand name capital, and so was used instead of flat fees. By focusing exclusively on the margins for cheating, Kenney and Klein overlook the fact that contingent pricing also aligns producer and exhibitor incentives as to *which* films should be shown, and for how long.

8 Retailers typically sign annual contracts with suppliers that specify various amounts for monthly delivery (the retailer can wait and submit individual orders as needed if it prefers, but, not surprisingly, the price paid per unit is higher). The uncertain nature of movie demand makes it comparable to the fashion clothing business: once fashion sellers are able to observe which lines sell and which do not, they adjust price and quantity accordingly; see Lazear (1986) and Pashigian (1988) for models of price adjustment, and Urban (1998) for a model of shelf-space allocation. See also Porteus (1990).

9 See Cassady (1959) and De Vany and Eckert (1991: 83–84). Cassady (1959: 382) writes: "block booking developed out of the need of distributors for a more efficient method of selling films."

10 All except the largest stones, which are sold on an individual basis for a nego-tiated price.

11 Kenney and Klein (1983: 521). The alternative to agreeing to blocks of films that had not been completed was to keep a season's worth of films (or part thereof) in a vault until exhibitors were ready to buy.

12 Kenney and Klein (1983: 522–523). Exhibitors were then organized by "runs,"

with first-run theaters showing films several weeks (or several months) before everyone else. See the discussion that follows for more detail.

13 For films sold on a revenue-sharing basis, the threat was not actually that "over-priced" films would be rejected ("over-priced" is hard to understand in the context of revenue sharing), but rather that films would be "overbought"; more would be booked *ex ante* than could be shown *ex post*, with the worst (as indicated by box office receipts) subsequently rejected.

14 Kenney and Klein (1983: 523). In fact, as is argued later, that penalty only applied to films canceled above and beyond a permitted amount. The existence of cancellation clauses, allowing a number of penalty-free cancellations from the block, was not recognized by Kenney and Klein. Penalty-free cancellations were also granted for a variety of other reasons.

15 Kenney and Klein (1983: footnote 70). Of course, the existence of this retaliatory mechanism raises questions as to why a rigid enforcement of blocks was necessary to overcome the oversearching problem in the first place.

16 *In the Matter of Famous Players-Lasky Corporation, et al.*, 11 FTC 187 (1927).

17 See Lewis (1933) and Koszarski (1990).

18 Lewis (1933: 7). A theater following a "one-change" policy (changing programs once per week) would need approximately fifty films per year if it showed single films and 100 if it showed double features. More common was a two- or a three-change policy, which meant that the theater showed a film for two to four days, and thus required 150–250 films per year.

19 Murphy (1992).

20 Ricketson (1938: 30). An industry spokesman appearing before the Supreme Court testified: "I can sell 40 pictures at $10 apiece if I can sell him 40. By selling one at a time (or selling a number of smaller groups) I cannot sell him at $400. He could buy the whole package at $400, throw half the films away, and be better off than if he'd had to buy them individually." Quoted in Chambers (1941).

21 Lewis (1933: 153).

22 See Merritt (1985) and Robert C. Allen (1985) for discussions of the nickelodeon.

23 When *The Great Train Robbery* was released in 1903, it astounded audiences by lasting a full fifteen minutes.

24 The records of the Biograph company indicate that, between 1900 and 1906, 1,035 of 1,809 films produced were non-narrative; see Spehr (1980: 421). As late as midway through the first decade, documentaries were still a staple; Allen (1985: 75–76) notes that documentary films (travelogues and newsreels) made up half of all American films produced between 1904 and 1906.

25 Photographs of early nickelodeons, such as in Merritt (1985: 84, 90) and Gomery (1992: 121) show either no film titles advertised, or the title listed on small placards, while large letters were used for such general announcements as "High Class Motion Pictures & Illustrated Songs," and "Motion Picture Subjects, 5 cents."

26 See, for example, Balio (1985a: 16) and Donahue (1987: 7).

27 The nickelodeons switched films at least weekly, and sometimes several times per week. The typical "show" consisted of a number of short films, lasting altogether for between thirty minutes and one hour. The audiences were also often treated to live entertainment: singing, music, and other performances. See Merritt (1985).

28 By 1907, between 125 and 150 exchanges operated around the country. See Balio (1985a: 17).

29 The following is from testimony given before the Federal Trade Commission in the 1920s: "The practice of block booking, in its essential substance, has

been rooted in the industry since its inception. The practice is directly evolved from the old service idea, under which entire programs were furnished to exhibitors, and which is frequently referred to as the 'program system'" (Lewis 1933: 147).

30 Section 5 of a typical exchange agreement specified that the exchange would receive "one or more prints of each and every subject regularly produced and offered for release by such manufacturer or importer." See Cassady (1959: 336), quoting from the court record.

31 A 1911 trade paper critic commented of one-reelers that: "There is too much evidence of 'cutting up' and 'cutting off' to the detriment of the continuity of the pictures, and this slaughtering of the subject only increases the ambiguity of the whole." Quoted in Janet Staiger (1985: 176).

32 The following plot descriptions pertain to popular one-reelers of 1908: two Irishmen at a lodge initiation fight each other with bricks and dynamite (*Casey Joined the Lodge*); two boys awaken a daydreaming policeman by setting him on fire (*A Policeman's Dream*); a political candidate has dirt and paste thrown at him, then his wife beats him (*The Candidate*); partygoers fall into a young gentleman's room when the floor caves in, and are beaten (*Noisy Neighbors*). See Merritt (1985: 88).

33 In fact, cameras were typically fixed in a static medium–long shot that left the faces of the actors difficult to distinguish. See Catherine E. Kerr (1990: 388).

34 For example, in 1909 the *New York Dramatic Mirror* sang the praises of the Selig Film Company as follows:

> There are several big dynamos to supply electric light and power, and in the far corner of the plant is a machine shop where inventors are constantly at work making improvements in projection and other details.... There is a most efficient staff and work proceeds in a most systematic manner. There is ... nothing wanted to make the best moving picture shows made anywhere on earth.
>
> Quoted in Kerr (1990: 392).

35 Lewis (1933: 7).

36 In fact, the films were sometimes so bad that some vaudeville theaters used them as "chasers"; they were played when the operators wanted to clear the house for a new group of patrons. See Allen (1985: 71).

37 Staiger (1985: 188).

38 Balio (1985b: 111).

39 D.W. Griffith's classic, *The Birth of a Nation*, opened on March 3, 1915 in New York and ran there for 802 straight performances. It broke box office records wherever it was shown (see Balio 1985b: 112–113).

40 Two alternatives preceded Paramount: selling film rights territory-by-territory to buyers who rented them out for a flat fee (the "state rights" method), and film exhibitions arranged by the producers themselves, who booked theaters on a one-off basis for a percentage of the gross revenues ("road shows"). Often, the film would be road shown in big cities, and then the rights would be sold territory-by-territory for the rest of the country. While these approaches worked fine for individual pictures, they were too cumbersome and costly for the distribution of film in quantity. See Balio (1985b).

41 Why Paramount first did this is open to question. It may have been a variation on the old vaudeville booking process; a new act performed by established artistes would open at a flagship theater and then move to other houses in order of prominence. See Allen (1985).

42 Zoning eventually became quite complex, and even gave theaters in certain cities prior rights over those in other cities. See Huettig (1944: 125–127).

43 It was this system that created the oversearching problem: first-run results were available before subsequent-run cinemas received and paid for films.

44 See Berg (1989: 49).

45 See Balio (1985b: 117).

46 For example, in 1917 an exhibitor in a town of 10,000 could book any given movie for $37.50 for one day, $45 for two days, and so forth, while an exhibitor in a town of 5,000 could book the same pictures for $25 for one day, $30 for two, and so forth. See "*Federal Trade Commission* v. *Famous Players-Lasky Corp., et al.*: Block Booking as Eliminating Competition, 1923–1928," *Harvard Bus. Rep. V. 8, Cases on the Motion Picture Industry* (1930: 231).

47 Ibid., p. 232. The following description of "star blocks" was given during testimony before the Federal Trade Commission: "The names of the particular pictures were still of no importance and the pictures were sold merely by the series or blocks in which the same star appeared.... [T]he exhibitor bought, for example, 6 Pickfords, 6 Harts, or 6 Clarks."

48 The 1939 MGM product offering, for example, consisted of four "super-specials" on which the rental rate was 40 percent of revenue; ten "lesser bombshells" with a 35 percent rental rate; another ten films at a 30 percent rate, and twenty B-pictures, mostly at flat rentals (these were used primarily as second features). See *Fortune*, Vol. 20, pp. 25–30, August 1939. Ricketson (1938: 32–33) lists the following hypothetical package of 52 pictures as typical: four pictures at 35 percent of gross receipts (which would revert to 30 percent if the theater did not earn one-third of film rental paid on each individual picture as profit), six pictures at 30 percent (falling to 25 percent under the same conditions), twelve pictures at 25 percent, and thirty pictures at flat rentals. He notes that the charges might fluctuate by plus-or-minus 5 percent, depending upon the size and bargaining power of the exhibitor.

49 Cassady (1933: 120) has described block booking as an "all or none" agreement but this was clearly untrue. For example, only half of all contracting exhibitors took the entire 1939 MGM line mentioned in the *Fortune* article (see the previous footnote), while fewer than 20 percent of 20th Century-Fox's 1938–1939 exhibitors accepted its full block of fifty-two films (1940 Congressional hearings referenced in Kenney and Klein (1983: 518). And of 322 separate Paramount contracts signed with plaintiff exhibitors for the 1920–1921, 1921–1922, and 1922–1923 seasons, only thirty-one were for the entire block of Paramount films offered, while ninety-eight were for a single picture each. See Lewis (1933: 157) citing testimony before the Federal Trade Commission.

50 See, for example, Federal Trade Commission (1930: 228). This also suggests a selling cost-based explanation for block sales.

51 In fact, even had it been possible to preview the films, exhibitor choice would have been "blind" in the sense that audience response would have remained unknown.

52 Kenney and Klein (1983: 521).

53 For films rented on a percentage-of-gross revenue basis, payment was due upon the last day of showing, or at the end of each day, if the producer so desired. For films rented out for a flat-fee payment was officially due three days before receipt of the print, but in fact was also often paid after the showing. This information is taken from contracts between the Warner Brothers Company and various independent theaters, as well as from descriptions in Ricketson (1938: 30–31) and Lewis (1933: 181–200).

54 See Donahue (1987: 22). Of course, the arbitration process may have been costly.

55 See Huettig (1944: 120).

56 The most prominent of those producers in UA's early days were its founders: Charlie Chaplin, Mary Pickford, Douglas Fairbanks, and D.W. Griffith.

57 Kenney and Klein (1983: 521).

58 Hanssen (this volume; Chapter 4) for an investigation of that change.

59 For example, the 1937 MGM film *Test Pilot* with Clark Gable, Myrna Loy, and Spencer Tracy rented out at 40 percent to the producer, while the same company's 1937 film *Man Proof*, also with Myrna Loy but co-starring lesser lights Franchot Tone and Walter Pidgeon, instead went for only 30 percent (information taken from Warner Brothers booking schedules; see below). "Sliding percentages," whereby the rental rate increased as revenue increased, were also occasionally used.

60 The reason for the first exception was that "B" films were primarily second features – double features were standard in the 1930s and 1940s – and showing two films on a revenue-sharing basis would have made it costly to determine the individual contributions of each. Small theaters did not lease on a revenue-sharing basis because the cost of monitoring to ensure honest reporting of attendance was too high relative to the revenue produced. Hannsen (2002) and Chapter 4 in this book.

61 See De Vany and Eckert (1991) and De Vany and Walls (1996, 1997) for a more detailed discussion of the optimization problem. See Huettig (1944: 31–38) for a brief history of the integration of production and exhibition.

62 See De Vany and Eckert (1991).

63 In fact, the long-term incentives should be the same even with flat rental fees, because the amount an exhibitor will pay depends upon the amount of revenue that will be generated. However, in the short run, a producer has a stronger incentive to extend a poor film's run if it is receiving a flat payment than if it receives a share of the revenue.

64 Like most producers, the majority of Warner Brothers cinemas were first-run; however, they retained holdings of second- and third-run theaters in Wisconsin. See Beaver (1983: 146–151) for a short history of Warner Brothers. The booking practices for these producer-owned chains do not appear to have differed in important ways from those of independent chains; see discussions in Lewis (1933: 71–75). For example, Lewis (1933: 110) describes how RKO's own theater division had the right to refuse to accept any RKO film that it considered "unsuitable" for exhibition.

65 There were 575 days of showings in excess of the original contract period, and 1,285 days of shortened showings.

66 I examined the relationship between days played and revenue earned by estimating a simple Ordinary Least Squares regression, with per-day revenue as my dependent variable, the number of days the film played as my right-hand-side variable of interest, and a dummy variable for weekend or holiday, the run designation, and theater dummies for each of the twenty-eight cinemas as control variables. Only "A" films – those booked on a percentage-of-gross basis – were included in the sample. I found each extra day of showing to be associated with $86 of additional per day revenue, nearly one-quarter of that of the average (the average film in this data set grossed $379 per day). The coefficient had a t-statistic of nearly 17.

67 It also meant that contracts had to be quite vague on exactly *when* an exhibitor received a given film, since if earlier-run theaters varied the number of days they kept a film (as they evidently did) no one could know for sure when that film would be ready for subsequent-run use. And so the contracts specified no dates, but instead promised simply to provide the exhibitor with fifteen days' notice of available play times and a thirty-day window within which it could choose its preferred dates. At regular intervals, the producer's

"booker" sent out notices of availability, which listed the current productions contracted for by each exhibitor and the dates available for showing. See Lewis (1933: 58) for a description.

68 The cancellation clause is discussed in Donahue (1987: 25), Huettig (1944: 120), and Whitney (1982: 167).

69 See Cathy Klaprat (1985: 355). Franklin (1927: 27), President of Fox Studio's West Coast theater holdings, described first runs as "affording independent theater owners an opportunity to gauge the public reaction to pictures presented, and serving as a guide to value." Perusing old issues of *Variety*, one finds such headlines as "*Narrow Street*, 2nd week, $13,650; Only Fell Off $200 at Piccadilly," "Women Off *Greed*; $9000 in Washington," and "*Narrow Street* Liked But Got $8000; *So Big* at $12,000," all from the January 21, 1925 issue. In the December 11, 1934 issue, one reads, "*Divorcee* Big in Denver, $10,000," "*Monte Cristo* Holds Second Week in Birmingham Despite All," and "*Veil* $8000 in Seattle; *Life* $5400." The articles list revenue totals for first-run showings in all the major cities around the United States.

70 The following is taken from the Standard Exhibition Contract (see *The 1929 Film Daily Yearbook*: 801–815):

> **Twentieth:** The Exhibitor shall have the right to exclude from the contract up to but not exceeding ten percent of the total number of such photoplays, but only if the Exhibitor shall give the Distributor written notice to such effect at any time not later than fourteen (14) days before the date fixed for the exhibition.

71 See Huettig (1944: 120).

72 See FBO Productions, Inc.: *Decrease of Number of Cancellations in Contract*, 1927, 391, 399–400 (1930), exhibits 3 and 4.

73 This was specified in the Standard Exhibition Contract, twenty-first clause (see *The 1929 Film Daily Yearbook*: 801–815).

74 See Klein and Leffler (1981). This was done in other ways as well; for example, De Vany and Eckert (1991: note 116) point out that film companies made *ex post* adjustments to rental terms when a block of films performed particularly badly – see also Cassady (1958: 176–177). Producers continue to do such things today – see next section and Kenney and Klein (1983: 530).

75 The categorization is insufficiently fine to determine what percentage of cancellations are explained by each cause individually; however, one can get a sense of the importance of the cancellation clause alone. If categories 3 through 6 are ignored (which involve causes of a different kind), category 1, which includes the cancellation clause, accounts for 69 percent of all cancellations. This means that, even if the cancellation clause explains as many as three-quarters of the total in category 1, it still accounts for only half of all the cancellations that occurred during the period. FBO's sales manager estimated that total cancellations amounted to 17 percent of sales on average; see FBO Productions (1930: 395).

76 FBO Productions (1930: 395–396).

77 FBO Productions (1930: 392–393), exhibit 1.

78 FBO Productions (1930: 395).

79 FBO Productions (1930: 396).

80 The boxes also contained contracts from the 1950s (by which time block booking was no longer used) and contracts from earlier periods that made no mention of the cancellation clause.

81 The reader will note the absence of negative values; of instances when more cancellations occurred than was contractually permitted. This may be due to the nature of the data. There are seven cinemas that I have not included in

Table 5.5 for which I have information on the number of films booked and the number canceled, but not information on the total number of cancellations allowed by contract. In each case, the number of films actually canceled was in excess of 10 percent of the total number originally booked. If 10 percent was indeed the contractually specified amount (as it was in nearly all the other instances) those cinemas would have canceled more films than allowed by contract, and thus would list negative values.

82 This is simply "overpricing" in a revenue-sharing context (see footnote 13).

83 "Entire" in the sense that bookings from each of the eight major film companies (Columbia, MGM, Paramount, RKO, Twentieth Century Fox, United Artists, Universal, and Warner Brothers) are available. The other eight theaters are missing information pertaining to particular companies – there would be complete data on all MGM and Paramount bookings, for example, but nothing on RKO bookings.

84 The number of available days varies by theater in part because some cinemas tended to close for several weeks in the summer, in part because not all showings were double features, and in part because cinemas varied in the number of B-films they bought from minor producers to show as second features.

85 United Artists only distributed the films of affiliated producers, while Universal was, along with Columbia, much smaller than the "big five" producers.

86 For discussions of the *Paramount* case and decision, see De Vany and Eckert (1991), Conant (1960), and Cassady (1954). Interestingly, although most exhibitors were apparently happy with the system of block booking (see what follows), the unhappy ones had complained to the court that the fewer the number of films they bought, the higher the per film price they were charged. Producers acknowledged that this was so, but defended themselves on the grounds that the fewer the pictures taken, the higher the selling cost per picture, as the argument that block booking was intended to reduce direct selling costs would suggest. See Federal Trade Commission (1930) for more detail.

87 See Sedgwick, Chapter 7 in this book.

88 Any theater interested in showing a particular film at a particular time in a particular area would submit a sealed bid, and the highest bidder would receive the film. The Court did not actually require a system of competitive bidding, but rather prohibited discrimination against small independent exhibitors. However, the only way to be *completely* sure of avoiding the charge of discrimination was to hold a competitive bid.

89 Both quotations from Whitney (1982: 184).

90 Conant (1960).

91 For example, in 1950, 3,700 theaters chose to book Paramount pictures in blocks with a right to cancel 20 percent; see *Variety*, September 20, 1950: 5.

92 Whitney (1982: 184).

93 The plan never came to fruition; see Whitney (1982: 179).

94 The following draws on conversations with Drew Devlin, President of Clark Film Buying, and Murphy (1992), Reardon (1992), and De Vany and Walls (1996)

95 Some cinemas in smaller towns receive films several weeks after the national release, usually for discounted rental terms. The smallest theaters in the smallest towns still receive films months after the initial opening, and still pay a flat rental fee.

96 See Reardon (1992: 312). *Armageddon*, for example, a high-budget, much-hyped film, was released on 3,000 screens at once. By contrast, *The Full Monty*, a relatively low-budget British film, was originally released on only 500 screens, and those mostly in larger towns. However, as its popularity grew, additional prints were made, and at its peak it was showing on close to 1,000

screens. On rare occasions, an "arty" film may have a single exclusive opening in New York or Los Angeles, and only open nationally once it has garnered sufficient publicity (*Hamlet*, with Mel Gibson, is an example).

97 Rates varying according to (1) the perceived importance of the film (big budget films may charge 70 percent, versus 50 or 60 percent for an average film), and (2) how long the theater plays it (rates typically fall by ten percentage points per week for at least the first three weeks). The percent-of-gross is adjusted upwards for very popular films through the use of an allowance for house expenses known as the "house nut." Most films do not garner revenue sufficient to render that allowance meaningful, but big hits like *Titanic* do.

98 Film contracts even contain "holdover clauses," which require a showing to continue as long as revenue is in excess of a specified amount. Furthermore, as an anonymous referee points out, distributors may permit a run to be abbreviated or a film to be double-billed if the film is performing more poorly than anticipated (this also happened in the days of block booking; see Table 5.3).

99 Production schedules are tracked by industry newspapers, such as *Variety*, and by the National Association of Theater Owners (NATO), the industry's trade organization.

100 These terms are rarely a surprise – big-budget films likely to be highly successful demand the top terms, lesser films lower terms, and so forth.

101 Some studios require exhibitors to sign a master agreement at the start of the year, which specifies standard obligations, while others list those obligations in contracts provided on a film-by-film basis. However, the difference is more apparent than real. Under the master agreement system, an order is followed by a confirmation note specifying the terms agreed to. That note generally arrives well after the film has begun to play, and often after the showing has been completed. The contract system instead follows the order with a contract, but that contract is short and of standard form, and specifies no more new information than the confirmation note (the contracts also arrive well after the film has begun to play). In addition, to protect themselves against law suits, most distributors continue to send out bid letters, and negotiations are carried out in the context of a bidding system even when individual dealings would be preferred by the affected exhibitors (or the theater is the only one in the town). I thank an anonymous referee for pointing this out.

102 Haggling is rare; similar movies entail similar terms, and producers and exhibitors have a long history of collaboration. As A. Alan Friedberg, former Chairman of Loew's Theaters, writes in Squire (1992): "Ours is an industry built on relationships evolving from trust, integrity, and loyalty," and then goes on to describe a series of "quid pro quos" between exhibitor and producer.

103 Producers and exhibitors dealt with each other year after year, with exhibitors buying roughly the same number of films on an annual basis; Kenney and Klein (1983: 521) compare it to a franchise relationship. The lawyer for an exhibitor trade association testified in the *Paramount* hearings: "[T]he relationship rests on a long-time course of business between the two parties [producer and exhibitor] ... and so the two by a course of dealing along those lines built up what somebody has called in his brief a circuitry of friendship. They rely on each other and trust each other in accounting matters as well as in the continued supply of film" (Kenney and Klein 1983: 552–554). Achieving higher-run designations (first, second, and third in particular) usually required substantial investment. Higher-run theater owners were willing to make these investments because the increase in revenue was higher still (Sharp 1969).

104 They suggest that rigid block booking reduced the amount of brand-name capital producers required, rather than, as here, that the prospect of repeat business influenced *exhibitor* incentives, and thus allowed a *flexible* application of block booking.

References

Allen, R. (1985) "The movies in vaudeville: historical context of the movies as popular entertainment," in T. Balio (ed.) *The American Film Industry*, Madison, WI: University of Wisconsin Press.

Balio, T. (1985a) "Novelty spawns a small business, 1894–1908," in T. Balio (ed.) *The American Film Industry*, Madison, WI: University of Wisconsin Press.

Balio, T. (1985b) "Struggles for control, 1908–1930," in T. Balio (ed.) *The American Film Industry*, Madison, WI: University of Wisconsin Press.

Beaver, F. (1983) *A History of the Motion Picture*, New York, NY: McGraw Hill.

Berg, A.S. (1989) *Goldwyn*, New York, NY: Knopf.

Cassady, R. (1933) "Some economic aspects of motion picture production and marketing," *Journal of Business*, 6: 113–131.

Cassady, R. (1958) "The impact of the Paramount decision on motion picture distribution and price making," *Southern California Law Review*, 31: 150–180.

Cassady, R. (1959) "Monopoly in motion picture production and distribution, 1908–1915," *Southern California Law Review*, 32: 325–390.

Chambers, R. (1941) "Block booking; blind selling," *Harvard Business Review*, 19: 496–507.

Conant, M. (1960) *Antitrust in the Motion Picture Industry*, Berkeley, CA: University of California Press.

De Vany, A. and Eckert, R. (1991) "Motion picture antitrust: the Paramount cases revisited," *Research in Law and Economics*, 14: 51–112.

De Vany, A. and Walls, W.D. (1996) "Bose–Einstein dynamics and adaptive contracting in the motion picture industry," *The Economic Journal*, 106: 1493–1514.

De Vany, A. and Walls, W.D. (1997) "The market for motion pictures: rank, revenue, and survival," *Economic Inquiry*, 35: 783–797.

Donahue, S. (1987) *American Film Distribution*, Ann Arbor, MI: UMI Research Press.

"*Federal Trade Commission* v. *Famous Players-Lasky Corp.* et al. (1930) Block Booking as Eliminating Competition, 1923–28," Harvard Business Reports, Vol. 8, *Cases on the Motion Picture Industry*, New York, NY: McGraw Hill, pp. 226–262.

Franklin, H. (1927) *Motion Picture Theater Management*, New York, NY: George H. Doran Co.

Friedberg, A. (1992) "The theatrical exhibitor," in J. Squire (ed.) *The Movie Business Book*, New York, NY: Simon and Schuster.

Gomery, D. (1992) *Shared Pleasures: A History of Movie Presentation in the United States*, Madison, WI: University of Wisconsin Press.

Hanssen, F.A. (2002) "Revenue-sharing in movie exhibition and the coming of sound," *Economic Inquiry*, 40: 380–402.

Harvard Business Reports, Vol. 8, Cases on the Motion Picture Industry (1930) "FBO Productions, Inc.: decrease of number of cancellations in contract, 1927," New York, NY: McGraw Hill.

Harvard Business Reports, Vol. 8, Cases on the Motion Picture Industry (1930) "Federal Trade Commission *v*. Famous Players-Lasky Corp., *et al.*: block booking as eliminating competition, 1923–28," *Harvard Business Reports, Vol. 8, Cases on the Motion Picture Industry*, New York, NY: McGraw Hill.

Huettig, M. (1944) *Economic Control of the Motion Picture Industry*, Philadelphia, PA: University of Pennsylvania Press.

Kenney, R. and Klein, B. (1983) "The economics of block booking," *Journal of Law and Economics*, 26: 497–540.

Kerr, C. (1990) "Incorporating the star: the intersection of business and aesthetic strategies in early American film," *Business History Review*, 64: 383–410.

Klaprat, C (1985) "The star as a market strategy," in T. Balio (ed.) *The American Film Industry*, Madison, WI: University of Wisconsin Press.

Klein, B. and Leffler, K. (1981) "The role of market forces in assuring contractual performance," *Journal of Political Economy*, 89: 615–641.

Koszarski, R. (1990) *An Evening's Entertainment: The Age of the Silent Feature Picture, 1915–1928*, New York, NY: Scribner and Sons.

Lazear, E. (1986) "Retail prices and clearance sales," *American Economic Review*, 76: 14–32.

Lewis, H. (1933) *The Motion Picture Industry*, New York, NY: D. Van Nostrand Co., Inc.

Merritt, R. (1985) "Nickelodeon theaters, 1905–1914: building an audience for the movies," in T. Balio (ed.) *The American Film Industry*, Madison, WI: University of Wisconsin Press.

Murphy, A.D. (1992) "Distribution and exhibition: an overview," in J. Squire (ed.) *The Movie Business Book*, New York, NY: Simon and Schuster.

Pashigian, P. (1988) "Demand uncertainty and sales: a study of fashion and mark-down price," *American Economic Review*, 78: 936–952.

Porteus, E. (1990) "Stochastic inventory theory," in D. Heyman and M. Sobel (eds) *Stochastic Models (Handbooks in Operations Research and Management Science, Vol. 2)*, Amsterdam: North Holland.

Reardon, D.B. (1992) "The studio distributor," in J. Squire (ed.) *The Movie Business Book*, New York, NY: Simon and Schuster.

Ricketson, F. (1938) *The Management of Motion Picture Theaters*, New York, NY: McGraw Hill.

Sharp, D. (1969) *The Picture Palace and Other Buildings for the Movies*, New York, NY: F.A. Praeger.

Spehr, P. (1980) "Filmmaking at the American Mutoscope and Biograph Company, 1900–1906," *Quarterly Journal of the Library of Congress*, 37: 419–432.

Staiger, J. (1985) "Blueprints for feature films: Hollywood's continuity scripts," in T. Balio (ed.) *The American Film Industry*, Madison, WI: University of Wisconsin Press.

Stigler, G. (1968) "United States v. Loew's Inc.: a note on block booking," in G. Stigler (ed.) *The Organization of Industry*, Chicago, IL: University of Chicago Press.

Urban, T. (1998) "An inventory-theoretic approach to product assortment and shelf space allocation," *Journal of Retailing*, 74: 15–35.

Whitney, S. (1982) "Antitrust policies and the motion picture industry," in G. Kindem (ed.) *The American Movie Industry*, Carbondale, IL: Southern Illinois University Press.

6　Warner Bros. in the inter-war years

Strategic responses to the risk environment of filmmaking[1]

Michael Pokorny and John Sedgwick

Film production is a manifestly risky activity. Each unit of output is unique, expensive to produce and has a limited life in the market place. Film-goers are attracted by films that offer 'surprises', although they are generally unable to articulate what they are looking for in the film-going experience – they will 'know it when they see it'. Thus film producers are engaged in a constant process of innovation, periodically producing 'hits', and even in a small number of cases developing successful 'hit' formulas, which can then be exploited, although generally for only a relatively short period of time. In between lie scattered large numbers of loss-making films.

However, while it is tempting to characterise the process of film production as an essentially random one, and a number of commentators have done so,[2] we would argue that the process is still capable of being viewed from a strategic perspective. This is the approach taken in this chapter. Specifically, we examine the film production experience of Warner Bros. in the inter-war period – 1921 to 1941 – but with a particular emphasis on the 1930s, when the 'talkie' had become the industry standard. We examine two aspects of Warners' strategic response to filmmaking – the manner in which production budgets were distributed amongst a wide range of film projects, and the manner in which stars were developed and used to attenuate some of the risks inherent in film production.

Until 1948, when a Federal Court ruling compelled Hollywood's major players to sell off their domestic cinema chains, the world market for films was dominated by five vertically integrated businesses. During the 1930s, MGM, Paramount, Fox (Twentieth Century Fox from 1935), RKO and Warner Bros. each produced an annual portfolio of over forty films, distributed world-wide through their own distribution organisations.[3] Each of these outputs was the subject of a severe amortisation schedule of between twelve to fifteen months.[4] It was not until the 1940s that re-issues became a more common practice. This portfolio would consist typically of three budget categories: super 'A's, films that were intended for lengthy runs in prime-location cinemas and exhibited as single features; 'A' features which served as the main attraction on a double-bill programme; and finally 'B'

features which were made to serve as second features on a double-bill programme.

Competition between the major players took the form of producing a
relatively small number of potential 'hit' films which might play on the
screens of rival corporations. This practice occurred because the dominant
body of assets owned by each of the vertically integrated players was not
their production studios but the real-estate value of their cinemas. Accordingly, at the margin for each of the vertically linked organisations, the
choice of foregoing the revenues generated by a 'hit' from a rival studio, at
the expense of a less popular film from its own stable, was irrational. 'B'
movies would not be expected to show on the screens of rival cinemas,
whilst the relative success of 'A' films depended on it. Herein lies the
source of strategic thinking for these combines. In needing to attract
paying audiences, the cinema chains required 'hit' productions. Yet from
Sedgwick's (2000) work on the consumption of films and stars in Britain
during the 1930s, only a small number of films could expect to become the
seasons' hits: between 1932 and 1937 only eight to fifteen films per season
– from a stock of releases which increased from 648 to 803 – earned more
than five times the mean box office take. The quest for 'hit' production
was elusive, yet necessary if the combine was not to become totally
dependent on the products of rival studios, with the consequent probability of being subjected to opportunistic behaviour, and explains the disproportionate budgets available for such gambles. As King (1986: 162) has
written: 'What the lucky producer (of a "hit" production) has, therefore, is
a monopoly (copy) right to a film which will give his company access to his
competitor's screen time for a price.'

Thus while a hit film can generate staggering revenues, the vast proportion of films do not achieve such a status. Although a high production
budget provides for a more flexible film production environment, this is
neither a necessary nor sufficient condition for hit production – the history
of filmmaking is littered with small-budget hits and large-budget flops.
However, *ex ante*, the production of a hit would generally be considered to
require a substantial production budget.

This chapter sets out to chart Warners' emergence during the 1920s, to
become, by the end of the decade, one of the major Hollywood players.
Based upon the recently discovered William Schaefer ledger of production
costs and distributor rentals of feature films released by Warners between
1922 and 1951,[5] it traces the studio's response to the rapid expansion in
domestic and overseas demand during that decade followed by, in marked
contrast, the Great Depression and subsequent slow and uncertain recovery up to 1941. From the ledger, it becomes clear that the size and organisation of Warner's filmmaking budget reflected strongly a changing set of
box office expectations on the part of its senior executives.

This chapter is structured as follows: the next section provides an
overview of the development of Warner Bros. in the inter-war years; this is

followed by a discussion of the relevant literature and theoretical approaches that provide the framework for examining Warners' strategic approach to film production during the 1930s; an analysis is then presented of the financial structure and performance of Warners' annual film port-folios, followed by an analysis of the manner in which Warners developed and deployed its stars and the impact that this had on the financial performance of its films; a final section draws some conclusions.

The emergence and survival of Warner Bros.

Warners transformed their position in the American film industry, during the 1920s, from a modest second-level producer with a small number of first-run cinemas and distribution exchanges into one of the five major players. It did so through adopting a strategy of vertical integration, the finance for which was organised by the Wall Street investment house of Goldman, Sachs and Co. The major events in this transformation were the take-over, in 1925, of Vitagraph with its Brooklyn studio and important US and overseas distribution exchanges; the agreements with Western Electric in 1925 and 1926 to first experiment with and then produce com-mercial films with soundtracks, resulting in the commercially successful exhibitions of *Don Juan* (1926) and *The Jazz Singer* (1927); the acquisition in 1929 of the Stanley cinema circuit of 300 east coast cinemas; and, between 1928 and 1929, the acquisition of First National's substantial pro-duction, distribution and exhibition assets. During this period, Warners' assets grew from $5 million in 1925 to $230 million by 1930.[6]

As pointed out above, this strategy of vertical integration adopted by Warners was common to the other four dominant firms in the industry. In order to finance this strategy, all five had become incorporated during the 1920s and to a greater or lesser extent had incurred debt. The cost associ-ated with re-equipping the studios and cinemas for sound had been particularly onerous coming as it did at the tail-end of the drive to acquire cinemas.[7] The basis for this expansion rested ultimately with the popular-ity of film at home and abroad and expectations of continued growth in demand. During the 1920s, cinema admissions in the USA doubled from a weekly figure of 40 million in 1922 to 80 million by 1929,[8] whilst real per-sonal disposable income increased by over one-third. The major players all had extensive world-wide distribution operations by the end of the decade reflecting the international phenomenon of film popularity.[9]

The dramatic downturn in economic activity in the USA between 1929 and 1933 found these firms in a particularly vulnerable state. This is reflected in Figure 6.1, which shows movements in the unemployment rate from 1922 to 1941, and compares these with movements in annual cinema admissions. Cinema attendances and box office receipts, in nominal terms, fell by one-third during these years as unemployment soared, although given the fall in the Consumer Price Index from 100 in 1929 to 75.6 by

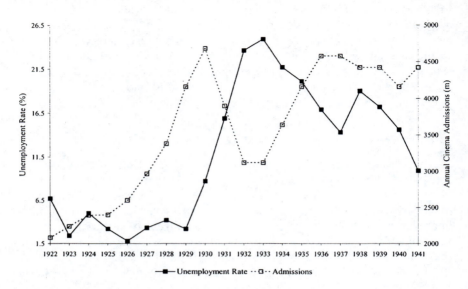

Figure 6.1 Unemployment rate and cinema admissions, USA, 1922 to 1941
        (source: Historical Statistics of the US 1975).

1933, the decline in real revenue (12 per cent) was not as dramatic. During
this time, personal disposable income almost halved although, of course,
this was mitigated by the fall in prices.

One important observation derived from Figure 6.1 concerns the resistance of the industry to the decline in economic activity; between 1929 and
1931 cinema admissions actually increased (as did box office revenue in
real terms). It was not until 1932 that the Depression began to make a
significant impact on the film industry. Certainly, as a proportion of overall
expenditure on recreational pursuits, cinema-going became relatively
more popular, increasing its share from 17 per cent in 1929 to 22 per cent
by 1931 before stabilising at 21 per cent from 1934 as recovery slowly
began to get underway.[10] The importance of cinema-going can be further
emphasised by considering expenditure on just spectator amusements
(cinema-going, theatre and spectator sports), and noting that cinema-going
accounted for 64 per cent of such expenditures in 1923, increasing to 82
per cent in 1930, a level which was maintained throughout the 1930s.[11]

Warners' reported profits fell from $14,514,628 in 1929 to a loss of over
$14 million in 1932.[12] However, whilst Paramount, Fox and RKO went into
receivership and changed their management teams substantially, allowing
financiers to take a much greater role at both the strategic and operational
level, Warners, along with MGM (Loews), maintained the confidence of
their shareholders and bankers and retained their management structures.[13] Warners' response to the recession was singular; overhead costs

were driven down through selling cinemas whilst operating costs were rigorously managed. Warners had developed a reputation for tight control of filmmaking budgets during the 1920s.[14] This served them in good stead during the height of the Depression. As Roddick (1983: 10) argues:

> (b)udgets could not continue to spiral and since the actual physical cost of filming had increased, a proportional reduction had to be made in non-technical costs – that is to say, in sets, schedules, stars and story material.... The new cost conscious budgeting and meticulous planning that would characterise the studio system through the 1930s had come to stay.

Theory and literature review

This chapter will examine two dimensions of Warners' strategic responses to the filmmaking environment it faced in the inter-war period. The first concerns the manner in which Warners attempted to control the financial risks it faced by developing portfolios of films and thereby spreading financial risks amongst and between various cost categories of films. The approach derives from the standard results of portfolio theory that are presented in the finance literature.[15] Thus we interpret Warners as investing in three cost categories of films – low, medium and high budget. These cost categories equate broadly to 'super A', 'A' and 'B' movies. Thus each season, given a global production budget, Warners had to decide the manner which this budget was to be distributed across these three budget categories. We interpret these three cost categories as 'assets' in which Warners invested, with low-budget films being relatively low risk, and high-budget production carrying relatively high risks. Thus Warners could be interpreted as having constructed a portfolio of films each season, the rate-of-return on this portfolio being a weighted average of the returns on the three 'assets'. But the central result of portfolio theory is that some control over the risk associated with the portfolio can be exercised via an appropriate diversification strategy – the risk on the portfolio is not just a direct function of the risk on each of the three assets, but depends also on the correlation between the risks on the assets. In other words, the process of portfolio construction can be interpreted as an exercise in maximising the expected return on the portfolio, for some given level of risk (or minimising risk at some given level of expected return), while fully exploiting the impact of diversification on risk. These ideas are explored in more detail in Sedgwick and Pokorny (1998).

The second dimension of Warners' filmmaking strategy that will be considered here is the manner in which stars were developed and deployed, and the impact that the associated strategies had on Warners' profitability.

Stars, it has been argued widely, serve to attenuate the risks associated with film production by locating new products in aesthetic and pleasure domains already familiar to audiences. Steven Albert (1998: 251 and Chapter 8 in this volume), for instance, argues: 'stars are important because they are the least noisy and most consistent marker for successful film types.' Tino Balio (1995: 144) goes so far as to claim that 'stars create(d) the market value of motion pictures'.

The importance attached to the notion of the 'movie star' has a long history in the industry, emerging during the years immediately before 1914. Indeed, the transformation of the industry from the studio-based structure of the 1930s, 1940s and 1950s to the freelance structure of today can be attributed in part to stars exploiting their growing market power. There was strong pressure exerted by stars to break free from the constraints placed upon them by the tightly specified, long-term contracts of the studio era, thereby allowing them to capture, through net profit contracts, the economic rents associated with their success.[16]

A number of studies have been published recently that have attempted to evaluate the precise impact that stars have on the success of film production. De Vany and Walls (1999), using a sample of over 2,000 films produced between 1984 and 1996, suggest that a strategy of using high-profile stars has limited and very uncertain returns. Thus while there is evidence that a very small number of stars can have a positive impact on profitability, this is not the norm. They conclude that given the extent to which film production is dominated by risk, there would appear to be no single strategy that can be adopted by film producers to control this risk, least of all the extensive use of stars. Indeed, they write: 'We conclude that the studio model of risk management lacks a foundation in theory or evidence. Revenue forecasts have zero precision, which is just a formal way of saying that "anything can happen"' (1999: 286). Ravid (1999), using a smaller sample, but a more extensive set of independent variables, reaches a similar conclusion. Albert (1998), on the other hand, while also concluding that it is only a small handful of stars that can be identified as being successful, argues that these stars none the less can be seen as being consistently successful, and therefore do represent the focus for a coherent risk-minimising strategy. This is consistent with Rosen's concept of 'super-stardom' where the combination of rising incomes and the widespread diffusion of technical progress is sufficient to generate an ever-growing consumer demand for quality, leading to 'the marked concentration of output on those few sellers who have the most talent' (1981: 847). Rosen, like Hamlen (1991, 1994), treats talent as an objective entity consisting of unique but measurable inputs that are not readily substitutable. Adler (1985), however, maintains that no difference in talent need be involved between stars and non-stars, hence drawing attention to the function of stars in lowering audience search costs. However, in contrast to De Vany and Walls and Ravid, Albert worked only with box office revenues rather than profits, which may explain, in part, his more positive conclusions (see Sedgwick and Pokorny 1999; Albert (1999)).

In terms of historical studies of stardom, these have tended to place less emphasis on detailed quantitative analyses, and have emphasised the broader context within which the star system operated. Thus stars could be interpreted as having been used to raise the profile of the industry as a whole and to maintain and extend this profile in the marketplace. As Kerr (1990: 387) argues, when explaining how Adolph Zukor and others reshaped the American film industry between 1912 and 1916:

> His product was the film star who became simultaneously a focal point for the construction of narratives within the film and for management coordination throughout the industry. The new star formed a synergistic link between film as an aesthetic form and as a product of corporate industry.

In evaluating stardom as a strategy, we will here do so within a film portfolio framework. Thus while it may well be the case that returns to stardom are difficult to identify on a film-by-film basis, studios produced portfolios of films, and the strategies that they adopted with regard to stardom must be evaluated within such a context. That is, we will here take as a point of contention the argument quoted earlier from De Vany and Walls that no sensible risk-averting strategy is available to film producers. The historical context allows for a deeper understanding of the business strategies employed during the period when Hollywood had evolved into a well-established and modern industry.

A portfolio theory of film production

Film budgets and returns

In order to convey the general risk environment of film production, Figure 6.2 presents a scattergraph of distributor rentals against production costs for all 871 films produced by Warners during the period from 1921/1922 to 1940/1941. The data are expressed in constant 1929 prices.

The obvious feature of Figure 6.2 is the positive association between production costs and both the level and variability of distributor rentals. Thus whilst higher-budget films tended to generate higher rentals, they did so with increasing uncertainty. However, the other feature of Figure 6.2 is that very high revenues were generated from some modestly budgeted films.[17]

While distributor rentals might have been a reasonable reflection of film popularity, they were a poor proxy for film profitability. The more popular a film, the higher were the distribution costs incurred in exhibiting it, which in turn impacted on profits. This is illustrated in Figure 6.3 which presents a scattergraph of film profits,[18] but in this case against total costs (the sum of production and distribution costs). Thus Figure 6.3 also

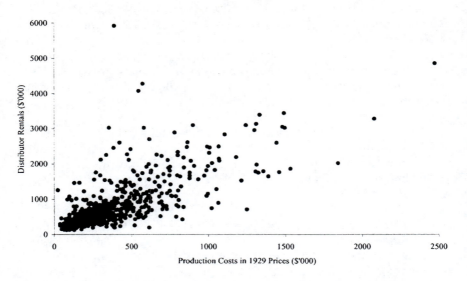

Figure 6.2 Scatter of distributor rentals against production costs, all films, 1921/1922 to 1940/1941 (source: William Schaefer ledger).

reflects, indirectly, the rates-of-return earned by the films (the ratio of profits to total costs), and highlights more starkly the conundrum which studio heads faced. Thus, whilst low-to-medium cost films were more reliable in the sense that they were less likely to make losses, they tended to generate only half of Warners' seasonal profits during the best box office years. Even though some low-cost films produced very high profits, these were relatively small in number and their overall contribution to annual profits was necessarily limited. Conversely, higher-cost films were more likely to generate high profits, but at an increasing risk of incurring losses. In the absence of any clear indication that profits were positively related to total costs, the decision to bet heavily on big budget productions would appear to be more inherently risky than the pursuit of a strategy based exclusively on low-to-medium-cost production. Indeed, the information contained in Figure 6.3 suggests that the premium-to-risk fell as total costs increased: not only does the variance of performance appear to increase with costs, but the average rate-of-return also appears to fall.

While Figures 6.2 and 6.3 reflect, in general terms, the nature of the risk environment of film production, they must also be interpreted within the context of the volatile economic environment of the data period. Table 6.1 charts the scale of the expansion of Warners' production operations during the 1920s culminating in the acquisition of First National in 1929 and the leap in film production costs associated with full sound production during the 1929/1930 season which was immediately followed by the stark financial/commercial impact of the onset of the Depression in the 1930/1931

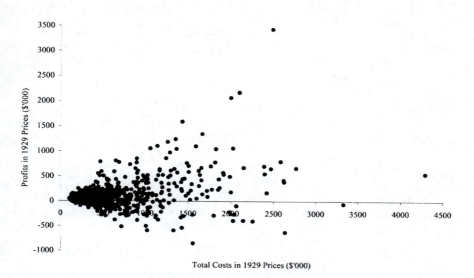

Figure 6.3 Scatter of film profits against total costs, all films, 1921/1922 to 1940/1941 (source: William Schaefer ledger).

season. Whilst the decline in Warners' film output can be partly explained by the rationalisation of production which followed the acquisition of First National,[19] the decline in cinema attendances from 1930, shown in Figure 6.1, led to a retrenchment across all Hollywood studios. Warners' rentals nearly halved for those films released between the 1929/1930 and 1930/1931 seasons.[20] Rentals continued to fall with the 1931/1932 batch of films and thereafter fluctuated widely around an upward trend. The 1937/1938 crisis in economic recovery is strongly reflected in the fall in rentals for both 1939/1940 and 1940/1941 releases.

From Table 6.1 the manner in which the scale of film production responded to the developing recession is clear, with the season's film portfolio budget cut back drastically between 1929/1930 and 1931/1932. However, note that even though film production continued to contract between 1931/1932 and 1932/1933, revenues began to recover. The period from 1933/1934 to 1937/1938 saw a steady increase in annual production budgets, suggesting a demand-led explanation of expansion in the industry, with a particularly sharp increase from 1936/1937 to 1937/1938. The latter coincided with the 1937/1938 recession and resulted in a severe squeeze on profits. In the latter part of the period, overall production costs were cut back somewhat as the studio sought to regain acceptable levels of profitability.

Table 6.1 also highlights the volatility of Warners' profit performance[21] over the period. The impact of the Depression is clearly reflected in the losses incurred on the 1930/1931 releases. There is a recovery with the

Table 6.1 Distributor rentals, costs and profits of films produced, 1921/1922 to 1940/1941 (1929 prices in $'000)

Season	Films produced	Total rentals	Production costs	Film profits	Rate-of-return (%)	Average production costs
1921/1922	3	1,197	268	497	71.0	89.2
1922/1923	6	2,173	803	569	35.5	133.9
1923/1924	13	5,203	2,450	810	18.4	188.4
1924/1925	23	5,851	2,337	1,349	30.0	101.6
1925/1926	45	9,964	5,251	963	10.7	116.7
1926/1927	29	11,109	4,814	2,166	24.2	166.0
1927/1928	38	14,936	3,957	5,554	59.2	104.1
1928/1929	36	35,025	6,657	15,776	82.0	184.9
1929/1930	82	51,996	25,133	7,408	16.6	306.5
1930/1931	60	29,385	21,260	−3,223	−9.9	354.3
1931/1932	52	28,559	16,348	1,397	5.1	314.4
1932/1933	56	43,465	15,431	12,050	38.4	275.6
1933/1934	54	38,698	16,851	7,460	23.9	312.1
1934/1935	54	47,479	20,136	9,719	25.7	372.9
1935/1936	58	44,509	19,468	8,489	23.6	335.7
1936/1937	58	40,967	20,649	4,947	13.7	356.0
1937/1938	56	46,350	28,079	645	1.4	501.4
1938/1939	53	53,602	26,244	7,285	15.7	495.2
1939/1940	47	46,097	25,574	3,110	7.2	544.1
1940/1941	48	47,324	22,658	6,970	17.3	472.0

Source: William Schaefer ledger.

1931/1932 releases, and a sharp increase in profitability for those films released in 1932/1933. The mid-1930s can be seen as a period of consolidation, recovery and rising expectations. However, the joint impact of rapidly increasing annual production budgets and the recession of 1937/1938 led to a dramatic downturn in profitability for the releases of those years, and resulted in a cut-back in annual studio budgets between 1938/1939 and 1940/1941, even though profits showed some signs of recovery.

Further insights are offered by considering *average* film production costs in Table 6.1. Apart from the increase in film budgets brought about by the transition to sound, it is interesting to note that average production costs actually increased between 1929/1930 and 1930/1931, despite the large fall in total production budgets. Thus the strategy employed was not so much a change in the nature of film production as such but rather a severe reduction in the number of films produced. In 1929/1930, eighty-two films were produced, followed by a cut back to sixty films in 1930/1931. There was a further reduction to fifty-two films in 1931/1932, and thereafter annual film production stabilised at between fifty-three to fifty-eight films, although only forty-seven to forty-eight films were produced in 1939/1940 and 1940/1941, respectively. These trends can be interpreted within a portfolio theory context. Thus, first, there is evidence from Table 6.1 that Warners' aggregate annual film production budget responded to the rate-of-return on the previous year's budget – high rates-of-return tending to result in expanding budgets in the following year, and low rates-of-return a contraction in production budgets.[22] Second, with the annual production budget having been determined, and within a context in which the number of films produced annually had stabilised to around fifty-five, a decision then had to be taken as to how this production budget was to be allocated amongst the various cost categories of films – the number of super 'A', 'A' and 'B' films to be produced.

Table 6.1 also highlights the much tighter cost controls which were exercised in the early 1930s and for the 1932/1933 releases in particular. Thus the outstanding profit performance of the 1932/1933 season can be explained in terms of the imposition of very tight cost controls, within an environment in which film revenues began to recover. It also highlights the apparent optimism which was felt in 1936, since both the studio budget and average film production costs for 1936/1937 and, in particular, the 1937/1938 releases, increased substantially. However, the poor performance in 1937/1938 did not lead to a marked reduction in average budgets but, rather, a smaller number of films in the next season's portfolio. This ties in with the tendency on the part of the major Hollywood studios, to concentrate on 'A'-type pictures and leaving 'B' production to Columbia, Universal and a set of 'poverty row' studios.[23]

Within this context of prudent financial control came a set of artistic and genre innovations which further differentiated Warners' product. Of the films themselves, Roddick (1983) has produced a careful and detailed assessment of the match between the system of production at Warners and the quality and characteristics of its output, maintaining that Warners produced a distinct, although changing, style of film during the 1930s. It became notable for producing films which were topical and hard hitting, with urban subjects and settings: crime, gangsterism, bootlegging, federal agents, prisons, night clubs, prostitution, newspapers and backstage intrigues provide recurring contexts, particularly during the first half of the decade. Such films could be made relatively cheaply and quickly, almost exclusively on the studio's stages, and often shot under night conditions requiring the minimum of detail to be shown, hence allowing backlot sets to be used time and again. A crop of new 'stars' emerged to carry these outputs with Joan Blondell, Bette Davis, Barbara Stanwyck, James Cagney, Edward G. Robinson, Paul Muni, Dick Powell and Humphrey Bogart featuring prominently.[24] From the data in Table 6.1, the strategy appears to have been brilliantly successful for, as we have seen, the losses of 1931/1932 were transformed into profits during the following season and provided Warners with an artistic and commercial base from which to develop. The quest for big budget 'hits' later in the decade led Warners to diversify into costume (historical) drama/adventure and biopics.[25] The organisation of human and physical capital was factory-like in form and intensity. Roddick (1983: 28) maintains that, more than any other studio, Warners' films:

> were strongly influenced by the economic and organisational system under which they were produced. The classic Hollywood style, with its insistence on the unproblematic, seamless narrative whose advancement is controlled by the destiny of one or more individual characters, was determined by the economics of the production system.

Yet its strategy for survival resulted in films of quality that audiences wanted to see. It was a factory geared to turning out product on a regular basis. But the product was in a sense artistic: if a work of art is defined not by the conditions of its production but by the circumstances of its consumption, then the product manufactured by Warners (and other studios) was undoubtedly art (Roddick 1983: 25).

In order to explore the manner in which Warners allocated its annual production budget across the various film budgetary categories, we first require a definition of what constitutes high-, medium- and low-budget production. First, in deriving such definitions it would not seem appropriate to use absolute cost criteria as a basis for doing so – the (real) cost of a high-budget film, for example, in the 1920s was presumably markedly different from the cost of high-budget film in the late 1930s. Rather, the approach adopted here is to define budgetary categories in relative cost terms, and in particular, to define high-budget films, in any given season, as those films that exceeded the average cost of all films produced in that season by 50 per cent or more. Medium-budget films are those that fall within the range of 75 per cent to 150 per cent of the average cost of all films produced in the season, and low-budget films are those costing less than 75 per cent of average cost. Such a partition produced 145 high-budget films, 336 medium-budget films and 390 low-budget films over the sample period. While there is an element of arbitrariness in such a partition – and in part its definition was conditioned by sample size requirements within each category, particularly the high-budget category – it at least provides some basis for disaggregating by budgetary category.[26]

Figures 6.4 to 6.6 present scattergraphs of film profits against total costs for high-, medium- and low-budget films. The nature of risk associated with each budgetary category is clearly apparent – higher-budget films exhibit markedly more variability in profit performance (both absolutely and relatively[27]) than lower-budget films. Additionally, higher-budget films were more likely to make losses than lower-budget films – 40 per cent of high-budget films made losses over the sample period compared with 31 per cent of medium-budget films and just 11 per cent of low-budget films. However, the attraction of high-budget production is also apparent from Figures 6.4 to 6.6 – high-budget films offered the possibility of generating

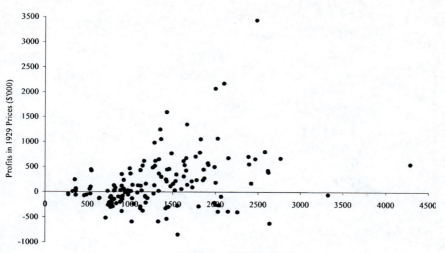

Figure 6.4 Scatter of profits against total costs, high-budget films, 1921/1922 to 1940/1941 (source: William Schaefer ledger).

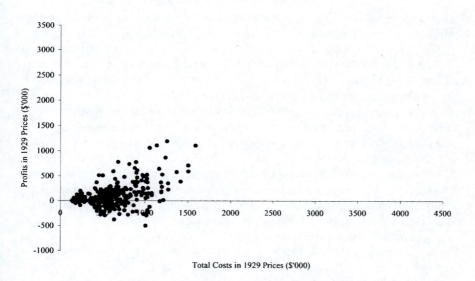

Figure 6.5 Scatter of profits against total costs, medium-budget films, 1921/1922 to 1940/1941 (source: William Schaefer ledger).

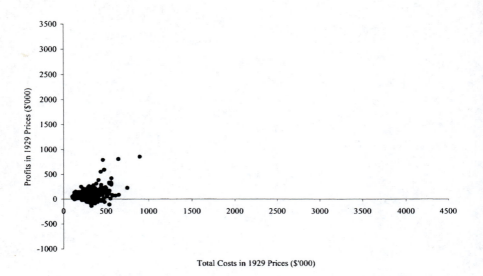

Figure 6.6 Scatter of profits against total costs, low-budget films, 1921/1922 to
1940/1941 (source: William Schaefer ledger).

very high profits, and therefore of making a substantial contribution to
annual profit targets, notwithstanding the obvious risks involved.

Therefore Warners' annual budgetary allocations can be characterised
as follows: an annual global production budget was first determined, presumably on the basis of the expected returns from film production, which
in turn was influenced largely by the rate-of-return performance on the
previous years' production budget; this budget then had to be distributed
across the three film budgetary categories, with the objective of maximising the rate-of-return on the global budget, but subject to the constraint of
an annual output of about fifty to fifty-five films. The risks associated with
high-budget production could be offset to some extent by the lower risks
associated with lower-budget production, and therefore an annual portfolio of films constructed on the basis of a balance of overall risk against
expected return on the portfolio. In other words, it was perfectly rational
and consistent to produce high-budget films, which generated low and
highly variable rates-of-return, while at the same time maximising the
rate-of-return on the aggregate production budget – a number of high-
budget films had to be produced in order to absorb the annual budget. The
key was getting the balance right between low-, medium- and high-budget
production, given the nature of the production constraints, and the distribution of risk across budgetary categories.

Table 6.2 presents the performance of each of the budgetary categories
over time, together with the extent to which Warners invested in each of
these categories (given the low level of film production in the early 1920s,

the first four data periods have been aggregated into a single data period). The most notable feature of Table 6.2 is the volatility in the rate-of-return performance of high-budget films in comparison with the relative stability in the performance of low-budget films and, to a lesser extent, medium-budget films. However, there were a number of years in which high-budget production was highly successful. This was certainly the case from the mid-1920s to the 1928/1929 season, which can be seen as the culmination of Warners' rapid growth during the 1920s. Thus, in the 1928/1929 season, all film categories generated outstanding rates-of-return, but none more so than the five high-budget films, which generated nearly half of the total profits for the season. The performance of high-budget films in 1928/1929 therefore illustrates starkly the clear advantages of this mode of production – by focusing substantial production resources on a small number of films, high levels of profits could be generated, reflecting the economies of scale that could be derived from high-budget production. Other successful years for high-budget production were 1932/1933, 1933/1934, 1938/1939 and 1940/1941, years in which high-budget production outperformed or matched performance in the other budgetary categories.

However, there were also periods in which high-budget production was manifestly unsuccessful, periods during which high-budget production generated substantial losses (1930/1931, 1931/1932 and 1937/1938), or, although profitable, generated markedly poorer performance than the other categories (1934/1935 to 1936/1937 and 1939/1940). These periods illustrate the risks associated with high-budget production. The success of high-budget production was clearly highly sensitive to the economic cycle. Thus while high-budget, high-profile film production had the potential to appeal to a wide audience base, any decline in this base could have disastrous consequences for profitability, given the substantial costs that were sunk in production. Lower-budget production, on the other hand, needed only to attract relatively modest demand to generate profits, although reduced demand would obviously impact on rate-of-return performance.

From Table 6.2 it is clear that Warners cut back its investment in high-budget films drastically in response to the onset of the Depression, with its survival during this period deriving from the relative success of lower-budget movie production. However, once the initial impact of the recession had been overcome, Warners expanded aggressively into high-budget production, investing upwards of half of annual production budgets. This expansion started in the 1932/1933 season, notwithstanding the poor performance of high-budget films in the previous season. In aggregate, the eight high-budget films in 1932/1933 were highly successful, but in fact this resulted from the performance of just two of these films[28] – the two most costly films – which generated 82 per cent of the high-budget profits, with highly variable performance amongst the remaining six films. It would appear that, as a result of the high level of risk to which Warners were exposed in 1932/1933, high-budget production was cut back somewhat in

Table 6.2 Budget allocations, profit contributions and rates-of-return by budget category

Year	High-budget films				Medium-budget films				Low-budget films			
	Number of films	Share of annual production budget	Proportionate contribution to annual profits/(losses)	Rate-of-return (%)	Number of films	Share of annual production budget	Proportionate contribution to annual profits/(losses)	Rate-of-return (%)	Number of films	Share of annual production budget	Proportionate contribution to annual profits/(losses)	Rate-of-return (%)
1921/1925	5	0.24	−0.01	−1.1	22	0.53	0.39	22.0	18	0.23	0.62	61.4
1925/1926	5	0.28	0.02	1.0	23	0.49	0.25	5.8	17	0.24	0.72	29.3
1926/1927	4	0.38	0.48	29.9	9	0.33	0.06	4.8	16	0.30	0.46	35.0
1927/1928	6	0.38	0.39	60.5	14	0.34	0.26	49.7	18	0.29	0.35	67.2
1928/1929	5	0.41	0.48	89.1	10	0.29	0.21	68.7	21	0.31	0.31	82.7
1929/1930	16	0.40	0.27	11.8	24	0.32	0.34	17.5	42	0.29	0.39	21.9
1930/1931	8	0.25	(0.58)	−25.1	32	0.54	(0.28)	−5.0	20	0.21	(0.13)	−6.2
1931/1932	2	0.07	−0.26	−23.9	37	0.76	0.79	5.3	13	0.17	0.47	13.5
1932/1933	8	0.26	0.36	48.9	30	0.60	0.43	29.1	18	0.14	0.22	52.5
1933/1934	4	0.19	0.26	31.1	31	0.59	0.53	21.9	19	0.22	0.20	22.3
1934/1935	10	0.42	0.25	16.3	17	0.33	0.48	35.4	27	0.25	0.27	27.0
1935/1936	12	0.47	0.26	13.7	15	0.29	0.30	24.5	31	0.24	0.44	39.3
1936/1937	16	0.55	0.15	3.9	13	0.27	0.40	20.1	29	0.18	0.45	30.6
1937/1938	12	0.55	−3.97	−10.8	12	0.25	0.27	1.5	32	0.20	4.70	28.0
1938/1939	10	0.39	0.44	17.5	19	0.42	0.42	15.8	24	0.19	0.14	11.8
1939/1940	10	0.48	0.24	3.7	14	0.33	0.21	4.7	23	0.18	0.55	20.0
1940/1941	12	0.53	0.57	18.5	14	0.32	0.30	16.3	22	0.15	0.13	14.9

Source: William Schaefer ledger.

the following season, to just four films, but with a markedly higher average production budget. Thereafter Warners returned to levels of high-budget production comparable to the pre-Depression period. This expansion into high-budget production was largely at the expense of low-budget production, as Warners attempted to compete with the market leaders MGM and Paramount in the super-A market. But, as Table 6.2 also makes clear, the obvious risks associated with super-A production were partially offset by the more stable returns in the lower-budget categories, and performance in these markets was crucial in the years in which high-budget films performed poorly. It is in this sense that high-budget production must be seen within context – within the context of a balanced annual portfolio of films, where successful medium- and low-budget production provided the flexibility to undertake risks in the super-A market.

Sedgwick and Pokorny (1998: 214–219) take this analysis a step further and demonstrate that the risk that Warners took on their annual film portfolios (measured in terms of the variability in the production costs across the portfolios) was in a broad sense positively related to the returns that those portfolios generated – there were returns to risk taking. However, Warners also adjusted its risk stance each year in response to the returns-to-risk that were achieved on the previous years' portfolio, and hence Warners' risk position could be interpreted as having evolved over time in a cyclical and strategic manner.

Stardom and the profitability of filmmaking

While a diversified production budget provided one strategy for attenuating the risk associated with film production, a perhaps more explicit (and a certainly more recognisable) strategy derived from the development and deployment of stars, a strategy that was well established in the studio system of the 1930s.

In order to gain some insight into the manner in which Warners deployed their stars during the studio era, we will here focus on the period 1931 to 1939, a period during which the star and studio system had reached its maturity and a period of considerable economic volatility, thereby providing a focused context for evaluating the various strategies associated with stardom. In Table 6.3 we present a set of statistical summaries, for those actors who appeared in films which in aggregate accounted for more than 2.5 per cent of total production budgets over the sample period.[29] A first observation which can be made from the table is how intensively many of these actors were worked during the period, with Blondell, Brent, Davis, Farrell and O'Brien appearing in over thirty productions for the studio, with another five featuring in more than twenty-five. In terms of the share of production costs, the leading actors were Powell (Dick), Brent, Davis, O'Brien, de Havilland and Blondell. In the cases of Blondell, Brent, Davis and O'Brien, this relatively large share of production costs

Table 6.3 Summary statistics of film appearances by actor 1931/1932 to 1938/1939 (1929 prices)

Actor	Number of films	Average production cost per film ($'000)	Percentage of films in which actor appeared that were high budget	Share of total production costs of films in which actor appeared (%)	Aggregate rate-of-return of films in which actor appeared (%)
Astor, M.	15	288.7	6.7	2.7	17.8
Blondell, J.	35	403.2	22.9	8.7	27.0
Bogart, H.	20	432.4	10.0	5.3	30.1
Brent, G.	32	465.5	25.0	9.1	12.2
Brown, J.E.	13	348.6	7.7	2.8	24.0
Cagney, J.	22	486.0	31.8	6.6	42.3
Davis, B.	33	444.2	18.2	9.0	22.9
de Havilland, O.	14	1,042.1	71.4	8.9	11.7
Dvorak, A.	20	262.5	5.0	3.2	26.5
Farrell, G.	37	256.0	10.8	5.8	27.8
Flynn, E.	12	989.2	66.7	7.3	23.8
Foran, D.	20	226.1	30.0	2.8	15.8
Francis, K.	28	421.7	25.0	7.2	14.3
Keeler, R.	8	734.7	100.0	3.6	33.9
Kibbee, G.	26	285.2	11.5	4.5	30.1
Lindsay, M.	28	354.7	17.9	6.1	29.9
Louise, A.	11	604.5	36.4	4.1	5.6
MacMahon, A.	18	292.2	16.7	3.2	34.2
Muni, P.	8	598.8	25.0	2.9	22.3
O'Brien, P.	31	472.3	22.6	9.0	20.5
Powell, D.	26	698.3	57.7	11.1	12.7
Rains, C.	11	1,123.0	72.7	7.6	1.1
Robinson, E.G.	14	454.0	14.3	3.9	26.9
Sheridan, A.	16	352.1	6.3	3.5	17.9
William, W.	28	271.0	7.1	4.7	22.5

Source: William Schaefer ledger.

derived from frequent appearances in medium-budget films, whereas in the case of de Havilland the large share derived from relatively few appearances in very high-budget films. Powell's large share derived from relatively frequent appearances in higher-budget films, particularly musicals. However, in terms of rates-of-return, these were relatively poor for those films in which Brent, de Havilland and Powell appeared. The highest rates-of-return were generated by films in which Cagney, MacMahon, Keeler, Kibbee, Bogart and Lindsay appeared. The real stars for the studio during these years were those artists whom they entrusted to carry their super-'A' productions: a list that narrows down to de Havilland, Flynn, Keeler, Powell and Rains, with a number of other actors experiencing shorter periods of 'superstardom' (see discussion of Table 6.4 below).

Of further note from Table 6.3 is that Rains appeared in the highest-budget films, but achieved the lowest rates-of-return. Similarly, Louise also appeared in relatively high-budget films, but these achieved a very low overall rate-of-return. Conversely, both Flynn and Keeler appeared in high-budget, high-rate-of-return films, although in the case of Keeler the films in which she appeared exhibited considerable variation in rate-of-return performance, reflecting her declining appeal after 1934.

In order to gain some insight into the variation in rates-of-return over time, Table 6.4 presents annual shares and rates-of-return for the more prominent actors from Table 6.3, and specifically, for those actors whose films accounted for more than 6.5 per cent of production budgets over the sample period. The table also shows, for each year, the average cost of the films in which each actor appeared relative to the average cost of all films produced in the given year (multiplied by 100), so that a value in excess of 150, for example, would indicate that the actor tended to appear in high-budget films in that year.

From Table 6.4 it can be seen that Blondell, Cagney and Davis achieved high and relatively consistent rates-of-return over the first half of the sample period, although there was considerable variation in budget shares from year to year. O'Brien and Powell also performed strongly during the early to mid-1930s, while Brent and Francis exhibited considerable variation in annual rates-of-return. Flynn, de Havilland and Rains were all introduced in the 1934/1935 season as high-profile stars (although at that stage they were relatively unknown), as Warners made a concerted move into high-budget film production (the average cost of the five most expensive films in 1934/1935 was $1,041,000 compared to $743,000 in the 1933/1934 season – see also Table 6.2). While the films in which de Havilland and Rains appeared generated high rates-of-return in this initial year, the performance of their films thereafter was much weaker, this being particularly so in the case of Rains. By contrast, Flynn exhibited consistent and strong performance even in the poor overall performance year of 1937/1938. Note also that, in order to accommodate these three new stars, a number of established actors experienced sharp reductions in their

Table 6.4 All films: share of annual production budgets, annual rates-of-return and relative average production costs by actor, 1931/1932 to 1938/1939

	1931/1932	1932/1933	1933/1934	1934/1935	1935/1936	1936/1937	1937/1938	1938/1939
Blondell								
Share (%)	10.7	11.4	17.8	5.7	10.2	12.3	3.5	3.6
Rate-of-return (%)	13.3	60.1	31.5	34.3	19.0	14.5	24.7	–8.6
Relative av. cost	92.8	106.9	136.8	77.2	147.3	178.7	98.4	95.6
Brent								
Share (%)	10.3	12.1	4.2	3.9	4.7	11.1	15.5	8.7
Rate-of-return (%)	7.5	43.4	14.3	20.2	11.6	13.5	–7.4	13.7
Relative av. cost	89.5	112.9	76.1	70.0	90.6	160.4	217.2	154.4
Cagney								
Share (%)	5.4	5.4	12.1	6.9	11.7	–	2.6	9.7
Rate-of-return (%)	36.3	34.5	53.9	80.4	18.5	–	–23.0	39.5
Relative av. cost	93.4	101.3	131.0	92.6	226.7	–	143.2	171.4
Davis								
Share (%)	7.3	10.5	8.6	4.7	8.6	4.4	8.3	17.3
Rate-of-return (%)	23.0	38.2	39.0	40.1	26.7	53.3	6.3	7.8
Relative av. cost	95.1	98.2	77.5	84.0	99.2	128.7	154.7	229.2
de Havilland								
Share (%)	–	–	–	16.7	13.1	2.9	19.0	10.0
Rate-of-return (%)	–	–	–	34.2	11.8	–27.2	–3.4	14.0
Relative av. cost	–	–	–	225.5	378.7	167.6	265.9	185.3

Flynn								
Share (%)	—	—	—	7.6	6.8	11.1	11.0	13.8
Rate-of-return (%)	—	—	—	24.7	31.1	23.7	16.8	26.4
Relative av. cost	—	—	—	205.4	396.2	214.9	307.5	183.3
Francis								
Share (%)	5.1	5.7	12.8	6.8	7.3	11.7	4.7	5.4
Rate-of-return (%)	1.0	48.2	32.3	8.9	28.1	4.4	−13.4	−9.8
Relative av. cost	89.7	106.7	138.1	122.6	140.3	169.7	87.6	71.0
O'Brien								
Share (%)	—	—	8.6	17.3	10.9	6.6	11.8	11.1
Rate-of-return (%)	—	—	43.5	37.2	26.3	5.6	−6.9	13.6
Relative av. cost	—	—	77.4	133.2	126.5	127.3	132.3	117.7
Powell, D.								
Share (%)	—	4.1	21.4	12.9	19.7	11.0	12.2	6.7
Rate-of-return (%)	—	28.3	39.0	27.0	2.4	10.3	−15.2	−12.6
Relative av. cost	—	115.9	192.6	174.6	229.0	212.0	228.4	118.8
Rains								
Share (%)	—	—	—	7.4	5.2	10.1	16.7	11.7
Rate-of-return (%)	—	—	—	24.2	−44.2	3.4	0.8	−0.6
Relative av. cost	—	—	—	399.1	304.1	195.1	311.8	206.7

budget shares between the 1933/1934 and 1934/1935 seasons, notably Blondell, Cagney, Davis, Francis and Powell.

The relative average cost data in Table 6.4 offer further insights into the manner in which Warners deployed their actors over the period. Thus Flynn, de Havilland and Rains were immediately placed in high-budget productions, their films being over twice as costly as the average in 1934/1935, and, in the case of Rains, four times as costly. This relative average cost index, therefore, can be interpreted as an index of 'stardom', in the sense that it reflects the relative level of investment that the studio was prepared to make in each actor. Interpreting (somewhat arbitrarily) a value for this index in the region of 200 or more as reflecting star-level investment, Flynn, de Havilland and Rains can be seen to have been used exclusively as stars. Powell could also be interpreted as a star, and certainly so from the mid-1930s. Brent and Cagney experienced brief periods of stardom. An interesting case is that of Bette Davis. Used in averagely costed productions for most of the sample period, productions that consistently generated high rates-of-return, it was only in the late 1930s that she attracted star-level investment.

Perhaps the most interesting aspect of these data, however, is how unsuccessful were the films in which many of these stars appeared, with the single and notable exception of Flynn. Thus, apart from initial success, the films of de Havilland and Rains were notably unsuccessful. The performance of Powell's films tended to decline as he attracted star-level investment, and Davis' films exhibited a sharp reduction in rates-of-return as the relative costs of these films were increased.

These conclusions are reinforced by decomposing the data in Table 6.4 into the high-budget films in which the actors appeared, and contrasting these with their appearances in medium- and low-budget films. This decomposition is shown in Tables 6.5 and 6.6 (where in Table 6.6 appearances in medium- and low-budget films have been aggregated). What is immediately obvious from Tables 6.5 and 6.6 is the much more stable performance of the medium- and low-budget films in which a number of the actors appeared, in contrast to the performance of their high-budget films. Thus Blondell appeared in consistently high-performing medium/low-budget films, but the relatively few high-budget films in which she appeared exhibited very variable performance. The most outstanding example was that of Davis – throughout the entire period her medium/low-budget films generated outstanding rates-of-return, but her high-budget films were manifestly unsuccessful, and particularly so in 1938/1939 season when Warners had made a substantial investment in her, giving her top billing in three of the season's four most costly films. The very poor performance of Rain's high-budget films is also emphasised in Table 6.5. In the case of Francis, both cost categories of her films performed poorly in the latter part of the data period, presumably reflecting a decline in her star power. This was similarly the case with Powell, although in his case this was probably more a reflection of the deteriorating performance of Warners' musicals over the period – twenty-one of the twenty-fix films in which Powell appeared were musicals.

Table 6.5 confirms the strong and consistent performance of Flynn's high-budget films, a performance that is unique amongst the actors analysed. Cagney presents an interesting example. Apart from two loss-making films – a high-budget film in the 1935/1936 season[30] and a medium-budget film in the 1937/1938 season – all his remaining twenty films generated high rates-of-return, a performance that was consistent as between his medium- and high-budget films. However, Warners would appear to have been somewhat ambivalent in investing in Cagney, and particularly so in the 1936/1937 and 1937/1938 seasons. In fact, the volatility of Cagney's production budget shares in Table 6.4 derived from a number of contract disputes between the actor and the studio, triggered by Cagney's dissatisfaction with the salary he was receiving relative to the manifest success of his films, and the high number of films in which he was required to appear. The resulting legal disputes resulted in Cagney making no appearances for the studio in the 1936/1937 season. Davis was involved in similar disputes in the latter half of the 1930s, resulting in her appearing in just two films in the 1936/1937 season, but thereafter, having won her battle with the studio, being promoted to star status. However, as Tables 6.4 and 6.5 suggest, this had a marked negative impact on the success of her films, as a result of the financial failure of her high-budget films, even though one of these – *Jezebel* – won her an Academy Award.[31]

In order to fully interpret the manner in which Warners invested in stars, it is necessary to consider the institutional framework within which this investment took place. Thus as a starting point it would seem reasonable to assume that the market value of a star as a commodity was determined predominantly by the relative box office success of his or her previous films. Accordingly, it could be expected that the value of a star who had appeared in a set of films with growing net box office returns would be rising, whilst that of a star whose films have performed relatively badly at the box office would be in decline. The ability of a contract to reflect this value is dependent upon its term structure. A seven-year-term contract held by a studio during the classical Hollywood period would be re-configured to reflect the rising value of a star.[32] Such a process favoured the studio, particularly where a significant portion of the term was still to run. A star in decline, on the other hand, was vulnerable to the decision not to continue with the option to retain her or his services.[33] In contrast, the rewards of a freelance star are much more likely to reflect market value, since rival producers will be engaged in a bidding game to secure his or her peculiar qualities.

Under the circumstance that the vertically integrated majors during the classical period required upwards of fifty films per season during the 1930s,

Table 6.5 High-budget films: share of annual high-budget (HB) production budgets, rates-of-return and number of high-budget films by actor, 1931/1932 to 1938/1939

	1931/1932	1932/1933	1933/1934	1934/1935	1935/1936	1936/1937	1937/1938	1938/1939
Blondell								
Share (%)	–	14.2	58.0	–	13.2	18.4	–	–
Rate-of-return (%)	–	103.8	34.0	–	9.1	7.8	–	–
Number of HB films	–	1	2	–	2	3	–	–
Brent								
Share (%)	–	14.4	–	–	–	11.3	24.6	18.1
Rate-of-return (%)	–	81.1	–	–	–	12.5	–8.8	20.2
Number of HB films	–	1	–	–	–	2	3	2
Cagney								
Share (%)	–	–	27.5	–	24.7	–	–	24.7
Rate-of-return (%)	–	–	52.5	–	18.5	–	–	39.5
Number of HB films	–	–	1	–	3	–	–	3
Davis								
Share (%)	–	11.2	–	–	6.7	–	8.4	36.9
Rate-of-return (%)	–	2.3	–	–	1.4	–	–10.8	0.1
Number of HB films	–	1	–	–	1	–	1	3
de Havilland								
Share (%)	–	–	–	32.5	27.5	5.2	30.8	21.2
Rate-of-return (%)	–	–	–	26.7	11.8	–27.2	–5.7	19.4
Number of HB films	–	–	–	2	2	1	3	2

Flynn								
Share (%)	–	–	–	14.8	14.4	20.1	16.0	22.1
Rate-of-return (%)	–	–	–	29.5	31.1	23.7	12.8	17.5
Number of HB films	–	–	–	1	1	3	1	2
Francis								
Share (%)	–	11.5	26.4	7.1	6.8	16.6	–	–
Rate-of-return (%)	–	46.7	43.2	13.1	37.9	–2.7	–	–
Number of HB films	–	1	1	1	1	3	–	–
O'Brien								
Share (%)	–	–	–	25.0	6.0	5.1	6.7	7.6
Rate-of-return (%)	–	–	–	16.3	38.1	–11.8	5.1	57.5
Number of HB films	–	–	–	3	1	1	1	1
Powell, D.								
Share (%)	–	–	84.4	25.1	38.3	19.8	17.7	–
Rate-of-return (%)	–	–	37.0	24.1	–3.6	10.3	–16.1	–
Number of HB films	–	–	3	3	4	3	2	–
Rains								
Share (%)	–	–	–	17.7	11.0	14.5	30.4	17.8
Rate-of-return (%)	–	–	–	24.2	–44.2	6.5	0.8	–23.6
Number of HB films	–	–	–	1	1	2	3	1

Table 6.6 Medium- and low-budget films: share of annual medium- and low-budget (M & LB) production budgets, rates-of-return and number of medium- and low-budget films by actor, 1931/1932 to 1938/1939

	1931/1932	1932/1933	1933/1934	1934/1935	1935/1936	1936/1937	1937/1938	1938/1939
Blondell								
Share (%)	11.4	10.4	8.1	9.8	7.4	4.8	7.8	5.9
Rate-of-return (%)	13.3	16.9	26.9	34.3	32.8	40.5	24.7	−8.6
Number of M & LB films	6	5	5	4	2	1	2	2
Brent								
Share (%)	11.0	11.2	5.2	6.7	8.9	10.8	4.4	2.7
Rate-of-return (%)	7.5	15.8	14.3	20.2	11.6	14.7	1.8	−22.1
Number of M & LB films	6	5	3	3	3	2	1	1
Cagney								
Share (%)	5.8	7.3	8.4	11.8	–	–	5.7	–
Rate-of-return (%)	32.3	34.5	55.0	80.4	–	–	−23.0	–
Number of M & LB films	3	3	4	4	–	–	1	–
Davis								
Share (%)	7.8	10.3	10.7	8.0	10.2	9.9	8.1	4.6
Rate-of-return (%)	23.0	48.4	30.9	40.1	38.7	53.3	24.2	39.2
Number of M & LB films	4	5	6	3	4	2	2	1
de Havilland								
Share (%)	–	–	–	5.4	–	–	4.6	3.6
Rate-of-return (%)	–	–	–	60.0	–	–	14.1	−10.9
Number of M & LB films	–	–	–	2	–	–	1	1

Flynn								
Share (%)	–	–	–	2.5	–	–	4.9	8.5
Rate-of-return (%)	–	–	–	0.0	–	–	30.9	39.5
Number of M & LB films	–	–	–	1	–	–	1	2
Francis								
Share (%) 5.5	5.5	3.8	9.5	6.6	7.7	5.6	10.4	8.8
Rate-of-return (%)	1.0	49.8	24.1	5.5	19.3	26.2	–13.4	–9.8
Number of M & LB films	3	2	4	2	2	1	3	4
O'Brien								
Share (%)	–	–	10.7	11.7	15.4	8.4	18.0	13.4
Rate-of-return (%)	–	–	43.5	60.6	21.7	16.7	–13.0	–11.0
Number of M & LB films	–	–	6	4	4	2	4	4
Powell, D.								
Share (%)	–	5.6	6.2	4.2	2.9	–	5.5	11.1
Rate-of-return (%)	–	28.3	45.2	38.4	52.3	–	–11.7	–12.6
Number of M & LB films	–	2	3	1	1	–	1	3
Rains								
Share (%)	–	–	–	–	–	4.7	–	7.7
Rate-of-return (%)	–	–	–	–	–	–9.8	–	25.6
Number of M & LB films	–	–	–	–	–	1	–	2

it is not surprising that the studios adopted a corporate approach to the resource-coordinating problem: they chose to internalise the process through a set of term contracts, rather than acquire human resources for the express purpose at hand through the market. This logic is apparent in studios' dealings with stars. The internal authority structure enabled studio executives to systematically plan for and direct the activities of those idiosyncratic assets under contract. (This often led to disagreements between stars and their executives concerning the appropriateness of the film vehicles to which the former were directed.) It also reduced the risks associated with not securing the contracts of desired artistes, where substitution was problematic, since studios maintained what were in effect stock companies of players.

In contrast, even where successful, the competitive market price necessary to secure a bundle of star and player inputs at any one moment, together with the additional transaction costs associated with constantly seeking such idiosyncratic inputs, project after project, through the market mechanism, imposed marked uncertainty upon the filmmaking process and may have significantly and adversely affected rates-of-return. In effect the major studios in the classical period were able to expropriate a proportion of the economic rents generated by their stars and in so doing attenuate the risks associated with film production. They did this by paying them less through their term contracts than the price that would have been necessary to secure their services on the open market. One measure of this was the fee obtained from loaning out a 'star' to another studio which invariably resulted in wages plus a payment to the home studio.[34]

The movements in actor budget shares in Table 6.4 would seem broadly consistent with such an interpretation of the resource-allocation process. Given that it seems reasonable to assume that Warners' annual production budgets expanded and contracted in response to the financial performance on the previous years' budget (see discussion of Tables 6.1 and 6.2), a similar process would appear to have taken place in the allocation of resources to actors. Thus up until the 1934/1935 season, the actor budget shares in Table 6.4 tended to increase in response to strong rate-of-return performance in the previous season – this would appear to have occurred in the cases of Blondell, Cagney, Francis and Powell, although this is not so apparent in the cases of Brent and Davis. The rapid movement into high-budget production in the 1934/1935 season led to some realignment in these shares, but thereafter similar trends can be observed – Brent, Francis and Powell all experienced initial increases in budget shares but declined thereafter as their films performed relatively poorly. De Havilland and Rains experienced relatively volatile share changes in response to the volatile rate-of-return performance of their films. Flynn experienced a steady increase in the budget shares of his films in response to their strong and consistent performance. The extent to which the profiles of Cagney and Davis are not fully consistent with such an interpretation can be explained by the contract disputes in which they were involved.

Pokorny and Sedgwick (2001: 169–172) examine these trends via the application of more rigorous statistical tools, which supports such an interpretation of the process by which resources were allocated to actors, and generalises to all the actors used by Warners over the data period.

Given that is seems reasonable to assume that Warners tended to invest in previously successful actors, the central issue is how profitable such a strategy proved to be. That is, to what extent can the rate-of-return performance of a film be explained in terms of the past success of the actors who appeared in the film, after having standardised for the range of other factors that may have impacted on film profitability?

These issues are examined in Pokorny and Sedgwick (2001: 173–179) within a regression model context. Thus the broad approach was to examine the extent to which the rate-of-return performance of a film could be attributed to the deployment of previously successful actors, directors and genres (defined in terms of rate-of-return and box-office performance). A range of other factors that might have contributed to film success was also included, such as the critical reception of the film and general economic conditions, so that a standardised framework was constructed in which the impact of stardom, if any, could be assessed.

Considering all the films that Warners produced over the period, there was evidence to suggest that there were indeed returns to stardom, in the sense that a strategy of directing resources to successful actors from the previous season impacted positively on film rate-of-return performance. However, this effect appeared to be restricted only to medium- and low-budget films, albeit that they accounted for 83 per cent of the films produced over the period and 61 per cent of production budgets. In the case of high-budget films, no returns to stardom could be identified. Indeed, there did not appear to be any identifiable and consistent strategy that proved to be successful in the production of high-budget films – high-budget production appeared to be dominated by high levels of uncertainty, reflecting the volatile nature of this category of film production. Medium- and low-budget production, by contrast, appeared to be characterised by a much more ordered and predictable production environment, in which a number of successful strategies could be identified. Investing in previously successful actors was certainly one of these strategies, but these also included the use of previously successful directors and genres.

The data presented in Tables 6.5 and 6.6 can now be seen to be consistent with such an interpretation. Table 6.6 reflects the consistent and high rate-of-return performance of most of Warners' prominent actors in medium- and low-budget films, in contrast to the volatile and often poor performance of these actors in high-budget films, as reflected in Table 6.5. Thus while high-budget films may have been more likely to have made a critical impact, such as the achievement of Academy Awards, such success did not necessarily translate into financial success, and certainly not in any predictable manner.

Conclusion

It is clear from the evidence presented here that Warners responded to changing economic and competitive circumstances in a strategic fashion: during the 1920s, expectations of an expanding market, principally at home but also overseas, led to a series of heroic corporate decisions in the direction of vertical integration, whilst the onset of the Depression caused it to produce fewer films and alter the cost, genre and star characteristics of its annual portfolio of films. Although it sold some cinemas during these lean years, the vertical structure of its business, like that of its main rivals, was left intact. In particular, three distinct stages can be distinguished during the 1930s: the period of survival following the onset of the Depression, when average film costs were reduced dramatically; the slow return to confidence as both annual portfolio and average film budgets crept up; and, finally, the move towards exclusive 'A' film production schedules at the end of the period.

In drawing attention to the variability and structure of production budgets through the application of portfolio theory, it is clear that during Hollywood's classical period Warners took a strategic approach to risk, both in terms of the global sum they were willing to invest for any single production season and the manner in which it was spread across the set of production projects. Warners could be interpreted as having adopted a retrospective approach to risk, where the financial performance of films in period $t-1$ proved to be a critical factor. This led to a cyclical pattern in annual film production budgets and risk taking which closely mirrored the behaviour of the US economy.

A similar approach could be identified with regard to the manner in which Warners deployed and developed their stars. Warners could be interpreted as having adopting an incremental approach to the development of their film portfolios, building on the success of their actors (and directors and genres), with such an approach appearing to have had a positive impact on film rate-of-return performance.

However, when a distinction is drawn between high-budget and medium-/low-budget film production, these positive effects that could be attributed to the exploitation of stardom were seen to have been derived exclusively from the production of medium-/low-budget films. In particular, the use of stars did not appear to have been an effective strategy in the production of high-budget films. In part, this could be explained by the fact that the production of high-budget films was necessarily risky and represented a major focus for innovation. Thus there is some evidence of there being returns to risk-taking behaviour in the production of high-budget films, but of negligible returns to an incremental approach. Perhaps this is to be expected, given the one-off nature of much high-budget production – the production of a high-budget 'hit' is a complex process and the relatively simple strategy of using high-profile stars to carry such productions is unlikely to have been successful in itself. In addition, Warners' expertise lay in the production of medium-to-high-/medium-budget films.

The conclusion which emerges is that the financial data on the performance of films produced by Warners during the 1930s indicate that studio investment in 'stars' and 'big-budget' vehicles in which they appeared is not explained by standard investment criteria: the additional expenditure on star qualities and expenditures associated with 'big-budget' films did not consistently generate sufficient box office revenues to justify this investment. Accordingly, the production of big-budget productions should be seen not as a business decision governed by a calculus based upon a probability distribution of risks, but rather as stand-alone investments, akin to product innovation, in which the producer's imagination is paramount. Nevertheless, and this is critical, such investments were made in a context of a portfolio of film products which, in effect, cushioned the gamble in this type of film.

Finally, to focus on particular stars and to evaluate their contribution to the profitability of specific films may be potentially misleading. The analysis here has demonstrated that there are clear returns to the use of previously successful actors, and particularly so in the production of medium-/low-budget films. That such a strategy must necessarily produce 'stars' is self-evident. However, to observe that some well-established stars did not have a significant impact on the financial success of the films in which they appear is not necessarily a rejection of value of stardom. Rather it may reflect the natural cyclical nature of stardom, in that it is inevitable that stars lose their star power, and therefore at some point cease to produce value added. Additionally, film production must also be seen within its institutional context, in the sense that any film is but a component of a portfolio of films. It is the manner in which risk is spread across this portfolio that is of relevance and, in turn, how the deployment of actors, amongst a range of strategies, can be used to attenuate this risk.

Notes

1 This chapter is a revised and combined reworking of Sedgwick and Pokorny (1998) and Pokorny and Sedgwick (2001).
2 See, for example, the work of De Vany and Walls (1996, 1997, 1999, 2002) all collected in De Vany (2004).
3 Annual Hollywood production declined steadily from the peak of 678 films in 1927 to 489 by 1932. Production lifted to around the 520 mark for the three years 1934–1936, but fell below 500 again towards the end of the 1930s. There were a number of forces at play in accounting for this decline, including the transformation to sound during the late 1920s and substantially enlarged

budgets per film towards the end of the 1930s. Undoubtedly, the severity of the Depression in the early 1930s was an important factor in an account of the fall between 1930–1932 (Finler 1988; *Film Daily Yearbooks*).

4 Greenwald (1950).

5 The authors are grateful to Mark Glancy for allowing us access to the complete Schaefer ledger in contrast to the selected details published in Glancy (1995).

6 See Gomery (1992), Izod (1988) and Roddick (1983).

7 Gomery (1992).

8 *Historical Statistics of the US* (1975), Series H.873.

9 See Thompson (1985).

10 *Historical Statistics of the US* (1975), Series H.878–893.

11 *Historical Statistics of the US* (1975), Series H.878–893.

12 MGM was the only studio that continued to make reported accounting profits during the height of the Depression. Warners' reported profits are listed in Finler (1988: 238) and can be found in detail in the *Motion Picture News*' yearbooks of the period.

13 See Balio (1995).

14 Roddick (1983).

15 For the detailed theoretical underpinnings of the approach, the interested reader should consult any standard text in Financial Accounting/Management, such as Brealey and Myers (2000).

16 This process was accentuated as a consequence of the dramatic decline in real box office revenues between 1946 and 1963, encouraging studios to off-load their stars in an effort to cut back on overhead costs. The widespread adoption of the net profit contract can be viewed as a means of transferring risk from the production company to the star. See Weinstein (1998, and Chapter 9 of this book), and Acheson and Maule (1994, and Chapter 11 of this book).

17 An extreme example is *The Singing Fool* (1928/1929), the highest-revenue-generating film over the period, which generated receipts of $5,916,000, from a production budget of just $388,000. This compares with the average production cost over the period of $326,000.

18 In order to estimate the net profit generated by a film, data on distribution costs are required. Unfortunately such data are not available for the films produced by Warners over the period. However, such data are available for the 1,130 films produced by MGM and RKO (see Glancy 1992 and Jewell 1994), allowing for the distribution costs, and hence net profits, of each of the Warners films to be estimated. Specifically, the distribution costs of a film are presumably directly related to the revenues generated by the film – the broader is the reach of the film, the higher are the distribution costs. It is presumably also the case that initial promotional expenditures will be determined as some (relatively small) proportion of production costs. Thus the distribution costs, D, of a film can be interpreted as being directly related to production costs, C, and the revenues, R, generated by the film, or $D = \alpha C + \beta R$. Using data on the 1,130 films produced by MGM and RKO produced estimates of 0.05 and 0.35 for α and β, respectively, with an R^2 value of 0.968 (see Pokorny and Sedgwick 2003 for further details). Using these estimates of α and β, the distribution costs for each of the Warners films could be estimated, and hence estimates of the net profits generated by these films.

19 Films continued to be presented under the First National trade name until 1941.

20 It is important to note that there is a mis-alignment between the Figure 6.1 and Table 6.1 dates. The latter represent the period of film release. Hence, given Warners' use of a fourteen-month amortisation schedule, the releases of one year would be expected to earn at least part of their box office revenue during

the following year. A further complicating factor in any time–series analysis is that the studio adopted a financial year which ended during the last week of August.

21 These profit/loss figures are not, of course, the same as those that were published in the Warner Bros. accounts for the period. They take no account of the company's accumulated assets and liabilities, and the accounting conventions applied to these. Also, they do not represent performance within the strict limits of a trading year, since films released in one season generated revenue during the following season. Rather, they are to be interpreted as reflecting Warner Bros.' annual performance with regard to its pure filmmaking activities.

22 See Sedgwick and Pokorny (1998: 210–211) for a more formal analysis.

23 Balio (1995: 29).

24 Glancy (1995: 61–62).

25 *Captain Blood* (1934/1935), *Anthony Adverse* (1935/1936), *The Charge of the Light Brigade* (1935/1936), *The Adventures of Robin Hood* (1937/1938), *The Prince and the Pauper* (1936/1937), *The Private Lives of Elizabeth and Essex* (1939/1940), *The Sea Hawk* (1939/1940), *The Life of Emile Zola* (1936/1937), and *The Story of Louis Pasteur* (1935/1936) are notable examples.

26 A number of alternative partitions were used. For example, the high-budget films in each year were also defined as the 20 per cent most expensive films in the year; medium budget as the next 40 per cent most expensive films; and low-budget as the remaining 40 per cent of films. Marginal changes to the relative average cost index cut off points were also experimented with. These different partitions did not produce significant changes in the statistical results that follow.

27 The standard deviation of profits for high-budget, medium-budget and low-budget films are, respectively, 544.1, 225.4 and 105.7, and the corresponding coefficients of variation are 2.87, 2.26 and 1.25.

28 *Gold Diggers of 1933* and *42nd Street*.

29 This can be justified in terms of identifying those actors whose performances were of overall importance to the studio. However, the string of actors who appeared in each of the 441 films released during the period have not been weighted according to their billing status.

30 This was *A Midsummer Night's Dream*, a highly critically acclaimed film, but a film that was unable to cover its high production and distribution costs, and a film that appears to have been made primarily to boost the cultural kudos and 'respectability' of the studio.

31 See Balio (1995: 159–161) for a fuller discussion of these events.

32 Weinstein (1998) confirms the generality of such contracts during the studio period. See also Chisholm (1993, 1997) For a general discussion of stardom during these years, see Sedgwick (2000: Chapter 9). Balio (1995: 155–161) gives an account of the typical life cycle of stars and details James Cagney's and Bette Davis' respective disputes with Warners during the mid-1930s. Also see Klein and Leffler (1981) on the economics of breaking contracts.

33 Where the star was on 'picture-deal' terms, the studio would cast the star in low-budget productions to encourage the star's agent to negotiate 'buying out' the contract (for example, Joan Crawford paid $200,000 in 1952 to be released from her contract with Warners). Where the contract had clauses giving the star approval of script and/or director and/or co-star and/or cinematographer and/or working conditions, the studio simply produced a flow of proposals that would be unacceptable to the star in the hope of forcing a buy-out (see Shipman 1989: 130–136).

34 See Sedgwick, op. cit., for a discussion of loan-outs. See also Balio (1995: 155–166) for a discussion of the life cycle of stars.

References

Acheson, K. and Maule, C. (1994) 'Understanding Hollywood's organization and continuing success', *Journal of Cultural Economics*, 18: 271–300.

Adler, M. (1985) 'Stardom and talent', *American Economic Review*, 75: 208–212.

Albert, S. (1998) 'Movie stars and the distribution of financially successful films in the motion picture industry', *Journal of Cultural Economics*, 22: 249–270.

Albert, S. (1999) 'Movie stars and the distribution of financially successful films in the motion picture industry – reply', *Journal of Cultural Economics*, 23: 325–329.

Balio, T. (ed.) (1995) *Grand Design: Hollywood as a Modern Business, 1930–39*, Berkeley, CA: University of California Press.

Brealey, Richard A. and Myers, Stewart C. (2000) *Principles of Corporate Finance*, 6th edn, London: Irwin McGraw Hill.

Chisholm, D. (1993) 'Asset specificity and long-term contracts: the case of the motion picture industry', *Eastern Economic Journal*, 19: 143–155.

Chisholm, D. (1997) 'Profit-sharing versus fixed payment contracts: evidence from the motion picture industry', *Journal of Law, Economics and Organization*, 13: 169–201.

De Vany, A. and Walls, W. (1996) 'Bose–Einstein dynamics and adaptive contracting in the motion picture industry', *Economic Journal*, 106: 1493–1514.

De Vany, A. and Walls, W. (1997) 'The market for motion pictures: rank, revenue, and survival', *Economic Inquiry*, 35: 783–797.

De Vany, A. and Walls, W.D. (1999) 'Uncertainty and the movie industry: does star power reduce the terror of the box office?' *Journal of Cultural Economics*, 23: 285–318.

De Vany, A. and Walls, W.D. (2002) 'Does Hollywood make too many R-rated movies? Risk, stochastic dominance, and the illusion of expectation', *Journal of Business*, 75: 425–451.

De Vany, A. (2004) *Hollywood Economics*, London: Routledge.

Finler, J. (1988) *The Hollywood Story*, New York, NY: Crown.

Glancy, H.M. (1992) 'MGM film grosses, 1924–1948: the Eddie Mannix ledger', *Historical Journal of Film, Radio and Television*, 12: 127–144.

Glancy, H.M. (1995) 'Warner Bros. film grosses, 1921–1951: the William Schaefer ledger', *Historical Journal of Film, Radio and Television*, 15: 55–74.

Greenwald, W. (1950) *The Motion Picture Industry: an Economic Study of the History and Practices of a Business*, Ph.D. dissertation, New York University.

Gomery, D. (1992) *Shared Pleasures: A History of Movie Presentation in the United States*, London: BFI.

Hamlen Jr., W. (1991) 'Superstardom in popular music: empirical evidence', *Review of Economics and Statistics*, 73: 729–733.

Hamlen Jr., W. (1994) 'Variety and superstardom in popular music', *Economic Inquiry*, 32: 395–406.

Izod, J. (1988) *Hollywood and the Box Office, 1895–1986*, Basingstoke: Macmillan.

Jewell, R.B. (1994) 'RKO film grosses, 1929–51: C.J. Trevlin ledger', *Historical Journal of Film, Radio and Television*, 14: 35–50.

Kerr, C. (1990) 'Incorporating the star: the intersection of business and aesthetic strategies in early American film', *Business History Review*, 64: 383–410.

King, B. (1986) 'Stardom as occupation', in P. Kerr (ed.) *The Hollywood Film Industry*, London: BFI.

Klein, B. and Leffler, K. (1981) 'The role of market forces in assuming contractual performance', *Journal of Political Economy*, 89: 615–641.

Pokorny, M. and Sedgwick, J. (2001) 'Stardom and the profitability of film making: Warner Bros. in the 1930s', *Journal of Cultural Economics*, 25: 157–184.

Pokorny, M. and Sedgwick, J. (2003) 'The long run characteristics of the US film industry', Paper presented to the 7th International Conference of the International Association for Arts and Cultural Management, Milan, Italy, June.

Ravid, S.A. (1999) 'Information, blockbusters and stars: a study of the film industry', *Journal of Business*, 72: 463–492.

Roddick, N. (1983) *A New Deal In Entertainment: Warner Bros. in the 1930s*, London: BFI.

Rosen, S. (1981) 'The economics of superstars', *American Economic Review*, 71: 845–858.

Sedgwick, J. (2000) *Popular Filmgoing During 1930s Britain: A Choice of Pleasures*, Exeter: Exeter University Press.

Sedgwick, J. and Pokorny, M. (1998) 'The risk environment of film making: Warner Bros. in the inter-war years', *Explorations in Economic History*, 35: 196–220.

Sedgwick, J. and Pokorny, M. (1999) 'Movie stars and the distribution of financially successful films in the motion picture industry: a comment', *Journal of Cultural Economics*, 23: 319–323.

Shipman, D. (1993) *The Great Movie Stars, Volume 1: The Golden Years*, London: Warner Books.

Thompson, K. (1985) *Exporting Entertainment: America in the World Film Market 1907–1934*, London: BFI.

United States: Bureau of the Census (1975) *Historical Statistics of the US: Colonial Times to 1970*, Washington, DC: US Department of Commerce, Bureau of the Census.

Weinstein, M. (1998) 'Profit sharing contracts in Hollywood', *Journal of Legal Studies*, 27: 67–112.

7 Product differentiation at the movies

Hollywood 1946 to 1965[1]

John Sedgwick

Popular film was a most important twentieth century commodity. It is worthy of study by the economic historian, not because it employed many people, which it did not, or because it contributed greatly to national income, which it did not, but because it attracted extremely large numbers of consumers to spend time voluntarily, in preference to other activities, experiencing some measure of well-being derived from sequences of moving images and their associated aesthetics.[2] Audiences across the globe now consume films through a variety of media, but in the years immediately following the end of the Second World War consumption was confined to cinemas alone. At that time US audiences, when counted by ticket admissions, were at an all time high with an annual count of four-and-a-half-billion (thirty-three visits per capita), dwarfing those attracted by other paid-for leisure activities.[3] After 1946, admissions fell continuously to a low point of 0.82 billion in 1972, followed by a gentle recovery. During this period, the mode of film consumption diversified from the cinema alone to home viewing on television sets, through the TV networks at first, and then video, cable and more recently satellite (Vogel 2001: chapter 2). Computer screens now constitute a third medium. Remarkably, during these changes, as before them, Hollywood has continued to dominate the global market for film (Aksoy and Robins 1992; Hoskins *et al.* 1997; Jarvie 1992; Storper 1994; Thompson 1985).

The American market for film entertainment was, and remains, by far the most important source of theatrical revenue for film producers, contributing approximately half the total world-wide sales in 1965. Unlike today, when approximately 70 per cent of film revenue is derived from non-theatrical sources, rental income from the box office was almost the sole source of revenue for production companies during the period under investigation.[4] Indeed, rental agreements with the TV networks did not start to make a significant contribution to the costs of film production until the widespread diffusion of colour television during the late 1960s and early 1970s (Izod 1988: 166–170). Before this, Hollywood's earnings from television came not so much from its library of vintage films locked away in studio vaults as from its production of contemporary made-for-TV films and celebrity shows (Gomery 1996: 407–408).

However, this strategic response to declining audience numbers was not unproblematic for the major studios. Extending their product portfolio to made-for-television programmes and films did not lessen the problem of how to compete effectively in the diminishing market for feature films and how, if possible, to arrest this decline. After all, making films, and distributing and screening them, had constituted the core business of Hollywood since the late 1910s (Balio 1993; Crafton 1997; Thompson 1985). In 1946 the principal studios dominated production and distribution, and five of them – Loew's/MGM, Paramount, RKO, Twentieth Century Fox and Warners – controlled a significant share of the first-run exhibition market from which they were compelled to disengage themselves as a result of the Supreme Court's *Paramount Divorcement* decree of 1948.[5] By 1965, most of the films released were made by production companies whose existence was short-lived, if not confined solely to the production of a single film output, and shown in divested cinemas.

The change in the organisational configuration of Hollywood is commonly explained as a consequence of the major studios no longer having a guaranteed retail outlet for their product (Izod 1988: 124–125; De Vany and Eckert 1991: 53–54). This chapter proposes a different explanation based upon the changing pattern of demand: namely, that during the period 1946 to 1965 not only did US box office revenues fall dramatically, but they became increasingly unequally distributed, so that whilst the rental income of the annual top-ten films held up over the period, films ranked in lower classifications performed progressively poorly. These changes made untenable the portfolio approach to risk that had characterised studio production during the preceding two decades: middle- and low-budget films could no longer be relied upon to attenuate the risks associated with big-budget production (Sedgwick and Pokorny 1998). The outcome of this was that studio production became increasingly focused on the production of 'hit' films. To make their films more attractive to audiences, studios spent increasing amounts in order to enhance production values, including the introduction of an array of visual and audio innovations (Belton 1992). Audiences for their part were becoming more occasional and selective. The evidence is that they responded to the perceived quality of certain 'event' films in relation to all other films. In the words of the movie mogul Darryl F. Zanuck:

> There is no such thing as a safe field. Theatregoers are more selective than ever before.... This does not mean that every picture we make must be a freak attraction completely off the beaten path but it does mean that it must have at least an idea that will lift it out of the commonplace.[6]

Whilst it may be true that demographic and other social changes lowered the average age of the audience over the period, leading to the rise in the number of films directed towards juvenile audiences, it was rare for one of these niche films to occupy an annual top-ten berth.[7] Market fragmentation can account for the emergence of the host of small-time opportunistic independent producers but it does not explain the central position retained by the major Hollywood studios.

The context

In the immediate post-war period, the United States experienced rapid social change occasioned by the growth in real disposable incomes, the build-up of wartime savings and the explosion in the birth rate. As Halberstam (1994: 118) has written: 'this was one of the great sellers' markets of all time. There was a desperate hunger for products after the long drought of fifteen years caused by the Depression and then World War Two.' The same author identifies the key symbolic products of the late 1940s and 1950s as cars, suburban (Levitt) homes – full of consumer durables, including televisions, bought at suburban (Korvettes) discount stores – fast foods (McDonald's) and advertising. To these should be added a whole range of outdoor recreation products including tourism, golf, gardening, participatory sports and fishing (Clawson and Knetch 1966; Oakley 1986; Rome 2001).

Cinema was not on this list. Indeed, audiences had stopped going to the cinema in large numbers. Referencing social survey evidence of 1948, Conant (1960: 12) identified the pressure on consumers' time as the most important factor in the decline of cinema attendances. Gomery (1992: 83) writes:

> When middle-class Americans moved to the suburbs in record numbers after the Second World War, they also abandoned propinquity to the matrix of downtown and neighbourhood movie theatres. In addition, these young adults, previously the most loyal fans, concentrated on raising families.

Table 7.1 reports the period as one of intensive urbanisation. The proportion of Americans living in urban areas, defined as cities with a population larger than 100,000, expanded from 46 per cent in 1950 to 58 per cent by 1970. More startling, however, is the growth in the number of Americans living in fringe areas of cities as opposed to city centres. Whilst the latter grew by 32 per cent over the period, the city fringe population grew by 161 per cent, a compound annual growth rate of over 5 per cent per year. Of course the record number of housing starts made this population movement to the suburbs possible, with the housing stock increasing by one-quarter during both the 1940s and 1950s (Rome 2001).[8] Alongside these

Table 7.1 Selected US population statistics, 1946–1970

Year	US population (000s) (1)	Urbanised areas – central cities (000s) (2)	Urbanised areas – urban fringe (000s) (3)	Persons aged under 5 (000s) (4)	Ages 5–14 (000s) (5)	Ages 15–24 (000s) (6)	Ages 25–34 (000s) (7)
1946	–	–	–	12,974	21,844	23,382	22,954
1950	151,684	48,337	20,872	16,331	24,477	22,260	23,932
1960	180,671	57,975	37,873	20,341	35,735	24,576	22,919
1970	204,879	63,922	54,525	17,156	40,733	36,496	25,293

Source: *Historical Statistics of the United States*, Chapter A, Series 29–42; Series 82–90; Series 288–319.

changes was the increase in home ownership, rising dramatically from 44 per cent in 1940 to 55 per cent in 1950 and to 62 per cent in 1960.[9] The change in lifestyle that went with suburbanisation is, of course, a subject for numerous films during the period.

The baby boom is captured in columns 4–7 of Table 7.1. The number of under-fives increased by 57 per cent during the fourteen years between 1946 and 1960, at a rate of 3.5 per cent per annum. Likewise the 5–14 age range also mushroomed – a 64 per cent growth between these same years at an annual rate of 3.9 per cent – whilst the next two age categories remained static. For men and women in their twenties and early thirties, there were many more children of pre-school and schooling age to be looked after.

Hence, whilst Americans had, on average, more leisure time at their disposal in the post-war period with the onset of institutional vacations and the decline in Saturday working, they found additional claims on their growing recreational budget through alternative recreational activities as well as family and house-owning responsibilities (Clawson and Knetsch 1966).[10] Between 1946 and 1950, cinema audiences declined by one-third, even though admission prices were falling in real terms.[11] From 1950 television became an additional attraction for Americans and the chief cause in the further decline of cinema numbers. The astonishing speed at which television services were diffused across the American population is captured in column 5 of Table 7.2. In 1950, less than 9 per cent of American households possessed a television, yet five years later the proportion had risen to 64 per cent. A Stanford Research Institute report showed that the diffusion of television accounted for more than 70 per cent of the drop in motion picture revenues in 1950 and 1951, falling to 60 per cent in 1952, 58 per cent in 1953 and 55.8 per cent in 1954. Interestingly, the growth in television viewing brought with it a demand for vintage films (Conant 1960: 13–14).[12]

In contrast to those exogenous factors responsible for the decline in audience numbers highlighted above, Sklar (1975) has focused attention on the contemporary reception of the product itself. Drawing upon scholarly work of the time, he reports a series of conflicting arguments. Whilst all contemporary commentators accepted Handel's findings – that younger people attended the cinema more regularly than older people, and that cinemagoers tended to have spent a longer period in education, and were of a higher socio-economic status but equally spread between the genders – they were interpreted in a variety of ways (Handel 1950). Lazarsfeld maintained that youth had become the chief arbiters of film success: they were its opinion leaders (Lazarsfeld 1947). The Riesmans concurred, arguing that the incipient orientation of filmmaking towards the taste of youth resulted in films that proved to be too fast and difficult to keep up with for older film-goers (Riesman and Riesman 1952). Seldes (1950), however, believed that pandering to youth had resulted in a lowering of

Table 7.2 Selected personal consumption statistics, 1946–1970 (all money values in US $millions, 1958 prices)

Year	Total personal consumption expenditure (1)	Recreational expenditure (2)	Total US box office (3)	Average weekly cinema attendance (millions) (4)	Households with TV sets (000s) (5)
1946	203,404	12,112	2,400	90	8
1950	230,409	13,446	1,660	60	3,875
1955	274,117	15,170	1,429	46	30,700
1960	316,075	17,779	924	40	45,750
1965	397,830	24,171	852	44	52,700

Source: *Historical Statistics of the United States*: Chapter G, Series 416 and 452; Chapter H, Series 874 and 884; Chapter R, Series 93–105. The price deflator used throughout the study is that given for Total Consumer Expenditure, Chapter E, Series 2.

cinematic standards and that it was this that had turned audiences away. Friedson (1954/1955) found that the cinema became a place where young people could be in a social setting of their own making, apart from the authority structures that normally governed their lives.

With the decline in attendances the proportion of young people in the audience increased, so that by 1957 three-quarters of audiences were under thirty and half under twenty years of age.[13] A criticism levelled at Hollywood was that the major studios failed to respond vigorously to this market information. Indeed Sklar (1975: 270–271) has argued that the logic of the situation demanded that Hollywood should have tried harder to attract less educated and lower income groups. However, such strategies were anathema to the studio moguls who conceived their audience to be essentially homogeneous, characterised by a range of 'middle-class' tastes that were known to, and intuitively understood by, them. This opinion is no doubt overstated. One has only to examine the great mix of film-types categorised by genre from, say, the mid-1920s to realise that 'old' Hollywood also produced films for niche markets (Maltby 1999). Nevertheless, it would also be true to say that middle- and big-budget films were designed to achieve maximum penetration in the market place and this was achievable only if audiences had a common conception of film quality. To assess the studios' strategic response to the declining market, it seems sensible to begin with the box office.

The data

In 1946 the weekly trade journal *Variety* published in either its first or second issue in January of each year an annual list of the most popular films released onto the American market, together with the rental incomes they generated for their distributors.[14] The data set of 1,820 films, with not less than sixty-one and not more than 130 top-ranking films recorded in each of the years of the study, provides a unique empirical source from which to study Hollywood during this time of declining theatrical audiences. The numbers of films reported each year – labelled by *Variety* as 'Top Grossers' – are found in column 1 of Table 7.3 and were selected on the grounds that they generated a threshold number of dollars at the US and Canadian box office, net of the exhibitor's take. In 1946 this threshold was $2.25 million.[15] The threshold was lowered to $2 million for the 1947 season; $1.5 million for 1948 and 1949; $1.25 million for 1950; and $1 million for the remaining years of the study. Initially, the reduction in the threshold more than counterbalanced the falling demand for films, because it admitted more films on to the 'Top Grossing' list during the period up to 1953. Thereafter, the number of films listed fell.

On the surface, the *Variety* returns might not appear to be a good basis for developing a thesis. They certainly were not produced from within an academy, or as the outcome of scientific method. The bases of the

Table 7.3 Box office revenues of 'Top Grossing Films', 1946–1965 (all money values in US $millions, 1958 prices)

Year	No. of films listed in Variety as 'Top Grossers' (1)	No. of 'Top Grossers' distributed by the major Hollywood studios[a] (2)	Net rental income of films listed in Variety (3)	Mean rental income of Variety listed films (4)	Total US box office (5)
1946	61	61	303.55	4.98	2,400.00
1947	75	75	329.27	4.39	2,046.21
1948	92	90	278.61	3.03	1,829.89
1949	89	86	246.14	2.77	1,776.01
1950	95	92	263.67	2.78	1,659.83
1951	130	130	277.40	2.13	1,478.56
1952	118	115	294.10	2.49	1,376.80
1953	131	129	329.67	2.52	1,294.44
1954	112	109	301.89	2.70	1,327.57
1955	107	103	341.97	3.20	1,428.88
1956	106	101	272.42	2.57	1,470.46
1957	95	92	293.27	3.09	1,152.51
1958	76	70	249.17	3.28	992.00
1959	82	79	224.89	2.74	945.71
1960	74	65	244.55	3.30	924.20
1961	75	71	235.90	3.15	886.43
1962	72	67	238.90	3.32	860.82
1963	77	68	301.31	3.91	852.03
1964	70	67	229.54	3.28	850.09
1965	83	79	355.07	4.28	852.02

Sources: Variety; Historical Statistics.

Notes

[a]Taken here to include Columbia, Disney, Loew's/MGM, Paramount, RKO, Twentieth Century Fox, United Artists, Universal and Warner Bros. The film rental data reported in Variety for any particular year included estimates for those films which were released during the year and were still on release. Occasionally, these films appeared as 'Top Grossers' during the following year with an updated figure. These films and their revenues have been attributed to the year of release. For the greater part of the period, re-releases were relatively uncommon with the life cycle of films on theatrical release being completed within fifteen months (Greenwald 1950). Only five re-releases made the Variety charts: Bridge on the River Kwai, reissued in 1964: Cinderella reissued in 1965; Gone With the Wind reissued in 1961; Hollywood Canteen reissued in 1954; and So Dear To My Heart reissued in 1964.

estimates were not recorded and hence are not transparent (Besas 2000: 281–283). Nevertheless, however imperfect they are, they are all that historians have to work on (Crafton 1997: 521). A two-fold case can be made to justify the use of the *Variety* lists. First, the trade treated the data with respect. It told a story about the relative and absolute popularity of films that accorded with the experience of those whose livelihoods were bound up in the film business. This is most important, since without such verity it seems highly unlikely that *Variety* would have continued to serve as the principal trade publication. Second, the reported rental incomes correlate, statistically, very strongly with the returns found in the business ledgers of three 'major' studios uncovered during the 1990s and published in part in microfiche form by the *Historical Journal of Film, Radio and Television*.[16]

From Table 7.3 it is clear that, whilst the total box office revenues of theatrical releases declined to about one-third of their starting value over the period, the rental income accruing to the distributors of those films found in the *Variety* lists experienced a much smaller decline. Some technical problems must be dealt with in analysing these two series. The *Variety* data include Canadian revenues, whereas the US Government statistics do not. This complicates the analysis but not damagingly, because of the relatively small size of the Canadian market.[17] A more serious difficulty is the point in the supply chain at which the data have been collected; in the case of *Variety*, the source is the rental incomes of the distribution companies, whilst the US Government data represent the box office revenue captured by exhibitors. Finler has suggested that the rental income constituted approximately half of the total box office gross, with the other half going to the exhibitor (Finler 1988: 276). The *Film Daily Yearbook* suggests that this proportion is a little above one-third.[18] As the figures stand in Table 7.3, it is apparent that the market share of *Variety*-listed films increases dramatically over the period. If the conservative assumption is made that rental incomes were half the annual box office revenue, the top films increased their share from 26 per cent in 1946 to 84 per cent by 1965.[19]

The period under investigation was notable for the increasing inequality of rental incomes. Table 7.4 shows the proportion of the rental income generated by the sixty top films for each year attributed to films ranked in sets of ten.[20] A first observation is the growing significance of the top-ranking films as money earners. Column 4 shows that the top-ten films significantly increased their share of the rental incomes generated by the top sixty films. This rose from approximately a quarter during the immediate post-war years to above 30 per cent during much of the 1950s, climbing to over 40 per cent for most of the years from 1957 onwards and peaking at 51 per cent in 1965. Further, the actual revenues that accrued to these films also rose in real terms, trending upwards from low post-war levels of less than $50 million in 1949 and 1951, to aggregate rental

Table 7.4 Proportional distribution of rental income of annual top-sixty films, 1946–1965 (column 1 in US $millions, 1958 prices)

Year	Top-sixty rental income (1)	Coefficient of variation (2)	Gini coefficient (3)	Films ranked 1 to 10 (4)	Films ranked 11 to 20 (5)	Films ranked 21 to 30 (6)	Films ranked 31 to 40 (7)	Films ranked 41 to 50 (8)	Films ranked 51 to 60 (9)
1946	300.35	0.29	0.11	0.25	0.19	0.17	0.14	0.13	0.11
1947	289.28	0.49	0.16	0.31	0.19	0.15	0.13	0.12	0.11
1948	211.42	0.24	0.10	0.24	0.19	0.16	0.14	0.14	0.13
1949	189.78	0.30	0.12	0.25	0.20	0.16	0.14	0.13	0.12
1950	201.63	0.53	0.15	0.31	0.17	0.15	0.14	0.12	0.11
1951	171.98	0.38	0.13	0.28	0.17	0.16	0.14	0.13	0.12
1952	210.06	0.79	0.21	0.37	0.16	0.14	0.12	0.11	0.09
1953	225.92	0.77	0.23	0.39	0.17	0.13	0.11	0.10	0.10
1954	226.54	0.51	0.18	0.31	0.20	0.16	0.13	0.11	0.10
1955	265.79	0.49	0.20	0.31	0.22	0.17	0.12	0.10	0.08
1956	211.02	0.52	0.21	0.33	0.22	0.16	0.11	0.10	0.09
1957	248.14	1.27	0.30	0.46	0.16	0.12	0.10	0.09	0.07
1958	231.07	0.87	0.29	0.43	0.18	0.13	0.11	0.08	0.07
1959	200.01	0.57	0.21	0.34	0.20	0.15	0.13	0.10	0.08
1960	228.08	1.26	0.29	0.44	0.17	0.13	0.11	0.08	0.07
1961	217.71	0.64	0.24	0.37	0.20	0.15	0.12	0.09	0.07
1962	225.82	0.88	0.27	0.41	0.19	0.15	0.11	0.08	0.06
1963	280.81	0.91	0.28	0.43	0.18	0.14	0.10	0.08	0.07
1964	219.09	0.75	0.24	0.37	0.20	0.16	0.12	0.09	0.07
1965	325.09	1.26	0.34	0.51	0.15	0.11	0.09	0.08	0.06

Source: *Variety*.

incomes of above \$100 million in 1957, 1958, 1960, 1963 and 1965. The peaks were generated by the extraordinary success of a small number of films. These films were: in the box-office year 1957, *The Ten Command-ments* (\$34.2 million) and *Around the World in 80 Days* (\$22 million); in 1958, *South Pacific* (\$17.5 million) and *Bridge on the River Kwai* (\$17.2 million); in 1960, *Ben Hur* (\$38 million); in 1962 *West Side Story* (\$22 million); in 1963 *Cleopatra* (\$23.5 million) and *How the West Was Won* (\$23 million); and in 1965, *The Sound of Music* (\$42.5 million), *Mary Poppins* (\$31 million), *My Fair Lady* (\$30 million) and *Goldfinger* (\$22 million). (The figures in parentheses represent the North American rental income reported in *Variety*.) However, this upward trend was highly volatile as is evident from the coefficient of variation statistic found in column 2, with marked falls in rental income being experienced in 1954, 1959, 1961 and 1964.[21]

The growth in the market share of the annual top-ten films over the period of this investigation was of course at the expense of the shares taken by the other categories. Distinctive downward trends are noticeable in films grouped into ranks lower than 20, with their market share falling by approximately one-third in the case of the films ranked 31 to 40 and by half in the bottom two categories. In 1946 the share of the top-ten films was a little over twice that of those ranked between 51st and 60th. By the 1960s the difference had increased to multiples of seven and above.[22] This growing inequality of rental incomes causes annual Gini coefficients to trend upwards over the period.[23]

The impact on the industry

During the two decades prior to the *Paramount* decree, Hollywood's prin-cipal studios had pursued a portfolio approach to risk management through the production of a range of films in which the higher risks associ-ated with big-budget production were offset by a greater number of middle- and low-budget films for which revenues were less variable and more evenly spread (Sedgwick and Pokorny 1998). The increasing skew of rental income reported in the previous section, manifest in the dramatic decline in the real earnings of sub-top twenty films, made portfolio pro-duction less tenable as the 1950s wore on, leading to the increase in independent production which Bordwell *et al.* (1985: 330–331) have termed the 'package-unit' system.

> Rather than an individual company containing the source of the labour and materials, the entire industry became the pool for these ... This system of production was intimately tied to the post-war industrial shift: instead of the mass production of many films by a few manufac-turing firms, now there was the specialised production of a few films by many independents. The majors acted as financiers and distributors.[24]

The trend in independent production, defined by Izod (1988: 125) as 'the work of companies that neither own nor are owned by a distribution company', is shown in Table 7.5. From the copyright ownership records it is clear that, for Loew's/MGM, Paramount, Twentieth Century Fox and Warners, the scale and importance of wholly in-house production fell. The main change occurred between 1956 and 1960 with the completion of the divestiture process, and accelerated during the next five-year period as the major studios transformed themselves into distributor-financiers handling annual portfolios of films in which investment risk was shared to an increasing degree with independent producers.[25] The studio that bucked the trend was Disney with its distribution arm Buena Vista. However, as is evident from a comparison of columns 1 and 2 in Table 7.5, whilst the major studios cut back on production, their share of the top end of the market as distributors remained dominant and continued to be so, as Aksoy and Robins (1992) have shown, for the remainder of the century. For these authors independent production was dependent on the major studios and should be seen as the consequence of their decision to produce, or co-finance, and distribute fewer but more costly films, a strategy designed to attract occasional film-goers back to the cinema by offering superior attractions.[26]

Product differentiation

In most product and service markets 'quality' goods have carried premium prices denoting the willingness of some consumers to pay higher prices for (presumably) perceived differences in utility. It is interesting to note that film exhibition has rarely engaged in this business practice, with admission prices in all but exceptional cases remaining invariant, irrespective of the film being shown.[27] Consequently, the question arises of how choices were made in the absence of relative price differentials among films shown in a locality.[28] If novelty is an irreducible characteristic of film as a commodity, it follows that, *ex ante*, consumers do not know fully what they want. De Vany and Walls (1996: 1493) express this point well when arguing: 'Film audiences make hits or flops and they do it, not by revealing preferences they already have, but by discovering what they like.'[29] Furthermore, film is an experience good: audiences cannot evaluate a particular film fully until they have experienced it (Nelson 1974). Implicit in these powerful ideas is the role of the film producer as an image entrepreneur, a person who is engaged in bringing to audiences pleasures that they could not fully imagine. As a rule Hollywood used stars, genres, directors, styles, story-line, story situation and ethos, together with enthralling technologies, in efforts to attract audiences by offering them strong novel pleasures whilst at the same time attenuating the risk associated with surprise (Sedgwick and Pokorny 1998: 196–198; Izod 1988: 56). The process was an interactive one with the production–distribution side of the industry engaged in three

Table 7.5 The 'major' studios' control of copyright

'Major' studios	No. of 'Top Grossing' films distributed (1)	No. of 'Top Grossing' films credited to the studio (2)	No. of 'Top Grossing' films where copyright owned by studio (3)	Ratio of column 3 to column 1 (4)
Columbia				
1946–1950	21	16	14	0.67
1951–1955	36	24	20	0.56
1956–1960	45	20	16	0.36
1961–1965	52	8	7	0.13
Disney/BV				
1954–1955	6	6	6	1.00
1956–1960	15	14	14	0.93[a]
1961–1965	25	25	25	1.00
Loew's/MGM				
1946–1950	87	85	86	0.99
1951–1955	97	96	96	0.99
1956–1960	65	38	31	0.48
1961–1965	63	13	18	0.29
Paramount				
1946–1950	63	59	51	0.81
1951–1955	85	62	67	0.79
1956–1960	56	20	23	0.41
1961–1965	44	6	6	0.14
RKO				
1946–1950	48	22	14	0.29
1951–1955	38	17	20	0.53
1956–1957	5	3	5	1.00
Twentieth Century Fox				
1946–1950	74	74	74	1.00
1951–1955	110	104	104	0.95
1956–1960	75	60	54	0.72
1961–1965	45	18	19	0.42
Universal				
1946–1950	33	27	24	0.73
1951–1955	88	88	88	1.00
1956–1960	44	38	40	0.91
1961–1965	44	10	13	0.30
Warners				
1946–1950	64	59	50	0.78
1951–1955	94	71	66	0.70
1956–1960	49	24	27	0.55
1961–1965	25	11	11	0.44
Total				
1946–1950	396	348	319	0.81
1951–1955	563	476	475	0.84
1956–1960	364	228	221	0.61
1961–1965	273	66	74	0.27

Source: *Library of Congress Catalog of Copyright Entries: Motion Pictures.*

Note

a The film that caused this proportion to fall below 1.0 was *The Big Fisherman* (1959).

types of activity: responding to consumer preferences as previously revealed; offering novelty; and finally, attempting to shape audience appetites, needs and expectations.

From the early years of film's existence as a commodity, audiences have been attracted to particular genres, such as westerns and musicals, as well as films with high levels of spectacle. During the period of this investigation, a number of new generic conventions emerged from the consumption interests of young people, in particular, rock and roll and sex (Docherty 1995). Nevertheless, as has been discussed, the growing unequal distribution of film revenues suggests that, increasingly, large-scale audiences were only attracted by the promise of extraordinary film experiences. One approach to analysing these differences in the alignment of audiences is provided by the distinction between vertical and horizontal forms of product differentiation. Waterson (1994: 106) provides a useful definition:

> If we consider a class of goods as being typified by a set of (desirable) characteristics, then two varieties are vertically differentiated when the first contains more of some or all characteristics than the second, so that all rational consumers given a free choice would opt for the first. They are horizontally differentiated when one contains more of some but fewer of other characteristics, so that two consumers exhibiting different tastes offered a free choice would not unambiguously plump for the same one.[30]

Horizontal product differentiation

Genre, in the words of Izod (1988: 56), enables 'the uniqueness of the product to be strikingly de-emphasized', serving to group films that share particular characteristic traits. In the spirit of Harold Hotelling, it is possible to conceive of genres, placed along a continuum, attracting particular audiences. Richard Maltby (1999: 4) has argued that:

> Classical Hollywood thus recognised a number of quite clearly differentiated groups of viewers and organised its output to provide a range of products that would appeal to different fractions of the audience. Movies were assembled to contain ingredients appealing to different generically defined areas of the audience, so that their marketing and exploitation could position each picture in relation to one or more of those 'taste' publics.

Genre classification, however, is not an exact science. Various agencies – audiences, the film trade, film critics, academics – have evolved distinctive genre systems for their own particular purposes.[31] Clearly, with such fluidity of usage, some form of working categorisation of genres will have to serve. The *Motion Picture Guide* provides a genre classification for each of its entries, and this has been used to provide an initial analysis of the sample of top-ranking films listed annually in *Variety*. The 1,820 films in the sample are differentiated under no less than 170 distinct genre categories, most of which are hybrid. For example, two films are classified as 'Adventure/History/Dramas', three films as 'Drama/History/Epics' and three as 'History/Drama/Adventures'. The assumptions made to reduce the categories to a manageable number for analytical purposes are: (1) that the forward slash commonly deployed in the *Guide* can be ignored as it is not at all clear that it is used consistently by its writers; and (2) that the ordering of the categorising terms used reflects the predominance of the first-listed term as a descriptor of the film in question. In this way the number of genre categories has been reduced to twenty-three, two of which – Cinerama and documentary – are not included in the *Motion Picture Guide*. These are listed in Table 7.6 along with the number of annual 'Top Grossing' films and top-ten films grouped under those headings for the period 1946 to 1965. Column 4 lists the genre categories identified by Maltby and Neale as those most commonly used as descriptors by audiences and personnel working in the film industry. Indeed, the correspondence between the most popular genre categories listed in column 2 and the Maltby/Neale categories is very close. Neale's list includes three genres not found in the *Motion Picture Guide* – the epic, the social problem film and the teen pic.[32] Conversely, the most frequently used genre categories in the *Guide*, but not found in the Maltby/Neale lists are fantasy, historical, romance and spy films. The principal genres were action/adventure, comedy, crime, drama, musicals, war and westerns. These seven genres accounted for 1,530 – 84 per cent – of the 1,820 top-ranking films. Three of the genres – crime, war and westerns – intimate a concern with killing and death, whilst comedy and musical genres suggest gaiety and light-heartedness, with drama and action/adventure lying somewhere in between. On this basis it is possible to think of these genres as being located along a continuum with comedy and war at the poles, with each genre being a near-neighbour of at least one but no more than two others. Films from genres which are close to one another along the continuum were more likely to be close substitutes for one another than those from more 'distant' genres.

These ideas are developed in Figure 7.1, which shows that the dominant genres can be organised empirically into four primary clusters of films in which drama is the common element. These clusters are drama–comedy–musical (944 films), drama–crime–war/western (878 films), drama–action/adventure–comedy (878 films) and drama–action/adventure–war/westerns (845 films). The numbers in parentheses are taken from Table 7.6 and represent the number of 'Top Grossing' films identified by the *Motion Picture Guide* belonging to each genre category. War and western films are placed together on the grounds that they often share common themes and thus might be considered very near neighbours. Under the proposed schema,

Table 7.6 Genre types and frequencies

Motion picture guide genre classification	Number of films in each genre category	Number of 'Top-ten' films in each genre category	The Maltby (1995)/ Neale (2000) classification
(1)	*(2)*	*(3)*	*(4)*
Action/adventure	127	12	✓
Animation	13	4	
Biblical	9	5	
Biography	25	2	✓
Children	7	1	
Comedy	343	49	✓
Crime	99	2	✓
Drama	408	44	✓
Fantasy	20	1	
Historical	57	13	
Horror	25	2	✓
Juvenile	4	0	
Musical	243	33	✓
Mystery	15	0	
Period	5	0	
Romance	39	3	
Sci-fi	24	1	✓
Spy	23	4	
Suspense/thriller	10	2	✓
War	93	9	✓
Westerns	217	9	✓
Cinerama*	4	4	
Documentary*	10	0	
Epic**			✓
Social Problem**			✓
Teen Pic**			✓
Total	1,820	200	

Sources: *Variety*; Maltby (1995); Neale (2000).

Notes
* Films listed in these two categories are not included in the *Motion Picture Guide*.
** Genres identified by Neale but not recognised as such by the *Motion Picture Guide*.

several genres are subsumed. For example, those films that the *Motion Picture Guide* identified as historical are closely associated with a parent genre found within one of the cluster groupings. Thus *War And Peace* (1956) is categorised as a 'historical drama' and can be located in the drama–action/adventure–war/western cluster. Biography and romance films can be similarly treated, so that, for example, the biography *Viva Zapata* (1952) may be thought of as being located in the same cluster as *War And Peace* whilst *Roman Holiday* (1953) classified as a 'romance/comedy' will be positioned on the drama–comedy line of the drama–comedy–musical cluster. Of the other notable generic categories, spy drama is closely associated to crime in the drama–crime–war/western cluster, along with horror and mystery, whereas science fiction is better located in the drama–action/adventure–war/western cluster. The clusters are intuitively conceived, based on the likelihood of near and distant neighbour characteristics attracting distinct 'taste publics'. The four clusters in Figure 7.1 contain broadly comparable numbers of films, which supports the idea of a range of audience tastes that are spread evenly across genres.

Table 7.7 provides an annual breakdown of the incidence of the *Motion Picture Guide* genre categories listed in Table 7.6. It is clear that whilst films entered under the comedy and drama genres maintain their numbers over the period, this is not true of the other initially very popular genre classifications, although it should be remembered that the number of films listed in *Variety* is not constant. Nevertheless, these films all grossed at least $1 million at the box office during their initial release or, exceptionally, year of their re-release. The demise of the action/adventure, musical and western during the latter years of the period is particularly noticeable and suggests a movement in taste preferences as new audiences emerged with different outlooks, concerns and interests.

Vertical product differentiation

The categorisation of films under particular genre headings is only part of the story. The exclusive use of genres as the choice criteria would indicate

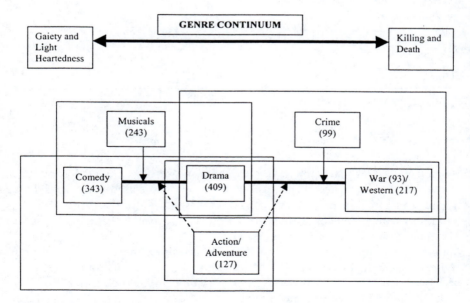

Figure 7.1 Distribution of 'Top Grossing Films' within genre clusters.

Table 7.7 Annual genre classifications of 'Top Grossing Films', 1946–1965

	No. of films	Action/adventure	Animation	Biblical	Biography	Children	Comedy	Crime	Drama	Fantasy	Historical	Horror	Juvenile	Musical	Mystery	Period	Romance	Sci-Fi	Spy	Suspense/Thriller	War	Westerns	Cinerama	Documentary
1946	61	2	1	0	0	0	7	7	12	0	1	0	0	12	1	2	2	0	4	2	1	7	0	0
1947	75	3	2	0	0	0	15	6	21	1	4	0	0	14	2	0	1	0	1	0	0	5	0	0
1948	92	3	1	0	0	0	18	14	24	0	0	0	0	17	1	1	1	0	1	0	1	10	0	0
1949	89	8	0	0	0	0	20	5	26	2	3	0	0	13	0	0	1	0	0	0	3	8	0	0
1950	95	4	1	1	2	0	17	6	21	2	3	0	0	21	0	0	1	1	1	0	7	11	0	0
1951	130	9	0	1	5	0	25	8	24	0	3	0	0	19	0	0	4	3	0	1	10	19	0	0
1952	118	13	0	0	2	1	20	3	19	0	4	0	0	16	0	0	2	0	6	2	6	20	1	0
1953	131	20	1	1	0	0	15	6	18	0	5	2	0	24	1	0	2	2	0	0	7	24	0	0
1954	112	16	0	0	1	0	13	9	13	1	6	2	0	16	3	0	3	1	0	1	5	22	1	2
1955	107	6	1	1	2	1	9	11	20	0	2	1	0	17	0	1	4	4	0	0	5	22	0	1
1956	106	7	0	0	5	0	11	3	28	0	2	1	0	14	2	0	1	4	2	1	6	20	1	0
1957	95	6	1	1	1	0	19	2	25	3	3	0	0	12	0	0	3	1	1	0	4	11	1	0
1958	76	2	0	1	2	0	13	2	25	2	2	3	0	6	1	0	3	1	0	0	10	6	0	0
1959	82	6	1	0	2	0	21	7	18	5	3	1	0	2	1	0	3	1	1	0	2	10	0	0
1960	74	4	0	0	2	1	15	3	18	0	1	3	0	7	1	0	2	2	0	0	6	2	0	1
1961	75	5	1	0	2	0	20	1	21	3	2	2	1	1	0	0	2	1	0	2	1	8	0	2
1962	72	4	0	1	0	1	16	4	21	1	5	3	0	10	0	1	2	0	1	0	4	2	0	1
1963	77	4	0	0	0	0	22	1	19	0	4	2	1	8	1	0	0	1	1	0	3	2	0	1
1964	70	2	2	1	0	2	23	1	16	0	1	2	1	4	0	0	0	2	2	0	4	3	0	2
1965	83	3	1	1	1	1	24	0	19	0	3	3	1	10	1	0	2	0	2	1	8	5	0	0
Total		127	13	9	25	7	343	99	408	20	57	25	4	243	15	5	39	24	23	10	93	217	4	10

Sources: *Variety; Motion Picture Guide.*

a horizontally differentiated market as described and analysed by means of Figure 7.1. However, quality differences exist *within* genres. For example, in 1952 of the twenty westerns listed as 'Top Grossers', *High Noon* (9th) was ranked above *Bend In The River* (14th) which, in turn, was ranked above *Westward The Women* (25th). If rental income is regarded as a proxy for popularity, the implication of these returns is that *High Noon* promised audiences a higher quality of experience than the other two films. 'Quality' in this circumstance refers to standards of pleasure anticipated by audiences. Hence, vertically differentiated markets consist of an array of commodities that can be ranked by criteria that are widely shared, so that, given a common price, a superior commodity would dominate all others in that set. The corollary to this is that, in markets where price differentiation prevails, consumers will reveal a willingness to pay for the extra quality offered by top-ranking commodities (Beath and Katsoulacos 1991; Sutton 1991; Waterson 1994). As was argued earlier, the 'system of provision' which has developed around film as a commodity has given emphasis to supply-side adaptability, rather than price flexibility, as the means for responding to variations in demand.[33] Films such as *Gone With the Wind* (1939), *The Sound of Music* (1965) and the more recent *Titanic* (1998) can be thought of as supreme examples of vertically differentiated film commodities: films that were considered to be attractions superior in almost all respects to other films on offer at the time by filmgoers at large, many of whom went only rarely to the movies.

Evidence for the co-existence of horizontal and vertical forms of differentiation is found in the skewed distribution of film revenues reported earlier in Table 7.4. This phenomenon is recognised widely across different periods and markets in film economics/history literature.[34] The disproportionate share of the market taken by the 'hits' of the season indicates that consumers enjoyed a particular quality of pleasure from such films. Moreover, the bunching of such attractions in favour of certain of the genres shown in column 3 of Table 7.6 suggests that the prospect of value-added pleasures offered by a 'hit' transcended particular genre preferences so that the holistic experience promised by a certain Film A was preferred to that offered by Films B to Z, irrespective of genre: 'hit' films promise a superior set of pleasures that attract *occasional* consumers – those drawn rarely to the cinema by specific attractions – and *regular* consumers, those whose film-going is more frequent but nevertheless selective. Hence a film such as *The Searchers* (ranked 11th in 1956), which generated a rental 2.67 times that of the median film for that year, must have attracted audiences other than dedicated 'western' film-goers.

Figure 7.2 illustrates this argument. Each vertical bar of the three diagrams represents a film from one of the major genres represented in Figure 7.1. The films are grouped by genre (arranged alphabetically) in descending order of the ratio of each film's rental income to the median film income for the selected years from the *Variety* sample of 'Top

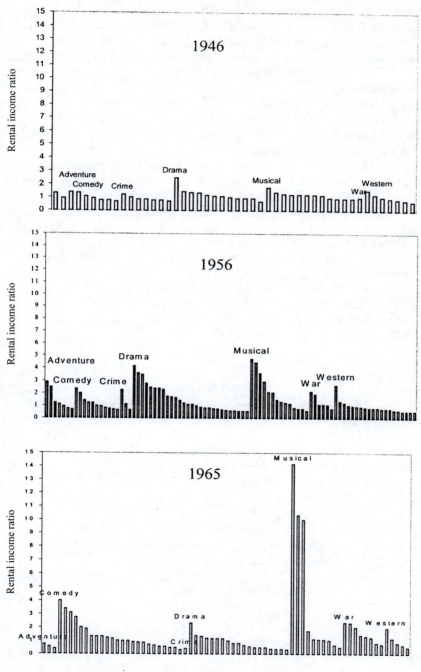

Figure 7.2 Distribution of genre preferences in 1946, 1956 and 1965.

Grossing' films. The growing inequality in the annual distribution of rental incomes is evident in that, for 1946, the distribution of rental incomes is much flatter than for the other two years, whilst that of 1965 is particularly skewed. This implies that film product at the top end of the market became more vertically differentiated over the period, and suggests that audiences were increasingly attracted to the cinema by films that could be marketed as 'special events'.

The generic composition of the top-ten ranking films over the period, set out in Table 7.6, serves to discriminate between those genres that were regularly associated with popular success and those that were not. The differences are striking when compared in the same table to the distribution of the 1,820 films across the *Motion Picture Guide* genre classifications. In Figure 7.1 the four clusters comprise films in numbers that are comparable between any one cluster and another. This is not the case in Figure 7.3, where 126 of the 200 top-ten grossing films – again not counting the minor genres – form the drama–comedy–musical cluster, compared to 105 films in the drama–action/adventure–comedy cluster, seventy-four in the drama–action/adventure–war/western cluster and sixty-four in the drama–action/adventure–crime cluster. Of further interest, when the analysis is confined to the highest-ranking films, is the greatly increased significance of films labelled 'historical'. Also, although numerically small, a high proportion of films from the animation, biblical and spy genres achieve top-ten success.

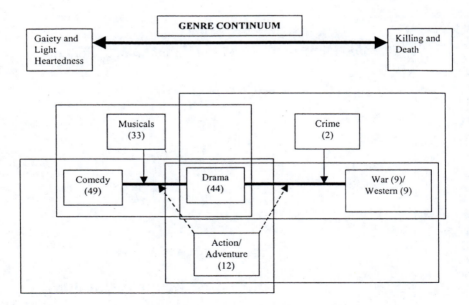

Figure 7.3 Distribution of top-ten films in genre clusters.

Stars as markers of quality

A crucial element in the metamorphosis of Hollywood away from the command structures of the old studio system to arm's length contracting based on particular projects was the release of stars from long-term contracts with the studios (Storper 1994; Weinstein 1998, Chapter 8). The growing absolute and relative value and importance of top-ten rental earnings during this period gave greater emphasis to the differentiating role played by stars (Bordwell *et al.* 1985: 332).

The function of providing information *ex ante* for audiences is the subject of a recent work on the phenomenon of stardom by Albert (1998: 251, Chapter 9) who argues that the previous successful performances of stars serve as markers for potential audiences, maintaining that 'stars are important ... because they are the least noisy and most consistent marker for successful film types'. The stochastic model he adopts predicts that 'the likelihood of a film of a particular type succeeding is proportional to all films of a similar type that have produced similar levels of success'.[35]

The probability of a star appearing in i successful films is $f(i)$ according to the model:

$$f(i) = 1/i(i + 1), \sum_{i=1}^{\infty} f(i) = 1.$$

The model predicts that half the stars will have only a single success, one-sixth will have two successes, one-twelfth will have three successes, and so on.

Looking at the principal star in each of top-twenty films for the period 1960 to 1995, Albert finds that there is good correspondence between predicted and actual results up to seven successes. However, the model is unsatisfactory because it greatly over-predicts the number of stars with high levels of success.[36] An allowance for the limited life and output of stars, made by assuming that they are subject to exponential decay, can remedy this fault so that the model predicts fewer stars with great success. It also improves the correspondence for stars with few successes so that there is sound ground to proceed with the analysis.

A broader enquiry than that undertaken by Albert is reported in Table 7.8, which reports the two leading stars of each film listed in the annual top ten, top twenty and top sixty films between 1946 to 1965.[37] It is clear that the great majority of the talent represented in Table 7.8 are not top-ranking stars. In the table, 684 (first or second credited) stars are shown to have appeared at least once in a top-sixty film, of which over half (366) were not credited with a leading role in a single top-twenty production, and just under three-quarters (481) did not appear in a top-ten production. Indeed, 332 stars appeared in one top-sixty film only. In contrast, the table also shows that a small number of stars had repeated top-ten successes. These are

Table 7.8 Distribution of stars by number of top ten, twenty and sixty films in which they appear

Top-ten films Star credits			Top-twenty films Star credits			Top-sixty films Star credits		
Films	Actual number	Expected number	Films	Actual number	Expected number	Films	Actual number	Expected number
1	128	102	1	176	159	1	332	342
2	32	34	2	57	53	2	117	114
3	13	17	3	24	27	3	52	57
4	15	10	4	19	16	4	50	34
5	9	7	5	10	11	5	20	23
6	2	5	6	9	8	6	25	16
7	1	4	7	5	6	7	10	12
8	0	3	8	1	4	8	11	10
>8	3	23	9	6	4	9	13	8
			10	3	3	10	5	6
			>10	8	29	11	7	5
						12	6	4
						13	5	4
						14	6	3
						>14	25	46
Total stars	203		Total stars	318		Total stars	684	

Note
The expected values are derived from the Yule distribution model. The expected numbers are rounded. The top-ten films for the twenty years (1946 to 1965) sum to 200. If each featured two stars the number of star berths would sum to 400. Accordingly, the annual list of top-twenty and top-sixty films would generate 800 and 2,400 star berths respectively. The actual number of berths occupied was 386,780 and 2,358 for the three lists, with the shortfall explained by the success of a small number of cinerama, documentary and animation films.

named in Table 7.9. However, as is evident, their success was not always consistent during the period 1946 to 1965. For example, whilst ten of Elizabeth Taylor's thirteen top-sixty films during the period were ranked in the top-ten of their respective release years, only five of James Stewart's thirty-one top-sixty films and two of Alan Ladd's twenty-four top-sixty films were similarly ranked.[38] All three were major stars, but as markers they generated different signal strengths to audiences. Indeed, it is apparent that no single template captures the 'hit' profiles of the stars listed in Table 7.9.

Figure 7.4 shows that each order of top-ten success corresponds to widely differing top-sixty levels of success, although a general upward trend can be observed. However, by dividing the stars into high-, medium- and low-volume categories it is possible to propose a taxonomy that distinguishes between high-volume frequent top-ten stars, such as Gregory Peck or John Wayne; medium-volume frequent top-ten stars, such as Elizabeth Taylor or Marlon Brando; high-volume, recurring top-ten stars, such as James Stewart or Doris Day; medium-volume, recurring top-ten stars, such as Rock Hudson or Tony Curtis; low-volume recurring top-ten stars, such as Ingrid Bergman or Grace Kelly; high-volume occasional top-ten stars, such as Clark Gable or Alan Ladd; medium-volume occasional top-ten stars, such as

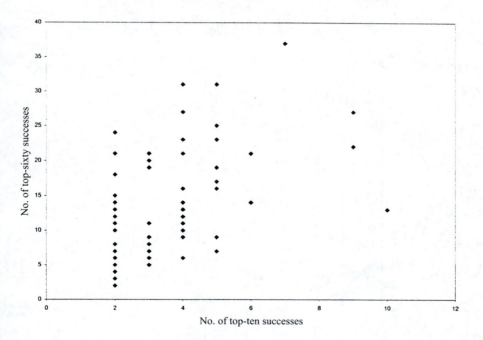

Figure 7.4 Top-ten against top-sixty star successes.

Notes
The diagram represents data found in Table 7.9. Multiple occupancy of a position is reported by a single point.

Table 7.9 Top-ranking stars, 1946–1965

Star	Top-ten films	Top-twenty films	Top-sixty films	Star	Top-ten films	Top-twenty films	Top-sixty films
Taylor, E.	10	11	13	Monroe, M.	3	5	7
Crosby, B.	9	14	22	Russell, J.	3	4	8
Peck, G.	9	14	27	Sellers, P.	3	4	5
Wayne, J.	7	17	37	Simmons, J.	3	5	6
Brando, M.	6	9	14	Wilde, Cornel	3	3	6
Grant, C.	6	14	21	Andrews, J.	2	2	4
Bergman, I.	5	8	9	Astaire, F.	2	5	12
Curtis, T.	5	6	17	Baker, C.	2	2	5
Day, D.	5	9	25	Bennett, Joan	2	2	4
Hudson, R.	5	10	19	Bogart, H.	2	4	15
MacMurray, F.	5	6	9	Clift, M.	2	4	5
McGuire, D.	5	5	7	Connery, S.	2	3	4
Sinatra, F.	5	13	23	de Havilland, O.	2	2	8
Stewart, J.	5	12	31	Fonda, H.	2	2	7
Turner, L.	5	9	16	Fontaine, J.	2	3	4
Brynner, Y.	4	4	13	Gable, C.	2	9	21
Burton, R.	4	6	9	Hepburn, K.	2	5	10
Douglas, K.	4	7	21	Howard, T.	2	2	4
Hepburn, A.	4	5	10	Hutton, B.	2	3	6

Name				Name			
Hope, B.	4	7	23	Jones, S.	2	3	4
Kelly, Grace	4	4	6	Kaye, D.	2	3	11
Kerr, D.	4	9	14	Kelly, Gene	2	5	11
Lancaster, B.	4	7	31	Kwan, N.	2	2	2
Lemmon, J.	4	6	13	Ladd, A.	2	4	24
Lewis, J.	4	10	27	Leigh, V.	2	2	4
Martin, D.	4	13	27	Lollobrigida, G.	2	2	5
Niven, D.	4	6	11	Loy, M.	2	3	5
Tracy, S.	4	10	16	Mason, J.	2	6	10
Webb, C.	4	5	11	Mitchum, R.	2	4	18
Wyman, J.	4	7	12	Newman, P.	2	6	14
Allyson, J.	3	4	11	Novak, K.	2	4	12
Cooper, G.	3	4	21	O'Toole, P.	2	4	4
Ferrer, J.	3	3	6	Parks, L.	2	2	3
Hayward, S.	3	6	19	Reynolds, D.	2	4	13
Heston, C.	3	4	9	Saint, E.M.	2	3	4
Holden, W.	3	9	20	Taylor, Robert	2	3	13
Keel, H.	3	3	9	Johnson, Van	2	5	10
MacLaine, S.	3	4	9	Williams, E.	2	4	12

Note

Gary Cooper died in 1961, Marilyn Monroe in 1962, Humphrey Bogart in 1957, Clark Gable in 1960 and Alan Ladd in 1964. The top-twenty column includes all top-ten films plus those ranked 11 to 20. Likewise with top-sixty films.

Humphrey Bogart or Robert Mitchum; and finally low-volume occasional top-ten stars, such as Peter O'Toole or Marilyn Monroe.[39] The personas of these listed stars served to differentiate films in that they offered audiences a distinctive experience, promising exceptional combinations of qualities which were widely perceived as being superior to those of actors starring in non-top-sixty films. Nevertheless, poll evidence tells us that each star also attracted distinctive audiences, or 'taste publics'.[40] For example, John Wayne can be considered to have been a superior box office star to Glenn Ford as a leading man in war/western/action type films in terms of the ratio of top-ten to top-sixty – that is, Wayne was a more potent vertically differentiating marker than Ford. However, the same could not be said of Wayne when compared to Cary Grant, a star of comparable vertical differentiating potency. Each occupied quite distinct territories along the characteristics continuum of leading men, which is to say that they were horizontally differentiating markers of quality. Accordingly, although leading stars differentiated films strongly, they did not do so monofactorially. Rather, it was their conjunction with other idiosyncratic and intangible inputs, such as director, screenplay and genre, which led to the success or otherwise of the films in which they starred. In other words, charisma needs good guidance, good story material and co-stars to work with, and an appropriate setting if it is to be fully effective.

Conclusion

Hollywood underwent dramatic change during the two decades following the Second World War as the supply side of the industry reacted to rapidly declining audiences. It can be argued in hindsight that the divestiture of cinemas, forced on Loew's/MGM, RKO, Paramount, Twentieth Century Fox and Warner Bros. through the *Paramount* decree of 1948, would have taken place anyway as audiences turned away from the cinema as a regular form of recreation. Evidence of the changing pattern of demand during the period emerges from the study of top-ranking film rental returns published annually by the trade journal *Variety*. The market was differentiated both horizontally and vertically, with stars and, to a lesser extent, genre, serving as markers. Audiences became increasingly attracted to particular films, rather than films in general. Such films, in providing extraordinary levels of utility, transcended traditional patterns of genre loyalty and achieved very high levels of market penetration. On the supply side, the growing inequality of the rank distribution of film rentals led to:

a   the growth in independent production;
b   the growth in the size of major-studio film budgets dedicated to 'hit' production; and
c   the transformation of these same studios into distributor–financier–producers.

Abandoning in-house portfolio production, Hollywood's major studios adopted a new strategy to reduce their exposure to risk whilst maintaining their dominance of markets. Bordwell *et al.* refer to this as the package-unit mode of production in which the studios as distributors organised production through market contract relations rather than in-house coordination. By changing in this way, Hollywood was able to retain its dominant collective position in the film business.

Notes

1 This chapter was previously published in the *Journal of Economic History*, 62, 3 (September 2002), © The Economic History Association. It was made possible by a grant from the Leverhulme Trust, for whom I was a Research Fellow between 2000–2001. I owe a great debt of thanks to Peter Armitage and Bernard Hrusa-Marlow for helping me shape the chapter. I also want to thank Sam Cameron, John Curran, Mark Glancy, Manfred Holler, Ian Jarvie, James Obelkevich, Mike Pokorny and Guglielmo Volpe for their critical contributions at various stages of the project. Comments from participants of seminars at Humbolt University, Berlin, and the Institute of Historical Research, London, and Southampton University, in the UK, also helped me form the final draft, as did the reviews of two anonymous referees.

2 In 1946 box office revenues constituted 1.1 per cent of Total Personal Consumption Expenditure in the USA, falling to 0.2 per cent by 1965 (*US Historical Statistics* 1975). It is interesting to note that not one of the seventeen chapters of Vol. III of Engerman and Gallman's (2000) recent *Economic History of the United States* takes a consumption perspective.

3 *Historical Statistics of the US* (1975: Series H 862–877).

4 See Vogel (2001: 58–63), *Film Daily Yearbook* (1966: 100).

5 Prior to divestiture the five 'majors' owned 70 per cent of first-run cinemas. See Conant (1960: 50). Also see De Vany and Eckert (1991).

6 Letter to Henry King, 14 June 1950, quoted in Custen (1997).

7 One that succeeded was the Beatles' film *A Hard Day's Night* which in 1964 was ranked 9th.

8 For an overview of the dramatic changes to the housing sector, see Rome (2001).

9 US Census Bureau: *Historical Census of Housing*.

10 Clawson and Knetsch (1966).

11 Conant (1960: Table 1) reports that average admission prices remained largely unchanged between 1946 and 1952 – hence falling in real terms. His own estimates of attendances is lower than that reported in official publications.

12 Ibid., pp. 13–14.

13 MPPA, *The Public Appraises the Movies*, p. 4, quoted in Belton (1992: 81).

14 To be shared subsequently with the producer according to contract.

15 The rentals do not contain overseas figures, estimated in 1961 to be approximately equal to domestic rentals. *Variety*, 10 January 1962: 13.

16 See Glancy (1992, 1995) and Jewell (1994). Glancy and Jewell have kindly made the full manuscripts available to the author.

17 Figures published in Vogel (2001: Table 2.4) indicate that rental incomes generated in Canada were less than 10 per cent of those in the USA.

18 The *Film Daily* figures (unattributed) are similar to those found in Vogel (2001: Table 2.4).

19 These shares are obtained by halving column 5 of Table 7.3 and expressing

rental income as a percentage. 'Conservative' because if the lower proportion is used, the market share of the 'Top Grossing' films would be even greater.

20 The top-sixty films have been used in order to standardise rental income observations across the period. These films took between 69 and 99 per cent of the rental incomes reported in Table 7.2.

21 Taking the top-sixty films only, the autocorrelation of the annual films with their one-year lagged values $(t-1)$ was very much lower $(r=0.11)$ than for similar series featuring the 10th film $(r=0.56)$ and median film $(r=0.60)$.

22 The Gini coefficient values would, of course, have been much higher had rental incomes of the full annual population of films released onto the American market been known.

23 In assessing the value of the Gini coefficient, it must be remembered that it is based on the truncated sample of the annual top-sixty films and would be very much nearer to 1 if computed for the whole population of annual releases.

24 Bordwell *et al.*, *Classical Hollywood Cinema*, pp. 330–331.

25 Information on the copyright ownership of films is found in the Library of Congress Catalog of Copyright Entries: Motion Pictures. I am indebted to Bernard Hrusa-Marlow for bringing this source to my attention.

26 See also Scott Berg (1989: 470).

27 For an explanation of the pricing practices in the industry, see Sedgwick (2000: 56–61).

28 In Sedgwick (2000: Chapter 1) a cognitive process is proposed in which audiences have prior commitments to quality and seek stimuli that are consonant with them, based on Gilad *et al.* (1987).

29 The article is reproduced in De Vany (2004: Chapter 2).

30 See also Beath and Katsoulacos (1991).

31 See Altman (1999); Neale (2000).

32 Neale op. cit., p. 51, adopts the eight genre types identified by Maltby and adds six more.

33 'Systems of provision' as an analytical framework for understanding historically specific relations between consumption and production is developed in Fine and Leopold (1993).

34 See Chapter 1 of this volume.

35 Albert draws on the work of Chung and Cox (1994) which in turn is based on a model first identified by Yule (1924) and later developed by Simon (1955).

36 The Yule distribution predicts that there should be thirty-five stars with eight or more successes in Albert's data and there are only seventeen. It implies there should be fourteen stars with over twenty successes and five with over fifty successes. In the sample the most successful star has nineteen successes. The distribution is based on a pure birth process (i.e. there is no allowance for death) and this long tail was the most desirable feature in the original applications of Simon (1955). In this context stars are not immortal and appear in a finite number of films during their career.

37 In identifying the top-twenty films of each season as being 'successful', Albert treats as equal the appearance of stars in films that earn quite different magnitudes of rental income. See Table 7.4. For this reason, the annual top-ten films – in keeping with the analysis on genre – might be thought of as a sample better suited to illustrate vertical differences between film characteristics.

38 Using the top-sixty films means that stars appearing in films that lie outside of this rank are not included in the analysis.

39 The following benchmarks are used: high volume, twenty films or more; medium volume, ten-to-nineteen films; low volume, less than ten films. The

frequency of top-ten success is also broken down into three groups: frequent, six films or more; recurring, four-to-five films; and occasional, two-to-three films.

40 See the *International Motion Picture Almanac* for each of the years in the investigation.

References

Aksoy, A. and Robins, K. (1992) 'Hollywood for the 21st century: global competition for critical mass in image markets', *Cambridge Journal of Economics*, 16: 1–22.

Albert, S. (1998) 'Movie stars and the distribution of financially successful films in the motion picture industry', *Journal of Cultural Economics*, 22: 249–270.

Altman, R. (1999) *Film/Genre*, London: BFI.

Balio, T. (1993) *Grand Design: Hollywood as a Modern Business Enterprise*, Berkeley, CA: University of California Press.

Beath, J. and Katsoulacos, Y. (1991) *The Economic Theory of Product Differentiation*, Cambridge: Cambridge University Press.

Belton, J. (1992) *Widescreen Cinema*, Cambridge, MA: Harvard University Press.

Besas, P. (2000) *Inside Variety: The Story of the Bible of Show Business, 1905–87*, New York, NY: Ars Millenii.

Bordwell, D., Staiger, J. and Thompson, K. (1985) *The Classical Hollywood Cinema: Film Style and Mode of Production to 1960*, London: RKP.

Chung, K. and Cox, R. (1994) 'A stochastic model of superstardom: an application of the Yule distribution', *The Review of Economics and Statistics*, 76: 771–775.

Clawson, M. and Knetch, J. (1966) *The Economics of Outdoor Recreation*, Baltimore, MA: Johns Hopkins University Press.

Conant, M. (1960) *Antitrust in the Motion Picture Industry*, Berkeley, CA: University of California Press.

Crafton, D. (1997) *The Talkies: American Cinema's Transition to Sound, 1926–1931*, Berkeley, CA: University of California Press.

Custen, G. (1997) *Twentieth Century's Fox and the Culture of Hollywood*, New York, NY: Basic Books.

De Vany, A. (2004) *Hollywood Economics: How Extreme Uncertainty Shapes the Film Industry*, London: Routledge.

De Vany, A. and Eckert, R. (1991) 'Motion picture antitrust: the Paramount cases revisited', *Research in Law and Economics*, 14: 51–112.

De Vany, A. and Walls, W. (1996) 'Bose–Einstein dynamics and adaptive contracting in the motion picture industry', *Economic Journal*, 106: 1493–1514.

De Vany, A. and Walls, W.D. (1999) 'Uncertainty and the movie industry: does star power reduce the terror of the box office?' *Journal of Cultural Economics*, 23: 285–318.

Docherty, T. (1995) 'Teenagers and teenpics, 1955–1957: a study in exploitation filmmaking', in J. Staiger (ed.) *The Studio System*, New Brunswick, NJ: Rutgers University Press.

Engerman, S. and Gallman, R. (2000) *The Cambridge Economic History of the United States, Volume III: the Twentieth Century*, Cambridge: Cambridge University Press.

Film Daily: Yearbooks, 1947–1966.

Fine, B. and Leopold, E. (1993) *The World of Consumption*, London: Routledge.

Finler, J. (1988) *The Hollywood Story*, New York, NY: Crown.

Friedson, E. (1954/1955) 'Consumption of the mass media by Polish–American children', *Quarterly Review of Film, Radio and Television*, 9: 92–101.

Gilad, B., Kaish, S. and Loab, P. (1987) 'Cognitive dissonance and utility maximization: a general framework', *Journal of Economic Behaviour and Organization*, 8: 61–73.

Glancy, H.M. (1992) 'MGM film grosses, 1924–1948: the Eddie Mannix ledger', *Historical Journal of Film, Radio and Television*, 12: 127–144.

Glancy, H.M. (1995) 'Warner Bros. film grosses, 1921–1951: the William Schaefer ledger', *Historical Journal of Film, Radio and Television*, 15: 55–74.

Gomery, D. (1992) *Shared Pleasures: a History of Movie Presentation in the United States*, London: BFI.

Gomery, D. (1996) 'Towards a new media economics', in D. Bordwell and N. Caroll (eds) *Post-Theory: Reconstructing Film Studies*, Madison, WI: University of Wisconsin Press.

Greenwald, W. (1950) *The Motion Picture Industry: an Economic Study of the History and Practices of a Business*, unpublished thesis, New York, NY: New York University.

Halliwell's Film Guide (1986) 5th edn, London: Guild.

Handel, L. (1950) *Hollywood Looks at its Audience*, Urbana, IL: University of Illinois Press.

Halberstam, D. (1994) *The Fifties*, New York, NY: Ballantine Books.

Hoskins, C., McFadyen, S. and Finn, A. (1997) *Global Television and Film*, Oxford: Oxford University Press.

International Motion Picture Almanac, vols 1946–1966.

Izod, J. (1988) *Hollywood and the Box-Office*, London: Macmillan.

Jarvie, I. (1992) *Hollywood's Overseas Campaign: the North Atlantic Movie Trade, 1920–1950*, Cambridge: Cambridge University Press.

Jewell, R. (1994) 'RKO film grosses, 1929–1951: the C.J. Trevlin ledger', *Historical Journal of Film, Radio and Television*, 14: 37–51.

Lazarsfeld, P. (1947) 'Audience research in the movie field', *Annals of the American Academy of Political and Social Science*, 254: 160–168.

Library of Congress Catalog of Copyright Entries, Motion Pictures, vols 1940–1949, 1950–1959, 1960–1969.

Maltby, R. (1995) *Hollywood Cinema*, Oxford: Blackwell.

Maltby, R. (1999) 'Sticks, hicks and flaps: classical Hollywood's generic conception of its audiences', in M. Stokes and R. Maltby (eds) *Identifying Hollywood's Audiences: Cultural Identity and the Movies*, London: BFI.

Motion Picture Guide (1986) Volumes I–IX (1927–84), Chicago, IL: Cinebooks.

Neale, S. (2000) *Genre and Hollywood*, London: BFI.

Nelson, R. (1974) 'Advertising as information', *Journal of Political Economy*, 81: 729–745.

Oakley, J. (1986) *God's Country: America in the Fifties*, New York, NY: Dember.

Riesman, D. and Riesman, E. (1952) 'Movies and audiences', *American Quarterly*, 4: 195–202.

Rome, A. (2001) *The Bulldozer in the Countryside: Suburban Sprawl and the Rise of American Environmentalism*, Cambridge: Cambridge University Press.

Scott Berg, A. (1989) *Goldwyn*, London: Hamish Hamilton.

Sedgwick, J. (2000) *Filmgoing in 1930s Britain: a Choice of Pleasures*, Exeter: Exeter University Press.

Sedgwick, J. and Pokorny, M. (1998) 'The risk environment of film-making: Warners in the inter-war period', *Explorations in Economic History*, 35: 196–220.

Seldes, G. (1950) *The Great Audience*, New York, NY: Viking.

Simon, H. (1955) 'On a class of skew distribution functions', *Biometrika*, 42: 425–440.

Sklar, R. (1975) *Movie-Made America: a Cultural History of American Movies*, New York, NY: Random House.

Sklar, R. (1999) 'Lost audience: 1950s spectatorship and historical reception studies', in M. Stokes and R. Maltby (eds) *Identifying Hollywood's Audiences: Cultural Identity and the Movies*, London: BFI.

Storper, M. (1994) 'The transition to flexible specialisation in the US film industry: external economies, the division of labour, and the crossing of industrial divides', in A. Amin (ed.) *Post-Fordism: a Reader*, Oxford: Oxford University Press.

Sutton, J. (1991) *Sunk Costs and Market Structure*, Cambridge, MA: MIT Press.

Thompson, K. (1985) *Exporting Entertainment: America in the World Film Market, 1907–1934*, London: BFI.

US Department of Commerce, Bureau of the Census (1975) *Historical Statistics of the US: Colonial Times to 1970*, Washington, DC.

Variety: 1946–1965.

Vogel, H. (2001) *Entertainment Industry Economics*, 5th edn, Cambridge: Cambridge University Press.

Waterson, M. (1994) 'Models of product differentiation', in J. Cable (ed.) *Current Issues in Industrial Economics*, Basingstoke: Macmillan.

Weinstein, M. (1998) 'Profit-sharing contracts in Hollywood: evolution and analysis', *Journal of Legal Studies*, 27: 67–112.

Yule, G. (1924) 'A mathematical theory of evolution based on the conclusions of Dr. J.C. Willis, F.R.S.', *Philosophical Transactions of the Royal Society*, B. 213: 21–87.

8 Movie stars and the distribution of financially successful films in the motion-picture industry[1]

Steven Albert

It has been argued that in the 1930s the popularity of films starring Mae West saved Paramount Studios from financial ruin, and that a succession of Deanna Durbin hits similarly kept Universal Studios afloat (Walker 1974; Morin 1960). In the 1940s and early 1950s, a majority of MGM's financial success was due to a string of films starring Clark Gable (Shipman 1979). Stars of the 1990s who, like Harrison Ford, are attached to a series of financial hits are still highly sought-after inputs (Brown 1995). Indeed, today the power wielded by movie stars underscores much of the motion picture industry. Producers, directors, writers and the stars themselves understand this. Saul Zaentz, independent producer of *One Flew Over the Cuckoo's Nest* and *The English Patient* relates: 'The studios? ... the first question is, "who's in it?"' (*The South Bank Show*, 1992). Says John Landis, director of hits *The Blues Brothers* and *Coming to America*: '...You ask them, "What do you think of the script?" And they answer, "If you can get Harrison Ford then it's a good script. If you can't then it's a bad one"' (Thomas 1996). Gary Fleder, director *of Things to Do in Denver When You're Dead*, comments on how he was able to finance this hip, off-beat US independent thriller: 'actors embrace it, and Miramax embraces that...' (Charity 1996). Peter Howitt, director and writer of *Sliding Doors*, also understands the actor's power to get movies made. He had no luck selling his screenplay until 'an agent showed the script to Gwyneth Paltrow. He thought she would like it. She did. Suddenly every major studio wanted to distribute the film' (*Sunday Times* 1998). Superstar Barbra Streisand comments: 'the audience buys my work because I have complete control' (Vincent 1996), while Robert De Niro describes his power to get films made for his long-time colleague and friend, acclaimed director Martin Scorsese: 'I told Marty, if he had trouble getting it off the ground and if he really wanted me to do it [*The Last Temptation of Christ*], I would've done it. It was something I was telling him as a friend; if he needed me, I was there' (Paris 1989).

However, no star guarantees a successful film. For example, the films *Havana* and *The Two Jakes* starred Hollywood giants Robert Redford and Jack Nicholson, respectively, and yet both were financial failures. With this seeming paradox in mind, we must ask: is there any evidence to support a system that relies so heavily on Hollywood movie stars?

Past economic and statistical analyses seem to answer, 'no'. Recently, De Vany and Walls (1996: 1493) have suggested that there is no known combination of release pattern, star, story and so on which will ensure a hit. They maintain that 'the crucial factor is this: nobody knows what makes a hit or when it will happen'. As far as stars are concerned, Kindem (1982) suggests only a weak impact of marquee value (a combination of star and other factors) to box office success, and this only during the studio era. Simonet (1980) and Garrison (1971), both using multiple regression analysis, conclude that movie stars, after the studio era, have very little impact on box office success. Miller and Shamsie (1996) suggest that stars during the studio era, while under long-term contracts, are weakly associated with revenues, while in the post-studio period they are not. Austin (1989) shows, using an audience survey, that the presence of stars is unimportant when deciding to attend a movie (see Austin 1989; cited in Jowett and Linton 1989: 39).

However, Prag and Casavant (1994) report a positive relation between the presence of stardom and revenues. They also report a positive relation between revenues and 'quality', revenues and the film being a sequel, and revenues and the film having won an Academy Award. When advertising is also included in their regression, the presence of stardom is no longer significant; only 'advertising', 'quality' and 'sequel' have a positive relation with a film's revenues. However, every independent variable shown by Prag and Casavant to have a significant positive relation to revenues is also shown to be related to stars (including advertising).[2] From this, one can argue that the relation between stars and revenues is the most important conclusion of Prag and Casavant's study.

Prag and Casavant, although contributing a very good start, use methods that, perhaps because of the exploratory nature of their study, do not reveal the full picture of why stars are so important to the film industry. Many questions remain. These include:

- What is the relation between stars and consumer behaviour?
- Is there any particular way in which stars are related to successful films? Do particular stars have more positive influence than others?
- Why do stars appear to be the most powerful influence over the film industry, in terms of which movie is made, who will contribute to its production and how it will be advertised?

This chapter explores film stars and successful films from a perspective that is significantly different from those cited above. Whereas those who employ regression analysis must use categorical variables to analyse the impact of stardom, like 'a rising or falling star' or 'an established star', the methods employed here allow us to investigate the relation between a host of *individual* stars and successful films, and investigate more than just their relation to revenues but the particular characteristics of their relationship to consumer choice.

Prag and Casavant, like many others, investigate stardom and power in relation to the star's ability to attract fans (1994: 227). I suggest there is more to it than that. This chapter argues that stars are important not only because they can attract a group of fans, but because they are the least noisy and most consistent marker for successful film types. And because of this they have not only drawing power, but also 'marking power'. This is an extremely useful tool for film producers when gauging the potential probability of a film being one of the few which are successful. And, I argue, this is an important reason why producers value stars and why stars, in many ways, define Hollywood.

Specifically, this chapter describes the motion picture industry using a stochastic consumer choice process wherein information of past successful film types influences the potential success of future films, and tests this by comparing the resulting predicted distribution of successful films with the actual distribution of successful films. I find that the distribution of successful films among film types is consistent with that predicted by a stochastic consumer choice process. And, because I use stars as markers of film types, my empirical results suggest the value of stars, as a group, is partly due to their marking successful film types in a consistent, predictable way. In other words, the power bestowed upon stars is a justified action based on an understanding of the characteristic connection between stars and consumer behaviour in the motion-picture industry.

Modelling a film market of film types

The theoretical section of this chapter is structured in two parts. The first develops a theory of consumer film choice as a mechanism based on past information of similar films. This generates a distribution of film types. The second part argues that the star is a marker of successful film types. The following sections explain each in turn and are followed by a brief summary of the theory.

Information and consumer choice in the film market

Before I construct a consumer choice mechanism of film types, it will be useful to briefly describe some of the underlying mechanisms of consumer choice of a particular film. It can be argued that a potential moviegoer will attend a film if the benefit of doing so is greater than the cost. If we assume the decision to attend a film is dependent upon revealed information, De Vany and Walls (1996) posit that person $n + 1$ will attend a film under the conditions that

$$E(b_{n+1}|\mathbf{s}_n) > c, \tag{8.1}$$

where the first term is the expectation of benefits to viewer $n+1$ from a particular film, conditional on the set of previous trials by other customers (s_n). This is the revealed information set that includes, among other things, friends' opinions and professional reviews. c is equal to the cost of seeing a film, which is the same for all customers.

In general, if information is positive, the expected benefits are greater than the costs and the consumer will purchase a ticket to view the film. If the information is negative, the expected benefits are below the costs and they will not purchase a ticket. In conjunction with the adaptive contracting policies of the film distributors, a positive information cascade will lead to a hit, and a negative information cascade will lead to a flop. This theory is designed to explain the mechanism behind the success or failure of a particular film, not a film type. With this in mind, let us look at a similar construction, only substituting film types for a particular film.

Imagine there are k film types. At time $t+1$, a particular film is released of a particular film type z. A consumer will see the film if

$$E(b_z | \mathbf{s}_t) > c, \tag{8.2}$$

where the first term is the expectation of benefits (b_z) of film type z conditional on information about similar film types from previous periods ($\mathbf{s}_{t, t-1, t-2, t-3, \ldots}$). This latter now becomes a revealed information set, which is based on a film's association with a particular film type. c is equal to the cost of seeing a film and is the same for all consumers. The information we assume the consumer uses in choosing to see a film is not just word of mouth about a particular film but also their own estimation of the probable benefits derived from such a film type. This is gained by information based on consumption in previous periods.

Because this model employs film types rather than specific films, consumers use different information than that in De Vany and Walls' model. In the De Vany and Walls case, information is gathered by potential consumers from reviews, word of mouth and so on about a particular film. For us, De Vany and Walls' information set designates a particular film as a particular successful film type. Once the film type is confirmed, the process implies that a consumer then makes a decision by using past information on the potential benefits of that film type and others like it. The decision process thus includes both the Baysian concepts of De Vany and Walls (continuously updated information designating a particular film into a particular film type) and a decision based on information from the consumer's past trials of different film types.

This model implies that the past success of a film type will impact future success and is in spirit with a class of distributions first established by Yule (1924) with their underlying stochastic processes made explicit by Simon (1955). This class of distributions has been found to have significance to a wide range of social phenomenon. Most important for this chapter, Chung and Cox (1994) have shown it to be descriptive in the accumulation of gold records in the music industry.[3]

For our purposes, the application of this stochastic process clarifies exactly what 'past information' is and how it effects the potential success or failure of a film. Consider a film industry that has produced k film types, each of which has generated at least one successful film. We can designate $f(i, k)$ as the number of different film types that have yielded exactly i successful films. That is, if there are 500 different film types that have generated exactly one successful film each, then $f(1, k) = 500$. If there are 200 different film types which have generated exactly two successful films each, then $f(2, k) = 200$, and so on. I now make an assumption based on what appears to be the assumption of the film industry. Namely, the likelihood of a film of a particular type succeeding is proportional to all films of a similar type which have produced similar levels of success. Formally:

Assumption 1:
> The probability that the next successful film is of the film type that has generated exactly i successes is proportional to $if(i, k)$, that is to the total number of films of the type that produces exactly i successes.

According to Simon (1955: 427), assumption 1 is much weaker than the assumption $(1')$ that the probability a particular film type will be successful is proportional to the number of its previous success, since it leaves open the possibility that, among all film types which have generated i successful movies, the probability of some producing another success may be much higher than others. So, for example, the probability that a particular film type will produce the next successful film may be higher if the film type has had more recent success compared to those that have not. Notice how this assumption is nearly identical to our discussion of the consumer choice mechanisms described above. A film will be successful depending upon how successful similar film types have been in the past. So the frequency of repeated success for film types will depend upon the stochastic decision-making process of the film-going audience (the use of past information) as described in assumption 1.

I further assume, not unlike producers in the film industry, that it is highly unlikely that the next successful film will be of a new film type. Namely:

Assumption 2:
> There is a constant probability, δ, which is very small, that the next successful film is of a new film type – a film type that is not represented by any of the k film types: i.e. $\delta \approx 0$

If these two assumptions correctly describe the ability of film types to produce many successful films, then the success of films themselves cannot be regarded as an entirely random process.

Simon (1955: 426 eq. 1.2, 428 eq. 2.12) shows that the probability mechanisms underlying these two assumptions lead to a class of functions given by

$$f(i) = AB(i, \rho + 1), \tag{8.3}$$

where A and ρ are constants and $B(i, \rho + 1)$ is the Beta function of $(i, \rho + 1)$, and where

$$\rho = 1/(1 - \delta). \tag{8.4}$$

He also shows that when $\delta = 0$ (as in our assumption 2; later in this chapter we will relax this assumption which will result in a different distribution), the steady-state distribution resulting from equation 8.3 (i.e. assumptions 1 and 2) can be approximated by (see Simon 1955: 426 eq. 1.6):

$$f(i) = 1/i(i + 1), \Sigma f(i) = 1, \tag{8.5}$$

where $f(i)$, in this context, is labelled as the proportion of film types which produce i successful films and the Σ is the summation over $i = 1$ to ∞. This means that the predicted proportion of film types that produce one successful film is equal to

$$f(1) = 1/1(1 + 1) = 0.50, \tag{8.6}$$

and the proportion of film types that produce two, three, four, etc. successful films are:

$$f(2) = 1/2(2 + 1) = 0.167, \tag{8.7}$$

$$f(3) = 1/3(3 + 1) = 0.083, \tag{8.8}$$

$$f(4) = 1/4(4 + 1) = 0.050, \tag{8.9}$$

etc.

This distribution results from the two assumptions above. It predicts the steady-state frequency distribution of successful film types, which would result from (i) a consumer choice mechanism based on information about films of the same type from previous periods, and (ii) that the probability of a successful film being of a new type is very small.

The actor as a marker for a particular 'film type'

Films can be characterised in many ways. They can be characterised by director, as do film theorists who promote the 'auteur' theory. They can be characterised by their year of production, as do those who distinguish films by the systems under which they were produced, like 'studio' and 'post-studio'. They can be characterised by story type, like 'action adventure', 'true life' or 'comedy', as many video stores do. They can be characterised by their use of lighting and visual aesthetics, as do those who label films 'film noir'. They can even be characterised by a combination of these things, like 'film noir of the 30s' or 'film noir of the 80s'. One can also characterise films by 'star' and an uncodifiable host of other inputs. Let us look at an example of how this might work.

Clint Eastwood's characters in the films *Dirty Harry* and *The Bridges of Madison County* can be seen as very different: mean, aggressive and young in the first, and nice, tender and old in the second. However, they can also be seen as similar: loner, self-assured and handsome in the first, and loner, self-assured and handsome in the second. The differences and similarities in the movies can go on and on: one was distributed in 1971 and the other in 1995 – very different. Yet, it can be argued, both addressed a baby-boomer age group's contemporary interests. The first addresses the baby boomer movie-going cohort when it was young and, at that time, wanted to be entertained by heroes who did what they had to regardless of the authorities in control. The second addresses the baby-boomer movie-going cohort when it was older, and, at that time, wanted to be entertained by the possibilities of love after the age of fifty.

The point is that how we identify similarities among films and what combination of characteristics work to engage an audience enough to buy tickets can be very subjective, and problematic for both the academic as well as the film producer. But some things stay constant, like the fact that Clint Eastwood starred in them. This is an objective fact that cannot be denied or argued about. This is the basis of the assumption which follows: that stars can mark a particular film type, even if the combination of other ingredients is difficult, if not impossible, to identify.

Consider this. An actor may be in many successful films for many reasons. He or she may consistently contribute talented acting skills or 'star quality', which have the potential to give films a unique quality enjoyed by audiences. In other words, the star personally affects the outcome of a film. They do this through an uncodifiable formula as they interact with various inputs. Their contribution produces a unique film type. Or, an actor may choose roles in films which are representative of a film type. In other words, some actors choose films that are of the type that produce repeated success. Alternatively, an actor may attract higher investment, including publicity, thus increasing the chance of success for a particular film type. Finally, an actor's attachment to a successful film type may be the result of a combination of these and other reasons.[4]

What this suggests is that, say, Clint Eastwood, through his talent, ability to choose, or ability to acquire investment, is a marker of many successful films which can then be characterised as a film type. If this is true, then, over time, the number of successful films in which Clint Eastwood stars will mimic a particular part of the distribution of successful film types resulting from the stochastic process discussed above. It does not mean that every film Clint Eastwood performs in is necessarily of that type. Indeed, some films in which Clint Eastwood performs, like 1990's *The Rookie*, may be failures. For it is not his mere presence alone which is sufficient for the production of a particular successful film type. Rather, it is his presence in combination with other immeasurable interactive components. If one gets the 'other things' right, and so long as the film type is one that the stochastic process has designated as a superstar (i.e. a film type that generates many successful films), one produces a successful film. Thus, some film types marked by particular actors will generate successful films year after year.

Other actors may, unfortunately for them, mark a film type which allows for only one successful film. This is necessarily so, because the film audience and its stochastic process based on past information generates a distribution of film types that have varying life spans.

The discussion above can be written into our third and final assumption:

Assumption 3:
  Actors mark particular successful film types.

Summary of the model

The audience chooses to see a film depending on past information about film types. Further, we assume that an actor becomes a marker for a particular film type. For example, if Clint Eastwood appears in fifteen successful films, we consider him a marker for a successful film type that generates fifteen successful films over time. Other actors will star in a different number of successful films. Some will star in fifteen, some in ten, some in five, some in three and so on, each actor marking a particular film type. Our theory predicts that of all the film types (as marked by actors) which generate success, there will be 50 per cent that generate only one successful film, because the consumer choice stochastic process predicts some 50 per cent of all film types are of this kind. And there will be fewer film types (marked by actors) which generate two successful films, because the consumer choice stochastic process predicts some 17 per cent of all film types of this kind, and so on.

If this is the case, then identifying actors (as a group) as markers is a useful tool for the film industry, to make predictions of the probable success of particular film projects. They give the film producer a key to understanding the potential rewards from investing in a film. This is because, if our assumptions are true, actors as markers will exhibit a consistent predictable relationship between themselves and consumer behaviour.

It is not clear whether the three assumptions provide a fair depiction of the market for movies. The rationality of (i) film types, (ii) a consumer choice stochastic process, and (iii) stars as 'markers' of film types can only be judged by 'the prescriptive power of their implications' (Chung and Cox 1994: 72), i.e. the distribution resulting from assumptions 1–3. In the following sections we examine whether the distribution is a good representation of the steady-state distribution of successful films among film types from 1960 to 1995, as marked by actors.

Empirical results

Data description and some initial results

A decision was made to limit the bulk of the discussion of this chapter to a period after the studio era,[5] though I do allude to results for the studio era when there is reason to do so. The total data set consists of a list of twenty films for each year between 1940 and 1955 and between 1960 and 1995 inclusive; a total of 960 films,[6] each marked by one starring actor. These are the top twenty films each year with regard to 'rentals'.[7] The data set was generated from each year's 'Big Rental Films of the Year in the US and Canada' list as reported by *Variety* in their 'Yearly Anniversary' issue. This series of lists was used because it is regarded as an industry standard and provides very reliable, consistent and comparable data over a long period of time.

There are approximately 450 films released in the United States each year (including both home and foreign produced). This number may vary slightly from year to year and from source to source, but differences vary by little more than ten to thirty films. I calculate that between 1960–1969 there were 443 films released per year; between 1970–1979, 476 films per year; between 1980–1989, 429 films per year and between 1990–1995, 420 films per year (*Variety* 12.30.87; Council of Europe 1994, table 4.6; Storper 1989, table 5; *Film Comment*, the last issue of each year 1974–1996). This means that the top-twenty films per year represent approximately 5 per cent of all films released in that given year, and are more successful than about 95 per cent of all movies released.[8]

Column 2 of Table 8.1 shows the distribution of film types (as marked by actors) which have generated at least one top-twenty film from 1960–1995.[9] Of the 283 different film types which generated at least one top-twenty film, 155 generated exactly one such film; fifty-two generated exactly two such films; twenty-four generated exactly three such films and so on, down to one superstar film type which generated nineteen top-twenty films (the film type marked by Clint Eastwood). One should note that although there are only fifty-four different film types (as marked by the actor) which generate four or more top-twenty films, they account for 365, or 53 per cent, of all top-twenty films. And those film types which

Table 8.1 Distribution of film types by the number of top-twenty films they generate, 1960–1995.

i number of top-twenty films	Number of film types generating exactly i number of top-twenty films			Percentage of film types generating exactly i number of top-twenty films		
	Actual number	Predicted by assump. 1–3	Predicted by assump. 1–3 with allowance for entry of new film types	Actual percentage	Predicted by assump. 1–3	Predicted by assump. 1–3 with allowance for entry of new film types
1	155	142	151	54.77	50.00	53.19
2	52	47	48	18.37	16.67	16.96
3	24	24	23	7.77	8.33	8.20
4	14	14	14	4.94	5.00	4.79
5	12	9	9	4.24	3.33	3.12
6	5	7	6	1.77	2.38	2.19
7	6	5	5	2.12	1.79	1.61
8	6	4	4	2.12	1.39	1.24
9	2	3	3	0.70	1.11	0.98
10	4	3	2	1.41	0.91	0.79
11	3	2	2	0.70	0.76	0.65
12	1	2	2	0.35	0.64	0.54
18	1	2	1	0.35	0.29	0.23
19	1	1	1	0.35	0.26	0.21

Source: *Variety*.

Notes
155 different film types produced exactly one top-twenty film each.
Fifty-two different film types produced exactly two top-twenty films each.

repeat success (a film type which generates at least two top-twenty films), account for some 80 per cent of all successful films. These results alone give some justification for the prevailing attitude in Hollywood that, in order to produce success, it is best to produce a film of the type that has had success already, or in other words, to hire a star who marks a film type that has been associated with a string of successful films in the past.

Empirical testing

Columns 5 and 6 of Table 8.1 compare the percentage of film types that actually generate i top-twenty films with the percentage predicted by assumptions 1–3. For example, the actual proportion of film types that generate exactly one top-twenty film was 54.77 per cent and the proportion predicted is 50 per cent. The actual proportion of film types which repeat success and generate exactly two top-fifty films is 18.37 per cent compared to the predicted proportion of 16.67 per cent, and so on. When comparing the actual percentages with the predicted percentages, it appears that the steady-state frequency distribution resulting from the stochastic process is very close to the actual frequency distribution of successful films (a top-twenty film) among film types (using the actor as the marker of that film type).

Columns 2 and 3 of Table 8.1 compare the actual number of film types which produce one, two, three, four, etc. top-twenty films with the number predicted by assumptions 1–3. The predicted number in column 3 is calculated by multiplying the predicted percentage by the total number of film types. The actual number of film types that generate exactly one top-twenty film was 155 and the number predicted is 142. The actual number of film types that repeat success and generate exactly two top-twenty films is fifty-two and the number predicted is forty-seven. The actual number of film types which generate exactly three top-twenty films is twenty-four and the number predicted is twenty-four, and so on. When comparing the actual numbers with the predicted numbers, it appears that the steady-state distribution resulting from assumptions 1–3 is very close to the actual steady-state distribution of successful films among film types.

Employing methods similar to Chung and Cox (1994), we can test whether this distribution describes our data by using the Chi-square goodness of fit test. The Chi-square statistic[10] in this instance is calculated by:

$$Q = \sum_{i=1}^{7}(\text{Actual}_i - \text{Predicted}_i)^2/\text{Predicted}_i = 3.660151, \tag{8.10}$$

which is well below $\chi^2_{0.95}(6) = 12.952$. Thus, because the actual distribution of successful film types (as marked by the actor) cannot be proven to be different to the steady-state distribution that is predicted by assumptions 1–3, we cannot reject the hypotheses that (i) there are film types, (ii) that actors are markers for such film types and (iii) that the success of films is determined by an underlying stochastic consumer choice process based on past information about film types.

Relaxing assumption 2

Although our results are very good, we can improve on them by relaxing assumption 2 and allowing a rate of entry for new film types. Recall that assumption 2 assumed that there was very little chance, approximately 0 per cent, that a new film type would generate a successful film. By relaxing this assumption, Simon (1955) shows that the predicted distribution is slightly altered. In short, the new predicted Yule distribution results in a greater percentage of film types that generate exactly one, two or three successful films at the expense of film types that produce four or more. These new distributions are similar to our original, in the sense that the past success of a film type will impact future success, and are calculated by the following formula

$$f(1) = 1/(2 - \delta), \tag{8.11}$$

and

$$f(i) = [(1 - \delta)(i - 1)/1 + (1 - \delta)i]f(i - 1), \tag{8.12}$$

where $0 < \delta < 1$ and is equal to the rate at which new film types are introduced (Simon 1955: 430 eq. 2.21, 429 eq. 2.11.)

Equations 8.11 and 8.12 imply that, for each new δ, there is a new distribution to compare to the actual distribution of successful films among film types. It makes intuitive sense that a predicted distribution that allows for the entry of new film types would better fit a data set that reflects successful film types over time, and indeed, this is the case. By calculating in a problem-solving manner, one can minimise the Chi-square goodness of fit value by adjusting δ. I have found that the Chi-square value is minimised when δ is equal to 0.12. The resulting Chi-square value is equal to 1.849439. So, a distribution that allows for new successful film types to be introduced at a rate of 12 per cent can be said with more confidence to be not unlike the actual distribution observed.

Columns 2 and 4 of Table 8.1 compare the actual number of film types which produce one, two, three, four, etc. top-twenty films with the number predicted by assumptions 1–3, with allowance for entry of new film types at a rate of 12 per cent. The actual number of film types that generate exactly one top-twenty film was 155 and the number predicted is 151. The actual number of film types that repeat success and generate exactly two top-twenty films is fifty-two and the number predicted is forty-eight. The actual number of film types which generate exactly three top-twenty films is twenty-four and the number predicted is twenty-three, and so on. When comparing the actual numbers with the predicted numbers, it appears that the steady-state distribution resulting from assumptions 1–3 with allowance for entry of new film types is very close to the actual steady-state distribution of successful films among film types.[11]

Testing other time frames

I have also tested the model using different time frames: the top-twenty films for a period representing the studio era, 1940–1955; and the top-twenty films for a period representing a contemporary post-studio era, 1980–1995. Both periods consist of sixteen years. Using Table 8.2 we can compare the percentage of film types that generated *i* successful films for the studio era with the contemporary post-studio era. Comparing columns 2 and 3 we see that during the studio era, 54.24 per cent of film types generated exactly one top-twenty film, compared to 55.00 per cent for the post-studio era. During the studio era, 16.10 per cent of film types generated exactly two top-twenty films, compared to 19.29 per cent for the post-studio era, and so on. The two distributions appear broadly similar.

Some observable differences do exist. For example, there is a higher percentage of film types during the post-studio era that generate exactly two successful films and there are more film types in the studio era that produce greater than five successful films. However, when testing for statistically significant differences, we cannot reject the hypothesis that the two distributions are the same. I test this by using the studio-era frequency distribution as the predicted distribution for the post-studio era. In other words, if the post-studio era were functioning in a similar manner to the studio era, then we would expect the studio era's percentages to be good predictors of the post-studio era's frequency distribution. This is the same method used to test the distribution predicted by assumptions 1–3. In this case, I have replaced the distribution predicted by assumptions 1–3 with the studio-era distribution.

Testing this new comparison yields a Chi-square statistic equal to 4.194255; well below the $\chi^2_{0.95}(4) = 9.488$. Thus, because the post-studio era distribution of successful film types cannot be proven to be different to the distribution as predicted by the observed studio era percentages, we cannot reject the hypothesis that, for the two periods, similar mechanisms underscore the distributions of successful film types as marked by actors. Testing the similarities between the predicted steady-state distribution of assumptions 1–3, given in column 8, with the actual distribution for the period 1940–1955 yields a Chi-square statistic equal to 1.373729, well below $\chi^2_{0.95}(3) = 7.815$; and for the period 1980–1995, a Chi-square statistic equal to 2.024055, well below $\chi^2_{0.95}(4) = 9.488$. In each case, we cannot reject our hypothesis that in both historical periods (i) there are film types, (ii) that actors are markers for such film types, and (iii) that the success of

Table 8.2 Frequency of film types when marked by actor, director or writer which generate at least one top-twenty film: 1940–1955 and 1980–1995

i number of successful films	Percentage of film types generating exactly i number of top-twenty films when marked by:						Percentage of film types generating exactly i number of top-twenty films predicted by assumptions 1–3
	Actors		Directors		Writers		
	Studio 1940–1955	Post-studio 1980–1995	Studio 1940–1955	Post-studio 1980–1995	Studio 1940–1955	Post-studio 1980–1995	
1	54.24	55.00	41.12	60.99	39.67	65.27	50.00
2	16.10	19.29	9.35	21.98	28.80	20.50	16.67
3	5.93	9.28	17.76	8.79	13.04	7.531	8.33
4	5.08	6.42	7.48	2.75	7.065	3.77	5.00
5	4.24	3.57	4.67	2.20	3.80	1.67	3.33
6	2.54	0.00	8.41	1.65	4.89	0.42	2.38
7	5.08	1.43	2.80	1.10	1.63	0.42	1.79
8	1.69	2.86	5.60	0.00	1.09	0.42	1.39
9	0.00	1.43	0.93	0.00			1.11
10	1.69	0.71	1.87	0.55			0.91
11	0.85						0.76
13	0.85						0.55
17	0.85						0.33

Source: Variety.

films is determined by an underlying stochastic consumer choice process based on past information about film types.

Using directors and writers as markers

The significance of our results, to some extent, can only be justified if other markers are inconsistent with our hypotheses. For example, it may be equally credible to use film directors or writers as markers of film types. I apply similar procedures to test these propositions.

Table 8.2 reports distributions when using the director and or writer(s) as a film type marker.[12] These are listed in columns 4–7. It is apparent that the actual percentages in both periods for both director and writer are distinctly different to those predicted by assumptions 1–3 (given in column 8). In testing that the actual distributions are the same as that predicted by assumptions 1–3, we find that for the directors working during the studio era, 1940–1955, the comparison yields a Chi-square statistic equal to 18.43753. This is greater than $\chi^2_{0.95}(3) = 7.1885$. For the years 1980–1995 it is equal to 10.06604, which is greater than $\chi^2_{0.95}(4) = 9.488$. In the end, we can reject the hypothesis that the distributions, the one predicted by the model and the actual distributions, are the same when directors are used for marking successful film types. We can also reject that the distributions are the same over time. Using the studio frequency distribution as the predicted distribution for the post-studio era, the Chi-square statistic is equal to 84.70154, which is greater than $\chi^2_{0.95}(7) = 14.067$.

Furthermore, it appears that successful films come from an increasingly diverse group of directors. Since the studio era, there appears to be an ever-increasing weight towards new entrants. Indeed, for 1980–1995, the Chi-square is minimised and becomes significant only if we relax assumption 2 and allow the entry of new directors at a rate of 37 per cent.[13]

Using another potential marker, 'writer', does no better than 'director'. In testing whether the actual distribution of successful films as marked by the writer is the same as that predicted by assumptions 1–3, we find that for the writers working during the studio era, 1940–1955, the comparison yields a Chi-square statistic equal to 31.28982, which is greater than $\chi^2_{0.95}(5) = 11.070$. For the years 1980–1995 it is equal to 19.99825, which is greater than $\chi^2_{0.95}(5) = 11.070$. In the end, we can reject the hypothesis that the distributions, the one predicted by the model and the actual distributions, are the same when writers are used for marking successful film types.

We can also reject that the distributions are the same over time. Using the studio frequency distribution as the predicted distribution for the post-studio era, the Chi-square statistic is equal to 83.13395, which is greater than $\chi^2_{0.95}(7) = 14.067$.

And, as with directors, there has been a distinct change in the distribution of success among writers, with an increased number of successful films being associated with a more diverse group of writers. Using similar methods as before, the Chi-square statistic is minimised only when there is an allowance for entry of new writers at a rate of 65 per cent.

With such inconsistent results for both directors and writers, it appears as if our hypotheses are not useful in describing the market mechanisms surrounding directors as a group and writers as a group, in the motion picture industry. It appears that the influences of the studio system were severe, and that once these disintegrated, a vast array of directors and writers could be seen to be associated with successful films. When comparing all three markers – actors, directors and writers – these results suggest that actors are, as a group, the only marker that is consistent over time and consistent with an underlying stochastic consumer choice process based on past information.

Conclusion and discussion

Recent work suggests that there is little Hollywood producers can do to ensure a successful film. However, many industry representatives believe that probabilities of success can be managed, though there has been little empirical evidence or theoretical modelling to suggest this. Perhaps the myriad of inputs that go into film production belies modelling. I take a new approach in examining the phenomenon of successful films, by using a 'marker' for a successful film type. The results suggest that the value of stars to the film industry may be more than simply their box office appeal, but also their usefulness in estimating probabilities of success.

This chapter is primarily concerned with the production of successful movies in the post-studio era: 1960–1995. It is based on a very simple premise: that consumers are more likely to choose a film of a type that has been successful in the past. The results suggest that stars mark successful film types in accordance with this type of consumer behaviour. And because of this, they wield not only audience drawing power but marking power as well. This cannot be rejected for the years 1960–1995, or for a representation of the studio era, 1940–1955, or for a strictly contemporary era, 1980–1995. Given the changes in government regulation, the advent of television, the change in contractual relations between studios and stars, the proliferation of cable television, the introduction of video cassettes, and the different levels in consumption, this consistency is quite remarkable.

The consumer choice stochastic process using actors as markers (i) predicts a particular distribution of successful films marked by actors, (ii) allows for failures by actors and, most importantly, (iii) provides a means by which investors/producers can calculate probabilities of success by using stars. All of these are evidenced in the US film industry.

We know that an established star does not ensure a successful film. Why? Because there are a host of other inputs that might make a film fail.

Yet, audiences consume film types as marked by stars when attached to the 'right' host of other things in a consistent way. The resulting consumption pattern provides information used to make decisions about advertising, production budgets and even whether to make the movie or not. Because of this, it makes sense for producers to use the presence of individual stars as a means to estimate the probability of a film succeeding. This is one reason why stars are so important to the film industry. They give the film producer one consistent way in which to understand consumption patterns in relation to successful films. Thus, in the film industry, a star is often the key ingredient to getting a film made. Not only because they have box office appeal, but also because they mark a known part of a consumer choice mechanism. It turns out that some can 'green light' expensive films, and others less expensive films, depending on the estimated part of the distribution they mark.

Of course, no one can exactly predict whether a particular film will be successful. The trick is to get the combination of inputs right. The producer's job is to manage that trick and their attempts are not always successful. But these findings suggest that the methods they employ – hiring a star and trying to get the 'other things right' – is a justifiable action. However, even if the star and other things are 'right', the stochastic process implies an end point to a particular 'winning streak'. In other words, not all film types can reproduce success ad infinitum. In this sense, producing films will always be a gamble. Does the successful film type marked by Tom Cruise have another success in it or not?

In a recent *New Yorker* article, industry executives were given the chance to reply to De Vany and Walls' findings on the apparent chaotic structure of the film industry. Universal executive Frank Biondi believes that the film industry is not as chaotic as it seems. He claims, 'there is a distribution of success in the movie business that can be impacted by management' (Cassidy 1997: 43). This chapter supports such an argument.

Mark Johnson, producer of *Good Morning Vietnam*, reveals that Hollywood producer Jeffrey Katzenberg, then chairman of Walt Disney Studios, 'is famous for putting figures on these films. . . . If *Good Morning Chicago* [the proposed sequel *to Good Morning Vietnam*] gets made with Robin Williams, it can arithmetically be worked out to do $12 million to $13 million its opening weekend – whether it's good or not. If the film doesn't work, it could do [a total of] $55 million; if it's pretty good, $75 million; if it's very good, $125 million. But if someone else [stars in] the film, those figures all change downward, not upward. So you kind of back yourself into a star' (Natalie 1989: 42). Katzenberg is relating his own intuitive sense not only about Robin Williams' box office appeal and the fact that a host of other factors are important in the film being either 'bad', 'good' or 'very good', but also about Williams' position as a marker within the film-type distribution. Robin Williams, like other stars, provides Katzenberg with a marker to make the estimations that he does.

Appendix

Appendix 8A.1 Markers of successful film types, 1960–1995

Actor/actress	Number of top-twenty films
Clint Eastwood	19
Paul Newman	18
John Wayne	12
Burt Reynolds	11
Barbra Streisand	11
Steve McQueen	10
Eddie Murphy	10
Robert Redford	10
Sylvester Stallone	10
Sean Connery	9
Harrison Ford	9
Chevy Chase	8
Tom Cruise	8
Tom Hanks	8
Charlton Heston	8
Jack Lemmon	8
Peter Sellers	8
Julie Andrews	7
Kevin Costner	7
Dustin Hoffman	7
Roger Moore	7
Arnold Schwarzenegger	7
Frank Sinatra	7
Warren Beatty	6
Jane Fonda	6
Bill Murray	6
Jack Nicholson	6
Al Pacino	6
Doris Day	5
Richard Dreyfuss	5
Henry Fonda	5
Mel Gibson	5
Goldie Hawn	5
Steve Martin	5
Gregory Peck	5
George C. Scott	5
William Shatner	5
John Travolta	5
Gene Wilder	5
Robin Williams	5

Source: *Variety.*

Notes

1 This chapter was originally published under the same title in the *Journal of Cultural Economics*, 22 (1998): 249–270.
2 They do not report that sequels and the presence of stars are related. Perhaps this is because their star variable is calculated along very broad terms (no star, rising or falling star, established star, more than one established star). However, if we take particular stars into account, there is some evidence that stars and sequels are related. Of the thirty-four sequels used in Prag and Casavant's database, approximately 60 per cent use the same star.
3 The paper by Chung and Cox (1994) is used as a blueprint for my analysis. I apply many of their methods, but employ a different model, which results in the same stochastic process. As in any application of a stochastic process, it is how the underlying phenomenon is modelled that produces unique results (Brock 1993). Therefore, the conclusion and content of this chapter are unique.
4 Talent or the ability to attach oneself to film types that generate many successful films may be the consequence of luck. We do not reject this, but rather accept it as a possible reason. The theory allows for all cultural considerations of why a particular actor might be talented or choose films of a particular type. It might be because he or she has a superior ability attained through hard work and know-how or that his or her instincts are good, that he or she is lucky, or reflects current societal tastes. The model and testable propositions are the same, regardless. Notice that this allows for superstars resulting due to a difference in talent as proposed by Rosen (1981) as well as superstars resulting by a random process as proposed by Adler (1985).
5 This is because much of the cultural studies literature points to various differences between two eras in the film industry arising from a series of events:

i) The US government applied pressure in the form of a 1940 consent decree which decreased the practice of block booking and the 1948 'Paramount Decision' (*US* v. *Paramount Pictures*, 334 US 131, 1948) which forced the divestiture of cinema chains and weakened Hollywood studios (Bordwell *et al.* 1985: 331; Pryluck 1986).
ii) The advent of television introduced new competition. In 1947 250,000 Americans owned TVs. By 1950 over one-quarter of US homes had televisions (8 million) which doubled to 50 per cent by 1952 and was up to 42.2 million by 1956 (Bernstein 1957). There was almost complete saturation by 1960.
iii) Studios, who had traditionally hired actors and actresses under seven-year contracts, began retreating from this policy after 1950 (Kindem 1982).
iv) In general, production was shifting to external independent companies (although distribution remained tightly controlled by studios) (Staiger 1985; Storper 1989).

These four factors combine to give two culturally and organisationally distinct periods in the film industry. First a studio era, followed by a post-studio era. Of more importance to this chapter, expenditure per inhabitant in 1989 dollars has been distinguished by several periods. Between the years 1929 and 1939, there was a relatively stable overall consumption hovering between $40 or $50 per head, and can be associated with the early decades of the studios' 'Golden era'. After 1939 the industry saw a dramatic rise in expenditure per head, reaching nearly $80 per head in 1946, and falling back to just under $40 per head by 1951. Another slight rise is seen between 1952 to 1956. By 1960 expenditure per head dropped and stabilised to approximately $15–$20 per head. For our purposes, then, the film industry is three different markets: 1929–1939; 1940–1956; and 1960 to the present.

6 Explanatory notes regarding data: (1) In each Anniversary issue of *Variety*, the year's rentals are given for films that earn over $1 million in rentals. (2) Because films have various release dates throughout the year and in order to provide more meaningful comparisons, I ascribed a film to a particular year by establishing which year it earned its greatest amount of rentals. So, some films may have been released in late 1985, but earned most of their rentals and had their longest run in 1986. In such cases these films were included in the year 1986. (3) Films receiving the exact same amount of rentals in a year were ranked equally. In the years in which this affected the bottom-ranking films – 1965, 1969, 1971, 1987 and 1988 – this policy increased the total number of films included for the year. (4) The data is restricted to the rentals earned at the time of initial release. It does not include cumulative tallies over time. For example, future earnings from art-house or festival screenings are not included in rentals received. (5) On rare occasions a blockbuster will earn enormous amounts of money spanning two years. For example, *Raiders of the Lost Ark* was released in June 1981 and made $90.434 million and its continued run in 1982 made a further $21.566 million. The 1982 taking would put it in the top-twenty for that year as well. Listing *Raiders* in both years would break up its initial release. This would show up in our results as consumers attending *Raiders* in 1982 based on the information from 1981. Although this might be the case (in that people were going to see the same film twice) there is no way to extract such knowledge. So I took the conservative approach and left *Raiders* in only one year. It is not clear what is the best approach, so in these rare cases, we underestimated people applying the consumer choice stochastic rule. Thus, if our results turn out to support the hypothesis that people see current films on past information of similar (in this case exactly the same) film types, the result would only be strengthened by approaching the data in the other way. (6) Reissues, a common practice wherein a popular film is re-released on a wide scale years after its initial release, were treated as any other release for that year. For example, *Gone with the Wind* was reissued several times. For each reissue, I included *Gone with the Wind* in the year in which it was reissued. This makes sense since we are concerned with consumer choice, and, so long as consumers choose among films that are released, reissues are among the possibilities. (7) Animated films are often at least one of the more popular films released in each year. For our purposes I did not know how to identify the star. Perhaps it is Disney, perhaps it is the lead character, so I excluded these from the data *after* calculating the top-twenty films. In this way some films were not elevated just because they were released in a year which happened to include many animated films. In any case, I analysed the data set when animated films were included and this made only insignificant changes in the final results.

7 A film's rentals are the amount theatre owners pay each motion picture company for showing the film and is usually 40 per cent to 50 per cent of the box office gross and therefore closely reflects the top-twenty grossing films per year. Earlier work has suggested that the correlation between rentals and gross is approximately 1 (Prag and Casavant 1994).

8 The amount of difference in rentals between the film ranked first and the film ranked twentieth is about six times. For example, for 1984 the number-one ranked film, *Ghostbusters*, received rentals equal to $120 million, while the twentieth-ranked film, *Bachelor Party*, received $19.07 million. This range, though, is misleading, as each year there is usually one to three blockbuster films that do exceptionally well. After that the spread between, say, the film ranked fifth and the film ranked fifteenth is much less. Our main concern is that the films receive rentals better than most films released. And any film in the top-twenty can be considered a success, when one takes into account that many

films that are released earn little more than \$1 million in rentals, and most earn even less than that, including many major studio releases.

9 A jury of three experts designated the films' lead actor: a cultural economist, a film theoretician and an independent film producer. When judges were unfamiliar with a film or were undecided about who should be designated the lead star, *Halliwell's Film and Video Guide 1998 edition* was consulted. This occurred in 13 per cent of the cases for the post-studio period and 44 per cent of the cases in the studio period.

10 Chi-square tests require that the predicted number be at least 5 so we use those observations wherein the predicted value is 5 or greater.

11 Results were also consistent with the stochastic process when altering the definition of a successful film. Testing the similarities between the predicted steady-state distribution of assumptions 1–3 and the actual distribution of successful films as defined by entry in the top-ten films yields a Chi-square statistic equal to 8.2775268, below $\chi^2_{0.95}(4) = 9.488$. Testing the similarities between the predicted steady-state distribution of assumptions 1–3 and the actual distribution of successful films as defined by entry in the top-forty films yields a Chi-square statistic equal to 5.12092, well below $\chi^2_{0.95}(9) = 16.919$.

12 In the case of writers, some films have more than one writer. In such cases, the writer with the most successful films was given credit. I included all writers that were associated with two or more successful films and excluded those writers who were co-contributors to a film script when another contributor was attached to two or more successful films. By using the data in this way one would expect an even greater chance that the distribution would resemble that predicted by assumptions 1–3.

13 One can imagine several reasons why this might be the case. One of the more interesting might be that the job of the director has become increasingly codified, perhaps due to the increase in film schools and the increased ability to copy the well-established filmic grammar developed during the studio era. For example, the angles, editing, lighting and suspense-generating techniques of Alfred Hitchcock are continually being copied. An interesting topic to investigate, but outside the scope of this chapter.

References

Adler, M. (1985) 'Stardom and Talent', *The American Economic Review*, 75: 208–212.

Austin, B. (1989) *Immediate Seating: A Look at Movie Audiences*, Belmont, CA: Wadworth Publishing Company.

Bernstein, I. (1957) *Hollywood at the Cross-roads: An Economic Study of the Motion Picture Industry*, Los Angeles, CA: Hollywood Film Council.

Bordwell, D., Staiger, J. and Thompson, K. (1985) *The Classical Hollywood Cinema*, London: Routledge & Kegan Paul.

Brock, W.A. (1993) 'Scaling laws for economists', Working Paper, University of Wisconsin at Madison.

Brown, C. (1995) 'City of fear', *Screen International*, 1018, 28 July: 8–10.

Cassidy, J. (1997) 'Chaos in Hollywood', *The New Yorker*, 73, 31 March: 36–44.

Charity, T. (1996) 'Dead Cert', *Time Out*, 1–8 May: 26.

Chung, K. and Cox, R. (1994) 'A stochastic model of super stardom: an application of the Yule distribution', *The Review of Economics and Statistics*, 76: 771–775.

Council of Europe (1994) *1994–1995 Statistical Yearbook: Cinema Television Video and New Media in Europe*, Council of Europe.

De Vany, A. and Walls, W.D. (1996) 'Bose–Einsetin dynamics and adaptive contracting in the motion picture industry', *The Economic Journal*, 106: 1493–1514.

Garrison, L.C. (1971) *Decision Processes in Motion Picture: A Study of Uncertainty*, unpublished thesis, Stanford University.

Halliwell's Film and Video Guide 1998 edition (1998) London: HarperCollins.

Jowett, G. and Linton, J. (1989) *Movies as Mass Communication*, Newbury Park, CA: Sage Publications.

Kindem, G. (1982) 'Hollywood's movie star system: a historical overview', in G. Kindem (ed.) *The American Film Industry*, Madison, WI: University of Wisconsin Press.

Miller, D. and Shamsie, J. (1996) 'The resource based view of the firm in two environments: the Hollywood film studios from 1936–1965', *The Academy of Management Journal*, 39: 519–543.

Morin, E. (1960) *The Stars*, New York, NY: Grove Press.

Natalie, R. (1989) 'The Price Club', *American Film*, June: 42–44, 65.

Paris, B. (1989) 'Maximum Expression', *American Film*, October: 32–39.

Prag, J. and Casavant, J. (1994) 'An empirical study of the determinants of revenues and marketing expenditures in the motion picture industry', *Journal of Cultural Economics*, 18: 217–235.

Pryluck, C. (1986) 'Industrialization of entertainment in the United States', in B. Austin (ed.) *Current Research in Film: Audiences, Economics and Law*, Vol. 2, Norwood, NJ: Ablex Publishing Corp.

Rosen, S. (1981) 'The economics of superstars', *The American Economic Review*, 71: 845–857.

Shipman, D. (1979) *The Great Movie Stars: The Golden Years*, New York, NY: St. Martin's Press.

Simon, H.A. (1955) 'On a class of skew distribution functions', *Biometrika*, 42: 425–440.

Simonet, T. (1980) *Regression Analysis of Prior Experience of Key Production Personnel as Predictors of Revenues from High Grossing Motion Pictures in American Release*, New York, NY: Arno Press.

The South Bank Show (1997) Televised interview, Director/Producer Tony Knox.

Staiger, J. (1985) 'The Hollywood mode of production, 1930–1960', in D. Bordwell, J. Staiger and K. Thompson (eds) *The Classical Hollywood Cinema: Film Style and Mode of Production to 1960*, London: Routledge & Kegan Paul.

Storper, M. (1989) 'The transition to flexible specialisation in the US film industry: external economies, the division of labour, and the crossing of industrial divides', *Cambridge Journal of Economics*, 13: 273–305.

Sunday Times (1998) 'The battle to make sliding doors', 22 March.

Thomas, C. (1996) 'Dumb, Dumber, Dumbest', *Flicks*, 9(8), August: 18.

Variety (1987) 'New U.S. Feature Film Releases', Wednesday, 30 December: 1.

Vincent, M. (1996) 'I always want total control', *The Times*, 2 December, Feature section: 15.

Walker, A. (1974) *Stardom, The Hollywood Phenomenon*, Harmondsworth: Penguin.

Yule, G.U. (1924) 'A mathematical theory of evolution based on the conclusions of Dr. J.C. Willis, F.R.S.', *Philosophical Transactions of the Royal Society* B, 213: 21–87.

9 Movie contracts

Is "net" "gross"?[1]

Mark Weinstein

One of my colleagues has suggested that the second easiest way to start a fight at a pool party on the west side of Los Angeles is to argue in favor of the two propositions presented in this article:

1 "net profits" contracts as used in Hollywood have been in use for more than sixty years, and
2 these contracts are reasonable responses to contracting problems that arise in the motion picture industry.

Litigation about employment contracts in Hollywood is widely reported.[2] These suits are usually brought by people who had contracted for a share of the "net profits" from a movie. After the movie is, arguably, successful the individual discovers that the "net profits" are small and perhaps zero. The common perception is that the studios use strange and arcane accounting practices to eliminate any profit. A contrast is often drawn between those who have little bargaining power – such as Art Buchwald – and sign contracts with "net profit" shares and big stars – such as Tom Hanks – who are able to sign for shares of the "gross." The latter are believed to be unaffected by studio chicanery. Indeed, the fact that some major stars get a percentage of the gross is considered one of the reasons the "net profits" are reduced (Abelson 1996). These claims are appealing to the public. The plaintiff is usually an individual who had a profit participation in a movie that has turned out to have large box office. How can *Batman* or *Forrest Gump* not be profitable? In reality, however, the term "net profits," as used in Hollywood to define a contingent compensation contract, is unrelated to "net profits" as defined by Generally Accepted Accounting Principles. "Net profits" is a contractually defined term, the meaning of which is well understood in the industry as this contractual form has been common there since at least the mid-1950s.[3] Moreover, it is similar to contractual forms in use since the 1920s as the integrated production–distribution–exhibition corporation that epitomized the "studio system" developed. It is difficult to see how a one-sided contractual form would survive such a long period.

This chapter examines profit- or revenue-sharing contracts in the movies. There has been virtually no analysis of the motion-picture industry or the contract forms used in the industry. Most who have written about the contracts used in the motion-picture industry have either been reporters, film historians, or legal professionals.[4] Thus, one of the objectives of this chapter is to present an analysis of the evolution of various sharing contracts used in Hollywood. I argue that the evolution is, in part, the result of changes in the economic and regulatory environment in which the studios do business. That is, as the underlying economics and industrial organization of the industry changed, the contract that best balanced the costs and benefits changed.

I proceed in the following manner. The first section develops an overview of the motion picture industry and some evidence on the historic performance of the studios. This is followed by a section that describes current sharing contracts in motion pictures and their historical development. I also point out that some aspects of the contract that were ruled unconscionable in the *Buchwald* decision in fact make it possible for participants to audit reasonably the payments they receive, thereby ensuring that the studio is keeping its side of the bargain.

The third section examines the potential economic rationales for these contracts. In fact, there are two issues that call for the application of economic reasoning. First, there is the question of why sharing contracts are used at all. That is, why does a presumably risk-averse individual take a contract that involves an uncertain payoff? There is, then, a second question, which is why a particular contract form is used. There are a number of competing hypotheses regarding these contracts. First, there is what I term the "rip-off" theory, to which I have already alluded. I argue that this is not an attractive rationale. In contrast to this view are a variety of analyses in which the contracts are the result of rational behavior. While others (e.g. Chisholm 1997) have analyzed the contract using a fairly standard principal–agent framework, I am dubious about that view. Rather, I propose that these contracts serve two potential roles.

First, the contracts may represent a risk-sharing device in which some of the risk of a movie is borne by those who sign these sharing contracts. This risk sharing may be optimal if the studio executive who signs the contract is risk averse (either because of risk aversion or because of a problem in the contract between the executive and the firm), or because it goes hand-in-glove with a reduced fixed payment to the "talent." In a studio, as in any large business, executives are often given a fixed budget with which to work and so often have an incentive to convert fixed costs (salaries) to variable costs (shares of receipts). That is, there are two reasons that behavior that appears to be due to risk aversion may arise. First, studio executives may actually be risk averse in a way that affects the contracts they write. Alternatively, as a result of the costs of monitoring studio executives, a system of fixed budgets for motion-picture production may provide an incentive for studio executives to reduce the fixed component of compensation by offering contingent compensation that, by definition, is risky.

Second, these contracts may serve to solve an asymmetric information problem between the studio and the actor. The actor may have private information about how interested he or she is in making this particular movie, and the studio may have private information about the likely success of the movie. In this case, a sharing contract may provide protection against the informationally advantaged party. These two hypotheses have not been previously developed in the literature concerning movie contracts. While these explanations are more relevant for those with more bargaining power, most of the litigation has been about those with relatively little bargaining power, who sign what are called "net profits" contracts. I present some analysis of their situation in the fourth section.

In summary, this chapter:

1   documents the long history of this contract form and presents evidence on its evolution;
2   suggests that the most common theories why these contracts exist are probably not valid; and
3   suggests some alternative hypotheses that are more consistent with industry practice.

The motion-picture industry

There are three well-defined stages in the motion-picture business: production, distribution and exhibition. Production involves making a completed master of the motion picture that is to be distributed and exhibited. This is a complicated process requiring the input of a myriad of talented people and fairly large sums of money.[5] The production of a movie is orchestrated by a "producer" who may or may not be the person with the "Produced by" credit on the film.

Distribution takes as input the completed motion-picture master from the producer. The distributor makes positive prints from the master and places them in the hands of the exhibitors. The distributor manages the physical flow of potentially thousands of copies of the movie, arranges promotional activities, and collects the moneys due it from the exhibitors. The distributor also forwards some of the moneys collected to individuals associated with the movie.

Exhibition refers to showing the movie to patrons. An exhibitor firm takes as inputs a copy of a completed motion picture, a movie theater that it owns or leases, and the various labor inputs (ticket takers, ushers, projectionists and so on) to produce seats at a showing of a movie. These seats are then sold to the public. As the structure of the industry has changed over time, some historical perspective is useful for readers who are not familiar with it.

The industry has gone through three main phases. Prior to about 1915, the industry was dominated by a large number of production companies that, for the most part, paid royalties to the trust that controlled all of the essential patents associated with movie-making. At the same time there was a set of smaller, independent production companies that operated outside of the trust. During the period from about 1915 to 1930, the industry became organized around a small number of vertically integrated firms that provided production, distribution, and exhibition. While many of the major stars had their own production companies before the rise of the "studio system," by the 1930s most, though not all, stars were salaried employees of the studios. The studio system ended with the *Paramount* decision in the late 1940s,[6] which forced the separation of exhibition from production and distribution. During the 1950s the studios evolved into what they are today, essentially distribution companies which provide financing to some producers ("studio productions"), provide distribution services for independent producers under long-term contract, and pick up partially or fully completed movies for distribution.

One way to get a feel for how the industry has performed over time is to examine the output and revenues of the industry. In Table 9.1, I present the number of movies released by the major studios during the sound era up to 1980. During the period from 1930 to 1942, the major studios released an average of 353 movies each year. War-related restrictions reduced the average to 264 over the period from 1943 to 1945. After the war output fluctuated in the late 1940s and then declined as the advent of television and changing demographics reduced demand. This is shown by the average output of only 119 a year over the period from 1971 to 1980. Figure 9.1 presents data on attendance and revenues for the major studios over the same period and tells a similar story with a significant decline in

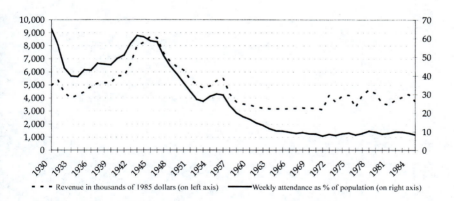

Figure 9.1 Average attendance and revenues, 1930–1985.

Table 9.1 Number of motion pictures released by each major studio, 1930–1980

Year	Studio											
	Columbia	MGM	Paramount	RKO	Fox	UA	Universal	Warners	Disney	TriStar	Orion	Total
1930	29	47	64	32	48	16	36	39				311
1931	31	46	62	33	48	13	23	24				280
1932	29	39	65	46	40	14	39	55				327
1933	32	42	58	48	50	16	37	55				338
1934	43	43	55	46	52	20	44	58				361
1935	49	47	63	40	52	19	37	49				356
1936	52	45	68	39	57	17	28	56				362
1937	52	51	61	53	61	25	37	68				408
1938	53	46	50	43	56	16	46	52				362
1939	55	50	58	49	59	18	46	53				388
1940	51	48	48	53	49	20	49	45				363
1941	61	47	45	44	50	26	58	48				379
1942	59	49	44	39	51	26	56	34				358
1943	47	33	30	44	33	28	53	21				289
1944	56	30	32	31	26	20	53	19				267
1945	38	33	23	33	27	17	46	19				236
1946	51	25	22	40	32	20	42	20				252
1947	49	29	29	36	27	26	33	20				249
1948	39	24	25	31	45	26	35	23				248
1949	52	30	21	25	31	21	29	25				234
1950	59	38	23	32	32	18	33	28				263
1951	63	41	29	36	39	46	39	27				320
1952	48	38	26	32	37	34	39	26				280
1953	47	44	26	25	39	49	43	28				301

Year											
1954	35	24	17	16	29	52	32	20	2		227
1955	38	23	20	13	29	35	34	23	4		219
1956	40	24	17	20	32	48	33	23	5		242
1957	46	29	20	21	50	54	39	29	4		292
1958	38	29	25		42	44	35	24	7		244
1959	36	25	18		34	40	18	18	5		194
1960	35	18	22		49	23	20	17	7		191
1961	28	21	15		35	33	19	16	7		174
1962	30	21	17		25	36	18	15	6		168
1963	19	35	17		18	23	17	13	6		148
1964	19	30	16		18	18	25	18	6		150
1965	29	28	24		26	19	26	15	3		170
1966	29	24	22		21	18	23	12	4		153
1967	22	21	30		19	19	25	21	5		162
1968	20	27	33		21	23	30	23	6		183
1969	21	16	21		18	31	26	21	3		157
1970	29	23	15		15	39	16	16	5		158
1971	32	18	21		13	25	17	17	6		149
1972	26	24	14		25	22	16	18	9		154
1973	19	15	27		15	19	16	21	7		139
1974	19	5	25		20	26	12	22	6		135
1975	17	4	12		17	23	9	15	6		103
1976	15	4	19		20	23	12	15	5		113
1977	10.5	3.5	14.5		14	10	14.5	11	7		85
1978	12	5	14		8	13	22	17	3		94
1979	20	3	14		13	18	15	10	5	4	102
1980	14	6	15		16	16	18	17	3	8	113

Sources: Joel Finler (1988); AMPAS *Annual Index to Motion Picture Credits* (various issues); Holliss and Sibley (1988).

attendance and (real) revenues in the 1950s. I return to this point, and its possible role in the kinds of contracts movie studios write, on pages 251–252.

Contracting in Hollywood

The net and gross participation contracts evolved over time. While it is a commonly held view that such participations are a recent development, this is not the case. As long as there have been studios, those with sufficient talent and bargaining power have been participating in the success of their movies. I start with an examination of a typical "net profits" contract, the one that was the subject of the *Buchwald* litigation.[7] Next I summarize the most common forms of contingent compensation that currently exist. I then turn to the changes in the form of the participation contracts that occurred as the studio era ended in an effort to trace the development of the contract form.

The Buchwald contract

The Buchwald contract is typical of the net-profits participation contracts that were written by the major studios in the mid-1980s. In 1983, Alain Bernheim contracted with Paramount Pictures Corporation for the possible development of a movie based on an idea of Art Buchwald's. This contract is a standard "net-profits" contract for a major studio production in the early 1980s.[8] A sharing contract in Hollywood defines two things. First, it defines a pool of funds from which participations are to be paid and, second, it defines the percentage of that pool that will go to the contracting party. Pool definitions generally fall into either of two categories, gross receipts or net profits.

The contract defines the gross receipts of the picture as the amount received by the distributor from various sources. Traditionally the main source of revenues was that part of the box office receipts (roughly 50 percent) that the theater rebates to the distributor. Other forms of exhibition (pay TV, network TV) are also accounted for, as is income from video-cassette and DVD sales, which has come to be as important as theatrical income.[9] Some individuals with sufficient bargaining power contract to share in the movie's gross receipts. While this participation may be from the first dollar of gross receipts ("first dollar gross"), more often it triggered by the gross achieving some predetermined dollar level or a multiple of the direct costs of production of the picture.[10]

The transformation of "gross receipts" to "net profits" requires subtracting a number of expense items. These fall into four categories. First, there are the distribution fees and expenses. These include:

1   the distribution fee (30 percent United States and Canada, 35 percent United Kingdom and 40 percent elsewhere);

2   direct advertising and publicity expenses;
3   the cost of prints; and
4   overhead charges of 10 percent of direct ad and publicity costs.

Next are the costs of getting the master print created. These include:

1   the direct costs of production (the "negative cost"), which includes all
    development and production costs, including all *gross* participations;[11]
2   the next item is the overhead charge, which is specified as 15 percent
    of the cost of production (including gross participations); and
3   interest expense.

Paramount subtracts from the revenues interest on the direct production
and overhead at the rate of 125 percent of prime. While the interest is
stated last, in fact it is recovered *before* any production costs are credited.
That is, if any funds from gross revenues remain in an accounting period
after paying of gross participations and the distribution-related expenses,
those funds are first used to pay off the outstanding interest bill, and only
after the interest is covered do they go to pay down the negative costs.[12]
Thus, the "net profit" is zero until the movie has recovered all the costs of
distribution, the overhead and the direct negative cost, and interest
charges on the negative costs and overhead.[13]

   The studio's revenues, then, come from four sources:

1   the studio receives a distribution fee which is a percentage of the rev-
    enues of the movie;
2   the studio recovers its direct expenses for prints and advertising and
    an overhead on advertising;
3   the studio recovers the direct costs of production, along with an over-
    head charge and an "interest" charge on the resources advances in
    making the movie; and, finally
4   the studio usually maintains a share of the net profits pool.

Thus a negative net-profits pool does *not* mean that the studio has not
made a profit on the movie as computed under Generally Accepted
Accounting Principles, or even an economic profit. For example, for the
purposes of financial reporting, there is no "interest" cost if the studio is
financed entirely with equity, though, to an economist, the opportunity
cost of equity capital is a cost of doing business. Alternatively, the actual
expenses for those items that are classified as overhead may differ from
that specified in the contract. Moreover, the distribution fee, which is
deducted before the computation of "net profit," is a revenue source to
the studio.

   One way to understand this contract is to look at it in the light of the
services provided by the modern studio. Consider an individual who has

an idea for a motion picture. In order to actually make and distribute the movie, she has two choices. On the one hand, she can avoid the studio completely. In that case, she must arrange financing, develop the idea into a script, hire a director, arrange for the actual production of the movie, and, finally, engage a distributor to distribute the motion picture. On the other hand, she can arrange for a studio to provide financing and other services. The producer, if she has little or no track record, might well end up with terms similar to that of Alain Bernheim in this case – an up-front payment and a percentage of the "net profits." In return, the studio finances all the costs of production, arranges for the resources needed to produce the film, and then distributes it.

If the studio's charges, including the interest rate and the distribution fee, are those that rule in a competitive market, then the producer should not prefer to produce the movie herself. The studio is providing an array of services, and charging market rates for them. Given the ease of contracting for services, the "one-stop shopping" nature of a studio production may even offer sufficient benefit that the studio's charges need not meet the market rate for each service in order to remain competitive.[14]

In *Buchwald*, some of the aspects of the contract that Judge Schneider found unconscionable were charging a fixed, predetermined overhead on production costs and advertising expenses, charging production overhead and interest on payments to gross participants, and charging interest at the rate of 125 percent of prime, rather than at Paramount's actual cost of funds. I believe that the judge was wrong in all of these cases. In any contract like this, which calls for some sharing of cash flows, there must be some way for the receiving party (in this case the performer or producer) to ensure herself that she is being paid in full. Further, the payer (the studio) may not want to reveal everything about its operations to the payee. The three clauses of the contract described above make it possible to audit the contract to ensure proper compliance without requiring the studio to divulge expenses or revenues for any other movie.

First, the overhead allocation on both the production cost and on the advertising expense is structured as a predetermined function of direct expenses. This is in contrast to normal cost accounting. Under normal cost accounting practices the overhead for a given picture depends on how costs are allocated across *all* of the pictures in a given year, and negative cost used in computing the contingent compensation would be a function of how many other productions were going on at the time. This means that it would be to the participant's advantage to have many other pictures under production to which overhead can be allocated. Moreover, auditing the contingent payment requires knowing the negative cost which, in turn, requires knowing the costs of each movie produced in a given year. Thus, it would be costly for the participant to ensure that she is getting the appropriate payment, and the studio would be required to reveal information on other movies. This means that in contracts that do not predetermine an overhead percentage, there might be no effective audit right for the participant. In the modern contract, of which Buchwald's is representative, detailed allocation of common costs is not required. This is in contrast to similar contracts from the 1920s, 1930s, and 1940s, which specified overhead charges as determined by the studio's accounting firm (Weinstein 1998: 81).

Because the gross participation payments are included in the negative cost of the movie, both overhead and interest are charged on them. Charging overhead on gross participation payments serves to provide, *ex ante*, the appropriate amount of overhead. This may seem odd. After all, how can the studio charge 15 percent overhead simply for writing a check? However, to the extent that the gross participation is a substitute for salary, adding the participation to the production costs makes sense. The purpose of the overhead allocation is to capture those costs associated with a given picture that are difficult and/or expensive to track. These are probably related to the "scale" of the movie. If a performer receives a gross participation, the fixed component of his salary understates his total compensation and this leads to an understatement of the "scale" of the movie.[15] Including the participation in the base used to calculate overhead offsets this bias. Further, it is reasonable to assume that an actor is more willing to take a participation rather than salary on a movie that has the backing of a major studio (the picture is more likely to actually get made and distributed, and when distributed will have the support of a major studio distribution system). Then one can easily imagine that, had the producer not had the support of the studio, she would have had to pay the star a larger salary during the cost of production and would have had to raise the funds for those payments. Thus the interest charge on the gross participation is simply a mechanism for the studio to capture the economic benefit that it provides to the producer.

Finally, there is the fact that the financing charge is a predetermined function of the prime rate and is not related to the studio's cost of funds. However, it does not make economic sense to tie the interest rate used for computing the participation to the interest rate the studio pays for borrowed funds. First, what would happen if a studio was flush with cash and had no net financing? That would not mean that the opportunity cost (the relevant economic cost) of the resources tied up in the movie was zero. Moreover, there is a real difference between any loan the studio makes from a lender and this contract. Because a negative net-profits pool does not permit the studio to recover from the participants, the "loan" associated with the movie is actually non-recourse and thus different in nature from any borrowings by the studio which are backed, in the end, by all of the studio's assets.

In fact, these clauses all contribute to an ability to determine separate contingent compensation pools for each picture, which allows the studio to maintain confidentiality from one movie to the other.[16] In effect, each movie is a separate firm, with its own "profit" statement. I examine the potential role of incentive contracts in this situation, after I turn to the evolution of the "net profits" contract.

"Net" and "gross" contracts

The contract in *Buchwald* is a "net" contract in that the contingent payment is a portion of the "net profits." This is in contrast with the "gross" contracts that big stars are able to get, which pay a percentage of the gross revenues, sometimes from the first dollar of studio receipts. However, as the description makes clear, the net profits participant does, in fact, get a percentage of the gross revenues, but only after the gross exceeds the direct and indirect costs of production and distribution and a distribution fee. There are also contracts that pay a percentage of gross revenues once gross revenues exceed a certain fixed dollar amount or once the gross exceeds a fixed multiple of production costs. Finally, there are some contracts that pay a fixed percentage of the gross after the gross has exceeded an amount equivalent to the point at which the net profits pool turns positive. This is equivalent to a net contract that, once the net profits pool has turned positive, has a zero distribution fee, expenses, and interest rate.

A useful way to look at the distinction between net and gross contracts is to focus on uncertainty about the level of gross receipts required to trigger payment. One can contract for a contingent payment once gross reaches a certain fixed dollar amount. In this case there is no uncertainty about how well the movie must do to generate a contingent payment, but there is, of course, still uncertainty about how well the movie actually *will* do. One could also write a contract in which the payoff is contingent on gross receipts reaching some multiple of production cost. Depending on the relation between box office and production costs, this may lead to different allocations of risk between the participant and the studio. Carrying this further, in the net-profits contract, the point at which payment will be triggered depends on the cost of production, period of production (which effects the "interest bill"), and the promotion and advertising expenditures. All of these expenditures are, to a greater or lesser extent, under the control of the studio. Thus, a potentially interesting question, and the focus of Goldberg (1997) is the question of why a contract that not only pays off fairly infrequently, but also allows one party to, in effect, alter the terms of trade *ex post*, continues to survive. I return to this question later in the chapter.

The economics of sharing contracts in Hollywood

In Weinstein (1998), I presented examples from old contracts to show that sharing contracts existed in the movie industry at least since the mid-1920s.

While they evolved over time, the main forms of sharing contract, the "net profits" and the "gross participation," existed by the early 1930s. We also know that they were uncommon, being reserved for only the most important talent in the industry.

In this section I examine alternative explanations for the use of sharing contracts in Hollywood. The most common economic explanation for sharing contracts in general is they serve to provide the appropriate alignment of incentives between the principal and agent, induce greater effort from the agent, and thus lead to higher total cash flows. I suggest that this is not the most likely explanation for the contracts in this industry. Before proceeding with the analysis, however, I examine some evidence on how the motion-picture industry changed after the studio era.

Changes in the industry following the demise of the studio system

Fewer pictures

One result of the demise of the studio system and the reduced demand for motion pictures was a reduction in the number of motion pictures distributed by the major studios. Table 9.1 shows the number of movies distributed by each "major" studio on an annual basis for the period 1930–1980. The number of releases reached a maximum of 408 in 1937. It declined slowly until the war limitations took effect in 1943, when the number of releases fell to 289 from 358 in 1942. The number of releases recovered from the mid-200s to reach the upper 200s, even passing 300 in 1951 and 1953 before beginning a fairly steady decline that bottoms out at eighty-five releases in 1977. Thus, the number of releases fell from the upper 300s in a typical year, to about 100, a decline of roughly 70 percent. One would expect, then, that studio revenues fell. In fact, Robins (1993) reports that not only did revenues drop, but so did box office revenues as a percentage of consumer spending, dropping to 0.2 percent in 1965 from 1.2 percent in 1946.

This reduction in the number of movies distributed, and total revenues, had a number of effects. There was an excess supply of physical motion picture studios. The land became more valuable for other uses and was often sold for development. The reduction also meant that it was no longer economical for the studios to employ large numbers of actors on salary as, in effect, a stock company. During the 1950s and 1960s, studios stopped placing new talent "under contract" and moved to a system where individual actors, producers, and directors were only hired for one (or a small number) of movies.[17] The number of actors under contract to major studios, which had been as high as 804 in 1944, fell to 164 in 1961 from 474 in 1949. Similar declines are also found in the 1949–1961 period for directors (to twenty-four in 1959, the last year available, from ninety-nine in 1949), producers (to fifty from 149), and writers (to 47 from ninety-one).[18] With fewer movies being made, it was no longer possible to predict accurately the demand for a given number of roles fit for actors/actresses with given characteristics. It can be argued that this reduced demand for motion pictures, rather than the *Paramount* decision, was the proximate cause of the decline of the studio system. Without the ability to amortize costs over a large number of movies, the "production line" approach that was one characteristic of the studio system was no longer optimal.

Not only did the major studios produce and/or distribute fewer movies after the demise of the studio system, but performers also appeared in fewer movies. Figure 9.2 presents the number of movies released in each year from 1933 to 1992 by the top-five finishers in the annual exhibitors' poll of the top box office attractions.[19]

Thus we see that not only were there few movies made after the studio system ended, but also that both non-stars (fewer were under contract) and stars made fewer movies.

Increased risk

Not only was there a decline in the number of movies produced during this period, but there was also a change in risk in the motion-picture business. One can argue from portfolio theory that with many fewer pictures coming out of any studio, the risk of the cash flows to a studio will go up. There is less diversification.[20] We have already seen this in Table 9.1. Moreover, the reduction in the number of releases understates the increased extent to which studio profit depends on a small number of films. Robins (1993) reports a secular increase in the concentration of revenues in a small number of films. In the late 1940s, the top 1 percent of

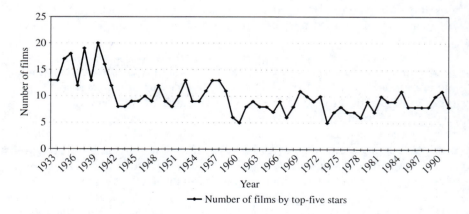

Figure 9.2 Number of films by top-five stars, 1933–1992.

films represented 2 percent to 3 percent of studio revenues; by the early 1960s, this had tripled, to an average of about 6 percent. This trend has continued in recent years. In 1993 the world-wide revenues for the top 1 percent (two films) of the 163 major-studio-released films were 13.8 percent of the total.[21] Not only is there less diversification at the studio level (fewer movies by the studio), but there is also, as we have seen, less diversification at the talent level. Further, the end of the studio era also saw increased turnover in top studio executives.[22]

We can also see the effect of increased risk at the level of the individual studio. Figure 9.3 presents an analysis of the data from the Schaefer ledger of Warner Brothers' releases over the period 1921 to 1960.[23] For each movie in the ledger I computed a "profit ratio": the ratio of net rental income to the production cost.[24] For each calendar year I computed the average and the coefficient of variation of that ratio for all Warner Brothers movies released during that year. Figure 9.3 presents the average ratio by year as well as the coefficient of variation. In order to highlight trends, we also present five-year moving averages of these variables. From this figure we see the increased profitability of the studio during the years leading up to and including the Second World War, with the profit ratio increasing by about 40 percent between 1938 and 1944 (to 2.62 from 1.98), before it declines to less than 1.61 in 1947 and recovers to about 2.8 by 1960. More dramatic changes occur in the coefficient of variation.[25] The coefficient of variation more than doubles during the post-Second World War period, increasing to 0.74 in 1960 from 0.32 in 1946.[26] As we shall see later in the chapter, this coincides with an increase in the use of sharing contracts.[27]

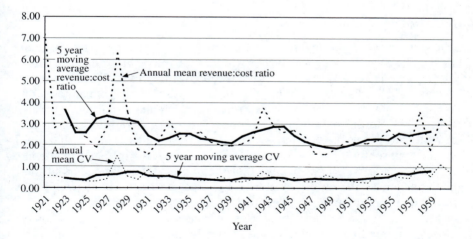

Figure 9.3 Analysis of ratio of gross revenues to negative cost: five-year moving average of mean and coefficient of variation.

Changed organization of production

Schatz (1988) notes that the studio era was characterized, at the most successful studios, by one or more strong central producers, such as Irving Thalberg at MGM. This central producer controlled the production of the movie, playing a very active role in pre- and post-production and truly shaping the movie. Directors, in this regime, simply shot enough good film for the central producer to work with. By the mid-1940s some directors, notably Alfred Hitchcock,[28] working within the studio, but not bound to it, would shoot much less film. This meant that Hitchcock, for example, was delivering a film that could not be significantly altered in the editing process, thus protecting his vision of the film from interference by the producer, in this case David O. Selznick.[29]

The demise of the studio system also had a more subtle effect on the organization of film production. During the studio era, the strong-central-producer system of movie-making was modeled on a production line. In part this was driven by a desire to get 40–60 films made in a given year for exhibition in the studio's (and others') theaters.[30] As the studio system died out, we have seen that there was a dramatic decrease in the number of films produced. Bordwell (1985) note that this removed a great deal of the pressure on film schedules.[31] As studios abandoned the production line as the model, more flexible forms of organization arose. Where once writers were kept away from the production side, by the late 1940s they were able to at least observe what was going on. This saw the rise of the multi-role individual, exemplified by Billy Wilder, who was a writer–director in the studio context. This movement was facilitated by a relaxation of job definition by the labor guilds.

Increased use of sharing contracts

There were some sharing contracts as early as the silent era (Weinstein 1998). The Shaeffer ledger indicates whether the movie had a direct participant (such as John Barrymore) or showed advances to independent producers, which implies a share. Figure 9.4 presents the percentage of Warner Brothers movies, by year of release, which had a sharing contract. It is clear from this data that the frequency of sharing contracts increased dramatically after the Second World War. It should be noted that the ledger apparently undercounts the number of movies with participants in the early years.[32] I do not believe that such understatement occurs in the later period, as the studio established a separate department to ensure payment of participations. The fact that studios established a formal department to handle participations is an indication that they had become more common. In any event, it is clear that, by the late 1950s, most movies had at least one sharing contract.

Although this graph suggests a decline in the use of sharing contracts in

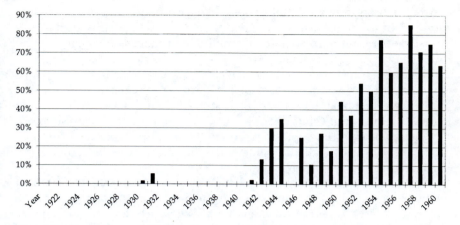

Figure 9.4 Percentage of Warner Bros. movies with sharing contracts by calendar
year of release.

the late 1950s, this dip was apparently temporary.[33] Today the vast majority of movies, especially those financed by a studio, do have participants of
either the net or gross variety.

Alternative explanations of the contract form

In this section I present the various alternative explanations for the survival of this contract form and evaluate the evidence supporting each
explanation.

"Studios rip off actors – and everyone else"

This is the essence of the trial court's finding in *Buchwald* (see note 7).
While this is not usually used as an explanation for sharing contracts in
general, it is the most popular explanation of the net-profits contract
form.[34] However, sharing contracts based on concepts similar to the
modern "net" and "gross" profits have been around since the dawn of the
studio era. Moreover, the motion-picture community is rather small, with
a limited number of agents and attorneys involved in drafting contracts. It
is difficult to imagine that the studios have been able to fool actors and
producers, and their agents and lawyers, for such a long period.[35]

There is another way in which the current contract gives the studio a
potential opportunity to enrich itself. It has been alleged that the contract
may provide an incentive for the studio to offer gross contracts to big stars
to the detriment of those with net contracts (Abelson 1996). The reason
for this is that in the usual contract the net participant has no control over
the studio or producer's freedom to sign major stars whose gross participa-

tions are treated as a negative cost and thus reduce the payoff to the net participant. To the extent that there are payments for major stars signed subsequent to the net participant, and there was some positive probability of a payoff to net participants, the studio or producer does not bear the full cost of the star's payment.

But, there is an offsetting effect which may work to the net participant's advantage. Consider the impact of having net profit participants on the movie. Assume that the studio is going to make a movie starring the current Governor of California. The producer, and the studio, must decide how much to invest in explosions. Assume that more explosions (production expense) leads – all else being equal – to more box office, albeit at a declining rate.[36]

First, as I have shown elsewhere (Weinstein 1998: 96), the optimal number expenditure on explosions, from the studio's point of view, is greater if there are net participants than if there are no net participants, and the effect is more pronounced as the overhead percentage, distribution fee, or percentage of the pool paid to participants increases.[37] If there are no net participants, the studio bears all the expense of increased spending on any factor of production; if there are net participants, the participants bear some of the cost. Thus, the presence of net-profits participants means that the studio does not internalize all of the cost, and thus overinvests in certain aspects of movie production. From this simple example we see that this effect has nothing to do with gross participants. The same incentive exists if the star's salary is fixed and also applies to the production budget.

Interestingly, however, if the big stars are paid a percentage of gross rather than a flat salary, the net participant may actually be better off. If there are no gross participants, the studio keeps all of the incremental revenues from increased expenditures on, say, special effects (less any share paid to net participants). However, if there are gross participants, the studio does not get all of the incremental revenues, but does bear all of the costs associated with increased production expense (again, less any effect on payments to net participants). Thus the studio will tend to cut back on these expenses, which will tend to ameliorate the overinvestment problem noted above.

This analysis also helps to explain why the percentage of net-profits contracts they pay off is fairly small. To the extent that a risk-neutral studio takes these effects into account, and there is no repetition of the game, it will reduce the anticipated net profits to a level below that which would be the case if there were no net-profits participants. However, if the studio may want to contract with the same people again, it might well choose not to go all the way to a zero expected net-profits pool. Moreover, even if it did, we would expect the studio to be wrong some of the time. Because the distribution of revenues is positively skewed, a given expected payoff will imply fewer (though larger) positive net-profits pools than would be the case if the distribution were symmetric. These arguments all suggest that what we should see is a situation where there are some positive net-profits pools, though they are not the norm.

The fundamental problem is that *someone* has to be given the right to choose the final cast and have decision-making authority during and after production. The studio is the ultimate residual claimant on the film, and as such it should not be surprising that the studio has the ultimate power to sign the star. This is similar to equity holders being given the right to manage the firm. The potential conflict arises because the studio, through its distribution function, collects a distribution fee that the net-profits participant never sees. To continue with the corporate finance analogy, this is akin to having the controlling shareholder also own most of the firm's outstanding debt. That shareholder may have an incentive to choose low-risk projects that benefit bondholders rather than stockholders. The distribution fee is like a prior claim on the cash flows from the movie, like debt service.

In the corporate law area, the conduct of shareholders in such a position is governed by the corporate law of the state of incorporation.[38] The issue here, however, is a matter of contract. A plaintiff could allege a violation of the implied covenant of good faith and fair dealing, or covenant of best efforts.[39] At issue here is how the court will fill in the missing blanks in the contract.[40] What would be the reasonable expectation of the contracting parties regarding the studio's freedom to sign a major star? The person who signs a net-profits contract knows full well, at the time the contract is signed, what the distribution fee is, and who has, traditionally, had control over casting the movie. Any *ex ante* benefit the studio might anticipate from later signing a big star is presumably reflected in the fixed component of the contract.[41] The only two alternatives to giving the studio power over casting are (1) a complete ban on subsequent budget changes, or (2) required consent of the net participant.[42] A complete ban on budget changes is almost certainly not value-maximizing because budget increases may actually serve to increase the size of the net-profits pool. While, in principle, the studio could give veto rights over subsequent third-party gross participations, or other changes, to *every* net participant, the contracting costs would be large. It is certainly impractical to give every net participant, from the author of the novel on which the movie is based, to the composer of the score, and beyond, this kind of control. Moreover, it would be impossible for the studio to convey to each previously signed net participant the information that it has regarding the benefits from hiring a new star without revealing to the industry at large, and perhaps more importantly to the star with whom it is negotiating, the benefit it expects to receive from the contract. Nor is it likely that the star would like to have the detailed terms of his contract appear on the front page of *Variety*. Thus it is reasonable to believe that both parties intended the studio to control casting.[43]

However, it is easy to overstate the importance of this possibility. Studios are notoriously unable to predict the success of a movie. To the extent that studio executives are reluctant to report losses, they will not offer big stars compensation sufficient to capture *all* of their incremental contribution to the movie. This reduces the likelihood that the big stars' compensation will, *ex ante*, reduce the net-profits pool. But, to the extent that this incentive to hire big stars is a problem, it appears to be a problem inherent in the nature of the business. The net participants want some promise of a back-end payment, which experience tells them will be small. The studio is not likely to provide a participation in the true economic profits of the movie because these cannot be determined without revealing everything about itself. The net-profits contract is a compromise.

These arguments are related to Golderg's (1997) analysis. He focuses on the question of why a net participant would sign a contract that provides opportunities for the studio to reduce her claim on the movie's proceeds. He argues that, in fact, such an arrangement serves both the studio and the participant. Goldberg starts by suggesting that net participants are usually people whose creative contribution comes early in the process of making the movie. He argues that it is in the studio's interest to keep these individuals motivated. However, after their contribution has been made, it is not optimal to keep them motivated, and value maximization is served by giving the studio the ability to, in effect, recontract with these people by changing the scale of production or including some gross participants. Of course, the studio cannot go too far in this direction and must maintain some reputation for "fair dealing," in the sense that it only adds gross participants to the extent this increases the total revenues by enough to offset the effects described earlier. If the studios always engaged in actions that eliminated any possibility of a positive net-profits pool, early signers would understand that there will not be any net profits and the agreements lose their ability to motivate. This is related to the point made above on studio incentives.

It is unlikely, however, that this is the complete story. First, it turns out that many people – for example, the composers who score the music for the movie, screenwriters doing rewrites, and many performers – sign on for, at best, a net-profits participation, *after* the star who will get a gross participation has already signed and the probability of reaching net has been diminished. Some of these people perform their function after the movie has finished production. This is inconsistent with the temporal ordering of net and gross participants that Goldberg postulates. Moreover, it turns out that many performers who get gross have a contract that may well be affected by the presence of other gross compensation contracts. Only a few performers get a percentage of the gross from the first dollar of revenues. Many gross contracts call for payment of a percentage of gross after a break-even point that is a function of the production budget, including the guarantee portion of any gross contract, and any gross payments made prior to the trigger point – the "cash break even." Thus, it turns out that, for many whose participation in the movie temporally *follows* that of most net participants, their contracts can be affected by other gross participations, though not to the extent that net participants can be affected.

Incentives in a principal–agent model

The theory. The standard incentive contracting problem (e.g. Hart and Holmström 1987) involves an employer (the principal) contracting with an employee (the agent). In this framework the principal wants to induce the appropriate amount of effort from the agent but cannot observe how hard the employee works (hidden action) and/or how skillful the agent is (hidden information). If the principal is less risk averse than the agent, then a sharing contract will induce the agent to work harder than would a contract with only fixed compensation. However, such a contract is costly to the principal, as the agent will require compensation for the fact that their share is risky. Thus, it will not be in the principal's economic interest to shift a sufficient amount of risk onto the agent (via an increased share of the profit) to induce first-best effort by the agent.

The motion-picture industry has some interesting features that make it difficult to fit into this framework. First is the fact that, while the basic technology of motion-picture production did not change from the 1930s to the 1970s, the sharing contract became much more common.[44] If optimal contract form is related to the technology of the industry, we would not have expected contract form to change over time. Moreover, to the extent that these contracts involve a contingent payment to offset a desire for shirking on the part of the agent, it is not clear what one means by shirking in the case of a motion-picture star. For example, consider the star who does not like the movie he is working on. While, in principle, a performer could shirk, the effect of this shirking would presumably simply be to make the star spend more time redoing scenes until he gets it right. Thus, the quickest way out of a bad situation may actually be to do it right the first time. Moreover, the motion-picture community is a rather small one, and it would be costly for a star to get a reputation of being difficult to work with. Recall that in the absence of the long-term contracts of the studio era, stars must recontract for each new movie. In that case, the labor market for stars may serve to provide a discipline through reputation effects.[45]

It is difficult to imagine that the "net-profits" pool provides much incentive to the performer. While it is certainly true that the studios pay out millions of dollars to individuals with net-profits contracts, it is also true that only a fairly small fraction of movies, between 10 percent and 20 percent, have a positive net-profits pool.[46] Consider the argument that the effort expended by a performer is not observable.[47] There is little evidence that this is the case. Directors are highly skilled, as are producers. Their success depends, in large part, on an ability to make the kind of subtle judgments about nuances of performance that make a movie a success, and can turn a performer into a star.[48]

Another problem with viewing the participations as incentive devices is that they often go to individuals who are not direct contributors to the motion picture. For example, recently both Alice Walker and William Groom have raised concerns about their shares in the profits from the movies based on their novels, *The Color Purple* and *Forrest Gump*, respectively. However, in neither case was the screenplay used actually the product of the novel's author.[49]

Chisholm (1997) presents an analysis of profit sharing in the motion-picture industry in the context of a standard principal–agent framework. She concludes that the contracts are consistent with an incentive contracting model in the presence of hidden action or hidden information. Her basic argument is that the contract is a solution to a moral hazard problem caused by the inability of the producer to actually observe the effort that the actor is expending in the motion picture. Her main empirical findings are that sharing contracts are more likely[50] for movies that: (1) take longer to make, (2) open at holiday time, or (3) were made later in her time period. Actors are more likely to get a sharing contract in a movie if they: (1) are male, (2) have worked with the producer before, (3) have been in more films, or (4) have had high revenues in their most recent film.

Chisholm's results can support our hypotheses as well as her principal–agent theory. In effect she is asking the hypothetical question: "What determines whether a given employee is paid a fixed salary or a profit share?" Her analysis omits the key variable that, according to our theory, determines whether someone is paid in cash or in percentage of the revenues or profits – the *anticipated* total compensation. The omitted variable, anticipated compensation in a fixed-salary contract, is likely to be correlated with all of the variables that Chisholm shows determine whether the star gets a sharing contract. The reason is simple. As long as the star's compensation is increasing with his experience and track record (as it almost certainly is), budget-constrained (or risk-averse) studio executives will find it most advantageous to give sharing contracts to the most expensive (most experienced) performers. The more highly paid the performer, the greater the incentive to turn a large fixed cost into a variable cost. This will induce a positive correlation between experience and the likelihood of a sharing contract. When one looks at Chisholm's results, each of the variables that she finds positively related to the likelihood of a sharing contract is also likely to be positively related to either the star's required compensation or the size of the movie's budget. Thus, Chisholm's main finding, which she interprets as evidence in favor of an incentive explanation which requires increased explicit incentives in the contract as performers age, is clearly also consistent with a risk-sharing or budget-constraints explanation. Indeed, when she includes variables designed to measure the financial state of the studio (a stronger studio should be less likely to grant a sharing contract) and the size of the production budget for the particular film (the more expensive the film, the more likely is a sharing contract), she finds results that are consistent in sign with the explanations I provide below.[51]

Frequent contracting. In order to understand why it is unlikely that the incentives provided by the "net-profits" pool are the main driving force in the contract form, it is important to recognize the role that frequent recontracting can play in providing incentives by an agent to perform to the best of his or her ability. As Eugene Fama (1980) pointed out in the context of the market for managerial labor, the *ex post* settling up that occurs on a return to the labor market may provide sufficient incentive for agents to avoid shirking. With the demise of the long-term contracts that prevailed during the studio era, stars (and others) are signed for limited deals, often a single picture. In that case an actor must perform at a sufficient level to convince producers and directors to hire him. These are highly skilled professionals who are aware of how the various elements (script, director, production values, performance) of a film work together and who can parse out the contribution that the performer made. Moreover, by judging the actor's work against those of other similar performers and against the actor's previous work, they can judge the extent to which he has been "walking through" a part. Finally, the motion-picture community is a fairly small one in which information travels quickly. Performers quickly develop a reputation, and this reputation is reflected in the wage they can earn.[52]

Grover (1991: 89) notes that when the newly installed team of Michael Eisner, Frank Wells, and Jeffrey Katzenberg at Disney were casting *Down and Out in Beverly Hills*, they took the opportunity to save on up-front expenses by hiring stars whose star had, so to speak, fallen. Bette Midler, who had been involved in series of unsuccessful movies, was signed for $600,000, exactly what her salary had been for her *first* movie. Richard Dreyfus, who had won an Oscar in 1979, was also signed for $600,000, half of his asking price of $1,200,000 at the time.[53] When there are short-term contracts and frequent visits to the labor markets, coupled with evaluation by skilled professionals and a small professional community so that the intangible aspects of working with a particular individual are revealed, there is no reason to view a contingent portion of the compensation as being primarily an incentive device.[54]

One might argue that, even if the incentive portion of the compensation is unimportant for actors and actresses, it is important for producers. Again, the importance of reputation in the industry suggests that this alone should be sufficient to induce producers to work hard.

Apparently risk-averse behavior

In some sense, explanations that rely on risk aversion are the least appealing explanations of all. The studios are publicly held and thus would be expected to be risk neutral. Moreover, risk aversion, like taste, is the last resort of economists because it explains too much. It is easy to use arguments based on one or the other party being risk-averse to explain almost any observation that troubles an economist. Even if managers are risk-averse, we would expect the shareholders to contract with managers so that this risk aversion will not manifest itself. However, such contracts may be difficult to enforce and thus managers have some freedom to spend shareholder money to avoid bearing risk.

We have already seen that one of the participants in the *Winchester '73* negotiations clearly states that a motivation for the contract was to get the actor, James Stewart, to bear risk with which the studio was not comfortable (Sattler 1990). To economists brought up in the principal–agent view of employment contracts, in which the principal is risk-neutral and the agent is risk-averse, this may seem strange. However, that model is inadequate because it ignores the role of the producer or studio executive.

Neither the actor nor the producer is, in fact, negotiating with a risk-neutral body of shareholders. They negotiate with studio executives. We have already seen evidence that the turnover of one of the most important executives, the head of production, has increased dramatically in the last forty years. Especially in the case of an established star, it is likely that the star is both wealthier and more secure in his or her position than the studio executive or producer with whom he or she is dealing. In that case, the star may, in fact, be less risk-averse than the studio executive and thus may be willing to bear risk that the studio executive may be interested in laying off. Chisholm (1997)[55] discusses, and dismisses, this possibility. However, her dismissal is not convincing.

Evidence from other industries provides support for the view that executives are reluctant to show losses. David Burgstahler and Ilia Dichev (1996) examine the cross-sectional distribution of earnings and earnings changes and present compelling evidence that firms report fewer small losses and small reductions in earnings than one would expect. This suggests that managers use what discretionary powers they have to avoid small losses. Larger losses are presumably beyond the range of management to avoid reporting without violating Generally Accepted Accounting Principles. In the motion-picture industry, substitution of profit or revenue sharing for fixed salary arguably serves the same purpose.[56]

There is certainly anecdotal evidence that increased risk, coupled with competition for limited studio funds, does play a role in the increased use of sharing contracts, which have the pleasant (from the studio's point of view) property that they only pay off when there is money to hand out from the picture's revenues. For example, the producers of *Forrest Gump* had great difficulty getting a studio to finance the movie until Tom Hanks and Robert Zemeckis agreed to make the movie for a (first-dollar) share of the gross with no up-front payment (Lippman 1995).[57] This reduced the amount that the studio would have to put up to make the movie. Moreover, we have already seen that risk in the motion-picture business increased after the Second World War when profit-sharing contracts became common.

More evidence consistent with the argument that risk has changed in the motion-picture industry is seen when we contrast the compensation of movie stars with that of stars in episodic television. With the decline in motion-picture production since the 1930s, and the rise of television, in a very real sense episodic television is today's version of the run-of-the-mill "A" and "B" movies that the studios cranked out during the studio era. That is, most of the major studio releases today would have been at the high end of studio-era releases, and the weekly television series embodies the more production-line approach that characterized most production during the studio era. When we look at compensation in episodic television, it turns out that stars of weekly series usually work for a fixed compensation per episode, with only the biggest stars getting percentage deals (Vogel 1986).[58] Thus, when we look at movies today, we are looking at what, in the studio era, would have been the most expensive movies with the biggest stars. The increase in the percentage of movies with sharing contracts in part reflects that change in the mix of movies released today as compared with the studio era. Not only are there fewer movies, implying less diversification, but, on average, each is more expensive than a studio-era production.

It must be understood, however, that while apparently risk-averse behavior may explain part of the use of sharing contracts, it cannot be the entire story. First, it says nothing about the contract terms that characterize the net-profits contract. Second, it can only be relevant for the few big stars who account for what are a significant portion of the movie's production budget.

Other possible explanations

Information asymmetry. Another possible explanation for the use of risk-sharing contracts could be an information asymmetry between the star and the studio or producer. At issue is the possibility that the studio (or its executive) is better informed about the likely market for a movie. Consider a case in which a star is negotiating with a producer for a given role. The producer may know, or the star may *think* the producer knows, more about the likely box office for the movie in question than the star. In that case, the star knows that, even if he and the studio could agree on the marginal contribution that the star adds to the movie, fixed-salary contracts put him at a disadvantage. The reason is that the studio has every incentive to understate the anticipated revenues from the film.

A contract calling for a profit share has the effect of protecting the actor against an informationally advantaged studio or producer. The risk that the actor must bear is, in effect, the compensation that the studio or producer earns for being informationally advantaged.

In this situation, the optimal contract between the studio and the actor may well involve both a fixed component and some sort of sharing rule, *even absent any desire to provide incentives to the actor.* Consider two polar cases and the countervailing incentives for truth-telling on the part of the studio. We have seen that if only a fixed compensation contract is available, the studio has an incentive to understate the likely market for the movie. In contrast, if the only contracts available included only a profit (or revenue) share, but no fixed component, the studio would have an incentive to *over*state the potential market for the movie to get the talent to sign for fewer points. Thus, the only contract that could possibly solve the information problem is a mixed contract with both fixed and variable compensation provisions.

While this story has some appeal, it is easy to overstate the ability of studio executives to predict the success or failure of a movie before it is made. The anecdotal evidence here is quite strong: simply recall *Ishtar*.[59] It is even hard to predict success after the movie is completed. The head of one theater chain, after attending a screening of *Star Wars*, told George Lucas that nobody would want to see the film (De Vany and Eckert 1991: 109). Moreover, it is not clear why the studio has an information advantage relative to at least major stars. Presumably the studio, in order to induce a major star to participate in a movie, will allow him and his agents to examine the same marketing data and have the same knowledge of potential cast that the studio does. Indeed it is not uncommon for major stars to get veto power over some other members of the cast and the director.

The information asymmetry may go the other way. In the case of *Forrest Gump*, Paramount would not commit to the full budget requested. The budget reduction was achieved by having the star (Tom Hanks) and director (Robert Zemeckis) agree to take no fixed compensation in return for a larger percentage of the gross (Lippman 1995). In effect, Hanks and Zemeckis agreed to provide some financing in return for a larger senior claim on the movie's cash flows. If we take this view, the question of why Paramount would view Hanks and Zemeckis as the lowest cost provider of capital is raised. After all, presumably Paramount could have gone to the capital markets. However, one effect of having the contracts structured this way is that, by agreeing to the reduced up-front payment, Hanks and Zemeckis are providing Paramount with information about how they expect the shoot to proceed. From Paramount's point of view it need not be the case that Hanks and Zemeckis know *more* than Paramount but only that their view of the likely success of the movie is based on different information than Paramount has. Structuring the compensation in this way reveals some of Hanks' and Zemeckis' private information to Paramount and thus may serve to reduce the risk to the studio. The studio, in effect, pays Hanks and Zemeckis for their information through the larger back-end.

Long-term relationships. If producers and studios are interested in maintaining good relations with the limited pool of very talented top per-formers, there is another role for sharing contracts. They bond the execu-tive. We see examples of a related phenomena, that studios provide expensive, non-contracted-for, bonuses when a film is successful. For example, it was reported that after the initial success of *The Firm*, the studio gave each of the major stars and the director a new car of a type featured in the movie (Flemming 1993).[60] Each car had a value of approxi-mately $100,000. While this was criticized in the press, it seems likely that the studio did have an interest in attracting major talent to work on future movies by showing a willingness to go beyond the letter of the contract. The studio has an incentive to remain on good terms with talented people that may lead to payments above and beyond the contract. In effect, the contract form that we see says to the talent: "If this movie does better than we expect, we will share that upside with you." This leaves, so to speak, a "good taste in the mouth." Such a good taste may be especially useful in an industry where a star who had signed a fixed compensation contract for a movie that was *ex post* highly successful, might believe that he or she had been taken advantage of.

Economizing on contracting costs. When there is frequent recontracting, the parties have incentives to economize on contracting costs. This will lead to standard-form contracts in the industry.[61] In the motion-picture business, this leads to "boilerplate" definitions of the participations.[62]

Moreover, in a world of imperfect and potentially asymmetric informa-tion, the contract form can be used as a screening device. For example, consider an actress who attaches a high opportunity cost to her time, perhaps because she is in great demand. A two-part compensation scheme, involving a fixed guarantee against a percentage of the gross or net revenue stream, has a certain appeal. First, it allows her to screen potential roles to ensure that the compensation meets her reservation utility; pro-ducers of movies unlikely to make full use of her talents will not find it worthwhile to meet the fixed component of her salary. The profit-sharing part of the contract ensures that she will earn the value of her marginal product if the movie turns out to be unusually successful. The same con-tract can be offered to all-comers, and the actress need not fear that she will not capture the *ex post* high marginal value of her role in a block-buster.[63] Thus, a contract that involves a fixed compensation and a per-centage, or a fixed compensation against a percentage, means that she can spend less time evaluating the likely market for the movie before deciding which movie to do, and can offer the same contract to all producers, thereby reducing contracting costs.

Summary of the evidence

At this point it is useful to consider the possible explanations for profit-sharing contracts in the movie business. The main possibility that has been presented is that these contracts, like other sharing contracts, lead to equilibria in which agents expend more effort and increase output or profits. I have, however, suggested that this paradigm in unlikely to provide an explanation for the sharing rule in the motion-picture industry. If it is not explained by incentives, then what causes it?

Recall that, although we have seen that, while profit-sharing contracts existed during the studio era, it is clearly the case that they are more common today. Also, we have seen that:

1   the structure of the typical "net-profits" contract is that it pays less than 20 percent of the time, depending on the relative expense of the movie;
2   studios have been known to give uncontracted "bonuses" to talented individuals when a picture is unusually successful; and
3   it is notoriously difficult to predict the profitability of a given movie.

The annual schedule of a movie studio is likely to be riskier now than it was during the studio era. This has translated into higher turnover of studio executives. To the extent that there is, in evaluating managers, an asymmetry between losses and foregone profits that leads managers to view losses as worse for their human capital than foregone profits, it is reasonable for studio executives to reduce fixed expenditures in movie budgets. This is reportedly the reason that Tom Hanks' and Robert Zemeckis' contracts for *Forrest Gump* included no fixed compensation (Lippman 1995). Thus, in effect, some of the risk associated with the movie is shifted from the studio executive to the star[64] – who may be wealthier and more able to bear risk.

Is there any evidence consistent with this story? Proven stars are likely to have high compensation. One prediction of this view is that bigger stars are more likely to have sharing contracts. When we examine Chisholm's study in this light, we see that the evidence is consistent with a simple alternative hypothesis to hers – bigger stars have more clout and require higher compensation and take this compensation in the form of a profit or revenue share. Why as contingent compensation? Increased risk and/or the normal budget process of a large corporation conspire to lead executives to reduce fixed costs. Bigger stars' contracts, if guaranteed, are bigger costs and hence are more likely to be the target of conversion to variable costs. Thus bigger stars are more likely to get sharing contracts. This is Chisholm's main result, and this result is consistent with the story I am telling in this section.

There is another type of evidence that is consistent with the view that sharing contracts in Hollywood are not primarily intended to align the incentives of performers with those of the studios. In none of my research in this area, neither in the studio archives nor in the media, have I seen any discussion of the possibility that a performer who is paid a percentage will work harder. However, in the executive compensation area, where stock options and other incentive plans are also common, the internal documents of the firm, and its proxy statements, when discussing these plans, virtually always provide a link between the contingent compensation and aligning managerial and shareholder interests.[65] Thus, if the participant's words in these situations are to be taken at face value, risk rather than incentives is the dominant force.

Summary and conclusions

This chapter has examined two aspects of contracting in the motion-picture industry. By examining the files of a major motion-picture studio from the dawn of the studio era, we have seen that the modern contracts that are so much in the news had clear antecedents in contracts that date back to the mid-1920s. Indeed, by 1930, at least one studio had written contracts that provided for shares of the two main varieties used today, net and gross. Thus the fact that these contracts were not in common use until the 1950s and 1960s cannot be attributed to a change in contracting technology. Further, we have seen that some of the aspects of the contract that were ruled unconscionable in *Buchwald* actually make the contracts more, rather than less, amenable to audit by the contracting party. Thus, all else equal, these clauses are actually more advantageous to the talent than alternative contract terms. We have also seen that the modern contract evolved to the form we see today, influenced by the studio's experience in dealing with independent, and quasi-independent (studio-sponsored) productions. It is also clear that the frequency of profit-sharing contracts is much higher now than it was at the height of the studio system. Thus any explanation of the economic role of these contracts must be consistent with their increased use after the late 1940s.

When we turn to the motivation for such contracts, we are on shakier ground (a Los Angeles metaphor). Recent developments in optimal contracting theory invite economists to view profit-sharing contracts in the context of principal–agent theory, with a risk-averse agent bearing some risk in order to provide the proper incentive if effort is unobservable or to sort out high- from low-quality agents if skill is unobservable. In this framework, the principal is usually, though not necessarily, risk-neutral. I argue, however, that incentive issues are unlikely to be the primary explanation of what is going on in the motion-picture industry. First, when I apply the model to actors, it is difficult to see what the unobservable characteristic is. Performers are closely monitored on the set by highly skilled directors and producers. Moreover, the prevalence of contracts that cover one, or at most only a few, movies means that actors must return to the labor market with great frequency. An actor who shirks, or presents other problems, will quickly find his or her market value diminished.

Finally, it is difficult to see why the appropriate model is one with risk-averse agent and a risk-neutral principal. The actor is, in fact, not negotiating with a studio but, rather, with a studio executive who is in a highly risky position and may have less personal wealth than the star. This leads to the possibility that the contract forms that are observed result from a desire by studios to maintain good relations with stars and a desire by studio executives to shift some risk to movie stars who may be less risk-averse owing to wealth and life cycle effects. The empirical evidence is consistent with either or both of these explanations.

Notes

1 A longer version of this chapter appeared as "Profit sharing contracts in Hollywood: evolution and analysis," *Journal of Legal Studies* 37 (1998): 67–112, © University of Chicago Press. I am indebted to many individuals, at USC and elsewhere, who helped me sort through my thinking on this subject and guided my research. I am specially indebted to Aton Arbisser, Harry DeAngelo, Linda DeAngelo, Victor Goldberg, Kevin Green, Richard Jewell, Ben Klein, Michael Knoll, Ananth Madhavan, Kevin Murphy, Pierce O'Donnel, Mel Sattler, Bobby Schwartz, Matthew Spitzer, Eric Talley, Jeremy Williams, Mark Zupan, and the staff of the Cinema Library at the University of Southern California. I would like to implicate all of them, but I cannot. I have received many useful comments from presentations at USC (Law and Business), Northwestern (Business), and Rochester and the Conference on Research Perspectives on the Management of Cultural Industries, Stern School of Management, New York University. The usual disclaimer applies. I first became interested in this subject when I consulted with counsel for Paramount Pictures Corporation and Warner Bros. Studios in litigation referred to herein.

2 Among the more widely known recent cases are: *Buchwald* v. *Paramount Pictures Corp. (second phase)* C706083, Cal. Super. Ct., L.A. Cty. (1990), *Batfilm Productions* v. *Warner Bros., Inc.*, BC051653 Cal. Super. Ct., L.A. Cty. (1994) and *Estate of Jim Garrison* v. *Warner Bros.*, et al. USDC, Cent. Dist. Cal. (1996). Monk (1995) reported that Winston Groom, the author of *Forrest Gump*, felt that he was not getting payments to which he was entitled.

3 "[N]et profit participations ... are negotiated contractual definitions which have evolved within the motion picture industry and have little to do with the real profit of a picture as measured by generally accepted accounting principles" (Brachman and Nochimson 1985: 1).

4 The economic analyses of the motion-picture industry that have been done either have been of the form of an industry study tabulating the size and influence of various facets of the entertainment industry (for example, Vogel 1986) or have concerned themselves with the *Paramount* decision and its fallout (for example, De Vany and Eckert 1991; Kenney and Klein 1983; Stigler 1968). The only economic analyses that focus on these contracts are Chisholm (1993, 1994, 1997) and Goldberg (1997). The main economic analyses of unpredictability at the box office are De Vany and Walls (1996, 1999), the implications of which are further explored in Sedgwick (2002).

5 In 1995, the average film released through members of the Motion Picture

Association, which includes virtually all firms of any stature in the industry, had a "negative cost" – the cost of making the master negative – of $36.4 million (MPAA 2002: 19). The average cost for prints, promotion, and advertising (PP&A) was $17.7 million (MPAA 2002: 20), for a total expense of $54 million. The aggregate box office for *all* films was $5.5 billion (MPAA 2002: 4) and 511 films were released (MPAA 2002: 12). Even if we assume that all box office went to MPAA films, the average domestic box office per film was only $23.5 million. Because the exhibitor returns roughly 50 percent of the box office to the studio, average *studio* gross from domestic theatrical distribution is less than $12 million per picture.

6 *United States* v. *Paramount Pictures, Inc.*, et. al., 334 US 331 (1948)
7 This well-known lawsuit concerned the motion picture *Coming to America*. The newspaper humorist Art Buchwald and his co-plaintiff Alain Bernheim alleged that the movie was based on a treatment that they had pitched to Paramount. In the first phase of the trial, the jury found this to be true. Since Buchwald and Bernheim had a net profits contract, they had to be paid their share of the "net profits" which were zero even though the movie had done well at the box office. In the second phase of the trial, the court found that the contract was unconscionable A contract is unconscionable when the court finds that it is so one-sided in its terms and in the conditions of its negotiation that it is unfair to enforce it (Chirelstein 1993: 68). Then, in a subsequent stage of the trial the court awarded damages by, in effect, rewriting the offensive clauses of the contract. After the verdict, Paramount appealed to a higher court. Before the appeal was heard, the two sides negotiated a settlement. For a presentation of the case from the viewpoint of the plaintiff's attorney, see O'Donnell and McDougal (1992).
8 Without commenting on how representative the contracts are, the complaint in *Garrison* presents net-profits definitions from each of the major studios and a table comparing their terms.
9 As with merchandising, the movies gross is credited with a percentage of the revenues from video-cassette sales, rather than crediting all the revenues to the gross and then later deducting all the costs. In effect, the studio contracts to "sell" the video-cassette rights for a 20 percent royalty. Often, the "purchaser" of the video-cassette rights is the studio, or an affiliate.
10 There are some small items subtracted from the gross receipts such as trade dues, contributions to the MPAA, etc. In the 1990s, I have been told that roughly twenty performers and five directors are able to get "first dollar" gross, although that number appears to be on the rise with some directors now getting paid at the level of the biggest stars (Thompson 2003).
11 Thus, for the purposes of computing the "net profit," there is no distinction between compensation paid as salary and compensation paid as a result of a "gross" participation. There is also a proviso that expenses cannot be counted as *both* a distribution and production expense ("no double deductions").
12 This is similar to the amortization of a loan in which the current payment is first applied to the interest and only if there are funds left over after bringing the interest up to date is the remainder applied to principal.
13 Although contracts written on the gross appear different from contracts written on the net-profits pool, one can always convert a "net-profits" contract into a contract written on the gross receipts. Of course, it will not be written on "first dollar" gross, but rather the contingent payment will be delayed until some multiple of production and distribution costs are recovered.
14 Actually, even if the studio simply charges market rates for its services, professionals may be willing to contract on different terms for a production that is

backed by a studio than for one without studio backing. A leading star, for example, is more confident that the movie will actually be finished and distributed, and hence may not require as much pay. Even those with relatively little bargaining power may work for less on a studio production because they do not bear the risk of non-completion or difficulties with payment for services. Also, considering the extent that working on studio production puts someone in contact with a diverse number of people who are involved in making a lot of movies, working on a studio production rather than an independent production may be a good career move. Thus, the backing of a major studio, per se, may reduce costs.

15 One problem with this view is that it implies that there should also be overhead charged on contingent payments made to "net profits" participants. This could lead to circularity problems in the definition of net profits and a similar result can be obtained by changing the percentage overhead charge to take this failure into account.

16 I am not contending that this is the only contract form that allows for determination of the profit or revenue share while maintaining the confidentiality of information about other movies. Tying the rate to the readily observable prime rate is, in fact, a way to avoid a costly "battle of the experts." Interestingly, this is another aspect of the contract that was found unconscionable.

17 The vestiges of the contract system survived into the mid-1960s when Harrison Ford was one of the last people hired on a contract basis by Columbia. The demise of the contract system was, however, widely recognized as a likely outcome of the *Paramount* decision. In the early 1950s, Dore Schary, then head of production at MGM, asserted that, while other studios might abandon the stock company, MGM would not. Of course, MGM eventually did just that. At this time a number of stars also became "free agents." The prime example of this was Jimmy Stewart, who was not tied to any studio in 1950 when he signed with Universal for *Winchester '73*. Clark Gable, no longer "The King," was released from his contract by MGM in 1954.

18 All data on the number of individuals under contract from various issues of *Film Daily Yearbook*.

19 The poll is taken annually by Quigley Publications, and is widely disseminated. Because the top stars are the result of a poll, they are not necessarily the top dollar-earners in a given year, though we suspect the correlation to be high. The films of the stars were taken from a number of sources. Sometimes the high rank is a result of a film that was released at the end of the previous year. In that case, a star may have no films released in the year they were voted one of the top-five attractions. As there is no clear bias for our purposes, we ignored this issue.

20 There are factors which offset the effect of fewer movies on studio risk. For example, during the studio era the censorship in place ensured that virtually all movies made would today be rated no worse than "PG-13." To the extent that studios are able to distribute movies aimed at different market segments, there may be more diversification today. Similarly, since studios no longer have the stock companies of performers under contract, they are less likely to be affected by the decreasing or increasing popularity of an individual performer. Even if these effects moderate the effect of the reduction in movie production on studio risk, evidence presented below suggests that risk has still gone up.

21 This is derived from data in *Motion Picture Investor* (1994). It is possible that the concentration ratio is affected by the fact that 1993 was the year in which *Jurassic Park* was released. However, even if we reduce *Jurassic Park's* worldwide revenues of $953.2 million (then the largest in motion-picture history; as

this is written, *The Lost World* has just opened to record box office) by 50 percent, the concentration ratio is 9 percent, which is still an increase. If we replace *Jurassic Park*'s revenues with those of *Mrs. Doubtfire*, the next highest revenue producer, the ratio is still over 8 percent.

22 Average tenure in office for executives in charge of production at the most stable studios (Warner's, Fox, Columbia, MGM, and Paramount) was around twenty years during the 1940s, and had declined to four years by the 1970s and 1980s. Moreover, turnover was higher at weaker studios. Thus, if studio heads do not like to get fired, risk also increased for studio executives as the studio system died. To the extent that executive turnover is associated with financial difficulty, it may be no surprise that Universal was the studio that negotiated the *Winchester '73* contract because, as one of the parties to the negotiations, they could not afford to pay James Stewart's normal salary. The studio (or its executives) could not bear the risk and laid it off on the actor

23 The Schaefer ledger is the data underlying Glancy (1995). It contains the net-rental income and production cost for every Warner Bros. movie from 1921 to 1960.

24 Of course, this does not capture the studio's actual profit on each movie. Among other problems with the data, it does not reflect distribution costs, nor does it capture any information regarding the timing of the cash flows. Sedgwick and Pokorny (1998) and Pokorny and Sedgwick in Chapter 6 of this volume estimate distribution costs to be 37 percent of the rental incomes generated through the box office.

25 Because the coefficient of variation is the ratio of the standard deviation to the mean, and the variable in question is the ratio of total gross to negative cost, simple scale changes should not affect the measure of risk that we report. The annual coefficients jump around quite a bit. This year-to-year fluctuation appears to be due to outliers in the ratio. In most years the ratio of the highest profit ratio for any movie that year to the second highest is less than two. The only exceptions are 1921 (the ratio of highest to second-highest profit ratio is 2.30), 1928 (3.57), 1930 (3.40), and 1959 (3.24). Figure 9.3 shows an increase in the coefficient of variation in the last three of these years.

26 In 1960, the ratio discussed in footnote 25 was 1.18, in 1946 it was 1.01, thus in neither year was the coefficient of variation driven by outliers.

27 This may overstate the risk increase. We are really interested in the *conditional* standard deviation. If the mix of movies made by Warner's changed over time, we could see an increase in the cross-section coefficient of variation even if there were no increase in the uncertainty about the revenues of any *individual* movie.

28 Schatz provides details on the relations between Hitchcock and David Selznick. Hitchcock was under contract to Selznick who would put together packages including the screenplay, director, and stars under contract to him (such as Ingrid Bergman). The movie would then be shot and distributed by a studio, with Selznick as the producer.

29 Whether or not this led to "better" films is an issue for film critics. The "New Wave" critics (Graham 1968) argued that it did, Schatz is not so sure.

30 It is tempting to conclude that studio *had* to put out enough films to fill the screens they owned. This is not true. No one studio could produce enough films to meet the demand in an era when double bills often changed twice a week. Moreover, because each studio's exhibition arms were strongest in different geographic locations, the studio would often prefer to have another major's theater chain do the exhibition. For example, Paramount had the best theaters (the Balaban and Katz chain) in Chicago, and other studios would want their pictures to play in Paramount's theaters there.

31 See also Paul and Kleingartner (1994) on the effect of changed production on labor relations in the motion-picture industry.

32 For example, the list omits the Jolson pictures and *Tiger Rose* which I know, from examination of the contracts, had participations.

33 Chisholm (1997) provides evidence that the trend toward increased use of sharing contracts continued to recent times.

34 Goldberg (1997) focuses on this issue.

35 Plaintiffs in *Garrison* allege collusion to get around the question of why studios do not compete by offering "fairer" contracts.

36 That is, going from no big special-effect explosion to one leads to more incremental ticket sales than going from 100 to 101 explosions

37 The incentive for the studio remains as long as there is any anticipated payment to net-profits participants. Of course this analysis is, in many ways, too simplistic, and is designed for only a limited purpose. We assume, for example, that the studio knows what the revenues from the movie will be. We also omit a participation constraint that, after adjusting for risk and monitoring costs, the compensation received by net participants must be the same as they would receive if paid a fixed salary. However, note (see Goldberg 1997) that the studio gets to choose the level of production expenses *after* the net participant has signed on. Also, we are only dealing with incremental changes in the movie budget. A big star's association with the movie might increase the likelihood that the movie will, in fact, be made and thus actually make the net participant *better* off.

38 In *Buchwald* the plaintiffs alleged that Paramount and the plaintiffs were joint venturers in the film *Coming to America*, which gave rise to a fiduciary obligation on Paramount. The judge dismissed that claim (*Buchwald* at 554).

39 The judge in *Buchwald* rejected these claims. A discussion of these concepts can be found in virtually any contracts book. See *Wood* v. *Lucy, Lady Duff-Gordon*, 222 New York 88 (N.Y. 1917), *Parev Products Co.* v. *I. Rokeach & Sons*, 124 F.2d. 147 (2d Cir. 1941) – in which the defendant introduced a new product which allegedly had the effect of reducing sales of a product licensed by, and hence royalties payable to, the plaintiff – may be closer to this situation. Moreover, the treatment of third-party gross participations as a component of negative cost was dealt with in *Alperson*, where it is expressly permitted.

40 For a discussion of default rules, see Ayres and Gertner (1989).

41 Holding variable costs constant.

42 It might be argued that a third alternative would forbid subsequent third-party gross participations unless a fixed payment is made to the net participant. However, this does not alleviate the problem. Any fixed payment would still provide an opportunity for the studio to exploit the net participant.

43 Moreover, even if it was found that the studio had violated its implied covenant of good faith and fair dealing, establishing damages would be difficult. The plaintiff would have to establish that the *ex ante* increase in box office from having a big star was not sufficient to lead to a larger net-profits pool. An interesting variant might occur if the big star changed the nature of the film. Consider the following hypothetical. The author of the play *Driving Miss Daisy* contracts with a studio to make a movie of the play. He may have an interest beside monetary gain. By the time the movie is made, however, Morgan Freeman has been replaced by Sylvester Stallone, Jessica Tandy has been replaced by Pam Grier, and a new subplot involves avoiding Chechin terrorists by various bits of derring-do. Would the author have a cause of action? *Parker* v. *Twentieth Century-Fox Film Corporation*, [3 Cal.3d. 176 (1970)] dealt in part with the question of whether a musical was sufficiently like a western that Shirley MacLaine Parker should have taken a proffered role in a western to

mitigate damages arising from the studio's decision not to make a musical that she had contracted to do.

44 Technological change in other industries could affect the motion-picture industry by changing, for example, demand for movies.

45 This point was made to me with some force by a number of people in the industry. The same argument was made in the context of managerial effort by Eugene Fama (1980) and further analyzed by Hart and Holmström (1987).

46 We can think of the net-profits participation as an option that is far out of the money; Gilson and Black (1995: 249) note that the vast majority of executive options have a striking price equal to the stock price when the option was granted. Deep out of the money options are rarely used in executive compensation packages, though this may be driven by tax considerations. It is also possible that, at least in that context, options with a low probability of actually paying off have little incentive effect.

47 It is unlikely that the sharing rule is needed to induce effort in promoting the motion picture. Promotional tours are observable and can easily be contracted for and monitored. Thus the non-observable effort is likely to be in the actual movie production.

48 However, shirking may still be possible if the star knows more than the director about what he or she is capable of. Sidney Lumet (1995: 64) writes that Marlon Brando will test a director early in the course of making a movie by presenting a deep and shallow performance on two takes of a scene. If the director cannot distinguish between the two, Brando effectively shirks for the rest of the movie. Of course, he is also pointing out that a skilled director can tell what kind of performance Brando is capable of.

49 Both movies were nominated for the Academy Award for Best Screenplay Adapted from Another Medium. In neither case was the novel's author credited with the screenplay.

50 Her sample size is limited to, at most, forty-three contracts. While her data set appears to be the best one in use, some important information is not there. For example, she is unable to distinguish between net profits and gross proceeds participations. Moreover, she excludes contracts where the star is also the producer – even though it is well known that, in many cases, the producer credit given to the star does not mean that the star served the traditional producer function. If such stars are atypical, and they almost certainly are, this biases her results.

51 See Table 3 of Chisholm (1997).

52 This is evidenced by *Welch* v. *Metro-Goldwyn-Mayer Film Co.*, 254 Cal. Rprtr. 645 (Cal. App. 2d. 1989). In that case the actress Raquel Welch was awarded punitive damages of $8 million for wrongful termination. "The evidence established that an accusation of breaking a contract would be very damaging to an actress's [sic] reputation, as people in the industry would assume that she was undependable" (*Welch* v. *Metro-Goldwyn-Mayer*: 652).

53 Dreyfus' problem stemmed, in part, from past cocaine addiction: "Disney became known as the 'Betty Ford Clinic' of Hollywood" (Grover 1991: 89).

54 Another way that frequent recontracting serves to foster information revelation is in the effect that it has on the incentives for the *evaluators* to truthfully report on the individuals in question. Because the evaluators will often have ongoing explicit and implicit business relations with those soliciting the evaluation, there is less incentive to lie about what an individual is like.

55 She presents some evidence consistent with this story, but argues that the evidence is very weak. However, given her small sample size (less than forty), the considerations about the relation between sample size and power raised in Brown (1986) suggest that the evidence is stronger than it appears.

56 "There is a general view among studio executives that gross participation deals significantly reduce the risk that a picture will not recover its costs" (Marcus 1991: 564). Note that the risk to be avoided is that of a loss, as opposed to variance of the payoff. This is consistent with the results of Burgstahler and Dichev (1997).

57 I have been told by executives who were at Paramount at that time that formal contract renegotiation actually took place after production had begun and it became apparent that the movie could not be made within the original production budget. The executives were unclear about whether the likely need for contract modification was foreseen prior to the start of production.

58 Also, "Participations in so-called pure or true gross receipts are rare in the television industry" (Levine and Meyer 1985: 12).

59 *Ishtar*, starring the major stars Warren Beatty and Dustin Hoffman, written by Elaine May, was viewed as a "can't miss" comedy. It was a disaster at the box office and is the classic example of how hard predicting success can be. See also De Vany and Walls (1996).

60 He also reports a similar occurrence in connection with *Lethal Weapon III*.

61 One former studio executive told me that, in the 1950s, when these contracts first became common, he found himself constantly making changes of a similar nature in each contract as requested by the various agents. He contacted all of the major agents and worked out a common form of contract, along with a personal pledge that if he changed any of the terms to be more favorable to the talent of *one* of the agents, he would change the terms of contract for *all* of the major agents. Of course, the viability of this "most favored agent" clause depended in part on the reputation of the executive (Sattler 1995).

62 Evidence from *Buchwald* indicated that Bernheim received the most of favorable of a limited set of contract definitions.

63 I have been told by people in the industry that this is essentially the case with the income that Jack Nicholson received for *Batman*. For that movie Nicholson received a guarantee of $5 million against an increasing percentage of the gross that led to him earning a reported $55 million dollars for playing "The Joker." At about the same time, Nicholson signed an essentially similar contract for *The Witches of Eastwick*, which only netted him his guarantee.

64 I use the term "star" to refer to high-quality directors and producers as well as actors and actresses.

65 This is verified by Kevin J. Murphy, an executive compensation *maven*.

References

Abelson, R. (1996) "The shell game of Hollywood 'net profits'," *New York Times*, March 4: D6.

Academy of Motion Picture Arts and Sciences (AMPAS) *Annual Index to Motion Picture Credits* (various issues).

Ayres, I. and Gertner, R. (1989) "Filling gaps in incomplete contracts: an economic theory of default rules," *Yale Law Journal*, 99: 87–130.

Balio, T. (1976) *United Artists: The Company Built by the Stars*, Madison, WI: University of Wisconsin Press.

Bordwell, D. (1985) *The Classical Hollywood Cinema, Part Five*, New York, NY: Routledge and Kegan Paul.

Brachman, L. and Nochimson, D. (1985) "Contingent compensation for theatrical motion pictures," Paper presented at 31st Annual Program, Legal Aspects of the Entertainment Industry, USC Law Center: Los Angeles, CA.

Brown, S. (1986) "Model selection in the federal courts: an application of the posterior odds ratio criterion," in P. Goel and A. Zellner (eds) *Bayesian Inference and Decision Techniques*, New York, NY: Elsevier.

Burgstahler, D. and Dichev, I. (1997) "Earnings management to avoid earnings decreases and losses," *Journal of Accounting and Economics*, 24: 99–126.

Chirelstein, M. (1993) *Concepts and Case Analysis in the Law of Contracts*, Westbury, NY: Foundation Press.

Chisholm, D. (1993) "Asset specificity and long-term contracts: the case of the motion-pictures industry," *Eastern Economic Journal*, 19: 143–155.

Chisholm, D. (1994) "The risk-premium hypothesis and two-part tariff contract design: some empirical evidence," working paper #94–28, MIT Department of Economics.

Chisholm, D. (1997) "Profit-sharing versus fixed-payment contracts: evidence from the motion-pictures industry," *Journal of Law and Economics & Organization*, 13: 169–201.

De Vany, A. and Eckert, R. (1991) "Motion picture antitrust: the Paramount cases revisited," *Research in Law and Economics*, 14: 51–112.

De Vany, A. and Walls, W. (1996) "Bose–Einstein dynamics and adaptive contracting in the motion picture industry," *Economic Journal*, 106: 1493–1514.

De Vany, A. and Walls, W. (1999) "Uncertainty and the movie industry: does star power reduce the terror of the box office?," *Journal of Cultural Economics*, 23: 235–318.

Fama, E. (1980) "Agency problems and the theory of the firm," *Journal of Political Economy*, 88: 288–307.

Film Daily Yearbook, various issues.

Finler, J. (1988) *The Hollywood Story*, New York, NY: Crown.

Flemming, M. (1993) "Dish: studio offers Mercedes moments to 'firm' folks," *Daily Variety*, July 8: 23.

Gilson, R. and Black, B. (1995) *The Law and Finance of Corporate Acquisitions*, 2nd edn, New York, NY: Foundation Press.

Glancy, H.M. (1992) "MGM film grosses, 1924–1948: the Eddie Mannix ledger," *Historical Journal of Film, Radio and Television*, 15: 127–144.

Glancy, H.M. (1995) "Warner Bros. film grosses, 1921–1951: the William Schaefer ledger," *Historical Journal of Film, Radio and Television*, 17: 55–73.

Goldberg, V. (1997) "The Net Profits Puzzle," *Columbia Law Review*, 97: 524–550.

Graham, P. (ed.) (1968) *The New Wave*, Garden City, NY: Doubleday.

Grover, R. (1991) *The Disney Touch: How a Daring Management Team Revived an Entertainment Empire*, Chicago, IL: Irwin.

Hart, O. and Holmström, B. (1987) "The theory of contracts," in T. Bewley (ed.) *Advances in Economic Theory*, Cambridge: Cambridge University Press.

Holliss, R. and Sibley, B. (1988) *The Disney Studio Story*, New York, NY: Crown.

Kenney, R. and Klein, B. (1983) "The economics of block booking," *Journal of Law and Economics*, 26: 497–540.

King, B. (1986) "Stardom as an occupation," in P. Kerr (ed.) *The Hollywood Film Industry*, London: Routledge and Kegan Paul.

Kitses, J. (1970) *Horizons West; Anthony Mann, Budd Boetticher, Sam Peckinpah: Studies of Authorship Within the Western*, Bloomington, IN: Indiana University Press.

Levine, A. and Meyer, B. (1985) "Contingent compensation in the television industry," Paper presented at 31st Annual Program, Legal Aspects of the Entertainment Industry, USC Law Center: Los Angeles, CA.

Lippman, J. (1995) "Star and director of 'Gump' took risk, reaped millions," *Wall Street Journal*, March 6: B1.

Lumet, S. (1995) *Making Movies*, New York, NY: Knopf.

Marcus, A. (1991) "Buchwald v. Paramount Pictures Corp. and the future of net profit," *Cardozo Arts and Entertainment Law Journal*, 9: 545–585.

Monk, N. (1995) "Now you see it, now you don't," *FORBES*, June 5: 42–43.

Motion Picture Association (2002) *U.S. Entertainment Industry: 2002 MPA Market Statistics*, Online, available at: http://www.mpaa.org/useconomicreview/2002/2002_Economic_Review.pdf (accessed 11 September 2003).

Motion Picture Investor (1994) "Motion picture grosses," April 30, 136: 3.

Murphy, K. (1996) personal conversation, Los Angeles, CA, August 5.

O'Donnell, P. and McDougal, D. (1992) *Fatal Subtraction: the Inside Story of Buchwald* v. *Paramount*, New York, NY: Doubleday.

Paul, A. and Kleingartner, A. (1994) "Flexible production and the transformation of industrial relations in the motion picture and television industry," *Industrial and Labor Relations Review*, 47: 663–678.

Robins, J. (1993) "Organization as strategy: restructuring production in the film industry," *Strategic Management Journal*, 14: 103–118.

Sattler, M. (1990) Declaration of Defendant Paramount Pictures Corporation Re: Phase II Hearing on Legal and Contractual Issues, *Buchwald* v. *Paramount*.

Sattler, M. (1995) Interview by author, Los Angeles, CA, May 1.

Schatz, T. (1988) *The Genius of the System: Hollywood Film Making in the Studio Era*, New York, NY: Pantheon.

Sedgwick, J. (2002) "Product differentiation at the movies: Hollywood, 1946–1995," *Journal of Economic History*, 62: 676–705.

Sedgwick, J. and Pokorny, M. (1998) "The risk environment of film-making: Warners in the inter-war period," *Explorations in Economic History*, 35: 196–220.

Stigler, G. (1968) "A note on block booking," in *The Organization of Industry*, Homewood, IL: R.D. Irwin.

Thompson, A. (2003) "Lord of the paycheck: film directors move up," *New York Times*, October 28: E1.

Tuska, J. (1985) *The American West in Film: Critical Approaches to the Western*, Westport, CT: Greenwood Press.

Vogel, H. (1986) *Entertainment Industry Economics: a Guide for Financial Analysis*, 3rd edn, Cambridge: Cambridge University Press.

Warner Brothers (1963) Contract with Bette Davis for *The Dead Pigeon*, dated January, 25. Warner Bros. Archives, University of Southern California Cinema Library.

Warner Brothers (undated) *Summary of Contract with Daryl F. Zanuck Productions*, prepared by P.D. Knecht, one page, Warner Bros. Archives, University of Southern California Cinema Library.

Weinstein, M. (1998) "Profit sharing contracts in Hollywood: evolution and analysis," *Journal of Legal Studies*, XXVII: 67–112.

Zagon, S. (1960) "Selected problems in theatrical and film distribution contracts," Paper presented at the Sixth Annual Program on Legal Aspects of the Entertainment Industry, USC School of Law: Los Angeles, CA.

10 Hollywood and the risk environment of movie production in the 1990s[1]

Michael Pokorny

Introduction

In terms of industrial organisation, the studios that constitute Hollywood today should be seen primarily as financier–distributors with production shared between a host of risk-takers through more-or-less complex contractual arrangements: what Bordwell *et al.* have termed the 'package-unit system'.[2] Also, they have become part of larger, vertically integrated entertainment–leisure–media conglomerates.[3] For Douglas Gomery, these new technologies, together with the changes in industrial organisation that have accompanied them, have strengthened rather than weakened Hollywood. He writes:

> At the heart of all of the billion-dollar mergers which have created today's Hollywood stands the realisation that this land rush for the take-over of five hundred [satellite TV] channels begins at Hollywood's doorstep. The new wonderland of video will make money for those who own the means of production. Without libraries of moving images and regular creation of new visual narratives, the promised electronic superhighway will simply be like fancy plumbing without water.[4]

This chapter focuses on the theatrical market for film for the period 1988 to 1999 and specifically on the role that financial risk played in the production process. This is to accept De Vany and Walls' assessment of film production as a risky business.[5] However, we build on and extend their characterisation of risk as being reflected primarily in the revenue performance of individual films, which has been widely interpreted as generating a production environment in which 'anything can happen': what Caves has termed the '"nobody knows" property'.[6] Treating the risks associated with film production as a single-shot game in which the risk and revenue performance of films are analysed atomistically runs counter to the contribution made by the theory of the firm to economic reasoning. Rather, the approach taken here is to bundle together the films distributed by the major Hollywood studios and treat these bundles as portfolios across which risk is distributed.[7] We find that there is strong evidence to support this hypothesis, which means that, although risky, the business environment of film production/distribution cannot be characterised as one of uncontrollable uncertainty. The chapter is organised as follows: the following section describes the data set and reports selected industry characteristics, including concentration characteristics; a section setting out the theoretical framework for the analysis then follows; the findings are then presented; and a final section concludes.

The film business

Table 10.1 presents summary information relating to the 'major' studios that form the focus of this study. It is clear from Table 10.1 that most of the 'majors' are diversified organisations, with film production being just one amongst a number of their activities. However, all the analyses presented here will be concerned only with film production activities, with Table 10.1 emphasising the context in which these analyses should be placed.

The process by which popular films are diffused across time and space is based on price-discriminatory practices, whereby audiences pay higher prices to see films at the cinema than when subsequently released through the ancillary markets of pay cable television, home video/DVD and free commercial television.[8] The importance of these markets has increased significantly since 1980, with home video in particular increasing its share of US film-industry revenues from 7 per cent to 38.2 per cent by 2000, whilst the share of the revenues generated through theatrical release has fallen from 52.4 per cent to 29.4 per cent.[9] Nevertheless, although its contribution to rental incomes has declined, theatrical release remains critically important as the showcase for popular films, determining prospective earnings in ancillary markets.

The data set from which the analyses presented in this chapter are derived was obtained from AC Nielsen/EDI Inc. The data set includes the box office revenues of all films released onto the North American market between 1988 and 1999 together with the distributors of each of these films. The data set also includes estimates of the production costs (negative costs) for just over half of these films. All re-releases were omitted from the data set, producing a data set containing 4,200 films, along with the North American box office revenues resulting from their initial release.

Table 10.2 presents some summary statistics derived from the data set. Only films costing $1,000,000 or more were included in the analyses (there were forty films which cost less than $1,000,000). Distributors are categorised as either 'majors' or 'non-majors'. Specifically, a 'major' distributor is defined as a distributor for which cost data are available for fifty or

Table 10.1 Major studios, 1988 to 1999

'Major' studios	Owner	Film revenues as % of corporate revenues[a]	Production and distribution companies
Disney	Walt Disney Company	44.8	Buena Vista, Touchstone Pictures, Hollywood Pictures, Miramax (from 1995)
Sony Pictures (formerly Columbia Pictures Entertainment)	Sony	7.3	Columbia Films, TriStar Films
MGM/UA	Metro-Golden-Mayer Inc. Acquired Orion in 1997	100	MGM/UA
Paramount	Viacom Inc.	71.5	
Twentieth Century Fox	News Corp.	31.1	Twentieth Century Fox
Universal (formerly MCA Inc.)	MCA Inc., then Seagrams Co. took a majority share in 1995 before Vivendi became the owner in 2000	60.9	Universal
Warner Bros.	Time Warner Inc.	45.1	Warner Bros., New Line.

Sources: Vogel (2001); [a]Litman (2001).

Table 10.2 Selected descriptive statistics, 1988 to 1999 (all money values in US $millions, 1987 prices)

| Year | Total US box office ($m) | US admissions (billions)[a] | Percentage of box office accounted for by majors plus Miramax and DreamWorks | Number of releases | Percentage of releases by majors plus Miramax and DreamWorks | Average negative cost of films released by majors ($m) | Average box office for films with cost data – majors ($m) | North American rate-of-return – majors (%) |
	(1)	(2)	(3)	(4)	(5)	(6)	(7)	(8)
1988	3,282	1.085	93.2	318	51.9	11.9	21.0	31
1989	3,652	1.263	95.7	307	53.7	13.6	22.7	33
1990	3,758	1.189	96.6	276	61.2	16.3	23.7	26
1991	3,462	1.141	97.1	301	60.1	15.7	22.5	29
1992	3,616	1.173	96.8	293	55.6	18.6	26.1	31
1993	3,788	1.244	96.1	329	54.4	16.7	27.2	36
1994	3,804	1.292	94.8	327	54.4	23.0	30.9	25
1995	3,913	1.263	95.0	364	50.8	23.2	30.5	30
1996	4,002	1.339	96.4	383	50.7	23.2	26.1	13
1997	4,418	1.388	94.7	404	43.3	29.3	33.7	19
1998	4,395	1.481	92.4	418	43.1	28.1	30.4	8
1999	4,817	1.465	93.6	444	39.6	25.7	32.9	23

Sources: AC Nielsen/EDI Inc; [a]Vogel (2001), Table 2.4.

more of its films over the data period, and for which these costs are available for at least 70 per cent of its films. The distributors that fall into this category are: Buena Vista (cost data available on 202 films), Columbia (81), MGM/UA (125), New Line (101), Orion (53), Paramount (161), Sony Pictures (122), TriStar (67), Twentieth Century Fox (157), Universal (165), Warner Bros. (224). This accounts for 1,458 films, 69 per cent of all the films for which cost data are available. The one large distributor excluded is Miramax – cost data are available on 148 of its films, but this only accounts for 55 per cent of its output, and consequently such coverage was considered as being potentially unrepresentative of its output. However, Miramax was included in analyses of film revenues and number of film releases, as was also the case with DreamWorks, a distributor that distributed just fourteen films over the data period, but films with high production budgets and high revenues.

Real box office revenues increased by 47 per cent over the period (column 1, Table 10.2), with some variation around this upward trend. Film releases increased by 40 per cent (column 4). These trends are also broadly replicated by the admissions data (column 2). In terms of market share, the majors (including Miramax and DreamWorks) are overwhelmingly dominant (column 3), consistently accounting for around 95 per cent of all film revenues. This is the case despite the fact that the majors typically accounted for little more than half of annual film releases, a proportion that declined to about 40 per cent at the end of the period (column 5). Presumably this is explained by the much higher budgets of the films produced by the majors (and the associated higher revenues), with these average budgets increasing at a greater rate over the period in comparison to the budgets of the non-majors. Thus from column 6 it can be seen that the average (real) budgets of the majors increased by 116 per cent. While extensive cost data are not available for the non-majors – only 29 per cent of the films produced by the non-majors have associated cost estimates – this restricted data set implied that average budgets for the non-major producers increased by only 71 per cent (data not shown).

Finally, column 8 presents a measure of the annual rates-of-return of the majors. This measure is derived from estimating rates-of-return on a film-by-film basis, and incorporates estimates of distributor rental incomes, therefore reflecting directly the rates-of-return earned by distributors. It estimates the returns to film distribution in the North American market only, and is based just on the profitability of theatrical exhibition. That is, the measure explicitly apportions costs (production costs and estimated distribution costs) to North American theatrical release, allowing the remaining costs to be apportioned to distribution in foreign theatrical markets and all remaining ancillary markets (although no attempt is made here to estimate rates-of-return in these ancillary markets). Appendix 10.1 to this chapter (pages 307–309) details the methodology employed, including the methodology that was used to estimate film distribution costs. That is, this rate-of-return measure only reflects film and distributor initial (theatrical) performance in the North American market. However, we would argue that such performance will be closely associated with the film's subsequent success in ancillary markets – indeed, success in ancillary markets will depend almost exclusively on success on initial theatrical release – and therefore this measure provides a consistent basis for comparative analyses. Thus from column 8 of Table 10.2, we can see that the aggregate rate-of-return performance of the majors has declined over time – from 31 per cent to 23 per cent, with particularly poor performances from 1996 to 1998.

Therefore the overall picture that emerges from Table 10.2 is of a market experiencing marked growth in demand, but one in which competitive pressures have increased over time, reflected in the declining margins experienced by the majors. It would appear that attempts at gaining competitive advantages were focused on rapidly expanding film budgets.

Table 10.3 presents performance and market-share data for the major distributors over the period. Thus note that three distributors – Columbia, Orion and TriStar – only distributed films in the first half of the data period, Columbia and TriStar having been acquired by Sony Pictures in 1994 and Orion by MGM/UA in 1997. Sony Pictures only began distributing films in 1994. Given the extent to which the major distributors dominate the market (see Table 10.2, column 3) we will hereinafter define the market purely in terms of the activities of these majors. Thus the last three rows of Table 10.3 disaggregate the data period into these three periods – the entire data period (1988 to 1999), the first half and the second half of the data period.[10] Thus in terms of the entire data period, the aggregate market rate-of-return achieved was 24 per cent, a performance level that was exceeded by Buena Vista, New Line, Paramount, Twentieth Century Fox and Universal, with MGM/UA and Warner Bros. exhibiting lower than market performance levels. MGM/UA exhibits particularly poor performance. Columbia, Orion and TriStar all exhibit similar performance levels, which are markedly lower than the aggregate rate-of-return of 31 per cent over the first half of the data period. Sony Pictures generates a marginally lower than market rate-of-return over the second half of the period, with market performance over this period having declined to 19 per cent. The market leaders in terms of performance were New Line, Paramount and Twentieth Century Fox, followed by Buena Vista and Universal.

In terms of market shares of the number of films distributed (column 2), the dominant distributors were Sony Pictures (over the second half of the data period), Warner Bros. and Buena Vista. These shares were also reflected in the share of box office revenues (column 4), although Buena Vista now has a larger share of revenues than Warner Bros. (in contrast to film shares), reflecting the superior rate-of-return performance of Buena Vista, which can also be seen in the lower proportion of costs expended by

Table 10.3 Performance and market shares of major distributors, 1988 to 1999

Distributor	Aggregate rate of return over data period (%) (1)	Number of films over data period (2)	Proportion of films over data period[a] (3)	Proportion of revenues over data period[a] (4)	Proportion of costs over data period[a] (5)	Data period (6)
Buena Vista	30	202	0.14	0.18	0.15	1988–1999
Columbia	17	81	0.10	0.08	0.10	1988–1993
MGM/UA	–1	125	0.09	0.04	0.07	1988–1999
New Line	32	101	0.07	0.05	0.04	1988–1999
Orion	17	53	0.05	0.03	0.03	1988–1996
Paramount	32	161	0.11	0.14	0.12	1988–1999
Sony Pictures	17	122	0.19	0.14	0.16	1994–1999
TriStar	21	67	0.08	0.09	0.11	1988–1993
Twentieth Century Fox	32	157	0.11	0.12	0.11	1988–1999
Universal	29	165	0.11	0.13	0.12	1988–1999
Warner Bros.	17	224	0.15	0.16	0.18	1988–1999
Market (1)	24	1,458				1988–1999
Market (2)	31	814				1988–1993
Market (3)	19	644				1994–1999

Note
[a]Proportions relate to period indicated in last column.

Buena Vista compared to Warner Bros. (column 5). MGM/UA's poor performance can be seen in its markedly higher share of costs compared to revenues. By contrast, New Line had a markedly higher share of films than of costs, reflecting the fact that it was a relatively low-budget distributor. Nonetheless, even as a low-budget distributor, it still generated high rate-of-return performance. Paramount's similar rate-of-return performance derived from its strategy of moderately high-budget production, given its marginally larger share of costs than of films.

A further insight into the performance of the majors over the data period can be derived by comparing the trends in the rates-of-return of each of the majors with the overall market trend shown in column 8 of Table 10.2. These comparisons are presented in Figures 10.1 to 10.11, in which each major's annual rates-of-return are superimposed on the market rates-of-return. The obvious feature of these comparisons is the marked variability of the individual rates-of-return as compared to the market rates. While this is not of itself necessarily surprising, given that the market rates are the outcome of an averaging process, it does empha-sise the volatility of the market, from a distributor's perspective, the market being subject to rapid changes in market shares from year to year. However, the more pertinent aspect of these comparisons is the extent to which each of the major's *levels* of performance compare to market performance. Consider first those distributors which distributed over the

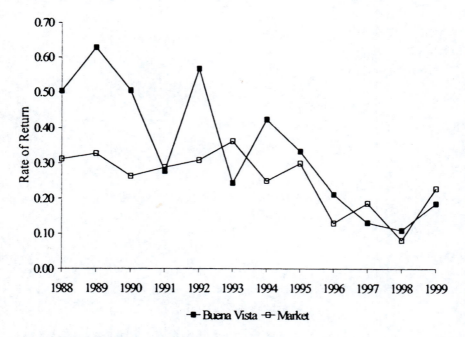

Figure 10.1 Buena Vista: annual rate-of-return.

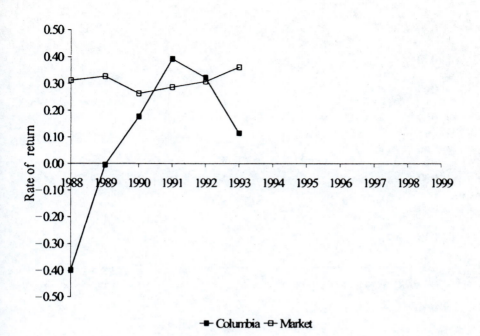

Figure 10.2 Columbia: annual rate-of-return.

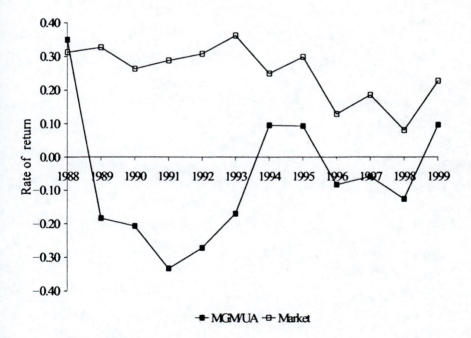

Figure 10.3 MGM/UA: annual rate-of-return.

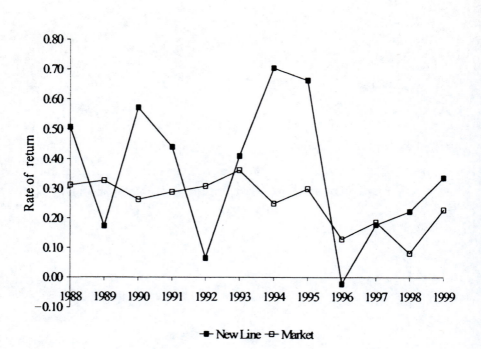

Figure 10.4 New Line: annual rate-of-return.

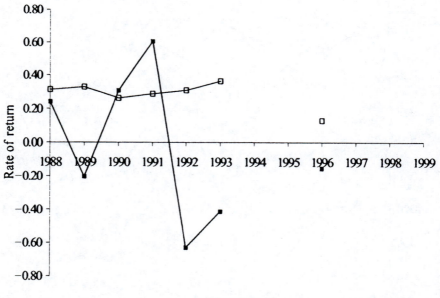

Figure 10.5 Orion: annual rate-of-return.

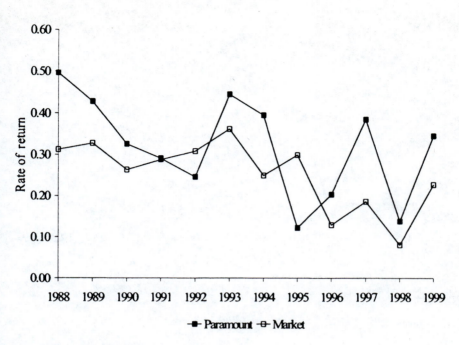

Figure 10.6 Paramount: annual rate-of-return.

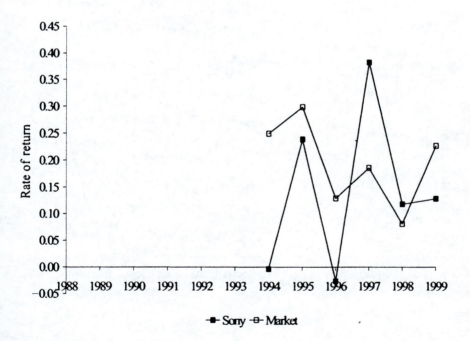

Figure 10.7 Sony: annual rate-of-return.

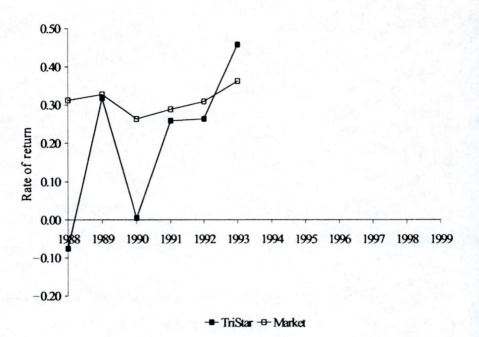

Figure 10.8 TriStar: annual rate-of-return.

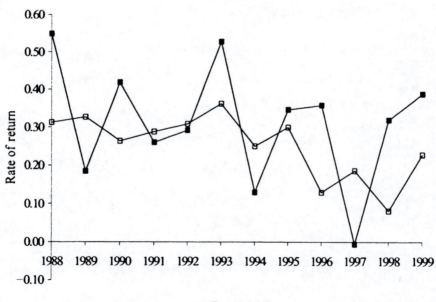

Figure 10.9 Twentieth Century Fox: annual rate-of-return.

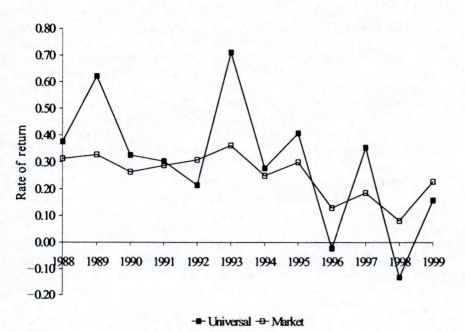

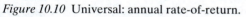

Figure 10.10 Universal: annual rate-of-return.

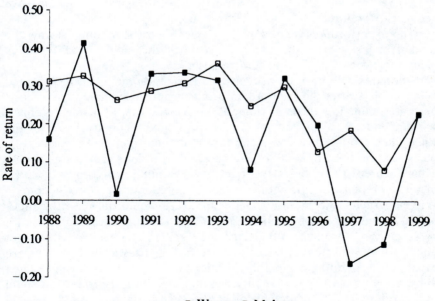

Figure 10.11 Warner Bros.: annual rate-of-return.

entire data period. Thus Buena Vista's strong overall performance (Figure 10.1) derives from outperforming the market in eight of the twelve years of the data period, and in the remaining four years only marginally underperforming the market. MGM/UA's difficulties are clear from Figure 10.3 – in only one year of the data period did it outperform the market (1988), and thereafter performance was markedly worse than market performance, although performance improved in the second half of the data period, where performance closely mirrored market trends, but nonetheless still fell markedly short of market levels. New Line (Figure 10.4) exhibits relatively variable annual performance, but outperforms the market in eight of the twelve years, whereas Paramount (Figure 10.6) mirrors market trends more closely, outperforming the market in ten out of twelve years. Twentieth Century Fox and Universal (Figures 10.9 and 10.10) exhibit similar trends, outperforming the market in seven and eight of the twelve years, respectively. Warners (Figure 10.11), by contrast, exhibits relatively variable performance, outperforming the market in just five of the twelve years, and in these cases just marginally so, and exhibiting marked underperformance in five of the remaining years. In the case of the remaining distributors, Columbia's poor performance (Figure 10.2) derives from relatively poor performance in four of its six years, despite rapidly improving performance, contrasting with Orion's more volatile and poor performance in its last three years (Figure 10.5). Although TriStar (Figure 10.8) only outperformed the market in one of its six years, it achieved near-market level performance in three of the remaining five years, its overall relatively poor performance being attributable to just two very poor performing years. Finally, Sony (Figure 10.7) outperforms the market in just two of the latter six years of the data period, although exhibiting broadly improving performance.

A broad insight into the risk environment of filmmaking can be gained via a simple scatter diagram of film profits against production costs (costs here are defined as those attributable to North American release only – see Appendix 10.1 for details). This is presented in Figure 10.12 for the 1,458 films produced by the majors over the data period. For contextual purposes, the titles of some of the better-known films are also indicated. Thus Figure 10.12 reflects the increasing variability of profits as costs increase, emphasising the nature of the risks of high-budget production.

A superficial interpretation of Figure 10.12 would question the rationale for high-budget production, given the increasing variability of profit performance as production budgets increase, the potential for high-budget films to make substantial losses and the fact that lower-budget films are capable of generating comparable levels of profits to many higher-budget films. Thus it is in this restricted sense that high-budget production could be considered to be irrational, or at the very least unappealing (Ravid 1999: 488). However, while high-budget production is manifestly riskier than lower-budget production, such risks should be evaluated within

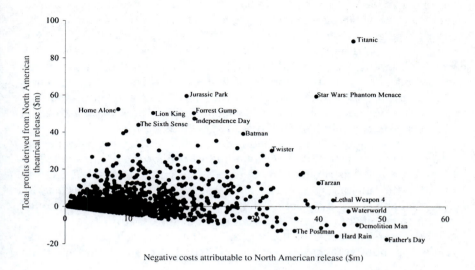

Figure 10.12 Distributor profits against negative costs, 1987 prices.

context – within the context of a given distributor's annual portfolio of films. In particular, the attraction of high-budget production is that a single successful high-budget film can make a substantial contribution to annual film profits, and hence to annual rate-of-return performance. Conversely, even a highly successful low-budget film can only ever hope to make a relatively modest contribution to aggregate profits, and hence only have a marginal impact on aggregate rate-of-return performance. For example, consider two high-budget films produced over the data period – Warner Bros.' *Batman* in 1989, at a real cost of $47m, and Paramount's *Hard Rain* in 1998, at a real cost of $48m. The North American rate-of-return for *Hard Rain* was a very poor −73 per cent, but *Batman* generated a rate-of-return of 83 per cent. In terms of annual rate-of-return performance, Paramount's aggregate rate-of-return performance in 1998 was 14 per cent, but would have been 28 per cent had *Hard Rain* not been produced. In the case of *Batman*, Warners' aggregate rate-of-return was 41 per cent in 1989, but would have been just 27 per cent had *Batman* not been produced. The most extreme example is that of *Titanic* – Paramount's aggregate rate-of-return in 1997 was 38 per cent, but would have been reduced to just 3 per cent without *Titanic*.[11] That is, a single strong-poor-performing high-budget film can have a marked impact on aggregate rate-of-return performance. Conversely, high-performing low-budget films would generally have a minimal impact on performance. For example, *The Wood*, distributed by Paramount in 1999, cost just $4m to produce, but generated a rate-of-return of 91 per cent, broadly equivalent to the rate generated by *Titanic*. Paramount's aggregate rate-of-return in 1999 was 35 per cent, but without *The Wood* this rate would have been reduced marginally to 33 per cent. In effect, high-budget film production offers a form of economies of scale – a single high-budget film project offers the potential for making a substantial contribution to total annual film profits, the equivalent of which could only be provided by a relatively large number of successful lower-budget projects. But there is, of course, the risk of high-budget films also generating substantial losses, and therefore a key element in the film production process is the manner in which film portfolios are constructed, with a view to distributing risk across the portfolio.

Given that film profitability had diminished markedly over the period (see column 8 of Table 10.2) and that a large proportion of films failed to break-even once distribution costs are factored in (of the 1,458 films produced by the majors, just 50 per cent generated profits), the business of film production and distribution described by De Vany and Walls would appear to be one of extreme uncertainty and contrasts strongly with other commentators' accounts of the 'majors' as powerful, self-confident focal points for industry behaviour.[12] Vogel (2001: 97) answers this apparent paradox, maintaining:

> The remarkable aspect of all this is that despite the potential for loss, most major studios, bolstered by distribution revenues related to library titles and television programmes have long been successfully engaged in this business. The existence of profitable studio enterprises in the face of apparent losses for the 'average' picture can be reconciled only when it is realised that the heart of a studio's business is distribution and financing and that, therefore, the brunt of marketing and production-cost risk is often deflected and/or transferred to (sometimes tax-sheltered) outside investors and producers.

However, we would argue that it is the manner in which the 'majors' organised their portfolios of films that is central here. Although contractual details with production companies, and thus the actual risk-stance taken on each film, are not in the public domain, a measure of the nature of the risks taken by the 'majors' can be realised through an examination of the spread of production costs across the films distributed by them annually. In doing this we are, in effect, assuming that distributors were fully responsible for financing the films they handled (which they were not), but justify this on the grounds that such a course allows us to make estimates of risk that otherwise would not be possible. Clearly, the results will exaggerate the risk position of the 'majors' but will do so consistently.

Theoretical framework

There are a number of straightforward strategies employed by producers in an attempt to attenuate risk. The use of established stars (directors, screenwriters) is an obvious one, although given the premiums that stars can command, such a strategy is not without its own risks. Indeed, Ravid (1999) and De Vany and Walls (1999) argue that the use of stars has an insignificant impact on film profitability, and at best, the use of stars might be argued to have a risk-minimising effect in the sense of guarding against film 'flops' (Ravid 1999). The production of sequels is a well-established strategy with a manifestly risk-minimising justification. Furthermore, the complex financing arrangements associated with much film production allow risk to be spread across investors (and in turn provide opportunities for investors to spread risk across a range of investments).

However, interpreting the process of film production as a series of one-off investments is restrictive as a context for evaluating the scope for risk-attenuating strategies. In particular, at a given point in time, the 'majors' will be handling a portfolio of films, at various stages of development and release, and it is the manner in which risk is spread across this portfolio that provides a more generalised analytical framework. While more generalised, such a framework is also a relatively complex one, given the range of risk-attenuating strategies that are available. Therefore the approach taken here will be to explore just one dimension of this investment decision. In particular, we will focus on the manner in which investment funds are spread across the film portfolio, and thus the extent to which the relationship between financial risk and return informs the portfolio-allocation process. As De Vany and Walls have demonstrated, the distributional properties of film revenues/profits/rates-of-return are such that they are essentially unpredictable, and the film investment decision cannot be derived from a calculus that is based on the analysis of the 'average' film, or the estimated distributional parameters of film financial performance.[13]

An obvious theoretical framework for exploring these issues is that of portfolio theory. Such a framework would imply that a film producer, in allocating funds across a range of film projects, will take into account the differing levels of risk associated with each project. Thus funds would be allocated in such a way that a trade-off is achieved between the expected return on the portfolio and the risk that is incurred. The basic result of portfolio theory is that the process of portfolio diversification exercises a measure of control over portfolio risk, not only by combining assets of varying levels of risk, but by exploiting the correlations between the returns on the assets that make up the portfolio.

This characterisation of the investment decision would appear to be particularly suited to the movie production process when seen from the film producer's/distributor's standpoint. While the production of a given film might be seen as risky, this is very much in a relative sense, with some film projects being markedly riskier than others. As Figure 10.12 emphasises, the production of high-budget films would be expected to be riskier than the production of lower-budget films, cet. par., by virtue of the fact that the performance of higher-budget films is markedly less predictable than that of lower budget films.

In order to develop this portfolio theory analogy of the film-investment decision, we require a definition of the appropriate 'asset'. In the limit, each film can be interpreted as an individual asset. However, such an interpretation would imply a highly precise and disaggregated approach to the film-investment decision. The approach taken here is to allocate films into three budgetary categories – high-budget, medium-budget and low-budget – and to argue that the film-production decision is conditioned by film producers' perceptions of the differing levels of risk associated with these three categories. Such a categorisation can be interpreted as broadly equivalent to the traditional categories of 'Super A', 'A' and 'B' movies. Specifically, high-budget films are defined, for each calendar year, as those films exceeding the average production costs of all films produced by the majors in that year by 50 per cent or more, medium-budget films are those whose production costs fell between 75 per cent and 150 per cent of average production costs, and low-budget films were those costing less than 75 per cent of average production costs. While such a categorisation has an element of arbitrariness, its main virtue is that it is relative in nature and therefore allows for the fact that the cost of a high-budget film, in terms of absolute (real) costs, would have increased markedly over the data period. Such a partition was also used by Pokorny and Sedgwick (2001).

However, we will not here develop this portfolio theory framework in any formal sense, but rather we will simply characterise film distributors/producers as constructing annual portfolios of films that consist of these three budgetary categories. We will now go on to examine the financial performance of each of the distributors over the data period, within the context of the structure of their annual film portfolios, and the performance of the 'assets' within these portfolios.

Empirical results

Table 10.4 shows, for each year over the data period, the proportion of production budgets allocated to each budgetary category and the proportionate contribution to profits of each category, together with rate-of-return performance within each of these categories.

The broad trends evident from these data are that the proportion of costs allocated to high-budget production increased over the period, at the expense of medium-budget production, and that high-budget films were the most successful in terms of financial performance – in aggregate, they generated the highest rate-of-return, generated 50 per cent of profits on the basis of absorbing just 42 per cent of production costs, and the proportion of profits contributed by high-budget films exceed the proportion of costs they absorbed in nine of the twelve years. Finally, while the rates-of-

Table 10.4 Annual budget allocations and performance by budget category, major distributors, 1988 to 1999

Year	High-budget films			Medium-budget films			Low-budget films		
	Proportion of costs (1)	Proportion of profits (2)	Nth Am rate-of-return (%) (3)	Proportion of costs (4)	Proportion of profits (5)	Nth Am rate-of-return (%) (6)	Proportion of costs (7)	Proportion of profits (8)	Nth Am rate-of-return (%) (9)
1988	0.37	0.45	37	0.45	0.42	29	0.18	0.13	24
1989	0.32	0.46	43	0.52	0.37	25	0.15	0.17	34
1990	0.37	0.27	20	0.44	0.58	33	0.19	0.16	22
1991	0.35	0.42	34	0.45	0.42	27	0.20	0.16	23
1992	0.45	0.43	30	0.31	0.34	33	0.23	0.23	30
1993	0.34	0.54	50	0.47	0.28	24	0.20	0.18	33
1994	0.29	0.39	32	0.56	0.35	17	0.15	0.26	37
1995	0.52	0.31	22	0.27	0.29	29	0.21	0.41	43
1996	0.44	1.13	33	0.40	−0.24	−8	0.16	0.11	8
1997	0.52	0.87	32	0.26	0.18	12	0.22	−0.05	−4
1998	0.54	0.60	10	0.25	0.01	0	0.21	0.38	12
1999	0.45	0.58	30	0.37	0.26	16	0.18	0.16	20
Entire period	0.42	0.50	30	0.38	0.31	20	0.19	0.19	23

return generated by high-budget films declined over the period, consistent with the overall decline in rate-of-return performance evidenced in Table 10.2, this decline was not quite so marked as the aggregate decline. By contrast, medium-budget films were relatively unsuccessful – they generated the lowest aggregate rate-of-return, their aggregate profit contribution was lower than the proportion of costs they absorbed, which was also the case in nine out of twelve years of the data period, and they exhibited a marked secular decline in rate-of-return performance. In the case of low-budget production, the proportion of costs they absorbed matched the proportion of profits they generated, and while low-budget rates-of-return increased strongly up to 1995, they declined markedly thereafter. That is, notwithstanding the risks associated with high-budget production, the majors would appear to have developed strategies to produce successful high-budget films, strategies that were able to accommodate those high-budget films that made substantial losses.

It is important to recognise that the importance of high-budget production to the financial success of the majors has been a feature of Hollywood in the post-war period. As Sedgwick (2002, and Chapter 7 in this book) has demonstrated, Hollywood's response to the upheavals in the movie industry in the post-war period was to focus on the production of high-budget 'hit' movies. While it took some time for such an approach to be successful, it represented the main thrust of movie production from the 1970s onwards, and has been a strategy that has been largely successful since that time. Indeed, it is useful to contrast the performance of the majors in the 1990s with their performance in the 1930s. Using a data set of 1,796 films produced by MGM, RKO and Warner Bros. over the thirteen-year period 1929/1930 to 1941/1942,[14] a similar categorisation to that presented in Table 10.4 can be derived (not presented here). While the scale of high-budget production was comparable between the two periods – 46 per cent of production budgets were absorbed by high-budget production during the 1930s, increasing from 36 per cent at the beginning of the period to 50 per cent at the end of the period – high-budget production during this period was largely unsuccessful. High-budget films generated just 29 per cent of North American profits over the period, generating a North American rate-of-return of just 9 per cent, compared to 12 per cent generated by medium-budget films and 20 per cent by low-budget films. The percentage contribution to profits of high-budget films exceeded the proportion of production budgets they absorbed in just one of the thirteen years of the data period (the last year, 1941/1942), compared to eight of the thirteen years for medium-budget films and twelve of the thirteen years for low-budget films. High-budget production was clearly subsidised by medium- and low-budget production. The success of medium- and low-budget films presumably derived from the prevalence and popularity of double-bill programming during the 1930s, an approach to exhibition that became increasingly less viable in the post-war period as television became the focus for productions with lower production values. Additionally, it might be conjectured that the approach to distributing high-budget films in the 1930s – initially exhibiting these in relatively high-price first-run cinemas, before they were shown in second-, third-, etc. run cinemas – restricted the revenue-generating potential of these films, and contrasts with the distribution practices of today where such films are exhibited as widely and rapidly as possible.

Returning to the 1990s, Table 10.5 shows, for each distributor, the proportion of production budgets allocated to each budgetary category, and the proportionate contribution to profits of each budgetary category over the entire data period, together with rate-of-return performance within each of these categories.

In terms of budgetary allocations, the high-budget distributors were Warners, Paramount, Twentieth Century Fox, Universal, TriStar, Buena Vista and Columbia, all of which allocated at least 42 per cent, in aggregate, to high-budget production (last row, Table 10.5). Both New Line and Orion were primarily medium-to-low-budget distributors, as was the case, to a somewhat lesser extent, with MGM/UA.

In terms of rate-of-return performance, Paramount, Twentieth Century Fox and Universal performed strongly within each of the three budgetary categories, exceeding or broadly matching market performance in all cases. Buena Vista performed strongly in the medium- and low-budget categories, but relatively poorly in the high-budget category. Warner Bros. performed relatively poorly throughout. The little high-budget production undertaken by New Line generated very poor performance, but this was compensated for by strong performance in both the medium- and low-budget categories. This was also the case for Orion, although its low-budget production performed relatively poorly. Columbia performed strongly in the medium-budget category, but relatively poorly in the other two categories, contrasting with TriStar's very poor medium-budget performance but strong performance in the other two categories. Both Sony and MGM/UA generated strong high-budget performance, but poor performance in the other two categories, this being particularly the case for MGM/UA for which these two categories were responsible for the overall losses incurred – that is, in aggregate, MGM/UA lost $6m over the data period, resulting from losses of $36m and $32m on medium- and low-budget production, respectively, even though profits of $62m were generated by high-budget production (note that this extreme imbalance produces somewhat perverse profit proportions). Table 10.5 also emphasises that high-budget films were the dominant source of distributor profits for those distributors involved in substantial high-budget production, apart from Buena Vista and Columbia.

However, while it was the case that high-budget production expanded over the period and became the dominant source of industry profits, success in the medium- and low-budget categories was still important in

Table 10.5 Budget allocations and performance by budget category, major distributors, 1988 to 1999

Year	High-budget films			Medium-budget films			Low-budget films		
	Proportion of costs (1)	Proportion of profits (2)	Nth Am rate-of-return (%) (3)	Proportion of costs (4)	Proportion of profits (5)	Nth Am rate-of-return (%) (6)	Proportion of costs (7)	Proportion of profits (8)	Nth Am rate-of-return (%) (9)
Buena Vista	0.42	0.29	24	0.41	0.50	34	0.17	0.21	32
Columbia	0.42	0.46	18	0.44	0.62	22	0.14	−0.08	−12
MGM/UA	0.30	−10.87	28	0.45	6.25	−12	0.26	5.62	−19
New Line	0.15	−0.07	−22	0.38	0.50	40	0.47	0.57	36
Orion	0.09	−0.09	−21	0.62	0.84	22	0.29	0.25	15
Paramount	0.49	0.65	41	0.32	0.18	19	0.19	0.16	27
Sony Pictures	0.38	0.56	27	0.34	0.24	12	0.27	0.20	11
TriStar	0.44	0.66	32	0.48	0.14	6	0.09	0.20	39
Twentieth Century Fox	0.46	0.52	38	0.35	0.28	25	0.19	0.21	31
Universal	0.46	0.55	36	0.37	0.22	18	0.17	0.22	34
Warner Bros.	0.50	0.66	22	0.37	0.26	13	0.13	0.08	11
Market	0.42	0.50	30	0.38	0.31	20	0.19	0.19	23

terms of aggregate rate-of-return performance. MGM/UA provides an extreme illustration of the success of high-budget production being entirely negated by poor performance in the medium- and low-budget categories, but this relationship holds more generally. Thus Figure 10.13 presents a simple scatter of the aggregate rate-of-return of each distributor over the sample period (column 1 of Table 10.3) against the rates-of-return achieved in the combined low- and medium-budget categories. Thus there is clear evidence of a strong positive association between the two rates-of-return (the corresponding correlation coefficient is 0.93). Indeed, the association is stronger still if just the first six years of the data period are considered, which provides a common time period for all ten distributors (recall that Sony only began distributing in the second half of the data period), where a correlation coefficient of 0.98 is produced. In other words, while clearly it is important to focus on the success of high-budget production, given the scale of sunk costs involved, a coherent film-production strategy also requires attention to be paid to the determinants of success in the lower-budget categories, which may well be quite different to those in the high-budget category.

Finally, a broad characterisation can be derived of the risks that each distributor took in the construction of its annual film portfolio, and the manner in which these risks evolved over time. We will here define risk in a very generalised manner and, in particular, we will interpret risk as being reflected in the variability of the production costs of the films included in any given annual film portfolio. That is, the wider the range of film budgets included in a portfolio, the greater is the risk incurred. We will

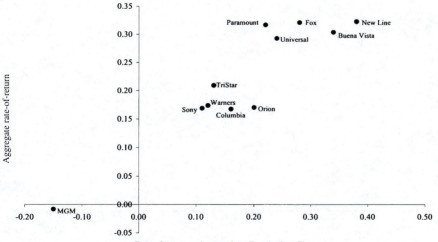

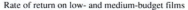

Figure 10.13 Distributor aggregate rates-of-return against rates-of-return on low- and medium-budget production.

measure variability as the simple standard deviation of the production budgets of the films in the portfolio. So, for example, consider the films distributed by Paramount in, say, 1996. Paramount distributed seventeen films in 1996, for which production cost data is available, with these costs (in 1987 prices) ranging from $8.5 million to $54.3 million, producing a standard deviation of $13.4 million. By contrast, New Line distributed ten films with estimated costs, in 1992, ranging from $3.6 million to $10.9 million (in 1987 prices), producing a standard deviation of $2.3 million. That is, we would interpret Paramount as having incurred a higher level of risk with the films it distributed in 1996 than the risk incurred by New Line with its 1992 films. It should be emphasised that this defini- tion of risk is a somewhat simplistic one, and certainly much simpler than the measure that would be used by the strict application of portfolio theory.[15] Thus the analysis presented here should be interpreted as indica- tive only.

We present in Figures 10.14 to 10.21 these annual standard deviations, for each of the eight distributors that were still distributing films at the end of the sample period. Also included in each of these graphs are the annual standard deviations of all the films distributed by the majors, thereby reflecting the aggregate level of risk adopted by the market as a whole. The graphs therefore provide a direct comparison of the risks undertaken by each of the majors relative to market risk.

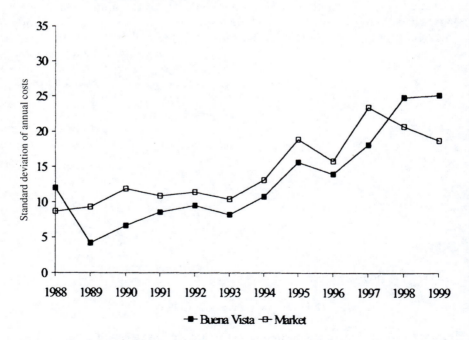

Figure 10.14 Buena Vista: standard deviation of annual film budgets.

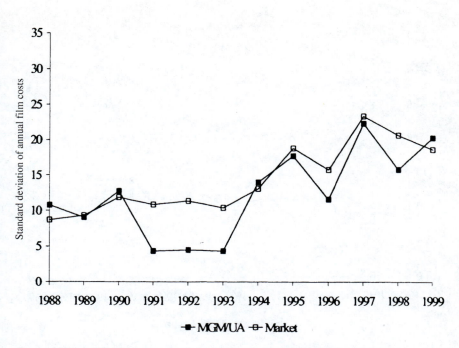

Figure 10.15 MGM/UA: standard deviation of annual film budgets.

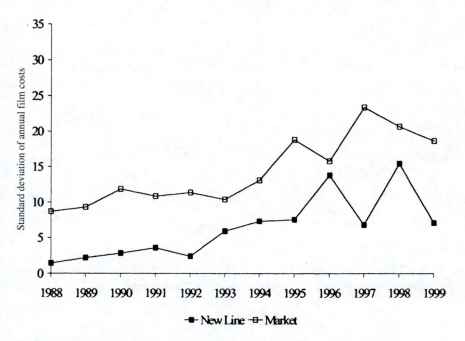

Figure 10.16 New Line: standard deviation of annual film budgets.

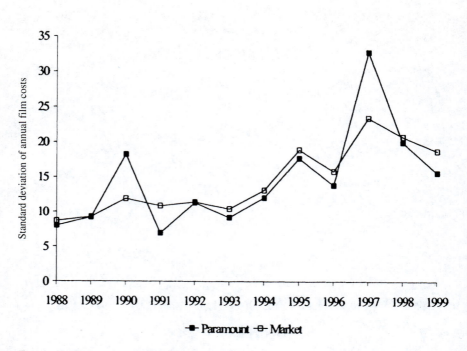

Figure 10.17 Paramount: standard deviation of annual film budgets.

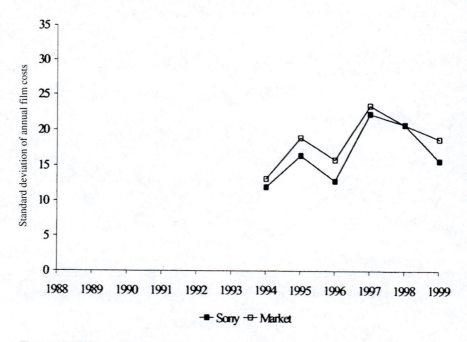

Figure 10.18 Sony: standard deviation of annual film budgets.

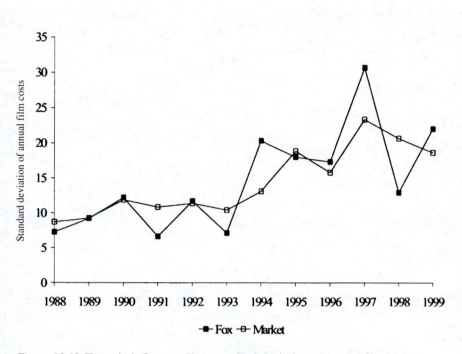

Figure 10.19 Twentieth Century Fox: standard deviation of annual film budgets.

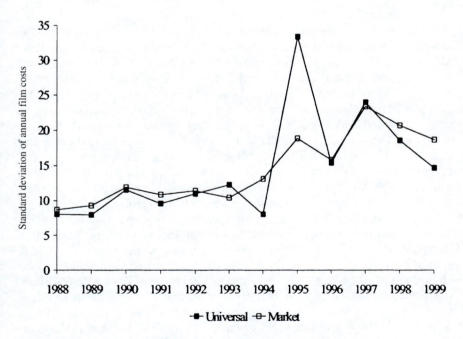

Figure 10.20 Universal: standard deviation of annual film budgets.

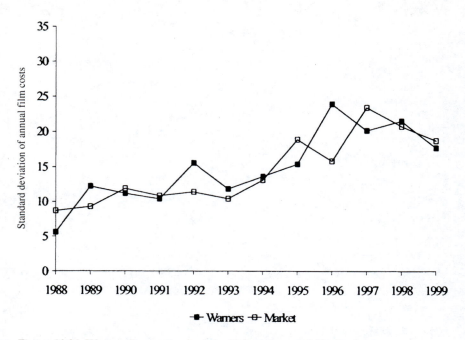

Figure 10.21 Warner Bros.: standard deviation of annual film budgets.

In terms of market risk, this can be seen to have increased over the sample period, reflecting the expansion in average production budgets, although this risk contracted marginally at the end of the period in response, presumably, to the relatively poor market rate-of-return performance in the late 1990s. In the case of Buena Vista (Figure 10.14) its risk position evolved closely in line with market movements, although in general Buena Vista adopted a lower risk stance. MGM/UA (Figure 10.15) exhibits relatively volatile changes in its risk position, which is the result of a high level of switching between budgetary categories from year to year. Thus a low-risk stance was adopted in the early 1990s, a period during which MGM/UA did not undertake any high-budget production, presumably in response to its poor rate-of-return performance in the pre-vious years (see Figure 10.3), a period during which about 40 per cent of its filmmaking budget was directed to high-budget production. Thereafter it expanded its risk position to broadly match market movements. While it is not possible to deduce the extent to which these somewhat erratic changes in MGM/UA's strategic responses explains its poor rate-of-return performance, Figure 10.15 is certainly suggestive of a degree of strategic inconsistency. New Line's relatively conservative risk stance is evident from Figure 10.16, given its focus on medium- and low-budget production. There were only two years in which it undertook high-budget production –

1996 and 1998 – in which just three and one high-budget films, respectively, were produced. All of these performed poorly, with the 1996 films all making losses and the 1998 film generating a rate-of-return of just 5 per cent. New Line's expanded risk position over the period resulted from an increase in medium-budget production at the expense of low-budget production. Paramount (Figure 10.17) followed market movements closely, apart from 1990 and 1997, when there was a marked shift to high-budget production.[16] Sony (Figure 10.18) mirrored market risk closely in the latter part of the period, whereas Twentieth Century Fox, although broadly following market risk in terms of trend and level, exhibits a degree of variation around this trend. Universal (Figure 10.20) closely follows market trends, apart from 1995, where there was a marked expansion into high-budget production. However, this was a result entirely of Universal's investment in *Waterworld*, a film that ran substantially over budget. Finally, Warner Bros. (Figure 10.21) exhibits a relatively conservative profile, implying that, while budgets expanded in line with market expansion, budgets were controlled relatively tightly, and risk-taking was kept to a minimum.

Thus a variety of strategic responses is evident from Figures 10.14 to 10.21. There is clear evidence of returns to risk-taking (the case of *Titanic* being an extreme example), and the dangers of risk-taking (the equally extreme *Waterworld*, a film which cost $129 million, but generated a North American rate-of-return of −8 per cent). However, the consideration of such one-off projects is misleading, and the emphasis here has been on the aggregate performance of film portfolios. While (successful) high-budget production offers the most direct route to profitability, the example of New Line illustrates that a low-risk, lower-budget approach can be equally successful. Similarly, the case of Warner Bros. illustrates that a high-budget, controlled-risk approach does not necessarily produce high aggregate rates-of-return.

Conclusion

This chapter has examined the process of film production with a particular emphasis on the financial structure of film portfolios. The approach taken has been to characterise film production as analogous to constructing an investment portfolio, in which risk is spread across the assets (films) in the portfolio, thereby allowing for some control to be exercised over the impact of risk. Specifically, a film portfolio was characterised as consisting of three assets – high-, medium- and low-budget films. However, it should be stressed that the approach here has focused on just one aspect of the film production process – the financial structure of film portfolios – and as such can only provide a partial analysis of the determinants of successful film production.

The focus for the analysis was the US film market in the 1990s. The market was one in which demand grew strongly, but one in which competitive pressures also increased, resulting in declining performance levels for individual producers/distributors. The risk taken by film distributors, annually, was measured simply as the standard deviation of the costs of the films in each annual film portfolio. Thus, an annual film portfolio that contains films with a wide range of production budgets is considered riskier than one in which the films have similar production budgets. In general this measure implied that distributors expanded their risk stances over the period, essentially (although not exclusively) via an increase in the extent of high-budget film production undertaken. However, this measure also indicated that there was considerable variability in the evolving risk profiles of distributors, implying a variety of strategic responses to tightening competitive pressures. In aggregate, there was evidence of returns to risk-taking, but this was not unambiguously the case – that is, there was evidence of high risk-taking distributors performing poorly and low risk-taking distributors performing strongly.

While the extent of high-budget production increased over the period, and high-budget films became the dominant source of industry profits, strong performance in the low- and medium-budget markets was also seen to be crucial for overall financial success. The poor overall financial performance of MGM/UA, in particular, and Sony and Warners, to a lesser extent, can be attributed to their poor performance in the lower-budget categories, notwithstanding relatively strong performance in the high-budget category.

A further feature of the market is that distributor annual rates-of-return can vary markedly from year to year. This is a reflection of the highly competitive nature of the market, notwithstanding its highly concentrated market structure, and success in the market can, and should, only be judged on the basis of an aggregate rate-of-return accumulated over a number of years, rather than rate-of-return performance in any one year.

Apart from one distributor, all the distributors were part of large conglomerates, in which film production was just one amongst a range of diversified activities. Thus the portfolio theory analogy could be extended to an analysis of corporate activity, in which risk is spread across these activities. It may be the case that film production tends to be a relatively risky activity, but diversification can be interpreted as allowing for some control of this risk, in aggregate. In addition, the outputs of the film production division are inputs into other divisions within the corporation, thereby exploiting the synergies between these divisions, providing a further focus for risk minimisation.

Therefore, to characterise the film industry as one involving unique and high levels of risk, on the basis of the potential for individual film projects to generate excessively high profits/losses, is to over-simplify the investment decision. An individual film project can only be assessed within a wider context of all associated film investment decisions – it may be perfectly rational to undertake a high-risk stance with regard to a single film project, within a diversified portfolio of films. In this sense, the film industry is little different from other industries which are characterised by high levels of research and development expenditures – success derives not so much from success on individual projects, but on the extent to which a range of projects can be supported contemporaneously, the manner in which risk is spread across these projects, and how risk-spreading strategies evolve over time.

Therefore it is clear that size matters – effective risk spreading can only occur within the context of a relatively large portfolio of films. It is not surprising, therefore, that Hollywood is dominated by a small number of large distributors/studios, which, in turn, are generally parts of large integrated conglomerates – the risks involved in one-off film production would be otherwise unsustainable.

Appendix 10.1

Estimating film profits and rates-of-return

In order to derive estimates of film profits and rates-of-return, estimates of film distribution costs are required. It would seem reasonable to assume that the distribution costs of a film are directly related to the revenues generated by the film – the broader is the reach of the film, the higher are the distribution costs. It is presumably also the case that initial promotional expenditures will be determined as some (relatively small) proportion of production costs. Thus the distribution costs, D, of a film can be interpreted as being directly related to negative costs, C, and the revenues, R, generated by the film, or:

$$D = \alpha C + \beta R \tag{10.1}$$

Thus estimates of α and β are required. For the 1930s, data are available on the 1,130 films produced by MGM and RKO, including data on profits and distribution costs, allowing for the direct estimation of equation (10.1). The revenue data for these films are distributor rentals. In fact, re-expressing equation (10.1) in terms of rates-of-return generated more statistically robust estimates of α and β, with an associated R^2 value of 0.968. The estimates of α and β so derived were 0.05 and 0.35, respectively (see Pokorny and Sedgwick 2003 for a more detailed discussion).

The issue, then, is whether these estimates of α and β are also appropriate for the 1990s. However, we first note that the revenue data in the Nielsen data set refer to box office revenues, rather than distributor rentals, and these revenues are for the North American market only. Thus the approach here will be to estimate film profitability with reference to performance in the North American market, and therefore to apportion costs to North American releases accordingly.

Vogel (2001)[17] provides annual estimates of the percentage of total box office that reverts to distributors as rental income. Thus applying these percentages to box office revenues of each of the films in the data set produces estimates of the rental incomes generated by these films in North America. Denote these estimated rental incomes as $\hat{R}_{NA}$. Second, we require estimates of film distribution costs. The approach taken here is to assume that, as in the 1930s, distribution costs are related to the production budget (initially) and thereafter evolve proportionately to revenues. However, data are not widely available for each film on revenues earned in both the North American and foreign markets – in terms of the 2,116 films in the data set for which cost data are available, foreign revenues are available for just 514 of these.[18] In all other cases it is assumed that foreign revenues accounted for 50 per cent of total revenues, given that, in aggregate, this was the case during the 1990s (Vogel 2001: Table 2.4). Thus estimated distribution costs are generated via:

$$\hat{D}_{NA} = (0.05 * \pi_{NA})C + 0.35\hat{R}_{NA} \tag{10.2}$$

where π_{NA} is the proportion of total box office generated in the USA for those 514 films for which foreign revenues are known, and in all other cases π_{NA} takes on the value 0.5. $\hat{R}_{NA}$ is estimated North American distributor rental.

Finally, in deriving film rates-of-return, the major difference between the 1930s and the 1990s is the role played by ancillary markets in the latter period (home video, television). Vogel (2001: Table 2.8) estimates that world-wide theatrical revenues accounted for about 52 per cent of total revenues in 1980, but had declined to about 30 per cent by 2000, with home video revenues increasing from 7 per cent to 38 per cent. Assuming that world-wide theatrical revenues accounted for an average of 40 per cent of total revenues during the 1990s, then North American film rates-of-return could be estimated via:[19]

$$RoR_{NA} = \frac{R_{NA} - ((0.4 * \pi_{NA} * C) + \hat{D}_{NA})}{(0.4 * \pi_{NA} * C) + \hat{D}_{NA}} \tag{10.3}$$

The application of equation (10.3) implies that 44 per cent of the 2,116 films that cost \$1 million or more, and for which cost and revenue data are available, broke even or better. This percentage is somewhat higher than the 30 per cent to 40 per cent that 'industry wisdom' would suggest (Vogel 2001: 35), but the measure does take explicit account of the revenues generated in ancillary markets, via just 40 per cent of production budgets being apportioned to world-wide theatrical release. However, it has been argued that a feature of the contemporary film industry is the increasing importance of marketing and distribution costs (Vogel 2001: 96), which would imply that equation (10.2) might underestimate these costs. Amending equation (10.2) to:

$$\hat{D}_{NA} = (0.05*\pi_{NA})C + 0.40\hat{R}_{NA} \tag{10.4}$$

and then substituting this second estimate of distribution costs into equation (10.3) results in 42 per cent of films breaking-even or better. Further, Vogel (2001)[20] has suggested that distribution costs were equivalent to about 45 per cent of negative costs throughout the 1990s. The application of equation (10.4) implies that, on average, these estimated North American distribution costs were equivalent to 47 per cent of negative costs attributable to North American distribution (that is, $\pi_{NA}*C$). Consequently, the rate-of-return measure used here for the 1990s will be that derived from equation (10.4) combined with equation (10.3), given the consistency between the implications of this measure and 'industry wisdom'. However, the extent to which this measure incorporates a number of approximations must be recognised, and hence the implications derived from it must be treated with some caution. Nonetheless, within an industry in which profitability data is very hard to come by, such an approximation at least provides a starting point for an evaluation of economic performance.

Notes

1 The author would like to acknowledge the contribution of John Sedgwick, who made extensive comments on earlier drafts of this chapter.
2 Bordwell *et al.* (1985: 330–331).
3 See Gomery (1998); Hoskins *et al.* (1997); Vogel (2001).
4 Gomery (1996: 408).
5 De Vany and Walls (1996)
6 De Vany and Walls (1999: 286; 2002: 450); Caves (2000: 3).
7 The work constitutes a development on earlier publications: see Pokorny and Sedgwick (2001) and Sedgwick and Pokorny (1998).
8 See Vogel (2001) for estimates of these prices in Table 2.6 and the temporal dimension of this distribution in Figure 3.2.
9 See Vogel (2001: Table 2.8). In 2000 the remaining 32 per cent of revenues came through pay cable (7.8 per cent), network TV (1.5 per cent), syndication (3.9 per cent), foreign TV (6.9 per cent) and made-for-TV films (12.3 per cent).
10 In the case of Orion, no cost data were available for 1994 and 1995, and data for just three films were available in 1996. That is, in effect, data for Orion were only available over the first half of the data period.
11 The profits derived from the production of *Titanic* is somewhat overstated for Paramount, as it only took a part interest in financing the film, after Twentieth Century Fox sold a stake in the film to Paramount, feeling that it needed to divest itself of some of the risk as the production budget began to run out of control.
12 Vogel (2001: 35).
13 See, for example, De Vany and Walls (2002).

14 See Glancy (1992, 1995) and Jewell (1994) for further details of this data set.
15 The interested reader is referred to any standard text in Financial Accounting/Finance, such as Brealey and Myers (2000).
16 Paramount's expanded risk position in 1997 is due entirely to the production of *Titanic*. However, as implied in note 11, Paramount's risk position in 1997 is somewhat overstated as the financing of *Titanic* was shared with Twentieth Century Fox.
17 Table 2.4: 52.
18 These were obtained from the website, worldwideboxoffice.com.
19 Note that an assumption of theatrical revenues accounting for 40 per cent of all revenues is a conservative one, in the sense that it is likely to understate the profits generated via theatrical release. That is, irrespective of whether theatrical revenues declined linearly or proportionally from 52 per cent of all revenues in 1980 to 30 per cent in 2000, 40 per cent would be about the maximum during the 1990s, and hence attributing 40 per cent of costs to theatrical release in equation (10.7) would, if anything, underestimate theatrical rates-of-return.
20 Table 3.2: 80.

References

Aksoy, A. and Robins, K. (1992) 'Hollywood for the 21st century: global competition for critical mass in image markets', *Cambridge Journal of Economics*, 16: 1–22.

Bordwell, D., Staiger, J. and Thompson, K. (1985) *The Classical Hollywood Cinema: Film Style and Mode of Production to 1960*, New York, NY: Columbia University Press.

Brealey, Richard A. and Myers, Stewart C. (2000) *Principles of Corporate Finance*, 6th edn, London: Irwin McGraw Hill.

Caves, R. (2000) *Creative Industries: Contacts Between Art and Commerce*, Cambridge, MA: Harvard University Press.

De Vany, A. and Walls, W. (1996) 'Bose–Einstein dynamics and adaptive contracting in the motion picture industry', *Economic Journal*, 106: 1493–1514.

De Vany, A. and Walls, W. (1997) 'The market for motion pictures: rank, revenue, and survival', *Economic Inquiry*, 35: 783–797.

De Vany, A. and Walls, W.D. (1999) 'Uncertainty and the movie industry: does star power reduce the terror of the box office?', *Journal of Cultural Economics*, 23: 285–318.

De Vany, A. and Walls, W.D. (2002) 'Does Hollywood make too many R-rated movies? Risk, stochastic dominance, and the illusion of expectation', *Journal of Business*, 75: 425–451.

Glancy, H.M. (1992) 'MGM film grosses, 1924–1948: the Eddie Mannix ledger', *Historical Journal of Film, Radio and Television*, 12: 127–144.

Glancy, H.M. (1995) 'Warner Bros. film grosses, 1921–1951: the William Schaefer ledger', *Historical Journal of Film, Radio and Television*, 15: 55–74.

Gomery, D. (1996) 'Towards a new media economics', in D. Bordwell and N. Carroll (eds) *Post-Theory: Reconstructing Film Studies*, Madison, WI: University of Wisconsin Press.

Gomery, D. (1998) 'Hollywood corporate business practice and periodizing contemporary film history', in S. Neale and M. Smith (eds) *Contemporary Hollywood Cinema*, London: Routledge.

Hoskins, C., McFadyen, S. and Finn, A. (1997) *Global Television and Film*, Oxford: Oxford University Press.

Jewell, R. (1994) 'RKO film grosses, 1929–1951: the C.J. Trevlin ledger', *Historical Journal of Film, Radio and Television*, 14: 37–51.

Litman, B. (2001) 'Motion picture entertainment', in W. Adams and J. Brock (eds) *The Structure of American Industry*, 10th edn, Upper Saddle River, NJ: Prentice Hall.

Maltby, R. (1998) 'Nobody knows everything', in S. Neale and M. Smith (eds) *Contemporary Hollywood Cinema*, London: Routledge.

Miller, D. and Shamsie, J. (1996) 'The resource-based view of the firm in two environments: the Hollywood film studios from 1936 to 1965', *Academy of Management Journal*, 39: 519–543.

Pokorny, M. and Sedgwick, J. (2001) 'Stardom and the profitability of filmmaking: Warner Bros. in the 1930s', *Journal of Cultural Economics*, 25: 157–184.

Pokorny, M. and Sedgwick, J (2003) 'The long run characteristics of the US film industry', paper presented to the 7th International Conference of the International Association for Arts and Cultural Management, Milan, Italy, June.

Ravid, S.A. (1999) 'Information, blockbusters and stars: a study of the film industry', *Journal of Business*, 72: 463–492.

Sedgwick, J. (2000) *Filmgoing in 1930s Britain: a Choice of Pleasures*, Exeter: Exeter University Press.

Sedgwick, J. (2002) 'Product differentiation at the movies: Hollywood, 1946–65', *Journal of Economic History*, 62: 676–704.

Sedgwick, J. and Pokorny, M. (1998) 'The risk environment of film-making: Warners in the inter-war period', *Explorations in Economic History*, 35: 196–220.

Storper, M. (1993) 'Flexible specialisation in Hollywood: a response to Aksoy and Robins', *Cambridge Journal of Economics*, 17: 479–484.

Storper, M. (1994) 'The transition to flexible specialisation in the US film industry: external economies, the division of labour, and the crossing of industrial divides', in A. Amin (ed.) *Post-Fordism: a Reader*, Oxford: Blackwell.

United States Bureau of the Census (1975) *Historical Statistics of the US: Colonial Times to 1970*, Washington, DC: US Department of Commerce, Bureau of the Census.

Vogel, H. (2001) *Entertainment Industry Economics*, 5th edn, Cambridge: Cambridge University Press.

Weinstein, M. (1998) 'Profit-sharing contracts in Hollywood: evolution and analysis', *Journal of Legal Studies*, 27: 67–112.

11 Understanding Hollywood's organisation and continuing success[1]

Keith Acheson and Christopher J. Maule

In Australia, Canada and western Europe, government support for the film and television industries is frequently justified on the grounds that, in its absence, theatrical and television screens would be inundated with films and programmes from the United States. Hollywood, as shorthand for the American industry, is seen to have captured most of its domestic and a large share of foreign markets.

The question we address has two parts. The first concerns how the internationally oriented segment of the industry copes with a unique mix of risk and informational challenges. The second is why institutions based in the United States were able to dominate the functions of distribution and finance and develop a product type that was successful in international markets. To address the first part, we describe and analyse the managerial responses and organisational arrangements that have emerged in the film and television industries over the past century. Integrative contractual networks and institutional relationships have evolved in response to the informational and risk environment in which films are made and distributed. With respect to American dominance, we argue that a flexible managerial culture and an open and innovative financial system allowed the American industry to take advantage of a series of historical events and technological developments.

Knight (1921: 268) recognised the importance of the internal workings of organisations in dealing with risk and uncertainty:

> When uncertainty is present, and the task of deciding what to do and how to do it takes the ascendancy over that of execution, the internal organization of the productive groups is no longer a matter of indifference or a mechanical detail.

Only recently has a literature developed in which firms are more than black boxes and managers more than robots making mechanical calculations of the first and second order conditions for maximising profit. Some argue that the economics of film and television is different from that of other industries (Cunningham and Turner 1993: 7). Our view is that each industry or sector has a unique configuration of economic, political, socio-cultural and technological conditions but commonalities remain important. Film financiers face risk, as do those who fund exploration for oil and minerals and the development of new computers, cars and drugs. Films carry cultural messages, but so do newspapers, magazines and books, as well as educational and religious institutions. Film production requires front-end sunk costs and sometimes suffers from the machinations of free riders, but so do the provision of justice, defence and health services. Each industry has idiosyncratic features that elicit particular contracting and institutional responses. The elements common to all industry analysis are a governance structure and culture for making and administering transactions, within and without. A complementary organisational culture, like mores and customs in a broader context, makes formal managerial systems work more effectively and frames responses to new challenges and opportunities.[2]

In the film industry, risk arises from the lack of knowledge *ex ante* about which films will attract viewers; difficulties in containing the costs of production; and piracy or theft of intellectual property rights.[3] How organisations, practices and contracts have reacted to risk has been affected by technology directly – sound, colour, television, video, laser disks, DVDs – and indirectly – communications and computer aids to management. A common feature across technologies has been the tendency to integrate organisationally, contractually and through ongoing business relations. Our discussion encompasses both film and television, but our emphasis is on the former. In our review of the international industry, "American" refers to a market orientation and process of extending the market for films rather than to ownership.[4] Historically, films made for mass consumption in the American market sold well in other English-language and foreign-language markets. With the coming of sound, the international influence of Hollywood was nourished by the dominant size of the English-language market, which supported its production of films with larger budgets and generally higher production values, facilitating their sale in foreign markets. The resulting exports exceeded the imports of productions from smaller language blocs. In turn, the Hollywood product dominated the English-language market. Experience and scale lowered the costs of dubbing into other languages, further expanding Hollywood's marketing reach.

The introduction of sound and colour were two important technological shocks for the film industry.[5] Recent developments in technology – Imax, satellite transmission, fibre optic cable, VCRs, DVDs, pay-per-view systems, digital signal transmission and compression, interactive multimedia systems, Internet delivery, and high-definition television add alternative distribution mechanisms. These developments are lengthening the post-release earnings profile of a film while encouraging more varied production. The new technologies add windows of exploitation to a current release and promote the re-release of old films[6] increasing the value of libraries. The DVD represents a quantum leap over video technology in portability, capacity, robustness and cost, and has resulted in a sequence of vertically differentiated releases.[7] When video recorders became popular, many low-budget films, and some high-budget animated films, were released directly on video cassettes.[8] The DVD makes the alternative of marketing some films directly to the public even more attractive.

Organisation and contracts adapt to technology. As video rentals and sales increased in value, the video release window was split into two – a video rental window and then a video sell-through window. To encourage video rental stores to offer more copies during the rental window, a sharing contract was developed. Before these changes could be fully absorbed and exploited, aggressive DVD pricing increased the importance of sell-through and decreased the attraction of sharing for rental outlets. As sell-through rises in importance, large discount retailers are emerging as major sources of film revenue in North America. New developments may facilitate separating sell-through and rental audiences. Disney has announced trials with a DVD that alters after it is removed from its packaging and has a playable life of two days. This allows rental without the pain of making returns. Rental outlets are also experiencing competition from Internet-based services.[9] As more formats become digitally based, transfer among complementary formats becomes less costly. The additional flexibility makes diverse offerings and the development of alternative distribution channels more economical.

Transactional issues in making a film

The decision to make a film is preceded by the selection of a concept from a large number of ideas and by the development of a viable script by one or more writers. The idea might originate with a book, play, news story, an earlier film or be developed from scratch by a writer, director, producer or actor. At any one time, writers are working on numerous ideas, only a few of which will ever become films.[10] Once a script is selected, a costly production process creates a film negative, from which an unlimited number of prints can be made at a relatively low cost. While the end product is tangible in the form of reels of film on which visual images and sound are captured, the ingredients are mainly intangible services. The managerial process of identifying the best set of inputs, arranging financing, establishing effective contractual incentives, coordinating production and containing costs is funnel-shaped, as depicted on the left-hand side of Figure 11.1.

In contrast, the right-hand side of the same figure shows film distribution as a mirror-image funnel, with the original negative being reproduced and rights licensed in a wide array of markets or windows – theatrical, television and home video – covering different geographical and linguistic markets for stipulated periods of time. Distribution is intertwined with

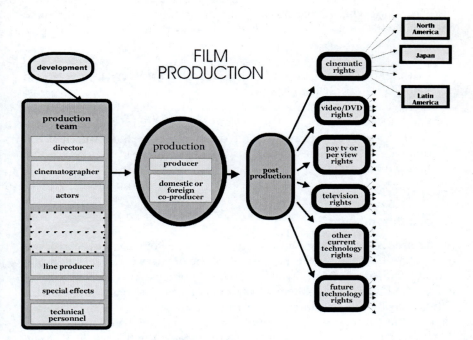

Figure 11.1 Film organisation.

production, as promotion of the film occurs while it is in the making through broadcast and press interviews and the distribution of promotional photographs.[11] Once a decision to shoot has been made, two documents, the script and the budget, provide planning tools.[12] The former supplies the information that allows costs to be estimated and the budget drawn up. Unlike the manufacture of a dress or car, where the end product conforms closely to a drawing or blueprint and the cost estimates are reliable, a film script evolves during the process of making the film and the only definitive script is the one written after the negative has been produced. According to director John Boorman (1985: 41):

> You work towards it, weave the themes into the characters and narrative, until, hopefully, they cannot be picked out of the fabric. Finally what you have made always surprises you, however close it is to intentions. If we knew exactly what we were trying to make in every detail, we would lack the heart to make it.[13]

Industry practice with respect to budgeting is to separate "above-the-line" costs of the story, director, cast and extras (essentially costs which vary from one film to another), and "below-the-line" costs of the remaining ingredients for production including fixed overheads and capital expenditure. The most challenging problem for the producer is coordinating and controlling the inputs covered by the "above-the-line" items. The producer

> is a creative administrator ... a judge of creativity. He guides and helps hundreds of people toward an objective that becomes increasingly clear-cut as the work proceeds from an idea, through its script and budget preparation, then to shooting (very tense and money hazardous), then to post-production (cost manageable and leisurely if you don't have a pressing air date or release deadline). It's like herding bees with a switch.
>
> (Houghton 1991: viii)

Risks in filmmaking

In the process of making and distributing a film, four sources of risk are encountered. At the outset there is risk at the creative level: selection of a concept and script results from a screening process and the exercise of judgement about what is likely to attract audiences and make money. This is followed by the risk intrinsic to production arising from the development of the concept, the creation of a budget and the negotiation of contracts for a range of goods and services needed to make the film. Some items are relatively easy to cost, such as transportation, studio time, equipment and wardrobe, but many of the expenditures are for labour services where there are two interrelated unknowns – how much of the service will be required and how well the service will be delivered. Other unknowns are how much time will have to be spent on shooting a scene, how many resources special effects will absorb, how cooperative and focused key personnel will be – opportunistic behaviour by members of the production group can have a marked effect on costs. To all of these must be added the extrinsic risk of production: adverse circumstances such as bad weather, illness, accidents, governmental actions and malfunctioning equipment.[14] Finally, once the film is made, there is the risk that it may be copied or sold illegally, causing financial losses to those who have legitimate claims on its income.

Some of these risks are due to a lack of knowledge or the inherent randomness of events. For example, no one knows with certainty the formula for picking a film that viewers will like or the length of development time for a new visual effect, or what the weather will be like when shooting occurs. Other sources of risk result not from general ignorance but from the asymmetric distribution of information. A lead actress knows what effort she is exerting and what the limits of her talent are with greater precision than does the director, although, conversely, directors can elicit a performance which surprises the actor and the audience. An exhibitor knows how many tickets are sold for the evening performance better than the distributor whose rental payment from the cinema depends on information about ticket sales. Risk arising from asymmetric information has been given different labels. When information about an individual's behaviour is better for the individual than for other affected parties, a moral hazard problem arises. When quality or personal characteristics are known less well by others who have an interest in knowing, the resulting problem is one of adverse selection. In either case, loss can arise from opportunistic behaviour, actions taken by the better informed that improve their own situation but impose damages on the less well-informed. Opportunism is economically inefficient because the benefits to those being "sharp" are less in total than the harm experienced by the individuals who are disadvantaged. Opportunities for opportunism in the film industry occur at a number of interfaces.

Examples of opportunism

Between the audience (viewer) and theatre, broadcaster or video rental outlet

The viewer may copy, rent or resell the material either in its original or in an edited form; while the supplier may provide a product of poor video or sound quality, misrepresent the quality and type of performance offered, or offer it in an unclean facility that is poorly heated or ventilated.

Between the theatre, broadcaster or video rental outlet and the distributor

The theatre owner may not honestly report the number of tickets sold or may show the film at a time other than agreed to by contract (Vogel 1986: 125–128); while the theatre or video store owner may make a copy of the film available to commercial pirates for illegal sale and distribution, or the broadcaster may broadcast the film more times than agreed to in the contract.

Between the distributor and the producer

A distributor acquires rights to license the film for cinematic exhibition, video and television release. If the film is finished, the uncertainty faced by the distributor concerns the market for a product that can be viewed and assessed before a deal is made. If the film is not finished, the distributor's risks are compounded by not knowing exactly what will be available to market. Early commitments by distributors are crucial to financing film production, not only for the financing directly provided, but for the signal sent to other financing sources that are not as knowledgeable about the business. The risk for the producer is that promises of payments will not be honoured.

Successful distribution also requires significant expenditures on promotion and advertising. For promotion to be effective, the timing and nature of initiatives by the cinemas showing the picture, by the distributor and by the writers, stars and directors of the film must be coordinated. Opportunism arises from the incentive to free ride on the efforts of others.[15]

Between the producer and project personnel

The producer chooses critical members of the team, such as a director, writer, cinematographer or leading actor, and with their input fills other production positions. In production, it is difficult to ensure that participants give their best efforts in directing, acting, lighting and camera work. The efforts must be coordinated with each other to make an effective whole. The key personnel can also be damaged by the failure of the producer to hire complementary resources of the promised quality and to meet implicit contractual obligations.

Once the budget is set and shooting begins, the producer is at the mercy of the director, and the director is at the mercy of those who can hold up production and cause budget overruns. After being reprimanded by the producer for exceeding the budget on the 1923 version of *The Ten Commandments*, Cecil B. De Mille is reported to have said: "What do you want me to do, stop shooting and release it as *The Five Commandments*?" (Laskey 1957: 168).[16] Michael Cimino overspent the budget in making *Heavens Gate* knowing that it would become increasingly difficult to fire him or terminate the project the more United Artists became financially committed to it (Bach 1985). Similarly, the director or the line producer has to deal with performers who, once hired, turn up late for work or do not want to rehearse, perform or reshoot a scene as the director wishes. The producer in turn is vulnerable to money being expended on items that increase the wealth of team members and make little contribution to the potential of the production.

Responses to opportunism and other risks in the film industry

Risks are mitigated but not removed by a web of contracts between organisations and between personnel and the producer, the pooling of risk within organisations, the appropriate choice of organisational form to cope with different problems, a complex set of professional relationships and reputations, government financing programmes, and industry associations that play an important role in lobbying for effective copyright protection and in enforcing the laws that exist.

Monitoring and contracting

The film producer contracts with suppliers of inputs and buyers of rights to distribute the end product. First consider production. The producer hires a line producer and a director who play integrative roles in the production. The line producer is in charge of the logistics of hiring inputs and ensuring that they are available when required. He or she also monitors and enforces contractual specifications and manages assets, such as inventories of film stock and props, which can be readily controlled using traditional techniques. The director provides both a creative vision and the managerial art of eliciting superior efforts from all of the key personnel. He or she employs more idiosyncratic techniques and skills to orchestrate the efforts of the key personnel. The importance of managerial techniques that vary with the people involved and the innovativeness of the project makes the outside assessment of film management as difficult as it is for research and development projects in industry or the university.[17] Since the director affects the performance of writers, actors, cinematographers, designers, composers and editors, opportunism by the director has a multiplied effect on the quality of the film.[18] To align more closely the interests of the producer and the director, the latter's contract usually defers some remuneration and makes it contingent on the film's commercial success. It is also common to grant shares in future revenues or net profits to other key personnel, particularly name writers or actors.[19]

In dealing with the key performers and technicians, the director has to counteract the opportunistic tendencies. Like a ballet teacher, she or he can cajole, praise, inspire, threaten, punish and reward persons in ways that lead to quality performances. A director may be given a daily quota of footage to be shot as a way of monitoring quantity of output. Because of the dangers of cost overrun, a producer will purchase a completion bond that ensures that the film is completed. If the triggering conditions are realised, the film is taken out of the hands of the original producer and given to a representative of the guarantor.[20]

With some projects, the director is also the writer and the creative thrust of the film is concentrated in one individual. Without a clever contract, the financier of a film may be at considerable risk, as is suggested by the following assessment of the terms of John Boorman's relationship with Goldcrest films for the making of *The Emerald Forest*:

> Boorman's deal with Goldcrest gave him absolute control over the production. He was co-writer, producer and director. Goldcrest was providing not only the production finance but the completion guarantee. Should the film go over the budget there would be nothing the company could do: they couldn't fire Boorman, since without him there was no movie; they couldn't appeal to the producer, since Boorman was his own producer; and they couldn't refer the problem

to an outside completion bond company, since they were providing the completion guarantee themselves. He really had the company by the balls...

(Eberts and Ilott 1990: 244)

Another factor that reduces opportunism in film production is the subjective monitoring of professional performance by peers and the adverse impact of being "sharp" on the reputation of the participants. Each film is a separate project and a career requires employment in a sequence of films. Team production makes the assignment of responsibility difficult but in a number of instances professional standards can be applied and distinctions made. It is common in the industry for a producer to seek information on an unknown applicant from other professionals in the field with whom he or she has worked or from those who have hired the applicant in the past. Assessment by specialised "juries" of critics or fellow professionals of the performance of functions within a film is encouraged by industry practice. Awards from peer or industry groups or praise for professional achievement in a trade journal review are made to, or about, individuals even in instances where the film in which the work appeared was a critical and box office failure. Despite such instances of individual recognition, there is often a halo effect from association with a successful film. In filmmaking, involvement is noted on posters and in credits at the end of the movie, and contracts often address the nature of the credit or listing. In the extreme, where separation of individual contributions is impossible, everyone can take credit for success and disavow responsibility for failure. In this case, reputation effects fail to discipline opportunism.[21]

With distribution, the relative exposure to opportunism by the producer and the distributor depends on the distribution contract. Consider the case of a project to make a film rather than to license a finished film. The distributor who pays everything upfront is vulnerable to the delivery of a product that meets the letter of the contract but has few of the elements that both parties would know are important for the commercial prospects of the film. If, instead, the distribution contract stipulates no upfront money but grants a share of the distribution income to the producer, the producer receives no direct financing help and is also vulnerable to the distributor not accurately reporting revenues.[22] The latter vulnerability is extended to key personnel that have contracted to share in future distribution income received by the producer from the distributor.

An independent producer of a feature film with international market potential can either contract with a major distributor and cover a large number of areas with one agreement or patch together a network of contracts with regional distributors. In either case, a typical contract is similar to one from the other. Revenue is shared according to a specified formula. Advances against this revenue are made that are non-recoverable if the film does not do well and the producer's share is less than the advance.

The distributor may guarantee a minimum number of screens on opening and outline a MAP (marketing, advertising and promotion) strategy. The advance helps to finance the film, while the promise of shares in future revenue provide an incentive for the production company to produce a film that not only meets contractual terms but has the intangible factors that enhance its commercial prospects. The contract specifies how the distributor and the producer share key managerial decisions, such as staffing, casting and control of the final cut, on the project.

To illustrate, consider the general features of agreements between the now bankrupt but once successful British independent film producer, Goldcrest, and the American studio, Warner Bros. Typically, Warner Bros. would advance 30 per cent of the budget against North American rights in perpetuity and more against other geographical areas. Goldcrest would receive 30 per cent of either the first $20 million of the distributor's gross (i.e. after the cinema exhibitors had taken their cut), or two-and-a-half times Warners' distribution expenses, whichever figure was the lower. For gross revenues received by the distributor over $20 million, Goldcrest's share was 30 per cent plus five percentage points for each additional five million dollars, e.g. 40 per cent for gross distribution revenues between 25 and 30 million dollars, up to a maximum share of 65 per cent. Goldcrest received 75 per cent of the gross in video and 70 per cent of the gross in syndicated television. Contracts for cable and network television called for 77.5 per cent of the initial block of revenue to be paid to the producer. To monitor and discipline against opportunism, key decisions on the budget, leading actors and the director had to be approved by both the producer and the distributor (Eberts and Ilott 1990: 359–360). For any project produced by Goldcrest and distributed by Warners the two companies were contractually integrated along important dimensions.

The amount of risk shifting between the producer and the distributor depends on the size of the advance and on the degree to which the shares owed to the producer by the distributor are cross-collateralised across different geographical areas and media. With cross-collateralisation, if the distributor collects less than the advance in one area or in one medium, the difference can be recouped from income generated by the film in other areas or other media. Contracts between an independent producer and a major studio usually have cross-collateralisation clauses.

With respect to their dealings with independent theatres in North America and many other markets, the major studios developed a form of quasi-vertical integration known as "block booking" and "blind bidding". The studios offered theatres a contract requiring them to rent a block of films before they were made and could be previewed. Typically, an exhibitor was granted the contractual right to reject some of the films in the block. By this means, the studio shared the risk with the cinema, but also ensured a steady flow of product to exhibitors who require new material to be available when the current movie's run is at an end. Block booking was prohibited in the United States by the *Paramount* decision of 1948, which culminated a set of related anti-trust proceedings that started well before the Second World War. Following later relaxation of these provisions, a number of American states have prohibited blind bidding; some require distributors to exhibit a film for exhibitors before licensing theatres.[23] Similar constraints on distributor–exhibitor contracts are imposed in a number of other countries. Nonetheless, distributors and exhibitors frequently re-establish relationships and practices that closely approximate block booking and blind bidding within the modified legal environment.

Whether covering an individual film or a block, North American contracts between a distributor and an exhibitor typically include complex sharing terms. The cinema pays the higher of a fixed percentage (typically 90 per cent in North America) on box office revenue minus the "nut", a fixed amount originally set to approximate the costs of making the cinema available for audiences during the week, or a schedule of percentage rates that start at a lower rate (typically 70 per cent), and decline in increments (typically 10 per cent) over the contracted run, applied to box office revenue with no "nut" deduction. The box office revenue of a film generally declines as the run at a cinema continues. The absolute amounts received by both the distributor and the cinema fall in this case but the share earned by the cinema owner often rises. The net transfer of risk between the distributor and the exhibitor has recently become more complicated by the distributor requiring a guaranteed minimum revenue from a cinema for the nominal run of a film. This guaranteed minimum is payable before the film is shown. Holdover clauses govern the extension of a run of a film that has succeeded in generating an agreed threshold level of box office revenue during its contracted run.

The risk of the exhibitor is also affected by whether the contract or extra-contractual understanding with the distributor grants exclusivity or at least stipulates a maximum number of cinemas to be licensed in the area it services. If an exhibitor can view a picture before committing to license it, a more precise estimate of revenue can be made. A blind contract, which is based on a cursory description of content, cast and staff of a work in process, must have offsetting advantages, such as a lower rental price, if an exhibitor agrees to it. From the supplier's perspective, blind contracting allows a film to be distributed more quickly after production is complete.

These complex sharing provisions and the discretion exercised by the parties in enforcing the letter of the contract, encouraged by the gains from continuous dealings, shape the incentives for distributors and cinema owners. In this vein, Kenney and Klein (1983) have argued that blind bidding and block booking (or informal arrangements that imitate these contractual practices) economise on distributors' inventory costs and restrict exhibitors' scope for the substitution of better films for films in the block. Where the exhibitor has some contractual freedom of choice, opportunistic substitution may occur as a result of monitoring the experience of other exhibitors or as a response to disappointing results during the opening days of the run. Some of the historical evidence is either unexplained by, or inconsistent with, this interpretation.

Hanssen (2000) notes that block booking was introduced when films were sold by the foot and exhibitors expended few resources on quality search. With the development of the feature film and the later introduction of sound, quality became an important issue to exhibitors. In this setting, if the Kenney–Klein hypothesis were correct, the right to reject a specified proportion of a distributor's block would have been fully exploited as exhibitors refused to show films revealed to be losers or curtailed their runs (Hanssen 2000). Full exploitation of the rejection right did not generally occur. Hanssen posits that block booking and revenue sharing provided a framework for determining an efficient timing for ending a current film's run and replacing it with another from the block supplier.[24] The efficiency of this arrangement depends on the block supplier providing the substitute film. If, instead, a film from another supplier replaced the current film, the block supplier would be damaged as it would lose a source of revenue and not share in the larger revenue generated by the film replacement. Hanssen's contract data reveal that exhibitors were most frequently replacing cancelled films or abbreviated runs with films from other distributors.

In response, Kenny and Klein (2000: 432) argue that after the *Paramount* decision made block booking illegal, distributors wrote contracts for each film that over-constrained exhibitors but relaxed these restrictions "when it was jointly profitable to do so".[25] Their thesis is that the value of preserving the distributor's reputational capital with potential exhibitors disciplines its discretionary easing of the constraints so that it is consistent with profit maximisation. This optimal alignment of incentives is a hypothesis to be tested. No evidence is given that profits are jointly maximised under current contracting, and no convincing evidence is likely if testing depends on quantifying the rather slippery concept of reputational capital.

Since producer/exhibitor contracts are conditioned on box office revenue, which the cinema owner knows with greater accuracy than the distributor, credible means of confirming box office revenue are required to make a sharing contract attractive to the distributor. Historically, numbered tickets and other control devices have been introduced to provide cheaper monitoring of box office figures. Trade journals also publish detailed figures on box office receipts, allowing the numbers to be inspected by a variety of knowledgeable people in the industry. Distributors that own cinemas can also compare the reported performance of a film placed in an independent theatre with box office figures at owned cinemas having similar characteristics.

In many countries, a substantial proportion of cinema revenue comes from the sale of food and drink to customers prior to the show and during intermission. The speed and reliability of the popcorn machine is often as important to economic viability as the quality of the picture being shown. Since the distributor does not share in revenues from concessions, a potential conflict of interest arises between the cinema owner and the distributor, as the former is willing to lower the price of tickets as long as the cinema's *share* of the box office revenue falls by less than the increase in concession profits. The distributor wants the cinema owner to price admission so as to maximise box office revenue rather than the joint profit from admissions and concessions. To protect their interests, distributors often include in the contract a minimum price requirement for a ticket. Although such clauses appear consistent with maximising joint wealth and preventing a source of dissipation from sharing,[26] the competition policy authorities have often taken a dim view of this practice.[27]

Organisational response

Integration of production, distribution and exhibition

In order to ensure an outlet for their films, the major studios not only produced and distributed films but owned theatres where they could be shown. Vertical integration provided a guaranteed outlet in major cities, and the theatres received an assured supply of films. At the same time, theatres and the associated real estate represented tangible assets, which could be used as security for loans from financial institutions unwilling to lend against the risky prospects of a film in development.

Vertical integration from production through distribution to exhibition reduced the risk of the films not having adequate screenings, and allowed producers to plan more effectively the timing of new releases and promotional campaigns. Firms that were not vertically integrated employed contracts, as discussed above, that resulted in quasi-integrated relations.

Although the American courts have viewed the industry's contracting practices and vertical ownership of cinemas as instruments of monopolisation, such arrangements have been defended as efficient innovations for dealing with the risk and informational characteristics of film exhibition and distribution. Whether the costs imposed on consumers by these practices outweighed the benefits is moot.[28] The concern of the competition authorities is the barrier to entry for independently produced and distributed films, if the majors control the cinematic distribution. The effect of this barrier has been reduced by the development of alternative distribution systems, in particular dedicated pay movie channels. Ironically, the most successful of these channels, Home Box Office in the United States and Canal Plus in Europe, vertically integrated and became major financiers and producers of films before being absorbed into larger entertainment complexes.

Another function for which contracts have become effective substitutes for vertical integration is that of production. Since the Second World War, the major studios have increasingly substituted for in-house production by contracting with independent producers.[29]

Integrating "the art and the brass": a historical perspective

Organisational structures have evolved to cope with the problems of making the right films and making the films right. Tension between the "art and the brass", the artistic and the business sides of filmmaking, has always existed because of the likelihood of failure and the difficulty of monitoring the expenditures and conduct of those making films. In 1941, an American film financier stated:

> The men on the West Coast are paid preposterous salaries because they have the kind of mad genius that's needed to put out films. I'd like to find executives who can cut Hollywood's costs without strangling the creative talents of the men who keep sending costs up. The moving picture industry needs men who can understand a balance sheet and a three-ring circus.
>
> (Rosten 1941: 251)

Joseph P. Kennedy examined the tension between the different cultures in a 1936 report prepared for the Paramount–Publix Corporation, which filed a petition for bankruptcy in 1933 and was reorganised in 1935. Despite noting egregious managerial shortcomings, Kennedy appreciated the creative peculiarities of filmmaking and concluded that there had been too much business interference with the production of movies. He recommended that the financiers appoint a chief of production as their agent to proceed without interference from the financiers, but with incentives to protect their financial interests.

> The New York executives learned that orthodox business practices may destroy unorthodox intangible assets: the creative urge.... They had instituted routine economies without understanding that Hollywood's producers, actors, directors and writers do not get fabulous salaries for their daily output, or their measurable diligence, or the decorum of their methods, or the regularity of their working hours ... movie making is not a systematised process in which ordered routine can prevail, or in which costs can be absolute and controlled. Too many things can and do go awry.... Movies are made by ideas and egos, not from blueprints and not with machines.
>
> (Rosten 1941: 255)

In response to the problem of disciplining creativity and managing risk, different types of organisational structures and contractual arrangements have evolved. In the United States, these arrangements have been identified with three periods associated with pre-studio (to about 1920), studio (approximately 1920 to 1960) and post-studio (since 1960) production. A finer, six-stage, categorisation depicts how specialisation and division of labour, from the "cameraman system", took place as the market grew, films became longer and more expensive to make, cost containment became more important, and viewers came to demand quality productions (Staiger 1985). The stages show the development of increasingly hierarchical organisations ending at the fifth stage with a studio organisation that is the equivalent of a multidivisional firm – a head office with a staff, below which are a number of producers each in charge of a series of directors.[30] The sixth stage depicts the "package unit system", agents working with independent producers and the studios used to provide financing and act as distributors.

Typical of the hierarchical (fifth-stage) studio organisation was MGM with its parent company, Loew's Inc. in New York, headed for many years by Nicholas Schenck. The studio was the responsibility of Louis B. Mayer, who operated with a central staff and a series of producers reporting to him. Each producer was responsible for the production of a number of films annually, using units consisting of directors, actors and the other resources outlined in the budget. Overall financial control was exercised from New York, while approval for the budgets and production of individual films took place in Hollywood.[31] As in any organisation, greater autonomy was experienced at the lower levels when the films were made within budget and resulted in a profit. Declining financial success, due either to inflated costs or insufficient revenues, would lead to greater head office control.

Organisational change in the United States has been affected by legal decisions, making long-term contracts with key personnel less effective, as well as anti-trust decisions governing the interface between distribution and exhibition. Another contributing factor has been the learning that occurred over time with respect to the effectiveness of contractual and relational integration as an alternative to integration by ownership. As a result, production, distribution and exhibition have become more organisationally fragmented while maintaining a systemic integrity. This controlled decentralisation has many advantages. For instance, the search process for new projects is more diffused and incorporates more independent sources of inspiration and ideas. Currently, independent producers and agents play a prominent role in assembling packages of directors, actors and scripts that are then presented to the studios for financing and distribution and compete with studio-developed projects. Studios no longer have a large number of production personnel on long-term contracts. Key creative people flow between projects that are linked to different studios. Similarly, the executives who are directly responsible for the slate of projects are more mobile than in the past. Frequent turnover of senior execu-

tives is a feature of the current Hollywood scene as the commercial for-
tunes of firms fluctuate, although executives are often recycled between
firms as the right mix is sought.[32] Even top executives may hold term contracts with clauses specifying the studio's conditional obligations if the
studio relationship is not renewed. When David Puttnam was Chairman of
Columbia Pictures in the mid-1980s, he held a three-year contract. He quit
to avoid being fired before the contract terminated and was consoled by a
$3 million dollar parachute. In doing so, he became the first studio head to
leave before any of his films were released (Yule 1989: 330). Some fired
studio heads are reabsorbed into the Hollywood industry as a result of the
network process noted by Storper and Christopherson (1987). Some of the
recent owners of studios – Trans America, Coca-Cola, Matsushita, Sony,
Seagrams and Vivendi – were successful in other activities. Their inexperi-
ence with the film industry may have added to the churning of managers.

What has been retained of the old studio system is an organisational
structure for monitoring films in which money has been invested and an
integrated approach to the choice of projects to back, promote and distribute. Over time, Hollywood has developed an organisational structure that
is effective in selecting persons who can manage the relationship among
different professional cultures – the financiers, those like Mayer in charge
of making the films, and the artistic talent and key inputs employed.

A portfolio of films

That many films lose money is a known risk to investors. According to
scriptwriter William Goldman, "Nobody knows anything – Not one person
in the entire motion picture field knows for a certainty what's going to
work. Every time out it's a guess – and, if you're lucky, an educated one"
(Goldman 1983: 39). The key phrase in Goldman's colourful description is
"educated guess". Jake Eberts provides a more balanced assessment that
"you had to do both: put your money into a portfolio of films, but choose
each film extremely carefully and make every effort you can to improve its
chances of success" (Eberts and Ilott 1990: 41).

In the early years of filmmaking, initial assessment was perfunctory as
the strong demand for new films meant that almost anything could be distributed and films were sold by the foot. Films were short and the industry
was characterised by small firms making relatively inexpensive films, which
were shown as part of programmes of slide presentations, lectures and
other live entertainment. With the introduction of the longer feature film,
and the hiring of highly paid stars, film costs rose and the probability distribution for commercial success of an individual film became more spread
out around the mean. Technological developments have increased the
viewing windows of a film and the development of ancillary revenue
sources. Box office revenues now represent a relatively low proportion of
the total revenue generated from a film project but success in this venue

promotes success in others. Consequently, the distribution of revenue from the cinematic release has a disproportionate effect in shaping the overall distribution of revenues.

On release, a film has a low probability of a blockbuster run and a high probability of disappointing box office results. Studio management is "well educated" about the uncertainty and international competition is sufficiently intense to motivate applying what it knows to reduce risk and raise its average return. Mobilising a studio's corporate "know how" requires that the studio influence development, control aspects of production as part of the financing/distribution contract and orchestrate the release. An intermediary that bought films for future delivery from independent producers, without becoming involved in influencing concept development and monitoring production, would realise the gain from pooling a number of such purchases but would end up with less attractive "lottery tickets" in its portfolio than a studio that integrated production and distribution.

Greater concentration in distribution than production makes it possible to offer cinemas a package of films. This bundling reduces transaction costs between the distributor and cinemas, increases the efficiency of a cinema's transition from one film to another, and reduces risk from portfolio effects. The Hollywood industry has prospered over time but the volatility of the box office share of each studio attests to the high level of uncertainty facing its portfolio of annual releases. Each year's production adds to a stock or library of films from which a stream of revenues is earned over the years. To an analyst, the distribution of overall profit on a project is of critical importance but difficult to estimate. On the revenue side, there are burgeoning sources of revenue associated with each film that have complex interconnections and are realised over a longer time horizon. On the cost side, data are scarcer and less reliable, particularly with respect to the additional costs of exploiting ancillary markets.

To reduce risk, large-budget films are often only innovative on the surface. Under this veneer lie concepts or formulae that have been successful in the past. Other factors that may contribute to risk reduction are the development of foreign markets, cross-marketing with ancillary products, branding, the inclusion of stars, editing of films for different markets and the pretesting of films during the editing process.

Developing foreign markets

An owner of a movie can generate additional revenues by exploiting the public good aspects of films and selling rights in all foreign markets in which the revenue outweighs the costs of distribution. Historically, French producers were among the first to recognise the value of foreign revenues, especially from the large American market. In turn, American producers soon recognised that Europe represented a lucrative market for their products. Until the coming of sound, language presented no barriers to exports, and where subtitles or intertitles were used they could be translated into different languages.

> By October 1906 it [Pathé] was exporting as many as 12 pictures a week and 75 copies of each film to the United States. . . . the American market by itself amortised the costs, however modest, of our negatives. We sold at least as many as in the rest of our offices. There were then fourteen. The columns of American receipts represented a net profit or nearly so.
>
> (Musser 1990: 488)[33]

Today, the high cost of feature films encourages producers to lock in a large proportion of the revenues from all forms of foreign market distribution – theatrical, television and home video. By timing releases in the different market windows, the risks associated with piracy can be reduced. The longer the delay between theatrical release in different countries, or between theatrical and home-video/DVD release, the greater is the opportunity for piracy.

Cross-marketing

Not only are revenues gleaned from exhibition in domestic and foreign markets but through economies of scope in markets that can be related to the film, its story or actors. Initially films were themselves cross-marketed with live entertainment in vaudeville settings. As actors gained popularity and notoriety, theatres could purchase items such as pillow cases with pictures of the stars which would be given or sold to fans (Bowser 1991: 115). Today, films are linked to records, compact discs, clothing, toys, comic strips, breakfast cereals, theme parks and the hardware that some firms produce. Universal's release of *Jurassic Park* in 1993 was accompanied by toy dinosaurs, cartoon characters, a theme park ride and the promotion of consumer-electronic gadgets developed by Matsushita, the parent company at that time. In its most recent Annual Report, Disney notes that retail sales of its Princess line of merchandise rose from $100 million in 2000 to $700 million in 2002.

Cross-marketing enables firms to garner revenues from related markets and increases the possibility of making profits on a film. The more successful a film is at the box office or on television, the more likely it is to make money in other markets. Success cross-fertilises success and any additional revenues are welcomed if they exceed the additional costs of the album, toy, electronic game or T-shirt. Increasingly, theatrical release is the vehicle to advertise and promote subsequent and related markets, in the same manner that the live rock concert is used to promote compact disc, tape and record sales.

Brand names

Risk can also be reduced if consumers believe that a film bearing the name of a particular producer or distributor will on average be better than one that does not. A brand name can also convey information about the type of film that a viewer will see. For example, that an animated film is from the Disney studio informs a moviegoer about treatment and production values. In earlier periods, different studios were associated with certain types of films – westerns, comedies, musicals, gangster movies. The studios also developed their own logos that facilitated brand recognition – the MGM lion, Paramount mountain, Fox searchlights and Warner shield. While originally these denoted films made by the studios, now they often mark films which have been financed and distributed by the studios but made by independent producers perhaps using the studio facilities.

Star appeal and sequel identification do for performers and a set of movies what brand names do for studios. They reduce uncertainty for viewers. In the 1930s and 1940s, the studios such as MGM invested in developing stars with the same calculation that an automotive manufacturer might apply to developing and promoting a new model. Then and now, a star helps "open" a film and seeds word-of-mouth dissemination of its value. However, the presence of a star does not ensure success. If the word-of-mouth response is negative, the film quickly dies.[34]

The advantages of a series for drawing customers was recognised early. Fox's Charlie Chan movies began in 1931 and lasted ten years. Later, Tarzan films were extremely profitable, as were the more modern variants, the James Bond, Rocky, Batman and Indiana Jones movies, the *Star Wars* trilogy, *The Matrix*, *Men in Black*, *Harry Potter* and *Lord of the Rings* sequences.[35] When stars were under contract to studios, more of the economic rents from sequels would accrue to the studio. Today, much of the rents accrue to the star, if he or she is crucial to the series, as was the case with the Rocky films. Predictably, many of the franchise series are not driven by a particular actor's presence.

Editing and pretesting of films

Editing, test marketing and sneak previews of a film reduce but do not eliminate risk. According to Francis Coppola, a director has several opportunities to create a picture:

> First, you write it. Second, you shoot it. Third, you edit it. Each is a creative process which depends on the ingredients you have in hand at the moment. At the picture's inception, you've got words and your imagination; in the middle ground, you've got actors and sets and a camera; at the end, you've got the film ... rigid in what is on it, flexible

in what order you put it together ... with music and sound embellishments coming up.

(Houghton 1991: 167)

New technologies have made editing easier by allowing the details of each frame to be altered, a far cry from the original editing by cutting and splicing existing film. In one sense, test marketing occurs from the outset of shooting when the director views the daily rushes to examine the adequacy of existing shots and to plan future scenes. This continues until the director's version of the film is compiled which may mean selecting 10,000 feet of film from ten or twenty times that amount. Reshooting a scene is always possible, but can be expensive if it means reassembling actors and a crew, especially if it is a location shoot.

A film can be test marketed by showing pre-release versions to selected audiences, assessing their reactions and making changes. But as director John Huston notes:

> Audiences are an enigma. There have been technical and scientific experiments aimed at analyzing the reaction of audiences, including measurements of heartbeats, skin temperatures and so forth. Not one of these experiments explains why an audience tends to react as though it had one body and mind
>
> (1980: 201)

Piracy

Like a book, music or computer software, films can be copied at low cost and distributed so that revenues do not flow to the owners of copyright. From the outset of the industry, illegal copying has been a problem with prints of films being duplicated and distributed for exhibition. Today, piracy is facilitated by the availability of video taping and the burning of DVDs from digital files that are "shared" on the Internet. Some entrepreneurs will videotape a film, usually a new release, from a theatrical screen, copy the tapes and resell them on the street.[36] The copies may include the sound of popcorn consumption and show persons crossing in front of the camera, but, if the film has time value to buyers, sales will be made. Illegal copying of tapes and DVDs, especially for sale in Eastern Europe and the former Soviet Union but also in developed and developing countries, is pervasive. A form of piracy occurs when a theatrical or television distributor purchases the rights to show the film a certain number of times, sharing revenues with the copyright owners, and then gives additional showings and pockets these revenues.

Producers may copy plots, scenes, characters and ideas from other movies for inclusion in their own productions and may make remakes of previous films. Copying ideas is not an infringement of copyright if the presentation or performance is different, and the rights to make remakes are often purchased.[37] However, if partial or complete scenes are duplicated from previous films, problems may arise as is occurring with samples taken from musical compositions.

Response by the industry to piracy has led to legal actions in the courts, establishment by the industry of a private police force to detect copiers and enforce the law, and lobbying governments to strengthen copyright laws and their enforcement and to impose a tax on blank tapes with revenues going to producers. Disney is especially aggressive in suing others who use its cartoon characters in any manner without permission. In Canada, the Film/Video Security Office of the Canadian Motion Picture Distributors Association has a full-time employee investigating piracy and working with the police to confiscate illegal tapes or DVDs from rental stores or retailers and prosecute offenders. Its activities are reported in trade magazines in order to discourage potential infringers. The International Intellectual Property Association is an alliance of eight US trade associations representing over 1,500 companies and promoting international protection of copyrighted works in different sectors.

The problem is not new. As early as 1907, producers established ownership by including trademarks in the filmed scenes, often on the walls of a set or on trees when the scene was shot outside. This "fence" did not prevent trespass:

> Fred Balshofer has recounted how he began his career in the motion picture business in the basement of Lubin's Philadelphia store, painstakingly brushing out the trademarks from every frame before proceeding to duplicate the films from such producers as George Méliès.
>
> (Bowser 1991: 138)

Today, the timing of the release of films in different markets and windows has been compressed, making it possible to reduce the rewards from piracy and discourage but not eliminate the practice.

Why Hollywood?

If over time Hollywood developed the organisational techniques that promoted and sustained its leadership internationally, why did other countries not emulate these practices? No patent or copyright protected the managerial skills. In fact, there was considerable freedom of movement of people and ideas as well as collaboration in co-producing films. In this section, we explore possible reasons why the organisational span was international and why the United States was and remains the centre of activity.[38] Our explanation of the latter rests on three pillars. The first is the cumulative impact of historical events, particularly the two world wars.

The second is the rapid commercialisation of new technologies made possible by the fortuitous conjunction of an aggressive, marketing oriented managerial culture and an open financial system. The third is the ethnic diversity, language homogeneity and size of the American market. In addition, we believe that the policies implemented by other countries in response to American success were counterproductive as measures to create a competing international system. We speculate that American organisational dominance arose from the interaction of the above factors and the informational efficiencies realised by an international distribution system.

In film, the original technological developments and the responses to them were spread over many countries. In the late 1880s significant hardware innovations were made in France, Great Britain and the United States. With respect to form and content, a French magician, Georges Méliès, filmed fairy tales and science fiction stories which he wrote, directed, acted in and for which he designed the settings, while the American Edwin Porter furthered the development of the narrative film. The hardware and content formats were quickly incorporated into film in a number of countries. Early moviemaking flourished in a number of European countries as well as in the United States, and up to about 1914 the majority of films shown in the United States were foreign productions. By 1918, however, the American producers had acquired the largest share of both their domestic market and the major foreign markets for film exhibition.[39]

Boosted by the 1914–1918 wartime destruction or curtailment of the industry in Europe, American producers enjoyed continuity of production and substantially reduced foreign competition. After the war, the reconstructing European industry had to contend with a large inventory of American films, which had not been shown in most foreign markets, and an American industry that had developed a competitive sharpness in its successful struggle to overcome the Edison trust.[40]

Important players among the independents, Fox, Laemmle, Loew and Zukor, were merchants with backgrounds in retail or wholesale trade, often in the poorer parts of cities where they serviced the mass market.[41] These entrepreneurs successfully tailored films for the large American mass market. In order to attract a mass audience in the United States, the films had to contain ingredients that appealed to a population made up of numerous ethnic and religious backgrounds. These multicultural "puddings" also proved tasty to foreign audiences. Since the costs of making prints available for overseas sales were small, foreign sales were often lucrative. In this silent era of films, language presented no barrier to international distribution, which was a relatively simple process not involving complex vertically integrated companies.

Hardware manufacturers searching to establish markets for their innovations found willing partners among the second tier of American firms.

Warner Brothers first introduced sound, followed by Fox in the late 1920s (Gomery 1976). The introduction of sound involved considerable investment by exhibitors and required coordination between the producers of films and the cinema owners. Similarly, a number of studios experimented with the two-strip Technicolor process at around the same time; Walt Disney, another smaller operator, introduced the more appealing three-colour process in 1932.[42] To ensure suitably equipped outlets for their output, the Hollywood firms expanded their ownership of cinemas domestically and abroad, as well as offering favourable financial terms for independent cinemas to convert their facilities.[43]

The potential *ex ante* of the new technologies was seen only dimly even by insiders. Initially, Warners had embraced sound as a way of saving on the costs of the musicians who accompanied screenings of their silent films but quickly recognised the potential of talk in movies with the release of *The Jazz Singer* in 1927. During the following year, eighty-five films were released with synchronised sound or part-talking, plus ten all-talking films. In 1929, 194 all-talking films were released in the USA.[44] In the United States, firms like Goldman, Sachs and Co. developed an intimate knowledge of the film business and provided important financial support for companies like Warners. In contrast, the views of many established financial institutions in Britain were reflected by the response given by Montagu Norman, governor of the Bank of England, to Lord Portal, chairman of the General Cinema Finance Corporation, when he sought advice on J. Arthur Rank's acquisition of Universal Studio's stock:

> "Wyndham, you're surely not going to interest yourself in that awful film industry?" Portal ... tried to make out a case, but Norman was adamant: "It's no good, Wyndham, it's unsound. And those dreadful people are not your class. Keep out of it!"
>
> (Wilcox 1969: 107)

Some established financial institutions did provide substantial funds to the film industry in England during the 1930s, but failed to develop the expertise that would have protected them from the opportunistic behaviour of less than scrupulous producers.

> The Westminster Bank managed to lose more than a million pounds while one small production company, with capital of less than £100, was able to persuade backers to advance it £200,000 for its never-to-be completed endeavours.
>
> (Macnab 1993: 18)

One aspect of the information obtained by Goldman, Sachs and Co. about Warners was its record of completing projects within budget. This was reinforced by the manner in which Warner Brothers developed "B" movies in the Depression years.

> Every means of avoiding retakes was exploited: stage business (entrances, exits, unnecessary transactions) was severely restricted to cut down the risk of fumbling. Crowded scenes were avoided to keep the wages bill low; extras if used were cheaper silent than speaking; actors were asked to wear their own clothes wherever possible (most B movies had present-day plots to reduce costs); sets were borrowed from other productions; and stock footage of places and events was cut in (often with massive errors of continuity) to save the expense of shooting them.
>
> (Izod 1988: 99–100)

With the need to market a steady flow of sophisticated sound and colour films, the Hollywood majors not only expanded their ownership of cinemas but developed forms of quasi-vertical integration by block booking and blind bidding contracts. These developments resulted in a protracted and costly interaction with the anti-trust authorities, as discussed above (pages 318–324). Nevertheless, the practices, or variants of them that were acceptable to the authorities, contributed to the rapid growth of the studios.

Sound also divided the world into linguistic markets. Again the United States was fortuitously positioned by having the largest national market in the English-language world, which in revenue terms was by far the largest linguistic market. The values that could be realised by selling rights to the different components of the English-language market around the world plus the lower values that could be picked up from foreign-language areas justified higher budgets and, on average, better production values. As occurred with silent films, American producers developed sound formats that appealed to different segments of the culturally diverse American market. These formats travelled well across the cultural differences in the English-language market and diminished the discount when transferred to foreign markets.

Hoskins and Mirus (1988) have stressed that the value attributed to audio-visual material varies across different cultures (they coined the term "cultural discount"). Musicals, westerns and gangster films, for example, lost less when dubbed or sub-titled, and became staples of the American production slates. The percentage of the international to the US box office revenue varies across films but its average has been rising. As a benchmark, the percentage for the forty films with the top international box office revenue of all time was 145.[45] It is very difficult to predict the percentage for particular films based on their content. *Pearl Harbor* (2001) has a lower than average percentage of 127 but *The Bodyguard*, which outgrossed *Pearl Harbor*, had a percentage of 237. Both these films have content that might be discounted outside of the United States. An Australian film, *Crocodile Dundee* (1986), did relatively better in the United States (ranked 76th) than internationally (ranked 131st) and had a lower percentage, 88, than *Pearl Harbor*.[46] In our opinion, the last example illustrates why it is difficult to find a systematic cultural discount in high-grossing films. By and large, these films, no matter where they are made, are produced with the international market in mind. For an Australian filmmaker making mass-market movies, the United States is an important part of his or her market.

The United States also benefited from the Second World War as it had from the First. A large inventory of American films produced in the war overhung the European markets, creating a hostile environment for these reconstructing industries. Many personnel who had moved to the United States before the war and during the hostilities did not return after the war, further strengthening the American industry. Although it was no secret that success depended on developing films that were attractive in world markets, the British industry with the second largest English-speaking domestic market, found it difficult to respond. Limbacher provides the following unflattering assessment of British pictures in comparison to the Hollywood product:

> 1) The action was too slow. 2) There was too much dialog. 3) The actors talked too fast and their accents and slang words were difficult to understand. 4) The actresses looked dowdy and the actors seemed effeminate. 5) The physical quality of the films often looked inferior to American productions.
>
> (Limbacher 1971: 10)

J. Arthur Rank, one of the few successful British film producers, owner of a vertically integrated operation and at one time a major shareholder of Universal Studios, was reported in 1945 to be

> Astounded by the efficiency of the American studio operation, he resolved to make more use of his influence at Universal by sending technicians, producers, directors and even stars to study American filmmaking at first hand.
>
> (Macnab 1993: 75)

British film producers may have improved their individual skills but they did not find a solution to the organisational problem.

In the period after the Second World War, the American studios became less vertically integrated, contracting out much of the production, and concentrating on financing and distribution. There appear to be natural efficiencies in integrating international distribution. An international distributor can marshal information from all or most potential markets and influence the choice of films to finance. The alternative is to patch together a number of independent regional distributors to cover world markets. Usually this is done in a sequence of contracts. A national distributor provides an advance and influences production content and timing. Other distributors sign on later and take content as given. They offer less, as a result of not being able to influence the film's content and style.

Distribution through a set of regional distributors has been artificially nourished by domestic policies that protect and promote national productions. These policies often include financial subsidies and require a national distribution contract. Occasionally a film, such as the Australian production, *Strictly Ballroom*, and the UK-produced *The Crying Game* and *Four Weddings and a Funeral*, breaks out to achieve considerable success internationally. However, such breakouts are relatively rare and cannot be relied on to fill the pipeline of films demanded by exhibitors around the globe.

When Rank sent producers, directors, technical personnel and stars to Hollywood to improve their skills, only part of the problem was addressed. One element that could not be learned by such a transfer was the relationship between production and financing controls. Accounts abound of, for example, Mayer and Thalberg's management of the MGM factory in Hollywood. Much less is known of the financial constraints placed on West Coast production by Schenck in New York. Nor is much known about the systems of routinely integrating information from the international distribution division when developing projects to finance. More will be learned on this account as we monitor the ability of recent and current foreign owners to manage the linkages between finance, distribution and production choice.

What we have been discussing is why American-produced, or more accurately studio-financed, films and the studio distribution system dominated international markets. This dominance related only to a certain type of product. Local and regional cinema co-existed with the international product and has been encouraged by national policies. The strength of the regional distributors is their knowledge of the local production and marketing scene. However, a coalition of regional distributors linked by contract has been generally revealed to be a less effective way of coordinating information for choosing and funding productions for world markets than integration through ownership, as occurred in Hollywood.

We do not expect the internationalisation of ownership in Hollywood to significantly change the experience of the typical viewer around the world. When under Japanese-ownership, Columbia Pictures and Universal Studios did not produce and distribute a stream of Japanese language art films. Nor has the line-up from Fox been dominated by fascinating but quirky Australian films. We do see the chance of significant change occurring as a response to new technological developments. An increased volume of audio-visual programming will be needed to satisfy the expanding cable, satellite broadcasting, Internet, and other new means of delivery. We anticipate that a number of internationally integrated distribution systems will be able to compete and survive in this environment. The dynamics of this greater competition may provide producers with more choices and viewers with more diverse viewing options.

Conclusion

The process of filmmaking has led to a set of organisational and contractual arrangements that have been adapted to changing technology and evolved over time to address the predominant risks faced by the industry, especially the risks of piracy, cost containment, opportunism, commercial failure and their interaction. We have analysed how the contractual nexus and institutional forms adopted by the industry helped manage these risks. The informational problems faced by the industry favoured integrated international marketing of films and related merchandise and close financial ties between the international distributors and producers. Whether this integration occurred through contract or ownership depended on the balance of advantages of the two modes and the stance of the competition policy authorities. Contract provides an effective alternative to ownership for film production and cinematic distribution, whereas large entities continue to dominate the distribution function. The fragmentation of production and exhibition windows is misleading as contractual and relational ties bind the atoms into an effective system.

Our conclusion is that the domination of the international aspects of the film industry by one system is based on the efficiency of that system. This conclusion is controversial. We do not claim to have proved it but to provide a perspective on the transactional problems of this industry that point in that direction. If one agrees with that conclusion and maintains the hypothesis that one system will dominate the international part of the film industry, a second question naturally presents itself. Why has this international system been dominated by Hollywood?

We argue that a number of factors contributed to American dominance. The Americans benefited from the two world wars by, at that time, creating an inventory of films available for release at the termination of hostilities and by attracting creative personnel from all corners of the world to reside and work in the United States. The United States was also the largest single market in the largest language market from a revenue perspective. At the same time, the United States had assimilated large blocks of viewers from different ethnic backgrounds. Films produced for this market had to cross cultural boundaries and therefore were easier to export. The American managerial and financial cultures were conducive to the development of contractual and institutional relationships that permitted the financing and distribution of films on a large scale. Outsiders to the established managerial groups were able to experiment with organisational form and attract funding. Temporary but effective linkages with manufacturing interests expedited the commercial exploitation of new technologies. Perhaps because the industry was successful internationally from the beginning, the United States government did not feel the need to adopt content quotas or distributional and cinematic restrictions. Such policies have been adopted at one time or another in one form or another by almost every other country. We believe these policies were not successful because they ignore the organisational basis for the American success.

With the rash of new technological developments, the organisational challenges facing production, distribution and exhibition remain but may appear in a different guise. Multiple channels of pay-per-view films provided by satellite broadcasters and cable systems as well as high-definition video and disk players provide new avenues for international distribution. The same technologies create new opportunities for piracy as well as novel defences against it, new ways for being opportunistic, and new methods for extracting revenues from viewers. The motion-picture industry has been active in supporting changes in patent, copyright and trade law to accommodate contractual procedures under the new circumstances. After the Uruguay Round, the WTO emerged as an integrated coordination and enforcement mechanism for trade in services as well as goods and copyright (Acheson and Maule 1994a, 1994b, 1999). These changes in law and international governance will be accompanied by significant changes in contracting practice and in institutional arrangements. The relatively low prices of DVDs, their mass marketing on the Internet and in large discount retailers, and the MPA's active support of costly litigation against file-swapping services and the publication of protective-code-breaking software are illustrative.

If the technologically driven increase in capacity results in an expansion of the international segment of the industry, competition from systems other than the American should develop. This competition will be good for consumers in terms of price but will still be based on mass-appeal formulaic audio-visual material. The experimental, novel and socially challenging content will emerge from the local and regional film segments as they do now. The two genres may not be as distinct as before. The international industry may provide a uniform skeleton on which local creators can add distinctive material or interacting viewers, choosing from locally or internationally provided menus, can make creative decisions.

Although we believe that our explanation of American dominance of the international film and television industry is coherent, other explanations could be proposed. What is not disputable is the fact of historical dominance. To our knowledge, no other industry has been persistently dominated in the same manner. The American advantage was achieved without a programme of subsidies, quotas and content rules[47] while in competition with industries of other countries supported by such policies.

One strength of our explanation is that it gives reasons for American success while explaining why the policies of other countries have had limited impact on international distribution.

Notes

1 We are grateful to Elizabet Filleul, Simon Grant, Peter Harcourt, Ian Jarvie, Janet Staiger and the editors of this volume for their comments and suggestions but absolve them of any responsibility for the views presented. An earlier version of this chapter was published in the *Journal of Cultural Economics*, 18 (1995: 271–300) and is reprinted with permission.
2 The context of transactions is emphasised by Chandler (1990).
3 Similar risks affect the undertaking of industrial research and development and academic research.
4 Sony, a Japanese firm, owns Columbia. An Australian-born American owns Fox. While we were revising this chapter, NBC repatriated Universal's film division, theme parks and US television holdings by purchasing them from Vivendi, a French company.
5 Until the widespread diffusion of commercial television in the 1950s, the film industry depended almost entirely on theatrical revenues. By 1992, of the $18.4 billion spent by consumers to watch films in the USA, 47.5 per cent went to the video rental and buy-through markets, 27.3 per cent to theatres and 25.2 per cent to pay-TV. This pattern was also representative of Europe and Japan. (*Wall Street Journal*, March 26, 1993: R6). In 2002, the MPA reports US box office of $9.5 billion and international box office of $9.6 billion and the Video Software Dealers Association (VSDA) refers to a $20 billion international home entertainment industry.
6 In 2000, for example, Disney released *Fantasia 2000*, an animated feature in the 70mm Imax format and later did the same for *Beauty and the Beast*, *Treasure Planet* and *The Lion King*.
7 New Line, for example, put out a basic DVD (two discs) of *Lord of the Rings: the Fellowship of the Ring* in August of 2002. A "platinum edition" with thirty minutes added to the film and thirty hours of complementary content and a "collector's DVD gift" with additional content were offered three months later. They retail for twice and four times the price of the basic version, respectively.
8 Disney Animation has released thirteen animated sequels theatrically or directly to video since 1994, which are expected to contribute profits of approximately $1 billion over their lifetime (Disney Annual Report 2002).
9 Netflix, for example, is one of a number of services operating in the United States. For a monthly fee of $20, a subscriber can rent any number of DVDs; however, only three can be checked out at the same time. Ordering and payment is done over the Internet; delivery and returns by mail. There are no late fees. By December of 2002, Walmart had announced the launch of a similar service and the Blockbuster video chain had introduced a monthly "all you can rent" plan (*Wired*, December 2002).
10 William Goldman notes: "One studio, and this is typical, recently announced that they had one hundred and eighty-three projects in development.... Of those one hundred and eighty-three projects, maybe ten, at the outside, will ever happen" (Goldman (1983: 92)).
11 Entertainment and current affair programmes provide thinly disguised advertising for current and future film and television productions.
12 Details of the budget process are discussed in Vogel (1986).
13 Other directors have different styles. John Huston and Alfred Hitchcock are

reported to have worked out most details of a film before shooting began. Steven Soderbergh describes working without a storyboard to preplan shooting sequences (*The Sunday Age*, Melbourne, November 21, 1993, Agenda: 7).

14 For disasters that occurred during the making of *The Emerald Forest*, see Eberts and Ilott (1990: 319).

15 Opportunism is often described in terms of shirking or appropriating ideas that are capitalised on outside the project, but it can take more subtle forms. The creative personnel may also not give a best effort from a commercial point of view for artistic or moral reasons. Successful management of film production involves mobilising these forces when they are present to achieve a better film and not permitting them to destroy its commercial viability.

16 Also quoted in Kent (1991: 200).

17 "Before he arrived he had already steeled himself for the age-old problem of applying financial disciplines to creative people.... In terms of controls on people the place was a bloody zoo" (Chippindale and Franks 1991: 151).

18 This may explain why the remuneration of directors is relatively high as compared to cinematographers and other key personnel. See Rosen's arguments re managerial "superstars" (1981).

19 If only incentive effects are addressed, free-rider problems can, in theory, be avoided by each member of the team making an upfront payment and being paid according to a schedule based on the team output. Each person is paid according to his or her marginal product at the efficient level of output. The upfront payments of the workers cover the deficit that is incurred when the producer pays each member of the team according to the steep schedule that induces the "right" amount of effort. When risk exists and the income levels of workers, or their tastes, make them more risk averse than the producer, the optimal design of a contract changes. It also changes when some monitoring is effective in reducing opportunism by either party. The optimal contracts between a principal and each of many agents involved in team production are characterised by more moderate shares and small or no upfront payments (McAfee and McMillan 1991). Such contracts more closely resemble those observed in the film industry, where shares of the agents add to less than 100 per cent and there are no upfront payments typically made by the workers.

20 In filming *The Adventures of Baron Munchausen*, director Terry Gilliam ended up working for the "supervising producer" appointed by the guarantor (Kent 1991: 184). For the final sequences of *The Emerald Forest*, Embassy, nervous about cost overruns, assigned an executive to approve every major decision taken by director John Boorman.

21 In notes to the unfinished novel, *The Last Tycoon*, F. Scott Fitzgerald wrote:

> The situation on the big lot was that every producer, director and scenarist there could adduce proof that he was a money-maker. With the initial distrust of the industry by business, with the weeding out of better men from the needs of speed, with emphasis as in a mining camp on the lower virtues ... it could fairly be said of all and by all of those that remained that they had made money.... There was not one of these men, no matter how low-grade or incompetent a fellow, who could not claim to have participated largely in success. This made difficulty in dealing with them.
>
> (Fitzgerald 1941: 160–161)

22 The producer can discount the contingent claim with a financial institution but at a heavy discount as most banks are less able to guard against opportunism in the industry than industry insiders such as distributors.

23 In the United States, a 1968 consent decree limited blind bidding by each studio to three films. This provision lapsed in early 1975. However, by the

beginning of 1983, twenty-two states had passed such legislation (Trotiner 1984: 162).

24 See Hanssen (Chapter 5 in this volume). Hanssen (2002) – see Chapter 4 of this volume – notes that sharing terms became common with the introduction of sound. He attributes the shift from a fixed payment by the exhibitor to the declining importance of the ancillary presentational services provided by the cinema when a soundtrack was integrated with the film.

25 Stigler (1963) showed that bundling sales into blocks could increase the ability of a licensor to extract revenue from buyers as compared to licensing each film individually.

26 The insight that parties to contracts would include constraining clauses that increase joint wealth derives from Coase (1960). Cheung (1969) provides an interesting analysis of how this perspective can be used to understand a persisting contractual form.

27 To illustrate, consider a series of Canadian competition cases. In 1977, Columbia Pictures Industries, Inc. pleaded guilty to not allowing a theatre owner to reduce prices and Warner Bros. Distributing (Canada) Limited was charged with "unlawfully attempting to discourage the reduction of the price of theatre admissions" by contracting with Famous Players, Canada's largest chain of cinemas, to suspend the senior citizen discount for a showing of *Barry Lyndon* at the Nelson Theatre in Ottawa. Two years later, United Artists Corporation was found guilty of contracting with Famous Players not to provide discounts of any kind. Bellevue Film Distributors Limited, which distributed Disney films in Canada, was also convicted of prohibiting cinema owners from giving children discounts.

28 The major American studios owned less than a majority of the theatres, but their venues were often the largest, best equipped and located in major cities. De Vany and Eckert (1991) have argued that, in the *Paramount* decisions, the American courts failed to recognise the efficiency aspects of block booking, blind bidding and other marketing practices.

29 See Sedgwick (2002: Table 5), reprinted in this volume, for a detailed account of this process during the years 1946 to 1965.

30 The stages are similar to those described in the evolution of firms from multidepartmental to multidivisional forms of organisation (Chandler 1990).

31 At MGM, Louis B. Mayer supervised a number of producers, five of whom participated in the company's profit-sharing plan (Gomery 1986: 69).

32 One consequence of turnover is that a new executive may not want the work of a past executive to succeed. If, on turnover, a film is incomplete, it may be starved for funds, and, if complete, not promoted.

33 This approach contrasts with the more recent attitudes of producers in countries with small markets, which are viewed as being an impediment to financing production. This is the case only if these producers decide to produce for their domestic market and not for the relevant world language markets.

34 The statistical literature provides equivocal support. De Vany and Walls (1996) state that movies often have fat-tailed distributions and infinite variances and (in 1999) estimate the effect of different stars on the probability of a box office hit and on profitability. Albert (1998) provides an alternative stochastic model in which a star provides information about the quality of the movie. In his words, the star is a marker for the potential viewer. Actors with more successes have more impact on the decision of viewers. The empirical frequencies are consistent with the expected theoretical distribution. (In a comment by Sedgwick and Pokorny 1999 and a reply by Albert 1999, there is an interesting discussion of some conceptual and measurement issues.) Pokorny and Sedgwick (2001), working with a database on Warner films from the 1930s, find that stars

had a significant effect on the profit measure for medium-/low-budget films but not on high-budget films. These studies refer to other earlier work.

35 Film sequels were the precursors to programme series on television.

36 The process is not unique. "Kineying" was used in Australia in the early days of television to make copies of live events by making film images from the television monitor (see Cunningham and Turner 1993: 25).

37 Rights to remakes of certain French films are reported to be about $1 million each. Examples include *Trois hommes et un couffin* remade as *Three Men and a Baby*, *Parfum de femme* as *Scent of a Woman*, *La femme Nikita* as *Point of No Return*, and *Le retour de Martin Guerre* as *Sommersby*, *Globe and Mail*, April 10, 1993, C3.

38 Jarvie (1992: 275) has addressed this question from a different but not contradictory perspective.

39 The available data for both the USA and selected European markets have been extracted from trade publications and customs records and ably presented in Thompson (1985).

40 The Motion Picture Patents Company was formed in 1908. It pooled key patents owned by Edison and others and, until 1911, had exclusive access to Eastman Kodak raw film stock. It licensed access to its technology and controlled distribution. The MPPC introduced renting rather than selling films, standardised exhibition practices, introduced pricing stipulations, runs and clearances in exhibition contracts, and classified theatres by size and location (Anderson 1985: 146). For the details of subsequent anti-trust actions, court decisions and consent decrees and different analyses of their efficacy see Conant (1960, 1985), Kenney and Klein (1983), Trotiner (1984), Borneman (1985) and De Vany and Eckert (1991).

41 William Fox (Fox Film Corporation) was associated with the garment trade on the east side of New York City; Carl Laemmle (Universal Pictures) had a background in mass-market retailing of clothes before entering the nickelodeon business; Marcus Loew (MGM) started vaudeville houses and music halls in the northeastern USA; and Adolph Zukor (Paramount) began as a fur merchant in New York. All entered the film industry at the distribution–exhibition end. The thrust of their approach is captured by a remark attributed to Louis B. Mayer: "I am reminded of the late Marcus Loew always pounding home ... that the picture business was a Woolworth business where they can bring the entire family" (Powdermaker 1950: 109).

42 Warner Bros. introduced the first all-talking-all-Technicolor film, *On with the Show*, in 1929.

43 Hanssen (2002) attributes the adoption of sharing contracts in distribution to the development of sound.

44 See Limbacher (1968).

45 Percentage is derived from the International and USA All-Time Box Office databases as of September 9, 2003 at http://www.imdb.com/Charts/.

46 The ratio has trended higher over time. *Crocodile Dundee* is one of the earlier films in the top 250 international box office films.

47 Jowett has argued that, when the United States had an industry-run production code, it shaped content and discouraged the importation of certain types of foreign films (Jowett 1990: 31). While the United States government argues that it does not subsidise film and television production, it used tax credits to fund production for about a decade (Vogel 1986: 99). Producers are also provided with American military facilities and personnel that can lead to considerable savings (we are grateful to Ian Jarvie for drawing this last point to our attention).

References

Acheson, K. and Maule, C. (1994a) "International regimes for trade, investment and labour mobility in the cultural industries", *Canadian Journal of Communication*, 19: 149–169.

Acheson, K. and Maule, C. (1994b) "Copyright and related rights: the international dimension", *Canadian Journal of Communication*, 19: 171–194.

Acheson, K. and Maule, C. (1999) *Much Ado about Culture: North American Trade Disputes*, Ann Arbor, MI: University of Michigan Press.

Albert, S. (1998) "Movie stars and the distribution of financially successful films in the motion picture industry", *Journal of Cultural Economics*, 22: 249–270.

Albert, S. (1999) "Reply: movie stars and the distribution of financially successful films in the motion picture industry", *Journal of Cultural Economics*, 23: 325–329.

Anderson, R. (1985) "The motion pictures patents company: a reevaluation", in T. Balio (ed.) *The American Film Industry*, Madison, WI: University of Wisconsin Press.

Bach, S. (1985) *Final Cut: Dreams and Disaster in the Making of Heaven's Gate*, New York, NY: New American Library.

Boorman, J. (1985) *Money Into Light – The Emerald Forest*, London: Faber and Faber.

Borneman, E. (1985) "United States versus Hollywood: the case study of an antitrust suit", in T. Balio (ed.) *The American Film Industry*, Madison, WI: University of Wisconsin Press.

Bowser, E. (1991) *The Transformation of Cinema, 1907–1915, Vol. 2, History of American Cinema*, New York, NY: Charles Scribner.

Chandler, A.D. (1990) *Strategy and Structure, Chapters in the History of the American Industrial Enterprise*, Cambridge, MA: MIT Press.

Cheung, S. (1969) *A Theory of Share Tenancy*, Chicago, IL: University of Chicago Press.

Chippindale, P. and Franks, S. (1991) *Dished: The Rise and Fall of British Satellite Broadcasting*, Sydney: Simon and Schuster.

Coase, R. (1960) "The problem of social cost", *Journal of Law and Economics*, 3: 1–44.

Conant, M. (1960) *Antitrust in the Motion Picture Industry*, Berkeley, CA: University of California Press.

Conant, M. (1985) "The Paramount decrees reconsidered", in T. Balio (ed.) *The American Film Industry*, Madison, WI: University of Wisconsin Press.

Cunningham, S. and Turner, G. (eds) (1993) *The Media in Australia: Industries, Texts, Audiences*, St. Leonards: Allen and Unwin.

De Vany, A. and Eckert, R. (1991) "Motion picture antitrust: the Paramount cases revisited", *Research in Law and Economics*, 14: 51–112.

De Vany, A. and Walls, D. (1996) "Bose–Einstein dynamics and adaptive contracting in the motion picture industry", *Economic Journal*, 106: 1493–1514.

De Vany, A. and Walls, D. (1999) "Uncertainty in the movie industry: does star power reduce the terror of the box office?", *Journal of Cultural Economics*, 23: 285–318.

Eberts, J. and Ilott, T. (1990) *My Indecision is Final: The Rise and Fall of Goldcrest Films*, London: Faber and Faber.

Fitzgerald, F. Scott (1941) *The Last Tycoon*, New York, NY: Scribner.

Goldman, W. (1983) *Adventures in the Screen Trade*, New York, NY: Warner Brothers.

Gomery, D. (1976) "Writing the history of the American film industry: Warner Brothers and sound", *Screen*, 17: 40–53.

Gomery, D. (1986) *The Hollywood Studio System*, London: British Film Institute/Macmillan.

Hanssen, F. (2000) "The block booking of films re-examined", *Journal of Law and Economics*, 43: 395–426.

Hanssen, F. (2002) "Revenue-sharing in movie exhibition and the arrival of sound", *Economic Inquiry*, 40: 380–402.

Hoskins, C. and Mirus, R. (1988) "Reasons for the US dominance of the international trade in television programs", *Media, Culture and Society*, 10: 499–515.

Houghton, B. (1991) *What a Producer Does: The Art of Moviemaking (Not the Business)*, Los Angeles, CA: Silman-James Press.

Huston, J. (1980) *An Open Book*, New York, NY: Ballantine.

Izod, J. (1988) *Hollywood and the Box Office, 1895–1986*, London: Macmillan.

Jarvie, I. (1992) *Hollywood's Overseas Campaign, The North Atlantic Movie Trade, 1920–1950*, Cambridge: Cambridge University Press.

Jowett, Garth S. (1990) "Moral responsibility and commercial entertainment: social control in the United States film industry, 1907–1968", *Historical Journal of Film, Radio and Television*, 10: 3–31.

Kenney, R. and Klein, B. (1983) "The economics of block booking", *The Journal of Law and Economics*, 21: 497–540.

Kenney, R. and Klein, B. (2000) "How block booking facilitated self-enforcing film contracts", *Journal of Law and Economics*, 43: 427–435.

Kent, N. (1991) *Naked Hollywood*, London: BBC Books.

Knight, F. (1921) *Risk, Uncertainty and Profits*, Cambridge, MA: Houghton Mifflin.

Laskey, J. (1957) *I Blow My Own Horn*, London: Victor Gollancz.

Limbacher, J. (1968) *Four Aspects of the Film*, New York, NY: Brussel and Brussel.

Limbacher, J. (1971) *The Influence of J. Arthur Rank*, London.

Macnab, G. (1993) *J. Arthur Rank and the British Film Industry*, London: Routledge.

McAfee, R. and McMillan, J. (1991) "Optimal contracts for teams", *International Economic Review*, 32: 561–577.

Musser, C. (1990) *The Emergence of Cinema: the American Screen to 1907, Vol. 1 of The History of the American Cinema*, New York, NY: Charles Scribner.

Pokorny, M. and Sedgwick, J. (2001) "Stardom and the profitability of film making: Warner Bros. in the 1930s", *Journal of Cultural Economics*, 25: 157–184.

Powdermaker, H. (1950) *Hollywood, the Dream Factory*, Boston, MA: Little, Brown.

Rosten, L. (1941) *Hollywood: The Movie Colony, The Movie Makers*, New York, NY: Harcourt Brace.

Rosen, S. (1981) "The economics of super-stars", *American Economic Review*, 71: 845–858.

Sedgwick, J. (2002) "Product differentiation at the movies: Hollywood, 1946–65", *Journal of Economic History*, 62: 676–704.

Sedgwick, J. and Pokorny, M. (1999) "Comment: movie stars and the distribution of financially successful films in the motion picture industry", *Journal of Cultural Economics*, 23: 319–323.

Staiger, J. (1985) "The Hollywood mode of production to 1930" and "The Hollywood mode of production, 1930–60", in D. Bordwell, J. Staiger and K. Thompson (eds) *The Classical Hollywood Cinema: Film Style and Mode of Production to 1960*, New York, NY: Columbia University Press.

Stigler, G. (1963) "United States vs. Loew's Inc.: a note on block booking", *The Supreme Court Review*: 152–157.

Storper, M. and Christopherson, S. (1987) "Flexible specialization and regional industrial agglomeration: the case of the U.S. motion picture industry", *Annals of the American Association of Geographers*, 77: 104–117.

Thompson, K. (1985) *Exporting Entertainment, America in the World Film Market 1907–34*, London: BFI Publishing.

Trotiner, G. (1984) "Coming to a theater near you: movie distributors challenge exhibitor instigated anti-blind statutes", *Cardozo Arts & Entertainment*, 3: 155–179.

Vogel, H. (1986) *Entertainment Industry Economics*, Cambridge: Cambridge University Press.

Wilcox, H. (1969) *25,000 Sunsets*, South Brunswick, NJ: A.F. Barnes.

Yule, A. (1989) *Fast Fade: David Puttnam, Columbia Pictures, and the Battle for Hollywood*, New York, NY: Delacorte Press.

Index